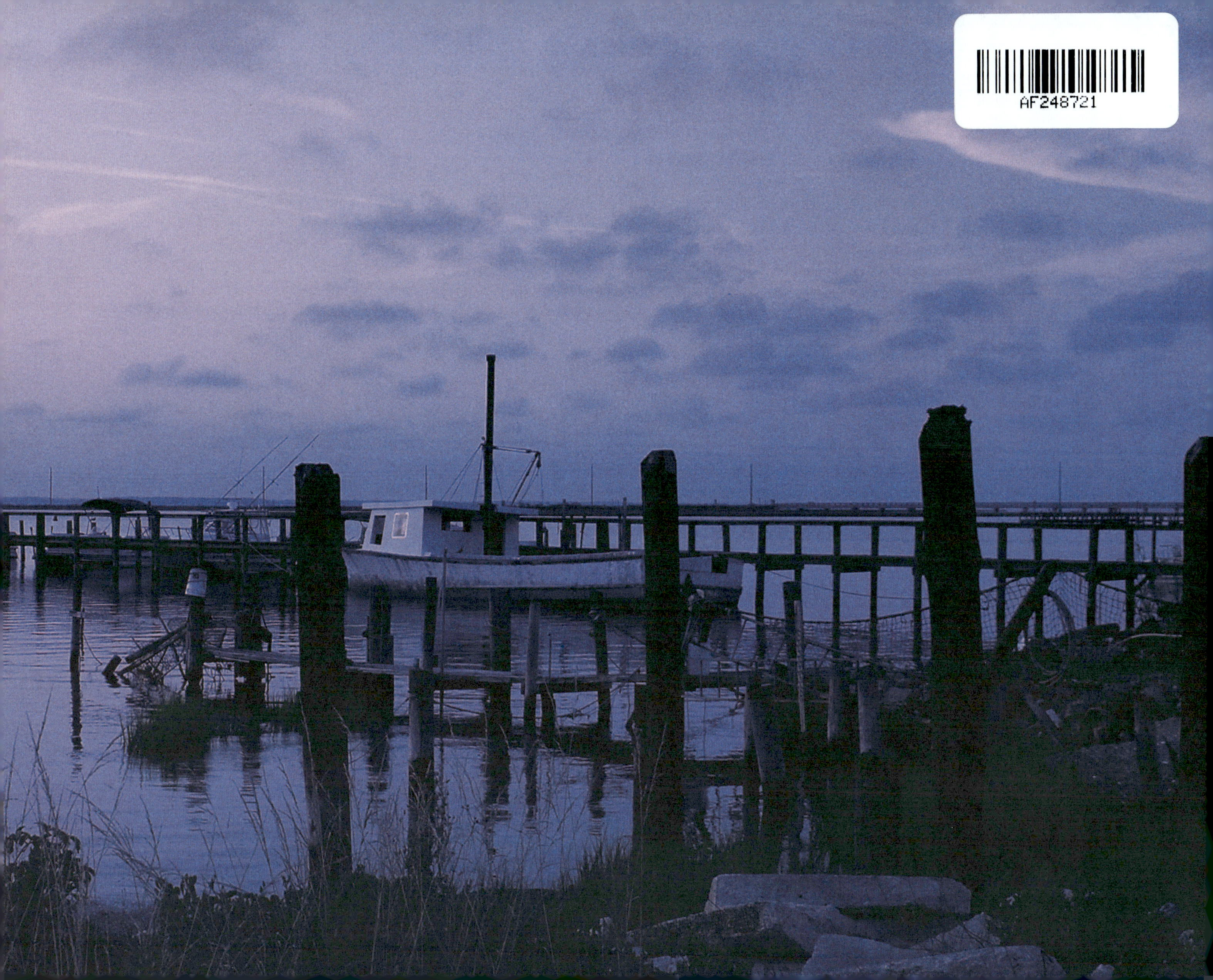
AF248721

Chincoteague Island

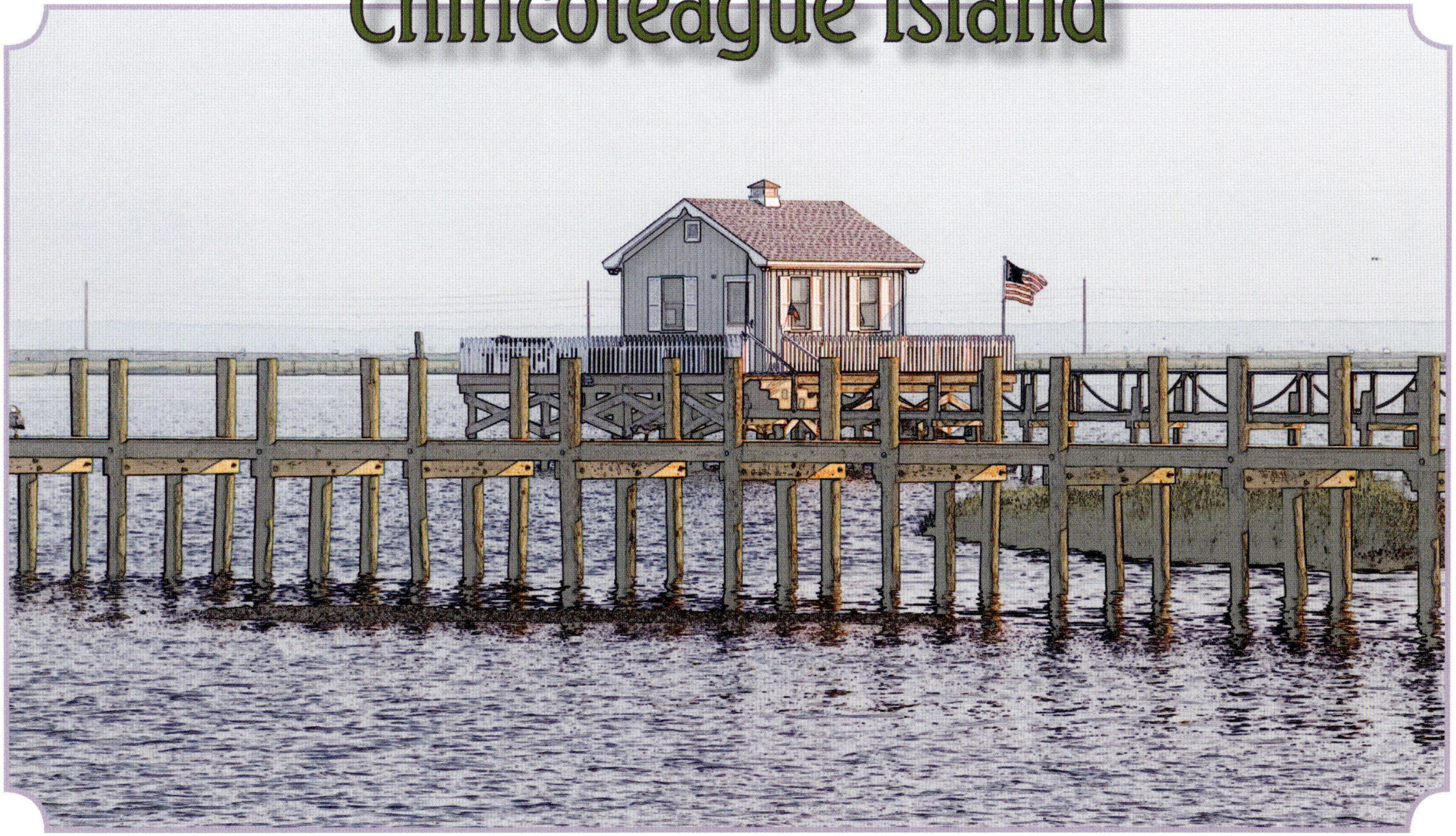

James Tigner, Jr.

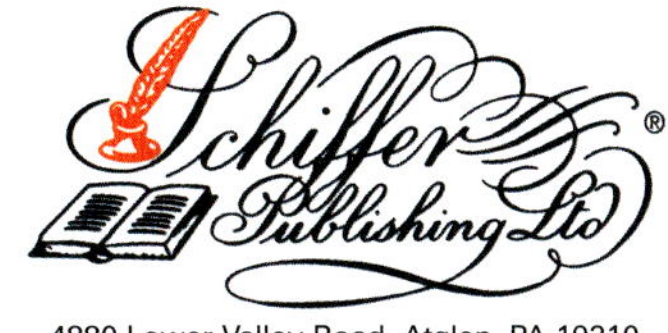

Schiffer Publishing Ltd

4880 Lower Valley Road, Atglen, PA 19310

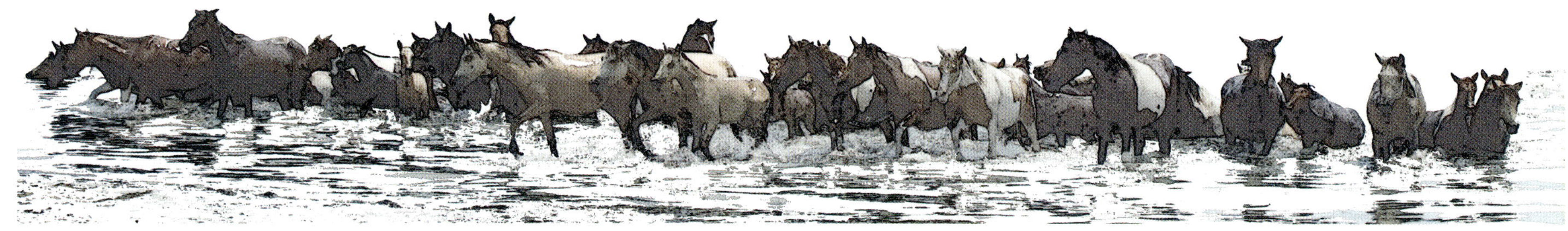

Other Schiffer Books by James Tigner, Jr.
Colonial Beach, Virginia: Playground of the Potomac
Greetings from Hampton Roads, Virginia.
Memories of Chesapeake Beach & North Beach, Maryland.
St. Michaels, Oxford, and the Talbot County Bayside.
Yesterday on the Chesapeake Bay.

Other Schiffer Books on Related Subjects
Newport News: A Vintage Postcard Tour. Harold Cones & John Bryant.

Copyright © 2008 by James Tigner, Jr.
Library of Congress Control Number: 2008921944

Designed by RoS
Type set in Seagull Hv BT/Zurich BT

ISBN: 978-0-7643-2919-7
Printed in China

Schiffer Books are available at special discounts for bulk purchases for sales promotions or premiums. Special editions, including personalized covers, corporate imprints, and excerpts can be created in large quantities for special needs. For more information contact the publisher:

Published by Schiffer Publishing Ltd.
4880 Lower Valley Road
Atglen, PA 19310
Phone: (610) 593-1777; Fax: (610) 593-2002
E-mail: Info@schifferbooks.com

For the largest selection of fine reference books on this and related subjects, please visit our web site at **www.schifferbooks.com**
We are always looking for people to write books on new and related subjects. If you have an idea for a book please contact us at the above address.

This book may be purchased from the publisher.
Include $3.95 for shipping.
Please try your bookstore first.
You may write for a free catalog.

In Europe, Schiffer books are distributed by
Bushwood Books
6 Marksbury Ave.
Kew Gardens
Surrey TW9 4JF England
Phone: 44 (0) 20 8392-8585; Fax: 44 (0) 20 8392-9876
E-mail: info@bushwoodbooks.co.uk
Website: www.bushwoodbooks.co.uk
Free postage in the U.K., Europe; air mail at cost.

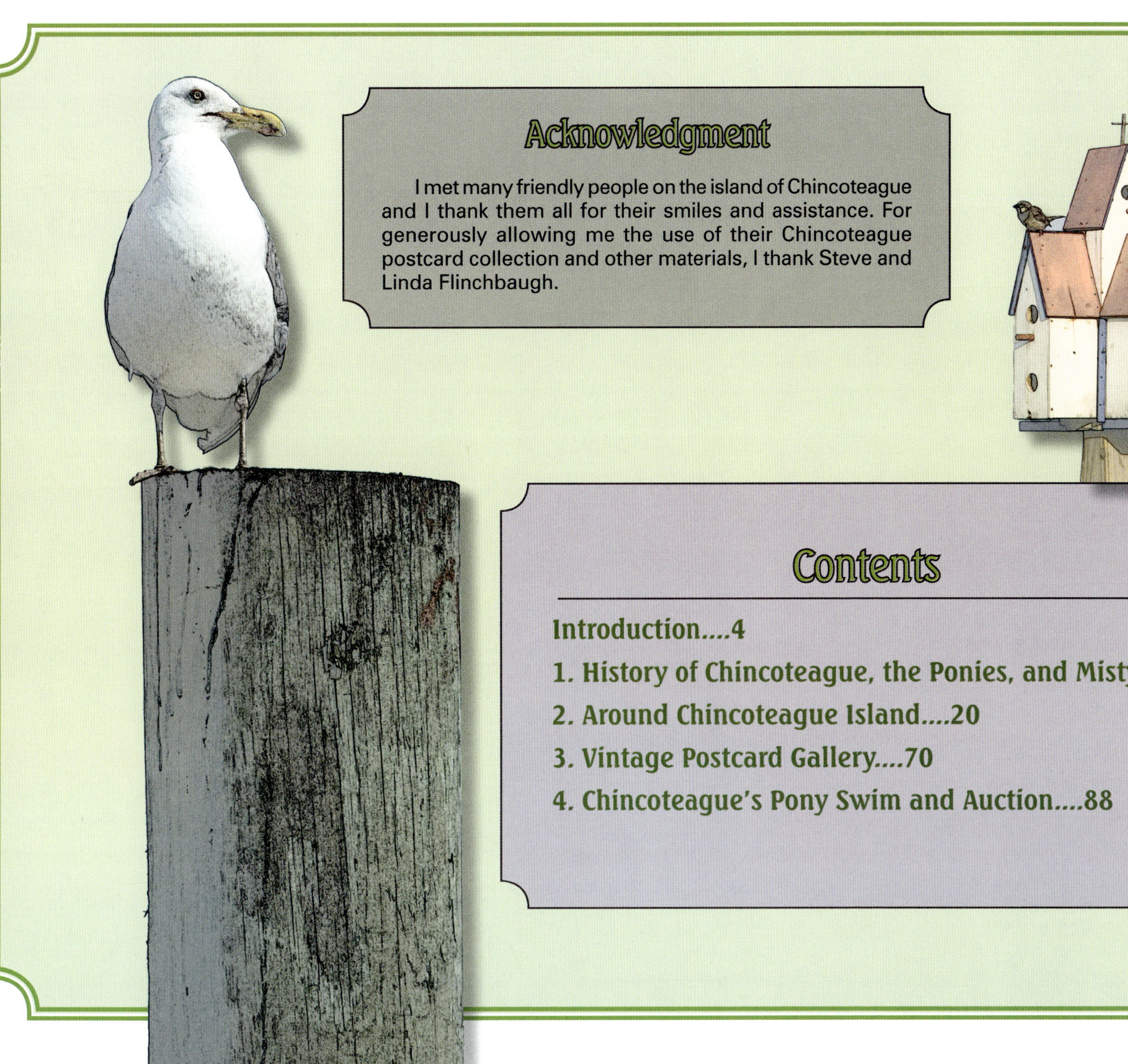

Acknowledgment

I met many friendly people on the island of Chincoteague and I thank them all for their smiles and assistance. For generously allowing me the use of their Chincoteague postcard collection and other materials, I thank Steve and Linda Flinchbaugh.

Contents

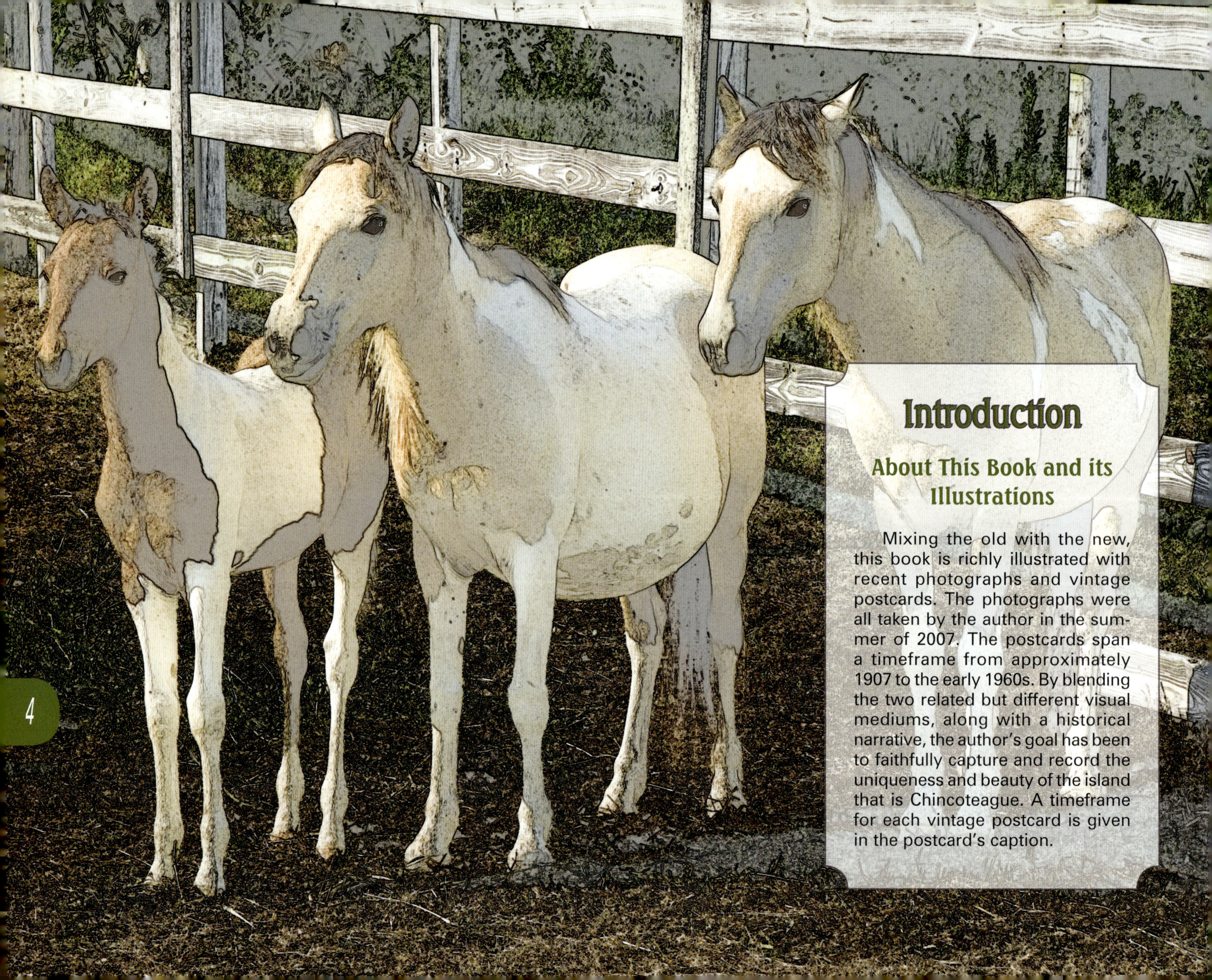

Introduction

About This Book and its Illustrations

Mixing the old with the new, this book is richly illustrated with recent photographs and vintage postcards. The photographs were all taken by the author in the summer of 2007. The postcards span a timeframe from approximately 1907 to the early 1960s. By blending the two related but different visual mediums, along with a historical narrative, the author's goal has been to faithfully capture and record the uniqueness and beauty of the island that is Chincoteague. A timeframe for each vintage postcard is given in the postcard's caption.

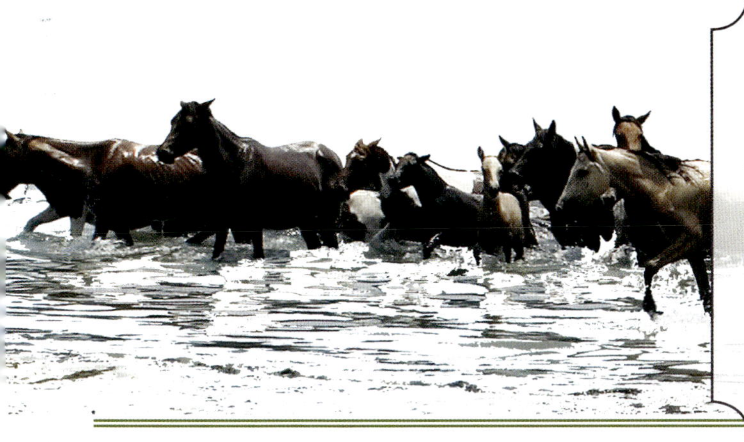

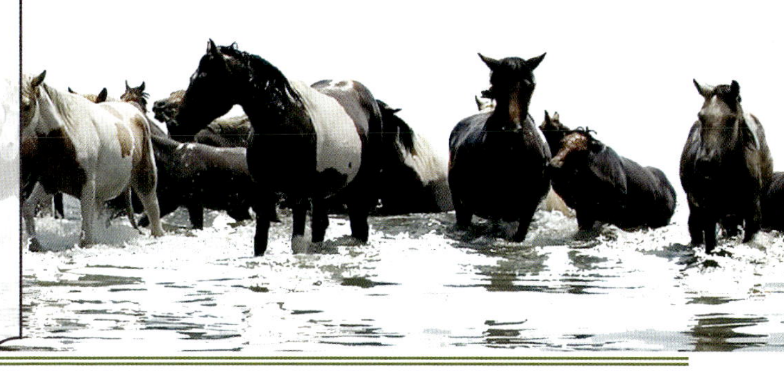

Unfold any modern Virginia highway map, put your finger on Richmond, slide your finger to the right until it reaches the Atlantic Ocean, then slide it upward and you will see the name Chincoteague. Located in the northeastern part of Accomack County, the Island of Chincoteague is located on the ocean side of Virginia's Eastern Shore. Chincoteague has the distinction of being Virginia's largest inhabited island and Chincoteague, the town, is the state's most eastern. Including the Wildcat Marsh area at its northern end, the island is roughly seven and one-half miles long and a mile and a half wide. The island is oriented lengthwise in a northeasterly to southwesterly direction. The island is approximately ten miles east of where the north-south Route 13 and the east-west Route 175 intersect. From Chincoteague, the first four miles of Route 175, the part that links Chincoteague with the mainland, is the John B. Whealton Causeway. The causeway is an alternating road and bridge system that stretches over the large, marshy area on Chincoteague's western side. The causeway has six bridges, five of which are in a fixed position, while the bridge closest to Chincoteague and spanning the Chincoteague Channel is a swing bridge. Locals however commonly refer to the swing bridge as a draw-bridge. Travel between Chincoteague Island and Assateague Island is by a two-lane bridge that spans the Assateague Channel.

Whether today Chincoteague Island should be considered a barrier island can be debated. Barrier islands are generally thought to be remote places, inhabited by wild creatures, swept by the sea, and dune covered. Years ago, the lower part of Chincoteague Island fronted directly on the ocean. However, for the last several centuries, the southern end of Assateague Island has been steadily growing lengthwise. The lower end of Assateague Island now completely separates Chincoteague Island from the Atlantic Ocean. Barrier island or not, the island of Chincoteague is really defined by the bodies of water that surround it. The Assateague Channel, a river-like causeway roughly a quarter-mile wide separates Chincoteague from Assateague on its eastern side. To Chincoteague's north and northeast is the large Chincoteague Bay. To the island's west is the Chincoteague Channel and several miles of varying marshland and open water areas beyond that. The Chincoteague Inlet separates the southern end of Chincoteague from the northern end of Wallops Island and the Tom's Cove portion of Assateague.

The island and town are named after the Chincoteague Indians who once roamed the area. Early writings sometimes refer to the Chincoteague Indians as the Gingoteagues. Some of those writings also say that Chincoteague is an Indian name meaning *"beautiful land across the waters."* Chincoteague historian Kirk Mariner contends that the name Chincoteague means *"large stream."* It is widely believed that the Indians (known to be nomadic) lived on the mainland in the vicinity of what is today Swan's Gut Creek, Wattsville, and Atlantic, but came to the island often in their canoes while on hunting and fishing excursions.

Not knowing its early history, it would be logical to assume that the island of Chincoteague was first populated by colonials wishing to take advantage of the many seafood harvesting opportunities that existed in the waters surrounding the island. That, however, was not the case. Early owners first looked upon the island as being desirable solely for the grazing of livestock, such as cattle, sheep, pigs, and horses. The island had a mixture of pasture and trees, and because it was entirely surrounded by water, the island was its own natural fence.

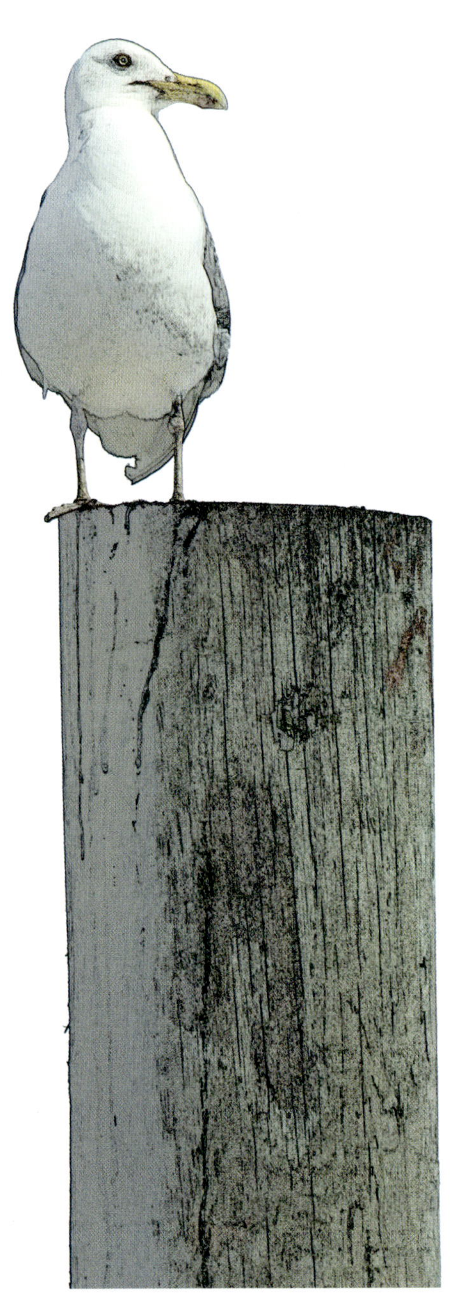

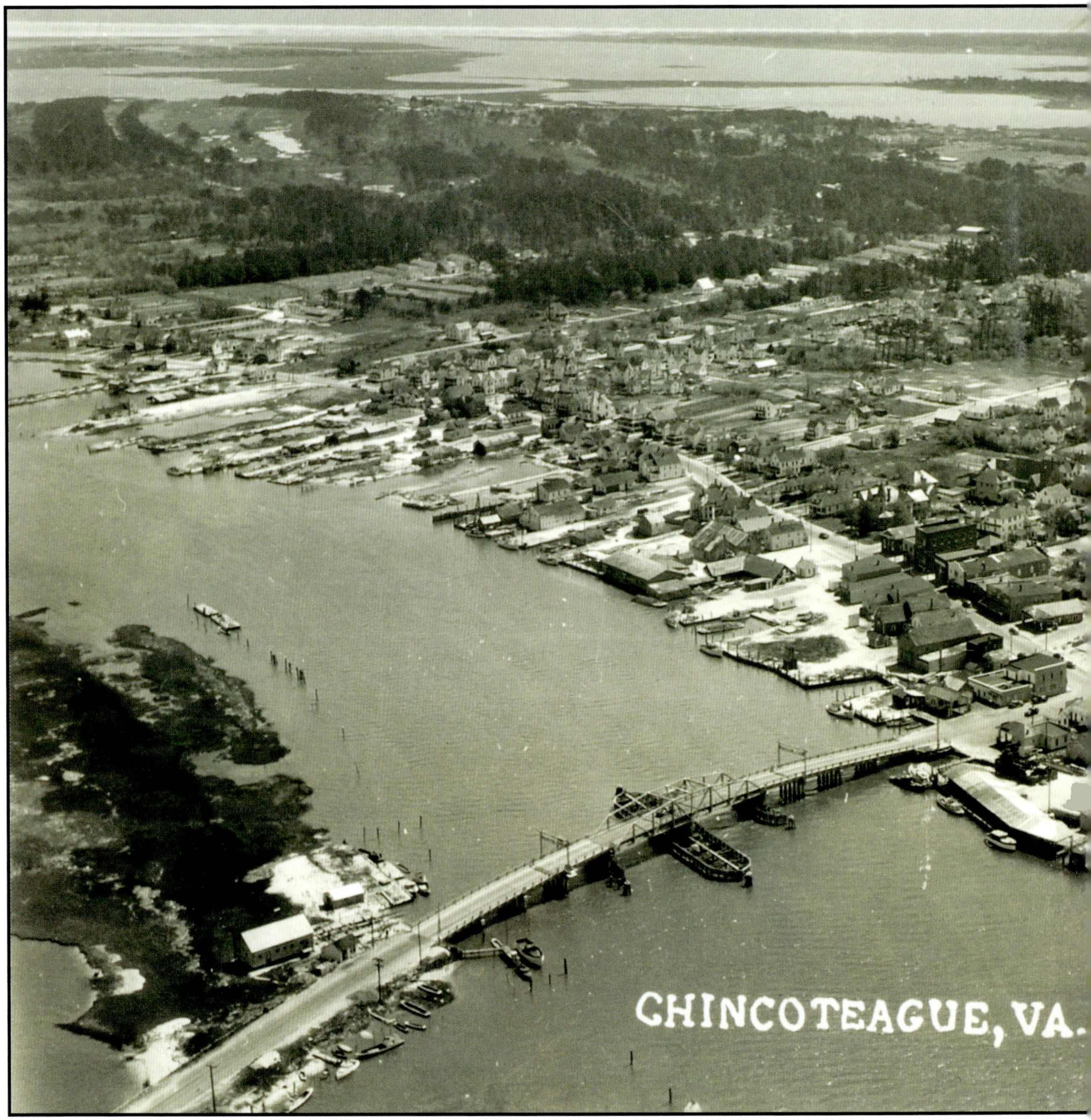

CHINCOTEAGUE, VA.

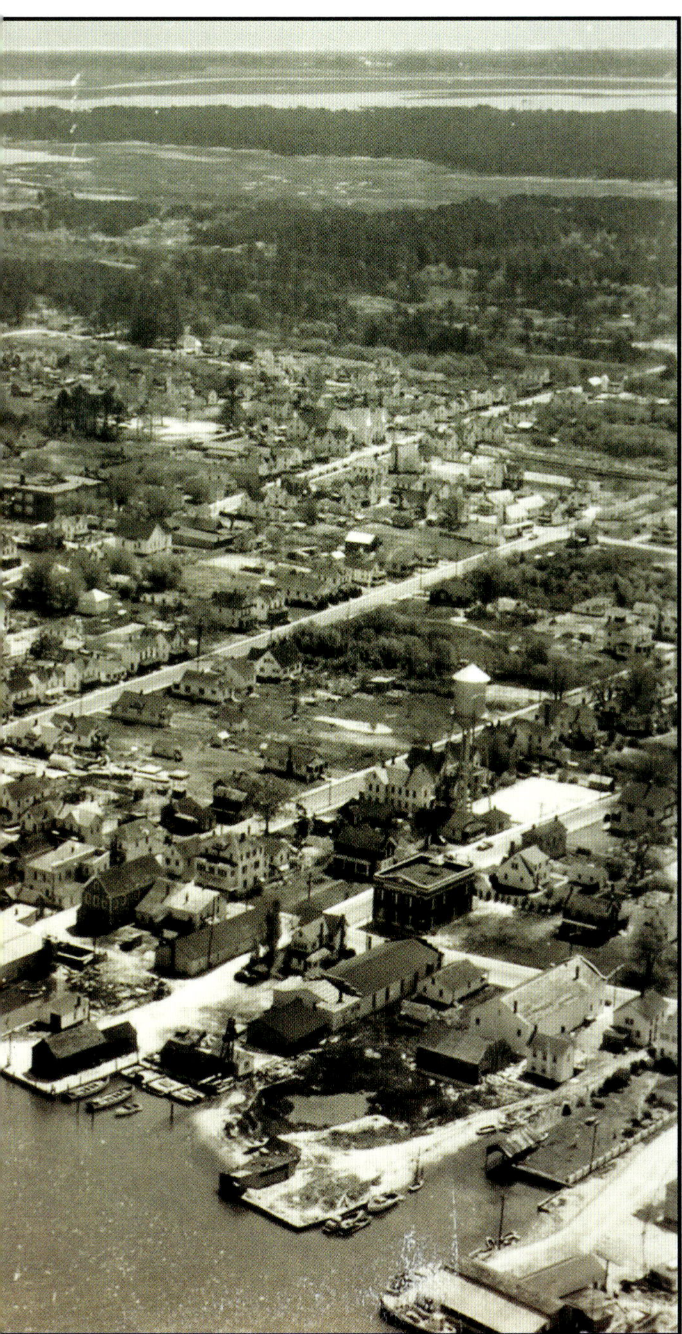
Aerial view of Chincoteague. Circa 1940s.

The first patent, or perhaps better stated as a "land grant," for Chincoteague Island was issued to Daniel Jenifer in 1671. Jenifer in turn passed it on to the husband of his stepdaughter, Thomas Welburn, in 1680. In an attempt to fulfill all the legal obligations needed to permanently hold onto the patent, Welburn had a small log house erected on the island and saw that someone lived in it for the specified legal time of one year. Welburn himself continued to live on the mainland. Unfortunately for Welburn, in 1691 the court ruled that his patent was invalid. The ruling was based on the fact that because Jenifer had never lived or built a home on the island, it was not a valid patent that he had passed onto Welburn. A new patent was issued to William Kendall for the northern half of the island and to John Robins for the southern half.

For the next seventy-five to one hundred years after the patents had been granted to Kendall and Robins, little in the way of change came to Chincoteague. The few families who lived on the island did so in relative obscurity. The years passed quietly and the island continued to be used for the grazing of livestock. At the same time nearby Assateague and Wallops Island, as well as other islands southward along the Virginia coast, were also being used for the same purpose. At the beginning of the nineteenth century, large tracts of land on Chincoteague began to be divided into parcels, and subsequently, smaller parcels. By the mid-nineteenth century, the free roaming herds of livestock on Chincoteague were a thing of the past and the island's inhabitants were vigorously looking toward the water for their livelihood. In other words, the island's economy had shifted from being land based to water based and the economic rewards of harvesting seafood from the surrounding waters, particularly oysters and clams, had been fully recognized by the islanders.

Chincoteague's longtime isolation from the mainland came to an end in 1876. In that year, the Dorcester Rail Road Company extended its tracks from Snow Hill, Maryland, down to just over the state border to Franklin City, Virginia. From Franklin City it was a straight shot and only five miles across Chincoteague Bay to Chincoteague. A small steamer began operating on a regular schedule between the two towns. In time, the railroad put a larger craft called the *Widgeon* on the route. The regular connection to the outside world brought about by the steamboat and railroad were to have profound effects upon the island of Chincoteague.

The waters surrounding Chincoteague held a bounty of seafood in the 1870s and it was a time when all seafood, particularly oysters, were in great demand in northern cities. Now the Chincoteague islanders had a reliable way to get their seafood to more distant and larger markets and to do so quickly and efficiently. Chincoteague oysters, especially those harvested from Tom's Cove, were soon recognized far and wide as being extra special and were highly prized for their tangy, salt water taste. The 1870s and 1880s were a time when Americans began traveling more than ever. Affluent urbanites eagerly sought escape from the sweltering heat in the big cities during the summer and often went on extended vacations. Many found their way to Chincoteague, liked what they saw, and stayed a couple of weeks, the entire summer, or decided to put down permanent roots. With its successful seafood industry, Chincoteague's economy boomed and its population steadily grew. Parcels of land were divided into building lots for homes. New commercial buildings were erected downtown. In 1890, the same year the town of Chincoteague acquired its first barbershop, about 500 barrels of oysters, bringing an average price of $3.00 a barrel, were being shipped daily to the mainland. The *Widgeon* was replaced by the larger, 100-foot steamer *Chincoteague* in 1893.

As Chincoteague celebrated the arrival of the twentieth century, horse and buggies were still the primary mode of transportation around the island and its downtown was being illuminated at night by new gas street lamps. The islands economy was still strongly centered around the harvesting and production of oysters, clams, and fish. Watermen worked long days just to keep up with the demand. In 1902 a telephone office was established and a dozen or so of the islanders had telephones installed in their homes. Rural mail delivery was begun on the island in 1905. The town was incorporated in 1908. Around 1910 the first automobiles were brought over from the mainland by boat. Since so many of the roads on Chincoteague were little more than horse and buggy paths and too primitive for the autos, and gasoline still had to be brought in by boat, they were of limited value at the time, beyond making heads turn. In 1914 an electric plant began producing electricity for the use of the islanders.

As Chincoteague entered into the 1920s, plans were already underway to build a causeway that would link the island to the Wattsville area on the mainland, a distance of roughly four miles. Supervising the project was John B Whealton, Jr., a one-time islander with many years experience in building roads in Florida and elsewhere, now returned. The project was one that he had dreamed of doing for years. The plan called for a roadbed to be built from dredged mud that would be contained between rows of wooden pilings and topped with a hard oyster shell surface. In addition it would be necessary to build six bridges. The bridge closest to the island, spanning Chincoteague Channel would be a suspension bridge. Work on the massive project began in March 1920. Two and a half years later, work on the *"Chincoteague Causeway"* was considered complete. The causeway officially opened to vehicular traffic on November 15, 1922.

The town of Chincoteague was hit with two devastating fires in the 1920s. The first fire occurred on September 5, 1920, and a number of buildings on Main Street were destroyed, including the island's premier hotel, the Atlantic. The second fire started on February 25, 1924. It destroyed a number of downtown buildings, including the Whealton Mercantile Store, a longtime fixture on the island such as the Atlantic Hotel had been. The town's small and poorly organized fire fighting force was unprepared to deal with either of these major blazes. As a result, in June 1925 the Chincoteague Volunteer Fire Company was organized. The new fire company's immediate need was for a fire truck and other firefighting equipment. It was decided that a carnival combining a pony penning and pony sale (the auction idea didn't start until later) might be a viable solution for raising the necessary funds. Plans were quickly formulated and the event was held at the end of July. A number of the ponies were sold and the event was considered a success.

The three days of pony-related activities, the highlight of the year on Chincoteague, have been held annually ever since, except for the war years of 1943 and 1944, and always occurs on the last Wednesday, Thursday, and Friday in July. The ponies on Assateague are rounded up in the days before the swim by "saltwater cowboys," the name given to the

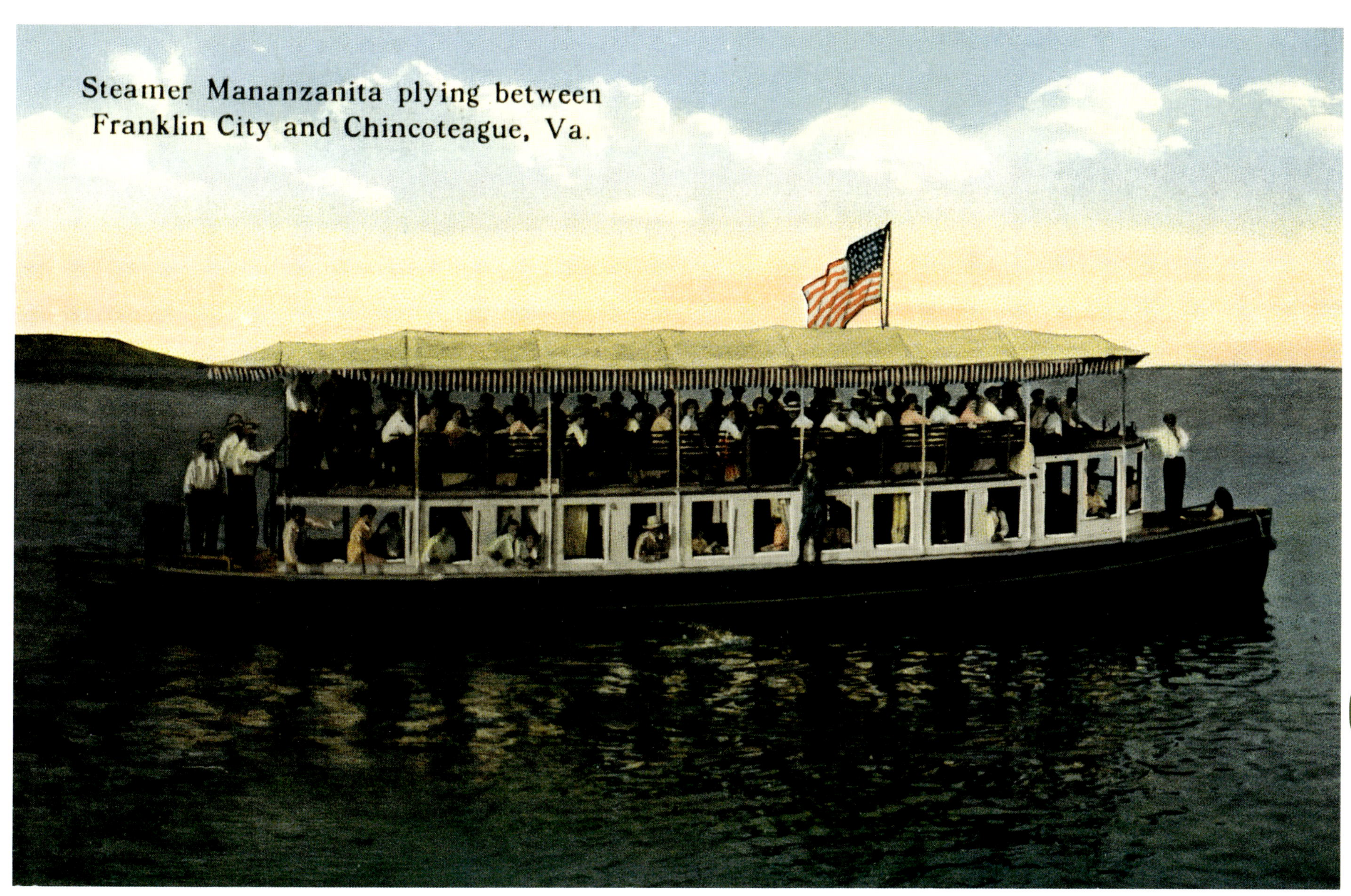

Steamer *Manzanita* plying between Franklin City and Chincoteague, Virginia. The vessel was 58 feet long. Circa 1913.

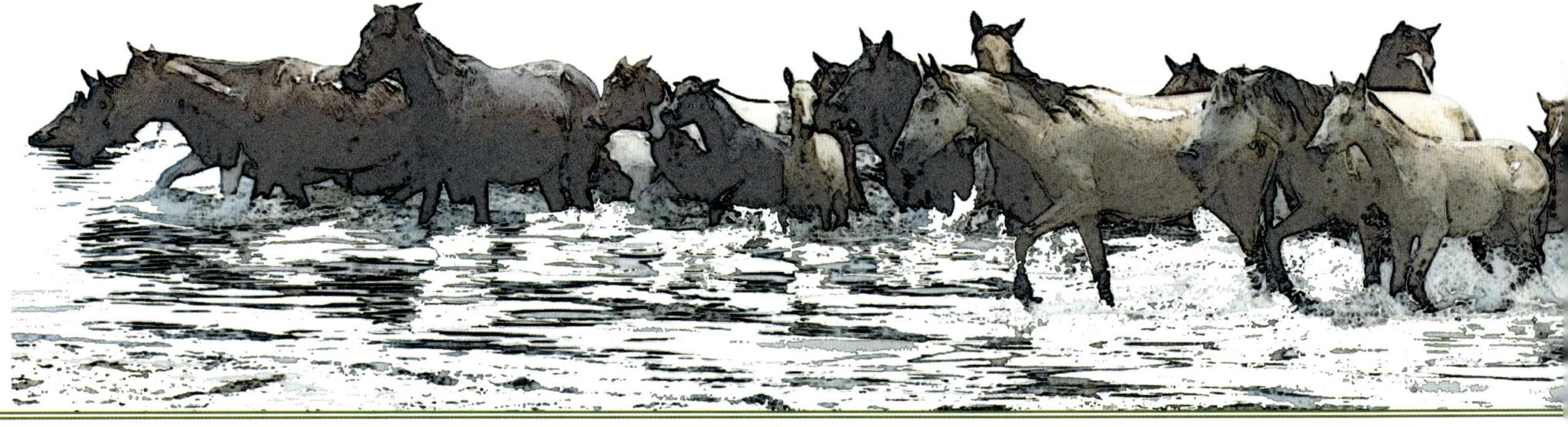

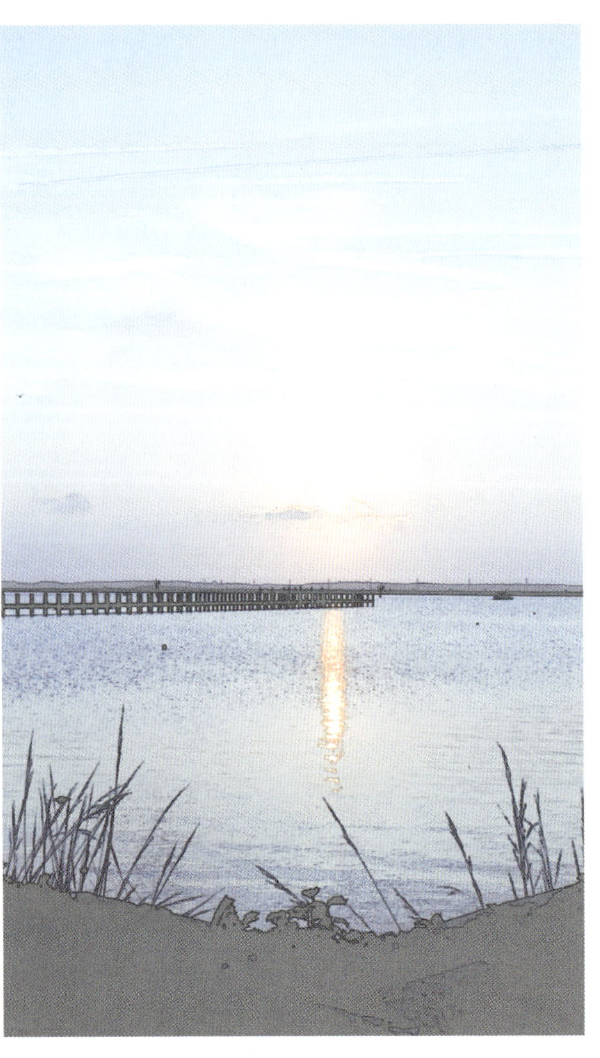

roundup men (all members of the volunteer fire department), and held in a big holding corral on Assateague Island. On Wednesday the "saltwater cowboys" swim the ponies as a group across the narrowest portion of Assateague Channel, which separates Assateague from Chincoteague. The exact time of the swim is not usually known until the day of the event, as it is important that it take place during a slack tide. Many of the newer born colts would not be able to survive the swim otherwise. Just the same, "saltwater cowboys" are close by in boats and ever alert and ready to rescue any pony needing assistance. Any colt too young to make the swim is brought across the channel in a barge with its mother. After the swim, which takes from five to ten minutes, the ponies are given roughly an hour to rest. Then they are paraded as a group, south on Ridge Road to Beebe Road and then up Main Street to the carnival grounds, the site of the auction.

In recent years as many as fifty thousand people have descended onto Chincoteague Island to watch the activities. Many spectators arrive well before sunrise and wait for hours just to have a front row view. The ponies come ashore at the end of Pony Swim Lane but many watch the activities from nearby Memorial Park or Tom's Cove Campground. Still others watch from the many boats that take their positions early in the day on either side of the swim area. In 2007 the fire company held its 82nd annual pony roundup, swim, and auction. It was estimated that thirty-five thousand spectators were on hand Wednesday morning to watch the ponies swim the 200 yards across the channel.

Once at the carnival grounds, the ponies are put in a big corral, watered, and fed baled hay. Curious onlookers and potential buyers line the fences taking pictures and discussing amongst themselves which pony is the cutest or looks the strongest. The fire department at one time branded the ponies on the front shoulder with the letter "F," but the practice has long since been determined to be unnecessary and has been abandoned. The auction starts at eight the next morning. There is limited bleacher style seating at the auction. Those who are in the know or are serious about buying a pony stake out their seats the day before with all sorts of imaginative ideas from beach towels wrapped around bleacher seats to hand printed signs with family names on them claiming territory. Anticipation fills the air on the day of the auction and it is both a happy and bittersweet, sad time. It's exciting to see the sometimes-feverish bidding on the young colts, but it's also the time when many of the colts are finally and forever separated from their mothers. If a colt is still too young

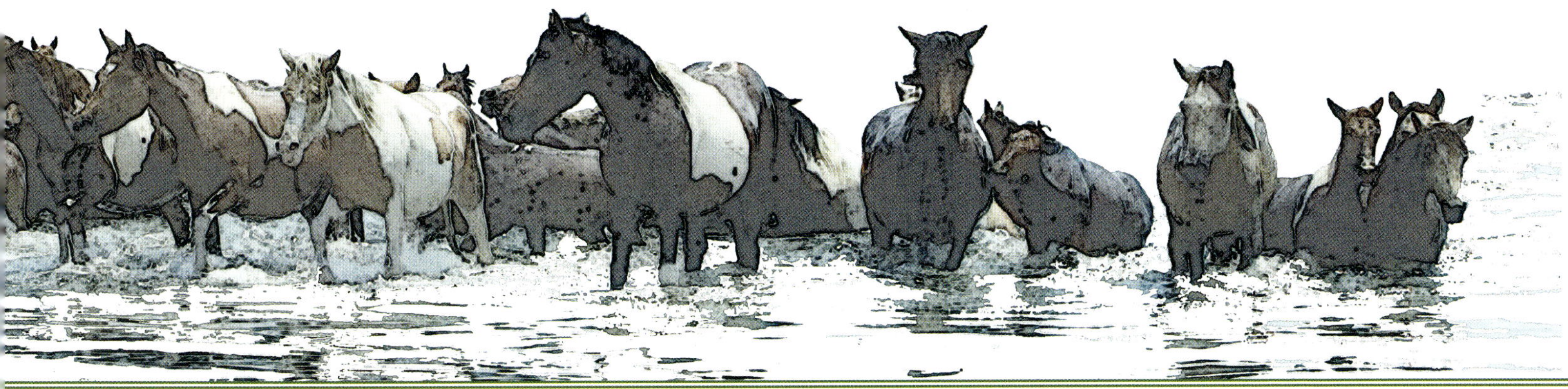

to leave its mother, it is still auctioned off. However, the high bidder must wait several months before they can take the colt home. It is interesting to note that in the early years of the pony auction, many who bought a young pony took it home in the backseat of their automobile. There are strict rules against that now and the ponies are treated very humanely by the fire department.

No one actually knows when the first pony penning took place. However, the earliest ones on Chincoteague and Assateague Islands are generally thought to date back to the late seventeenth century. The original purpose of the pony penning appears to have been for the islanders to determine how many horses there were, to determine ownership of the horses, to hot-iron brand them, and to select which horses were to be sold, domesticated, removed or added to the herd. The early accounts that we have of pony pennings are sometimes contradictory, and at best can only be interpreted in a general sense. Some accounts appear to speak of Assateague Island as being Chincoteague Island, or speak of the two islands as if they were one. In some of these early accounts June is given as the month for pony penning, in other accounts the event is said to occur in August. Still though, no matter where or what part of the summer, just as they are today, pony pennings were a high energy, festive time, eagerly anticipated, and attended by not just locals but by curious onlookers from far and wide.

In 1835 Thompson Holmes wrote to the editor of the *Farmers' Register* his thoughts on pony penning at the time and what he remembered them to be like thirty years previous. He writes that pony pennings previously occurred on many of the islands, but currently, *"The horses have been gradually diminishing in number, by neglect, until on one island, they are nearly extinct; and the rustic splendor, the crowds, and wild festivity of the Assateague horse-pennings, scarcely retain a shadow of their ancient glory."* He goes on to speak of how there once were large crowds as *"the multitudes of both sexes"* came to watch the events from up to fifty miles in each direction. Then he adds, *"All the beauty and fashion of a certain order of the female population, who had funds, or favorites to command a passage, were sure to be there."* Obviously Holmes thought more of the *"horse-pennings"* he had seen years ago than the ones he was witnessing in recent years. The fact that most of the residents of Chincoteague by 1835 were in one way or the other making their livelihood from the harvesting of seafood perhaps had something to do with the *"horse-pennings"* at the time lacking *"their ancient glory."*

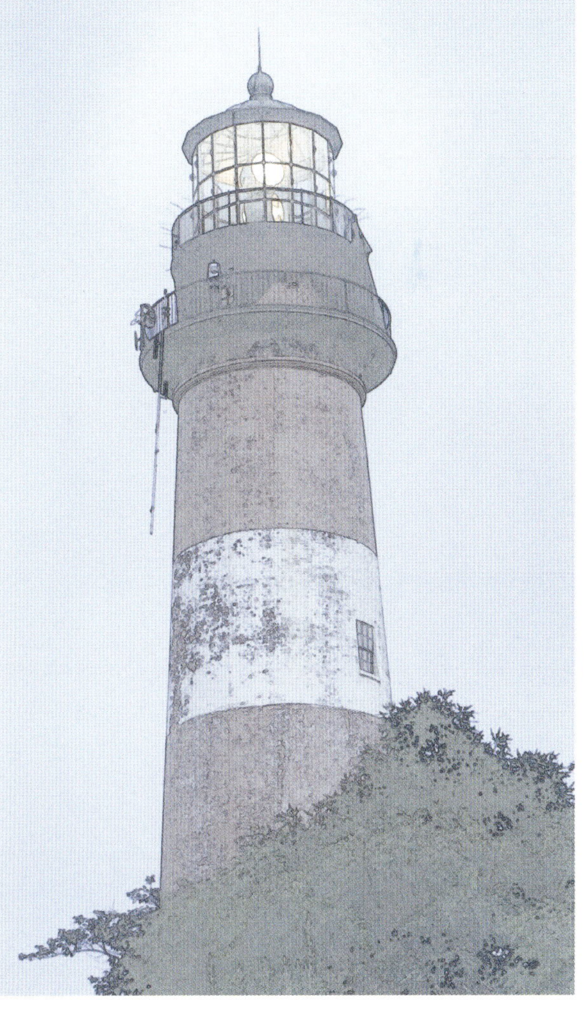

Misty of Chincoteague on her second birthday, July 20, 1948. Circa 1948.

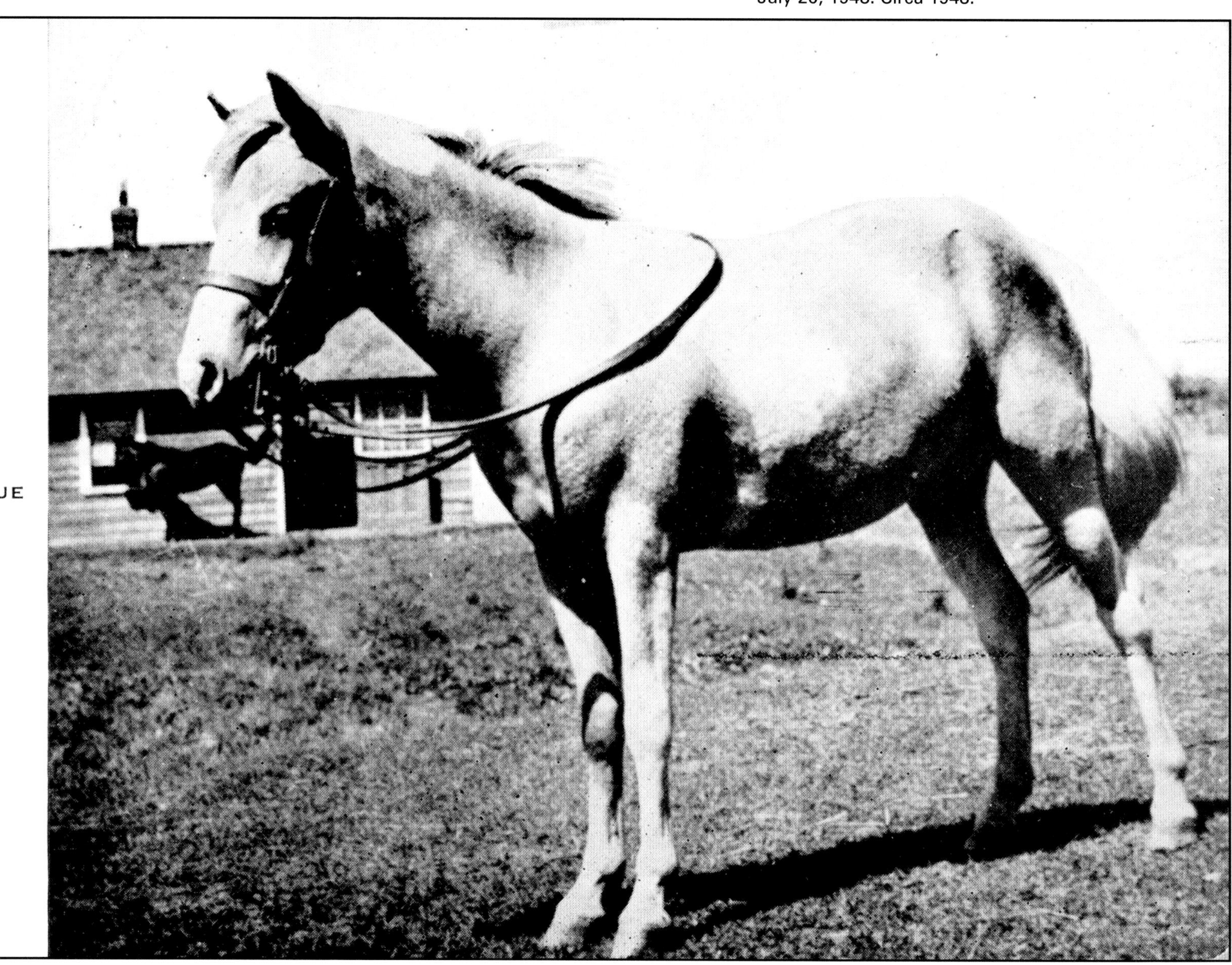

For many, their first awareness of the island of Chincoteague came, and continues to come, from a book about a pony. In 1946, an author from the Midwest made her first trip to Chincoteague and booked a room at the establishment of Miss Molly Rowley (now Miss Molly's Inn) on Main Street. The author had come to Chincoteague with the intent of gathering background information for a children's book she intended to write about the wild ponies on Assateague and the pony penning and sale held each summer on Chincoteague by the fire department. She soon crossed paths with Clarence Beebe and his two young grandchildren, Maureen and Paul. Clarence Beebe bred, raised, and sold ponies on his small ranch toward the southern end of the island. The author became enamored with a newborn filly named Misty. The author some years later described Misty this way, *"She was curiously marked. That splash of gold around one eye gave her a clownish look. Her body color was a coppery Palomino, and the white marking over her withers and down her left side took on the shape of a map of America. The map looked superimposed, like a permanent saddle pad."*

The author pleaded her case with Grandpa, as Clarence Beebe was known, that she needed Misty with her back at her home, called Mole Meadow, near Wayne, Illinois, to write the children's book. She offered one hundred and fifty dollars for the pony, a generous sum at the time. She promised to include Maureen and Paul in the plot line of the book. She also promised to return Misty at some later date so

she could be bred. Grandpa Beebe eventually agreed to sell Misty to the author, but the pony would have to stay on Chincoteague at the Beebe Ranch until she was weaned. Then he would ship the pony to Illinois. After her stay on the island, the author returned to Mole Meadow with a basic outline for the story and waited for Misty to arrive. True to his word, Grandpa Beebe shipped the pony by rail to the author and it was not long thereafter that Marguerite Henry finished writing her now famous book, *Misty of Chincoteague*. The book was very well received and in 1948 was designated a "Newbery Honor Book" for children's literature by the American Library Association. The popularity of the book also focused worldwide attention on Chincoteague Island. In a very real sense, the success of the book ushered in Chincoteague's tourist industry.

Ten years after the book *Misty of Chincoteague* was published, Marguerite Henry sent Misty back to the Beebe Ranch on Chincoteague to be bred. It was not too long after Misty's return that Grandpa Clarence Beebe passed on. Misty was put in the confident care of Ralph and Jeanette Beebe, Grandpa's son and daughter-in-law. It was national news when Misty gave birth to her first foal, a colt on April 6, 1960. The author's publisher sponsored a contest with a one thousand dollar prize for the best name submitted for the colt. Thousands of names were submitted from all over the country. Ten names were carefully chosen from a list of 1700 of the best names. Those ten names were dropped in a hat and a winner was picked.

Two little twin girls, Carol and Cheryl Costello from Wessington Springs, South Dakota, won the prize with their submission of the name Phantom Wings.

A film crew came to Chincoteague in the summer of 1960 and spent six weeks filming *Misty*, a movie based on the *Misty of Chincoteague* book. Misty was too old at the time to do any of her own acting. A little filly named Emma played the role of newborn Misty. Misty's second foal was born on March 21, 1961. Marguerite Henry offered the name Wisp O' Mist, a carryover submission from the earlier contest, and Wisp O' Mist the filly was so named. Later that year there were two premier showings of the movie *Misty*, one in Hollywood and the other on Chincoteague. On June 14, 1961, Misty was paraded up Main Street and made a grand appearance for the Chincoteague premier at the Island Theater (now the Roxy Theatre). Both Marguerite Henry and the book's illustrator, Wesley Dennis, took part in the festivities. A crowd watched and clapped as Misty left her front hoof prints in wet cement in front of the theater. In a touching moment, Marguerite wrote "Misty" next to the hoof prints.

Misty was pregnant with her third foal when the storm of the century struck Chincoteague. The 1962 storm, now known as the Ash Wednesday Storm, wreacked havoc along the Atlantic Coast from the Outer Banks of North Carolina to New York's Long Island. Most of the storm's destruction was done on March 7th, Ash Wednesday. Because of the severe flooding, Chincoteague had to be evacuated. Just before they were airlifted out by a helicopter, the Beebe's moved Misty from her stall to the kitchen in their house. For three days Misty stayed in the Beebe's kitchen while the weather outside threatened, with only the family cat to keep her company. After the storm calmed and the water subsided, the island was such a mess that Misty was temporarily moved to the mainland to have her colt. On March 11, 1962, Misty gave birth to a little filly, appropriately named Stormy. Marguerite Henry went on to write a book featuring Stormy. *Stormy, Misty's Foal* was published in 1963.

The storm damage inflicted on Chincoteague was overwhelming. On Assateague, half of the wild ponies owned by the fire department had perished. A sickening number of ponies had also been done in by the storm at the Beebe Ranch. It was a somber time on Chincoteague and prospects looked very bleak for a pony penning in the summer. Thanks to the urging of Bob Radnitz, the producer of the movie *Misty*, 20th Century Fox came to the aid of the islanders in a big way. The studio agreed to let any theater show the movie for free if the proceeds from the showing were donated to a fund to help replenish the herd by buying back a number of the ponies sold in past years. To the delight and fascination of both parents and children, Misty and Stormy made personal appearances at a number of the showings within driving distance. Then in late July, miracle of miracles, the annual pony penning took place.

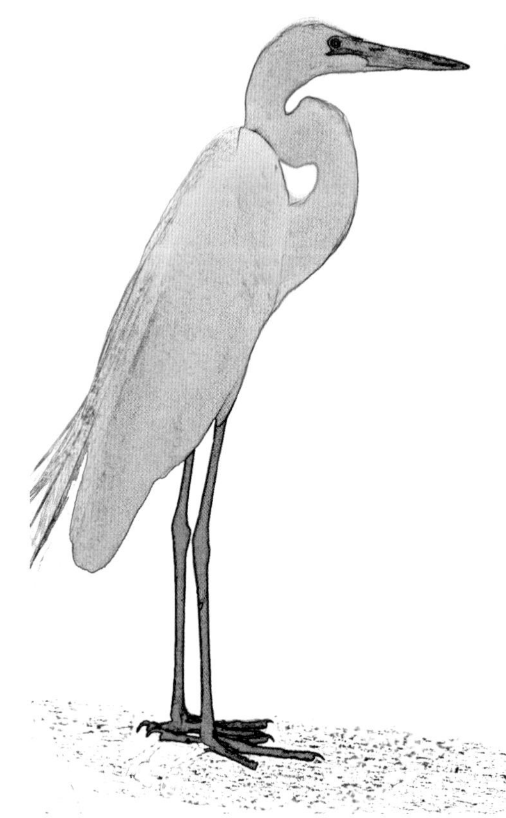

The Chincoteague ponies are both a hardy and smart breed. Perhaps because survival on the coastal island of Assateague has never been easy for the ponies, they have evolved that way. Even in the best of conditions, there is only a limited supply of food and fresh water. Harsh winters, summer droughts, coastal storms, and even hurricanes take a toll on the animals. There are two herds of ponies on Assateague, the Maryland herd and the Virginia herd. A fence at the Maryland-Virginia border is maintained to keep the two herds from mixing. The National Park Service manages the herd in Maryland. The Chincoteague Volunteer Fire Company owns and manages the Virginia herd.

The Chincoteague pony (horse) is smaller than the average horse, being on average 13 to 14.2 hands high. The ponies often have a bloated belly look to them. This is because their diet is rich in salt and the ponies tend to drink double what other horses drink. Their diet on the island consists primarily of saltmarsh cordgrass, American beach grass, seaweed, bayberry twigs, greenbrier stems, and occasionally poison ivy. The smallness of the ponies is attributed to poor breeding practices, where the ponies were allowed to inbreed. Other factors perhaps contributing to the ponies' smaller size are their lean diet and the harsh coastal environment, particularly in winter. Originally the ponies were an overall solid color that ranged from black to sorrel (reddish brown) to bay (brown and black). With the introduction of other horse breeds,

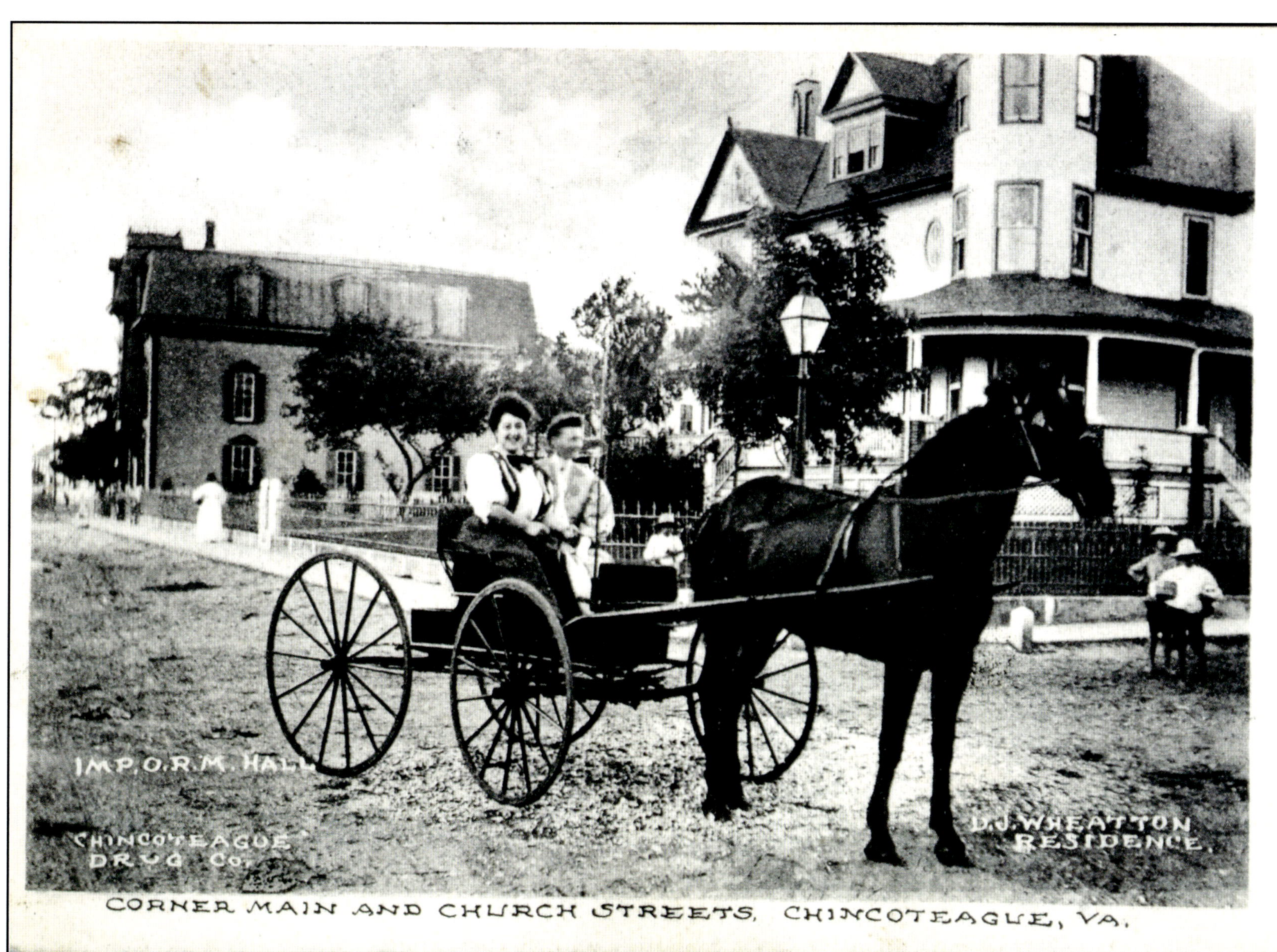

Corner of Main and Church Streets. The building to the left in the background is the lodge of the Imperial Order of Red Men. To the right is the residence of D. J. Whealton, built in 1902. Postmarked 1907.

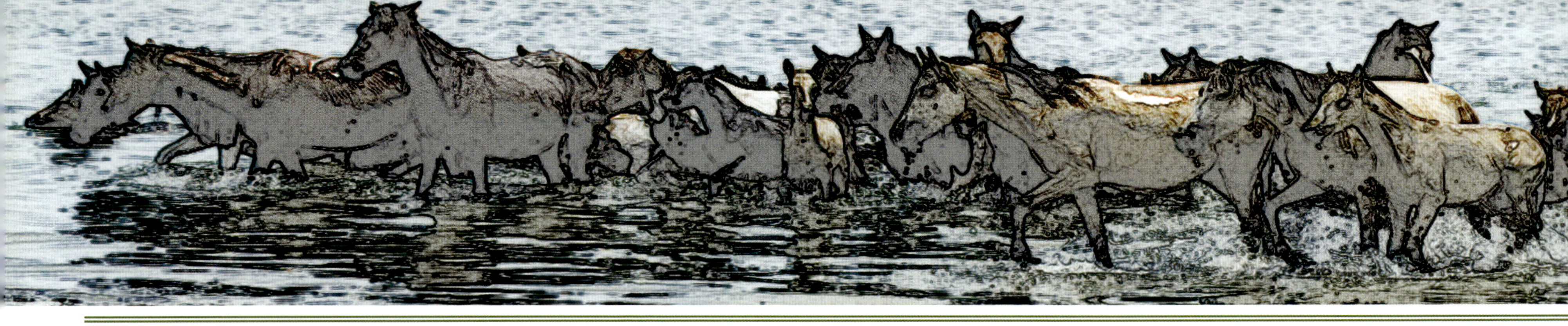

like mustangs and welsh, to the Assateague herds, many of the ponies today have a pinto (patches of color) and palomino (varying color) look to them.

A newspaper article published in May of 1890 describes the ponies as follows: *"As captured in the pen the pony stands not far from 12 hands high, and weighs, perhaps, 450 pounds. He is too big bellied to be handsome, but his legs, neck, and head are never ungraceful. They are various colors, generally red, brown, or brownish gray. They are always wicked looking little rascals, but, when properly broken, become perfectly safe for women and children to use, and on the mainland are very popular for dog carts and for saddle ponies for young people."* A newspaper article a year later in 1891 describes the ponies this way: *"They are hardy as a Shetland pony, docile as an ox and fleet as the wind. In winter their coats are as shaggy as a bear's."* Another description of the ponies is given in a 1924 newspaper article: *"The ponies are of superior intelligence, indicated by their wise foreheads and intelligent eyes. Their intelligence is much above that of the standard bred horse. In the beginning they were of an undesirable solid color of sorrel. After they were located by the white men, they were bred by better standard males and became more perfect in form and desirable in color."*

In the opening pages of *Misty of Chincoteague*, Paul asks Grandpa *"Is it true about the Spanish galleon and the ponies?"* Grandpa replies, *"Course it's true!"* Then Maureen, Paul's younger sister, asks, *"Then it's not a legend?"* Grandpa's response to the inquisitive two youngsters is: *"Course it's a legend. But legends be the only stories as is true!"*

There are a number of different theories, or perhaps better stated, *"legends be the only stories as is true"* as to where the Chincoteague ponies, as they are known today, came from and how and when they ended up roaming the wilds of the barrier island of Assateague. There is little more than hearsay to support any of the theories and the topic is one that will forever be discussed and debated.

The more romantic theories all center on Spanish shipwrecks. Years ago locals spoke of a Spanish galleon that had wrecked in the sixteenth century in the vicinity of Assateague's Maryland-Virginia border, spilling its cargo of horses in the process. It has been said that when the first white men came to the area they were told about the shipwreck by Indians using sign language. David Watson, the first keeper of the Assateague lighthouse (built 1833) popularized the story that the Spanish ship that foundered at this location was the *Greyhound*. Early visitors to Assateague reported seeing timbers from a wrecked ship in the area. The only hint we have today which

even remotely suggests this story may have some truth to it is that in the vicinity of Pope Bay and Pope Island there is a long sandbar known as Spanish Bar. Apparently at one time there was also a geographic feature in the area with the name Spanish Point. One variation of the story has it that the vessel (whatever its name) was transporting Arabian horses; the other variation is that the vessel was transporting Mustang horses.

Then there is the *San Lorenzo*, a Spanish merchant ship. Apparently Spanish records survive that indicate the vessel wrecked off Assateague while en route to Spain in 1820. Said to be onboard, in addition to much gold and silver, were ninety-five very small and very blind ponies being transported to Spain for work in the mines. Where along the Assateague coast the *San Lorenzo* foundered and also how much, if any, of her cargo was recovered is not known. It should also be pointed out that before the big storm of 1933 created Ocean City Inlet in Maryland, Assateague was a much longer island and included all of Ocean City, Maryland. All indications are that ponies were roaming Assateague way before 1820. However, it is possible that at least a few of the blind ponies from the shipwreck survived and mated with the existing herd.

In the opening pages of *Misty of Chincoteague* we are told that the ponies were *"Moor ponies"* and they were being trans-

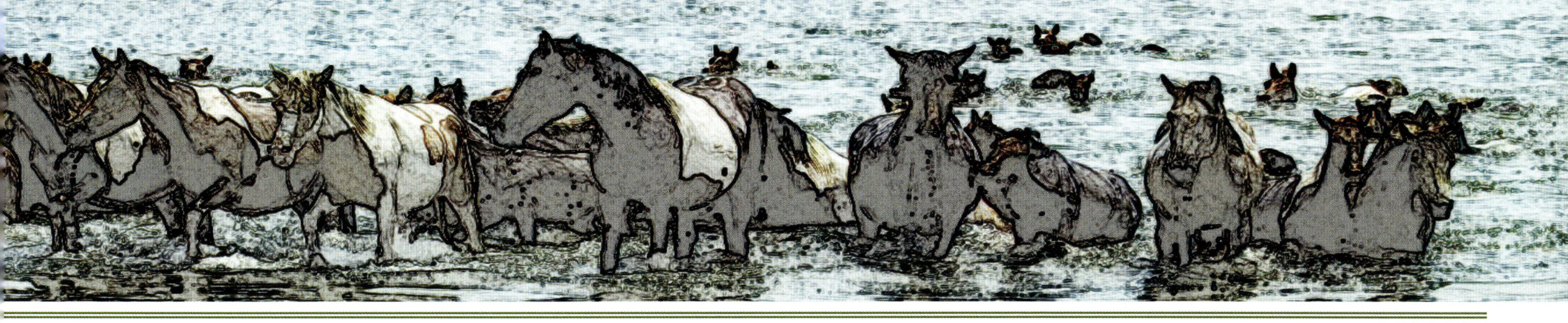

ported to Peru in the cargo hold of a Spanish galleon named *Santo Cristo*. During a storm, the galleon struck a shoal and broke up off the shore of Assateague Island. The ponies, after spending *"forty days and forty nights"* in the drab and damp recesses of the galleon, gained their freedom and swam to shore. On Assateague they quickly adapted to their new surroundings. If the ponies, technically horses, as they resemble ponies only in size, were Moorish, then their lineage must date back to the eighth century when Moors invaded a part of Spain. The invading Moors occupied an area in the southern region of the country that is still known today as Andalusia.

Yet another variation on the Spanish galleon theory is that the horses came from the *La Galga*. It is believed that the Spanish galleon *La Galga* foundered off of Assateague in 1750 in the vicinity of the present day Maryland-Virginia border. Divers have found no evidence of the shipwreck to date. One theory is that the wreck site, and perhaps a portion of the galleon itself, lies buried beneath the sands of Assateague on the bayside of the island and close to Virginia Creek. Unfortunately, this suspected location is not searchable, as it is on protected government land.

Another theory is that the ponies were purposely put ashore by pirates or escaped from one of the many pirate ships that are thought to have sailed and sometimes anchored along the deserted Assateague shores. Here again, this theory has a ring of romanticism associated with it. Yet, there just is no hard evidence. However, there is a small and insignificant island on the bay side of Assateague Island and in the vicinity of Green Run that is called Pirate Island.

Then there is the theory that places the origin of the ponies to the time when the Indians still roamed Assateague. Supposedly an English ship sailing to one of the early colonial settlements in Virginia, perhaps in the James River area, ran afoul on the shoals along the southern portion of Assateague Island. The Indians, still friendly at the time, rescued the passengers and crew and helped them to find their way across land and eventually to their destination, but the beach-horses (beachers), as the ponies were referred to before the Misty phenomenon, were left behind to fend for themselves. Again, there is no hard evidence to give credence to this event other than the recorded sightings of ponies on Assateague Island as early as the mid-seventeenth century.

Assateague Island is a narrow, dune swept barrier island that fronts directly on the Atlantic Ocean for almost thirty-eight miles and extends today from Ocean City Inlet in Maryland to Chincoteague Inlet in Virginia. The island varies in width from one-fifth of a mile to one and a half miles, except at its lower end where it is over two miles wide. The fact that its Maryland portion lies in close proximity to the mainland and its Virginia portion lies in close proximity to Chincoteague Island is good credence for the next theory. Although void of any romanticism, it is likely that the horses were purposely deposited on the island beginning in the mid-seventeenth century so that they could graze and also so that their owners could avoid fencing and taxation laws being imposed on livestock at the time.

Who does not want to believe a pirate story? The theory that the horses came from a Spanish galleon is so romantic it makes for a great introduction to a children's book. It is that romanticism which only makes one wish to believe it as truth all the more. Since the success of the *Misty of Chincoteague* book and then the *Misty* movie, the Spanish galleon theory is the one most often recounted. No matter from where or how they arrived, the Chincoteague ponies have been roaming wild on Assateague Island for well over 200 years. Whether they arrived by Spanish galleon in the sixteenth century, or by pirate ship, or by an English ship, or were purposely placed on the island in the seventeenth century we will never know. Because the Chincoteague ponies have characteristics of several different breeds, I suspect the truth may perhaps reside in more than one of the *"legends be the only stories as is true."*

Chincoteague's economy these days is fueled by tourism. The island draws visitors for many reasons. Anglers come for the great fishing on Chincoteague Bay and the Atlantic Ocean, sun worshipers for the ocean fronting beach on nearby Assateague Island. Then there are those who are lured to Chincoteague after reading about its small island charm in the Sunday sections of large urban area newspapers. Still others come for the decoy and hunting lore associated with the island. Then there are the devoted pony lovers. They come to see the famous Chincoteague ponies and to see where Misty, the most famous Chincoteague pony of them all, lived.

The Virginia portion of Assateague Island, with its National Seashore and National Wildlife Refuge status, is perhaps the single biggest draw. Thousands descend on its beach every day during the summer like the many crescent waves that wash its shore. Once across the drawbridge and on Chincoteague Island, the route to Assateague is up Main Street and then right onto Maddox Boulevard, past the ranks of souvenir and gift shops. These shops sell everything from summer clothing and island mementos to regional artwork, plus all the necessities for a day at the beach such as suntan lotion, beach chairs, sand buckets, towels, drinks, and snacks. Also available are pony-related souvenirs such as T shirts with ponies silk screened on them, books that talk about ponies, and videos that show ponies, as well as other souvenirs having to do with the yearly pony roundup and auction. In the midst of this menagerie of Chincoteague pony memorabilia, Misty items are interspersed.

In the book and in real life, the story of Misty is really of those who loved her unconditionally. For that reason Misty today is a symbol for all that is wonderful and beautiful. In this all too often abrasive and puncturing world, we are fortunate to have a Misty. From my visits I know that much of the good that Misty represents can still be found on her little island of Chincoteague.

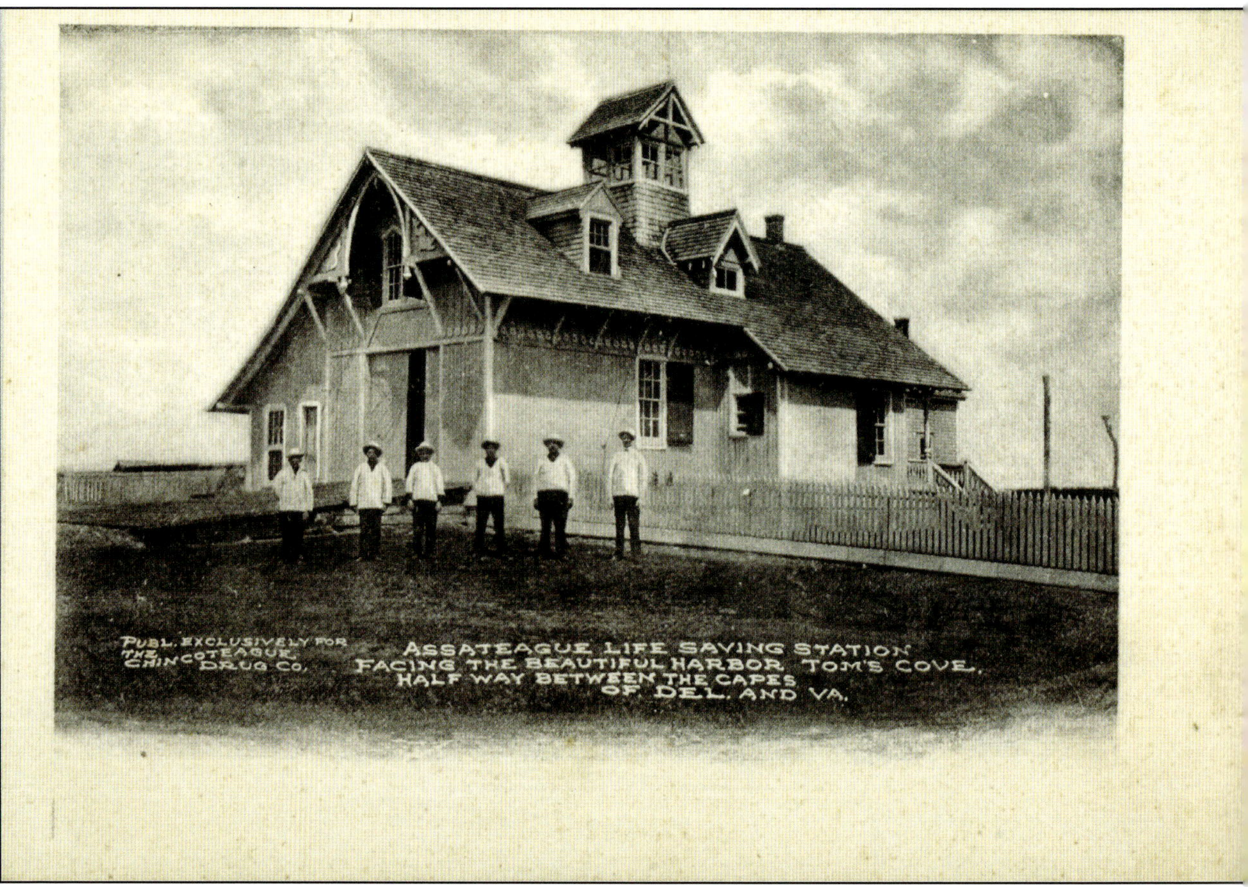

The Assateague Life Saving Station. Circa 1907.

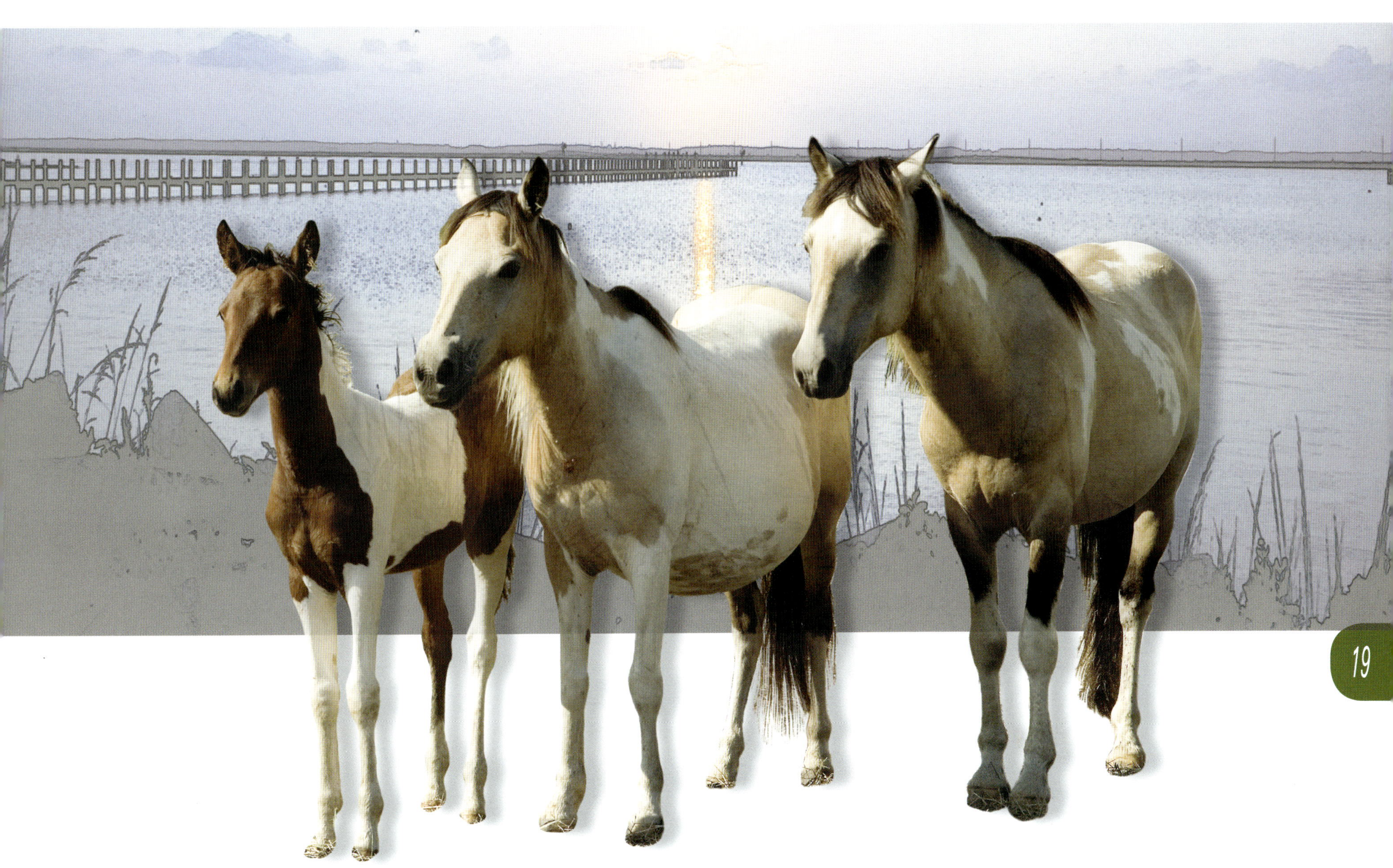

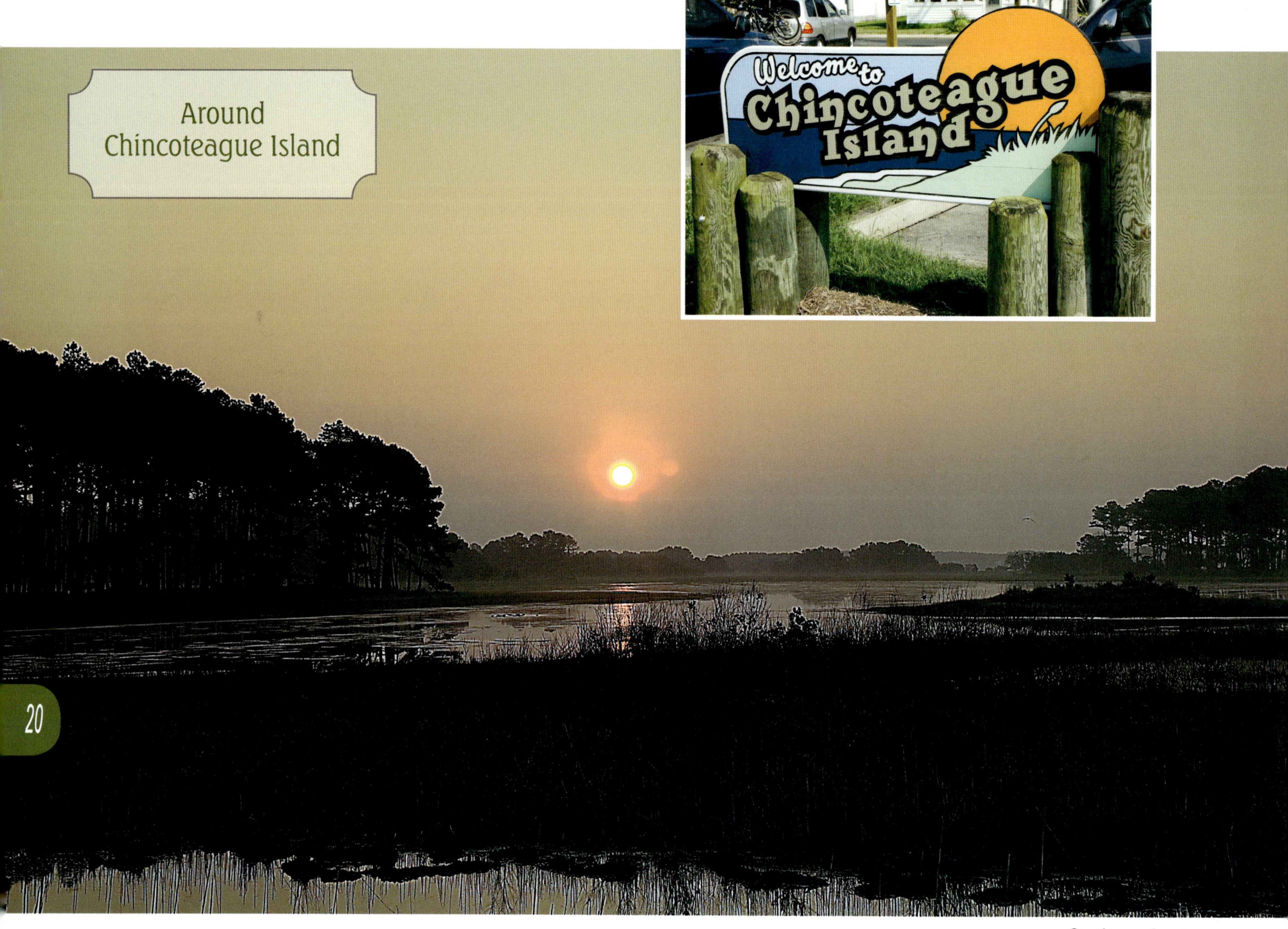

Around Chincoteague Island

Sunrise on Assateague.

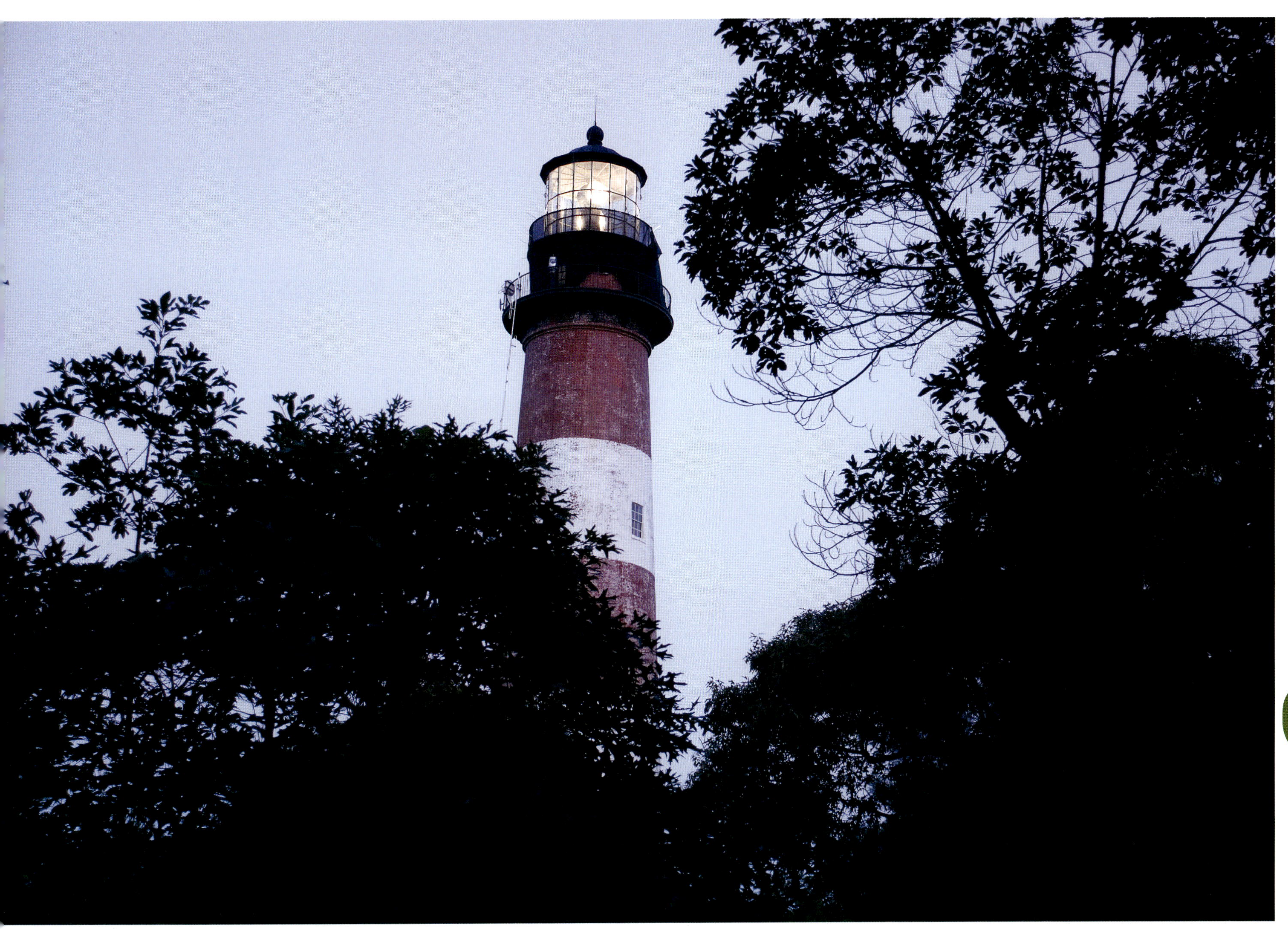

Assateague Lighthouse

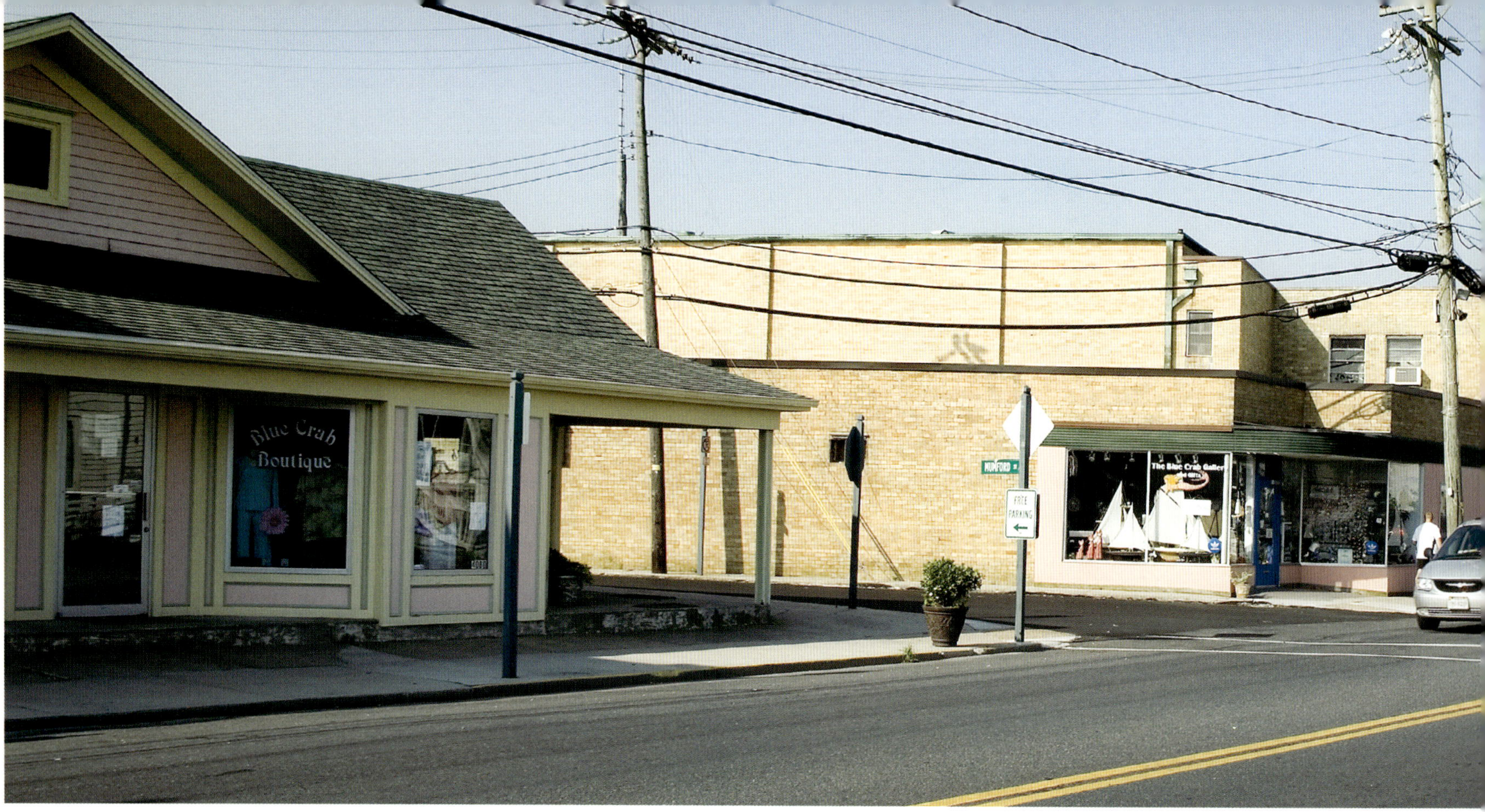

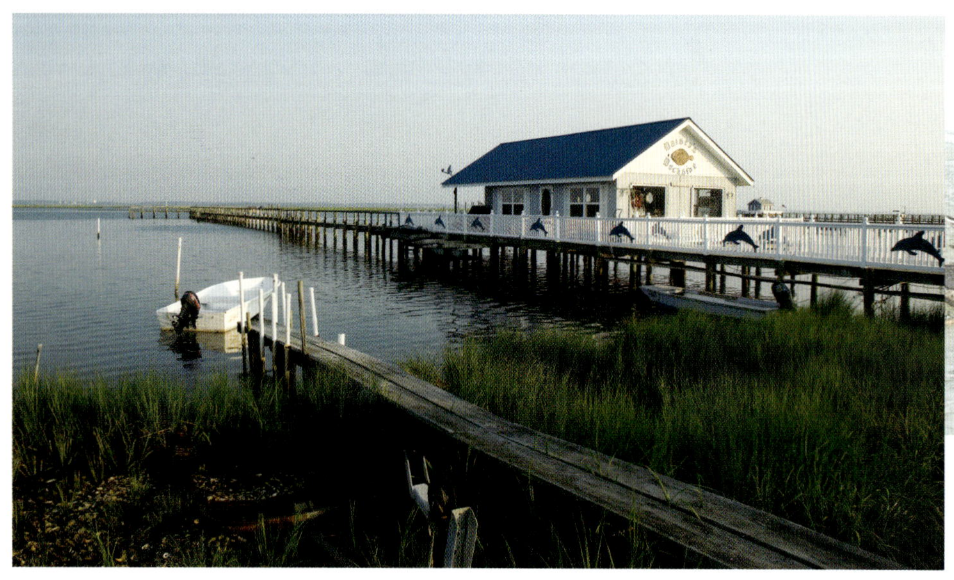

Main Street

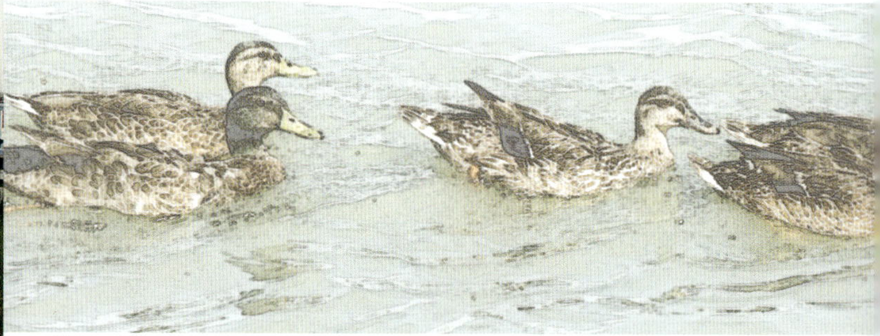

Early morning on Chincoteague.

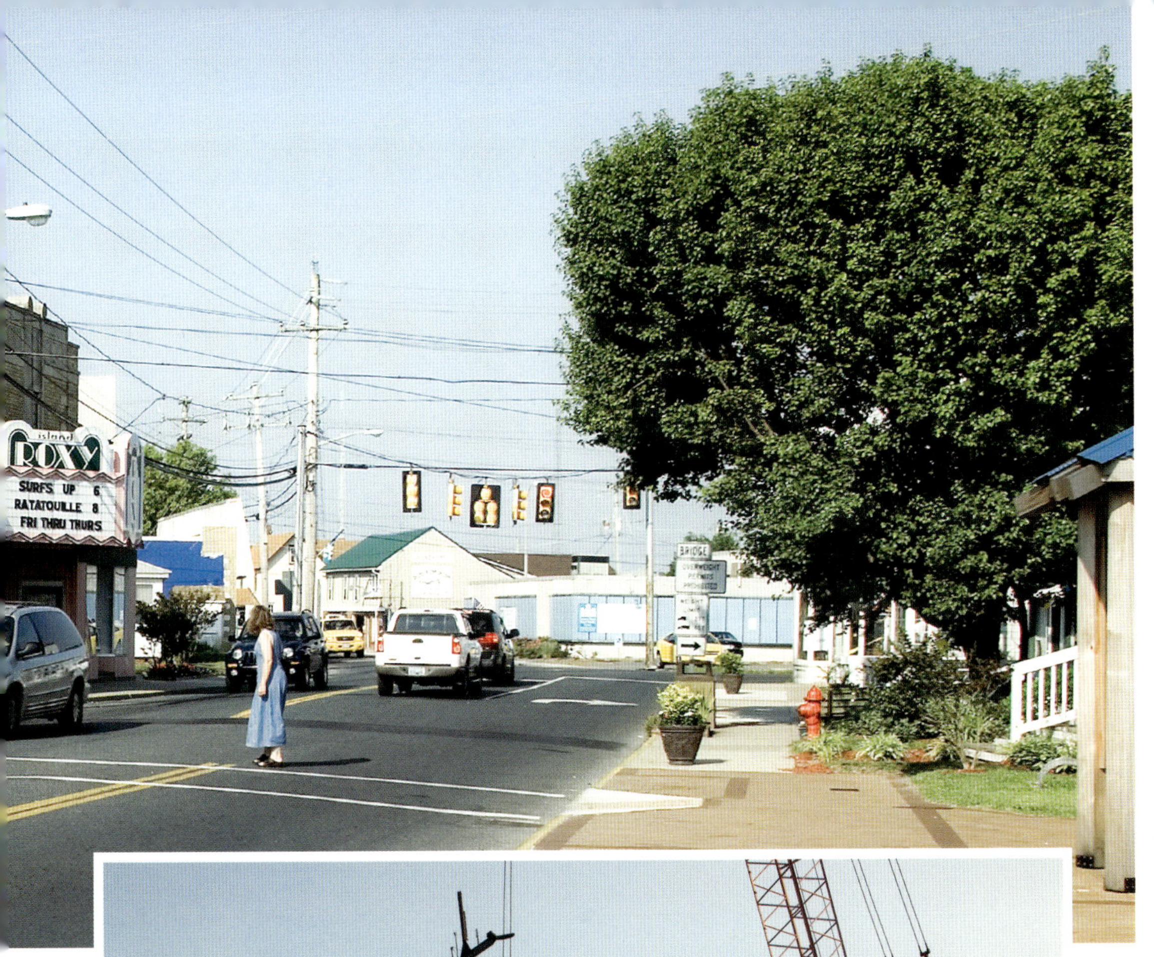

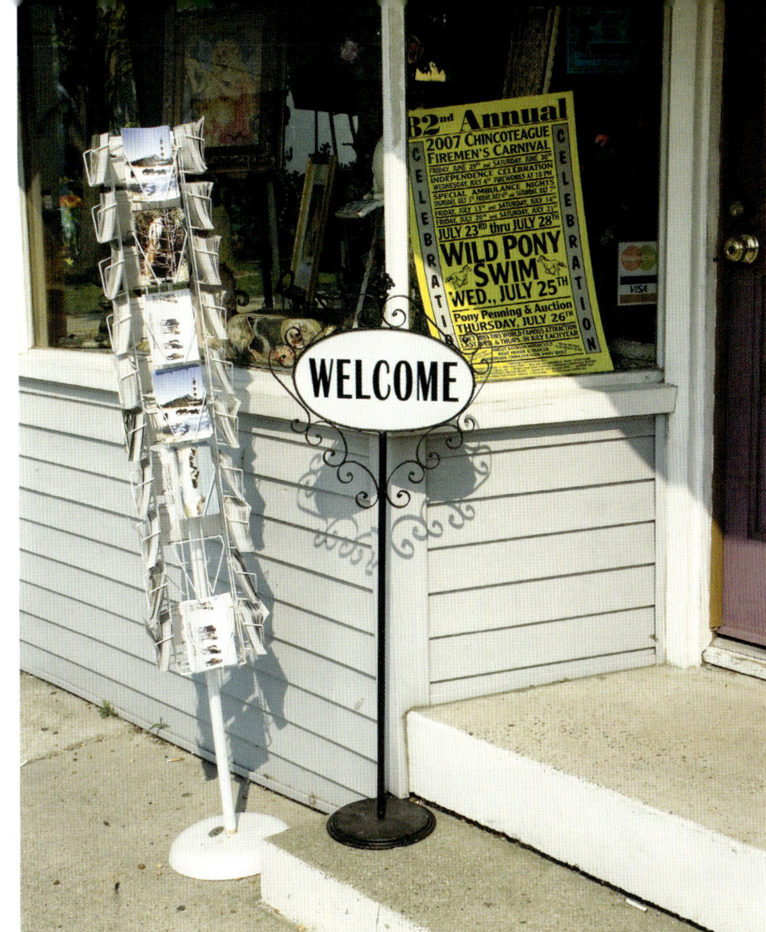
32nd Annual
2007 CHINCOTEAGUE
FIREMEN'S CARNIVAL
WILD PONY
SWIM
WED., JULY 25TH
Pony Penning & Auction
THURSDAY, JULY 26TH
JULY 23RD thru JULY 28TH
WELCOME
VISA

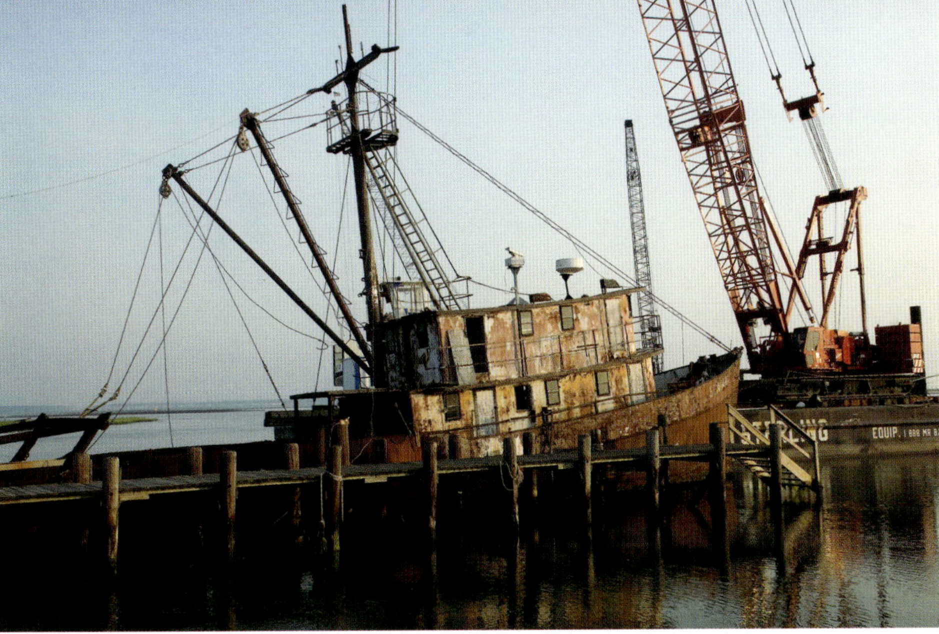

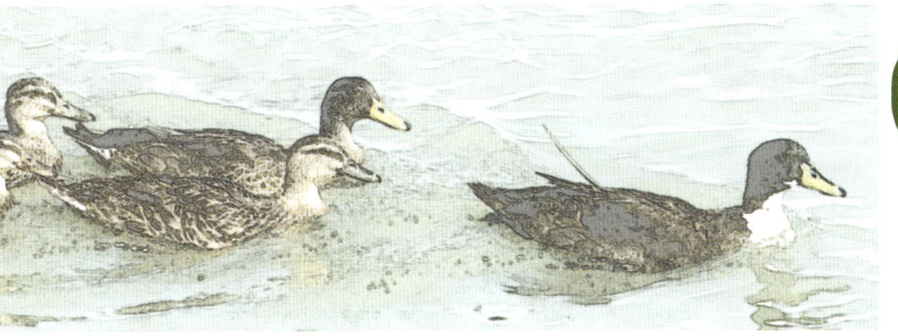

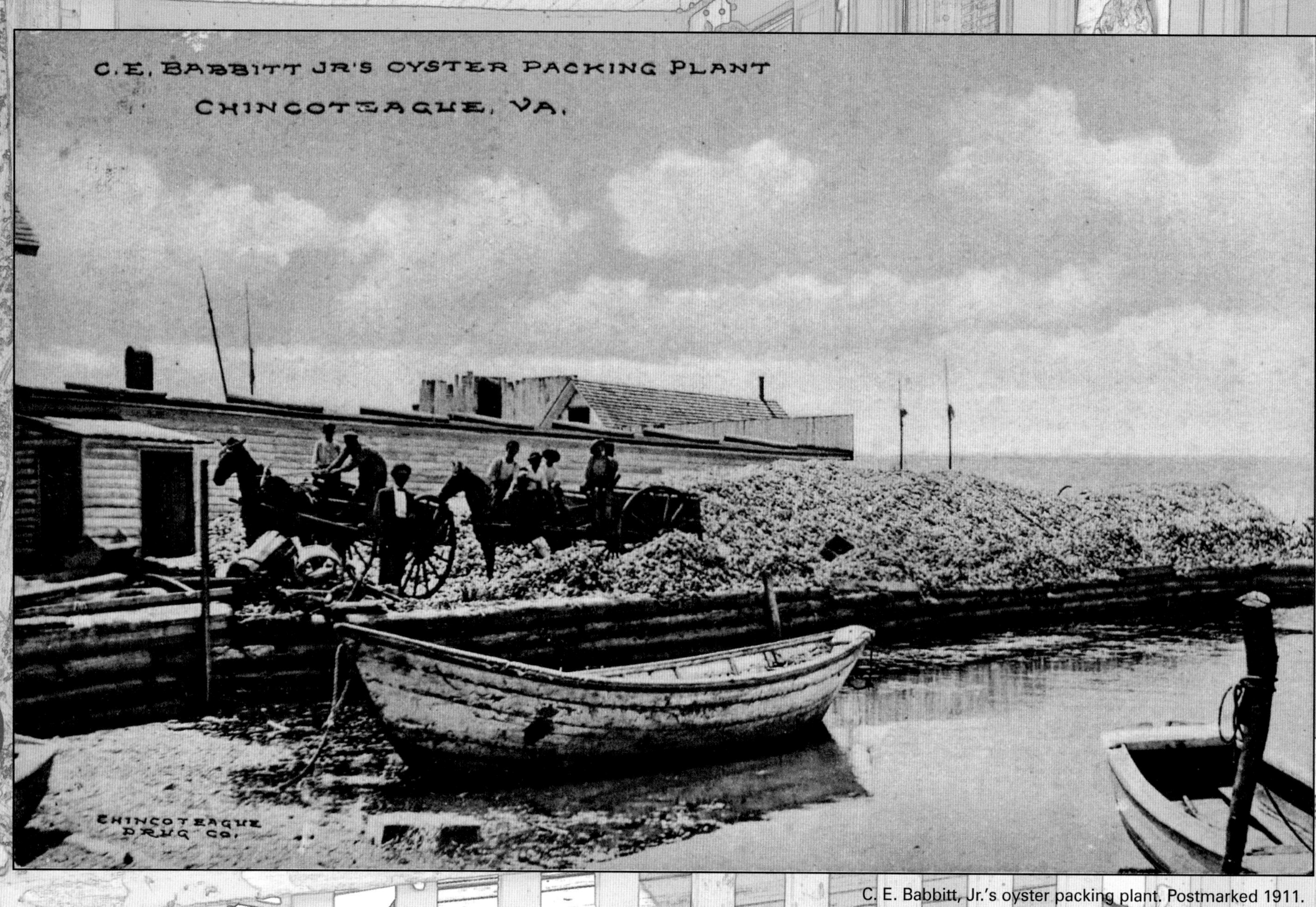

C. E. Babbitt, Jr.'s oyster packing plant. Postmarked 1911.

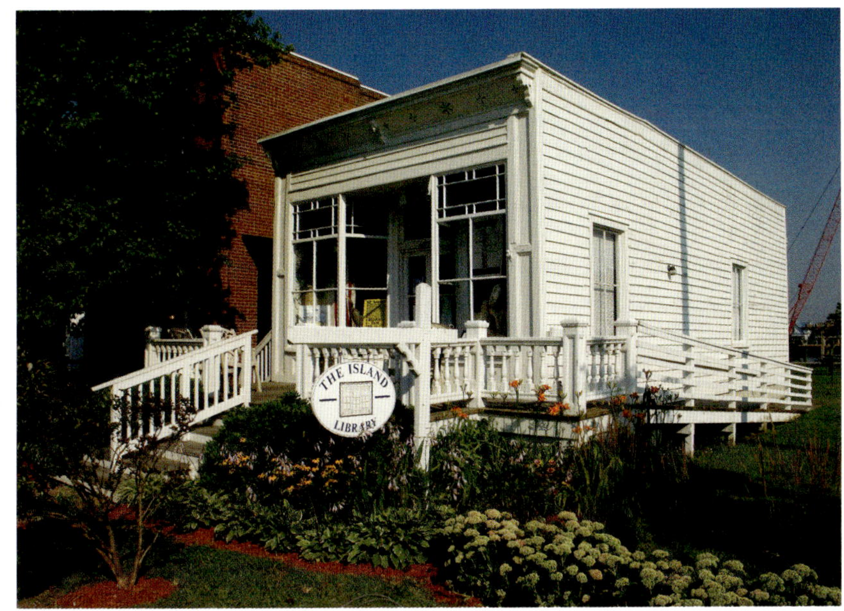

Library on Main Street.

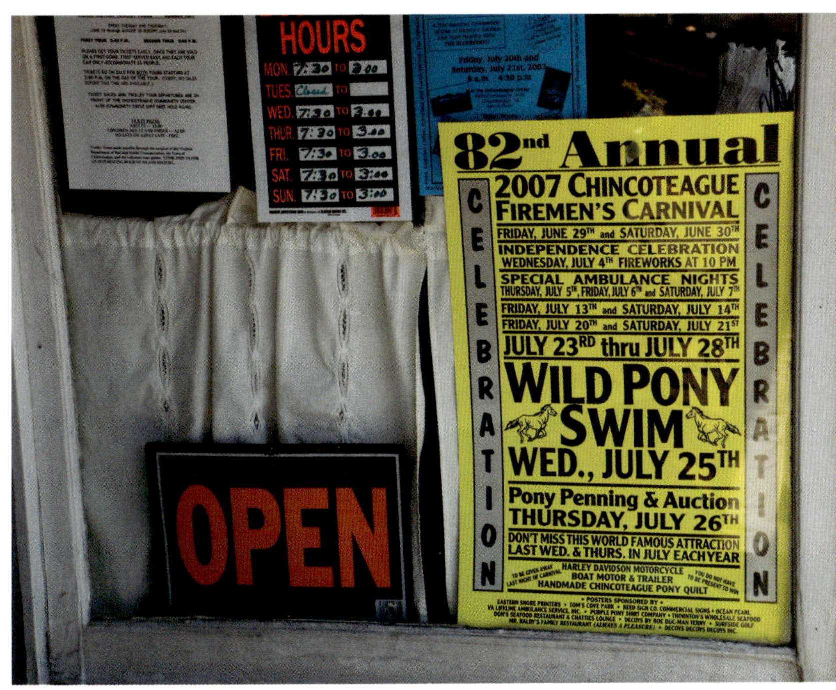

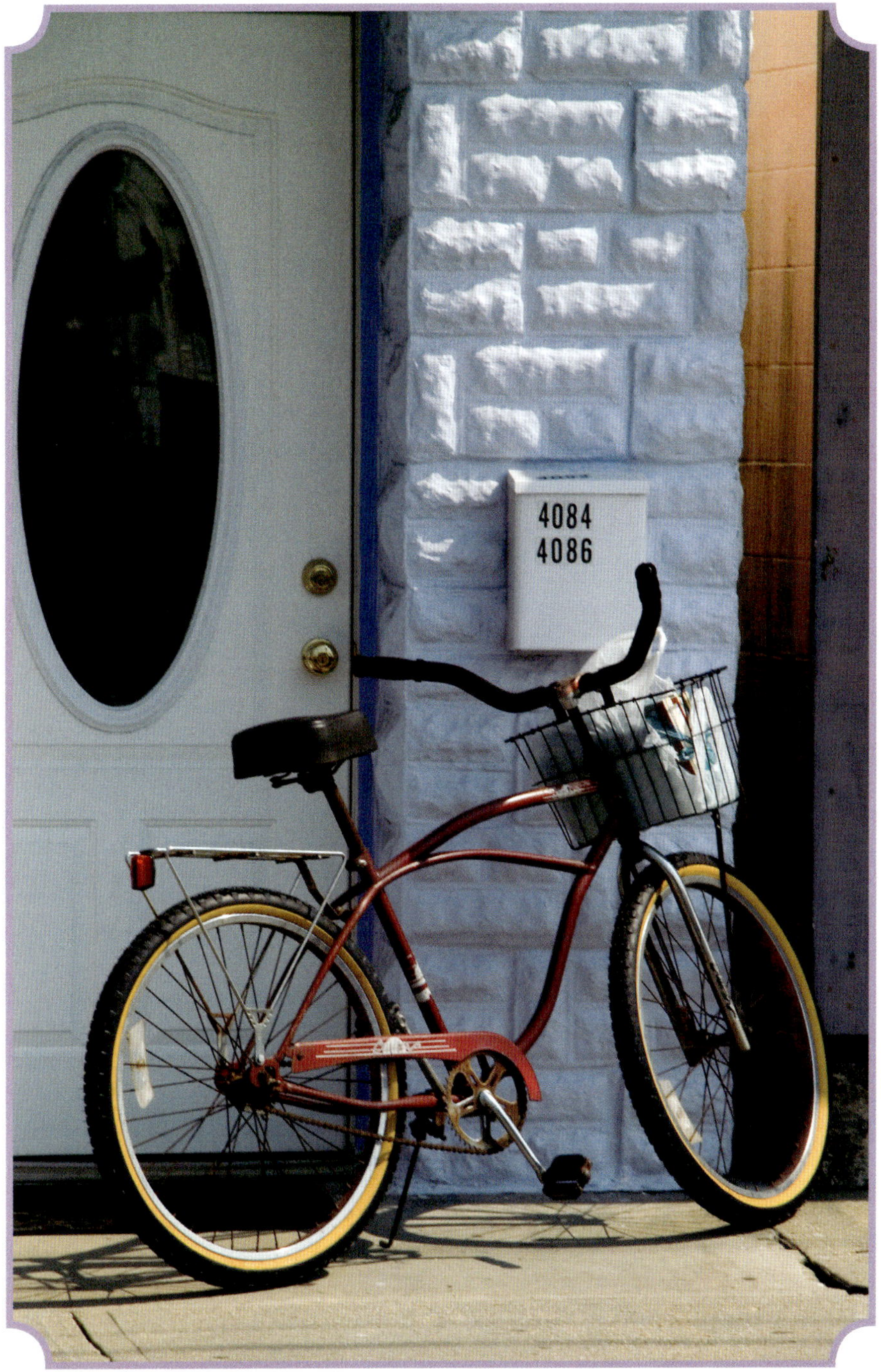

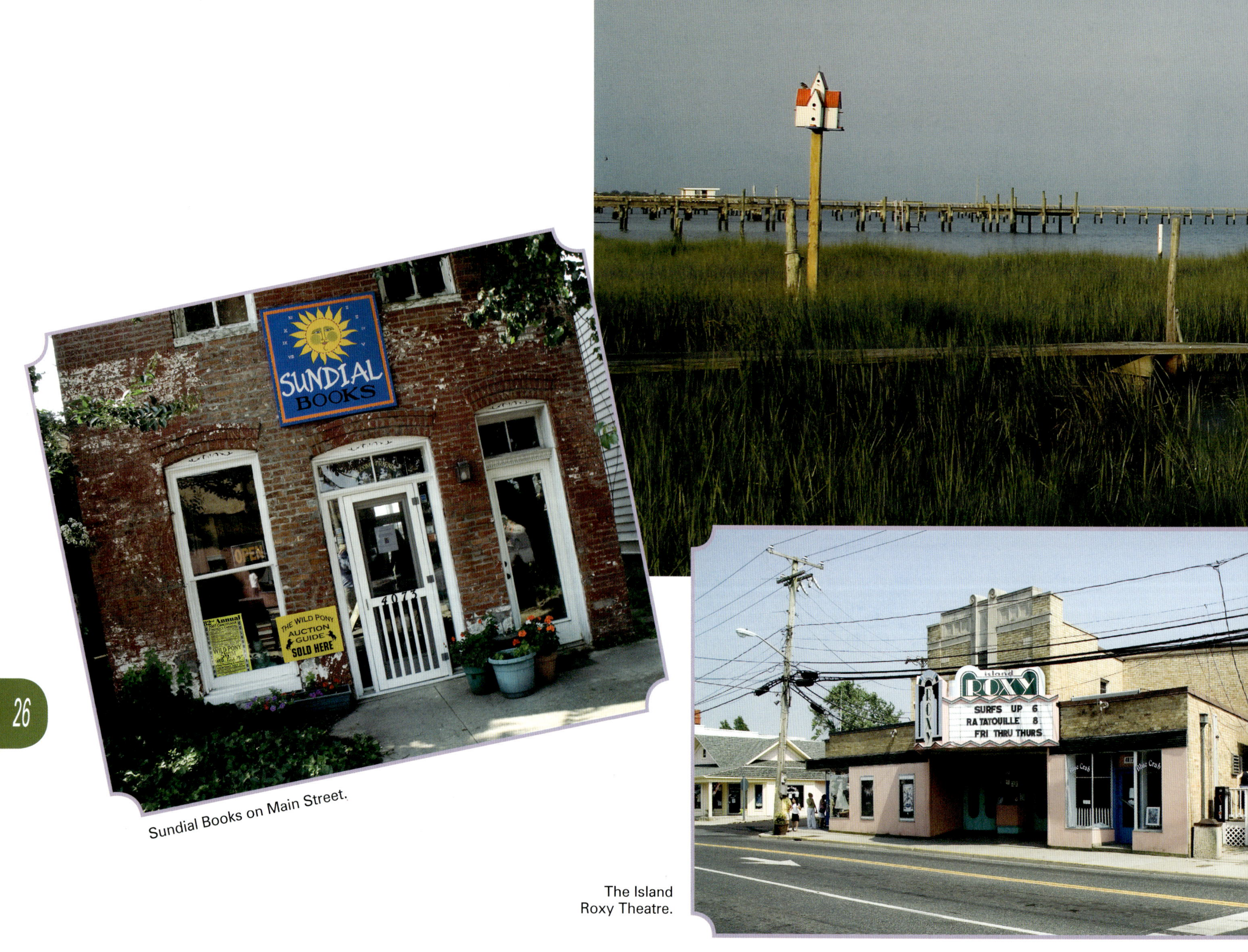

Sundial Books on Main Street.

The Island
Roxy Theatre.

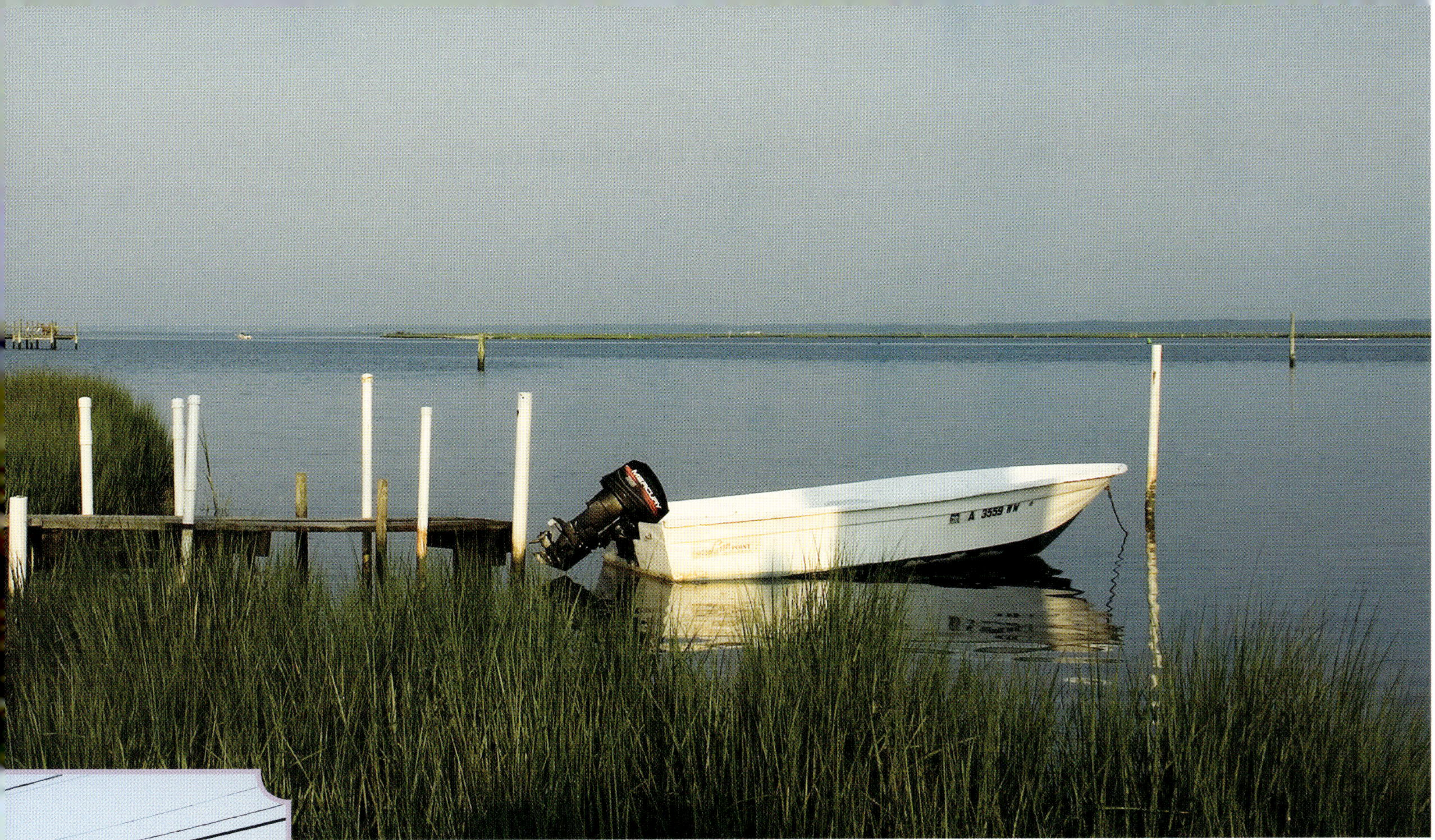

Sunrise on Chincoteague's western shore.

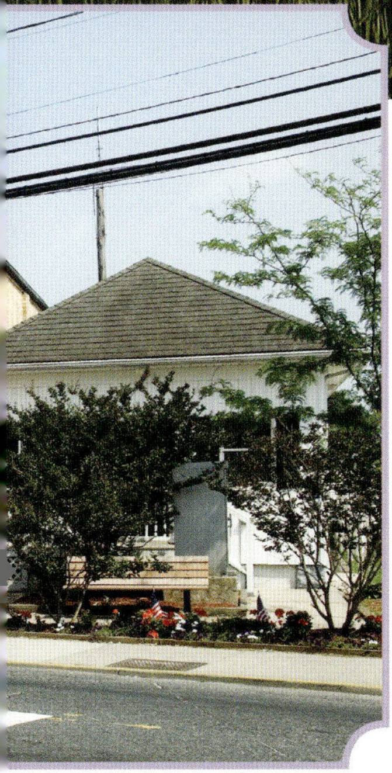

Sidewalk in front of the Island Roxy Theatre.

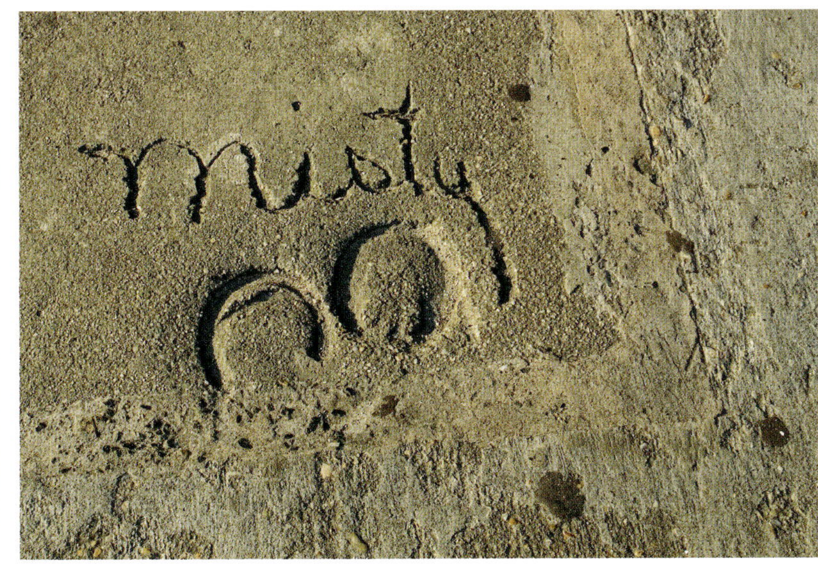

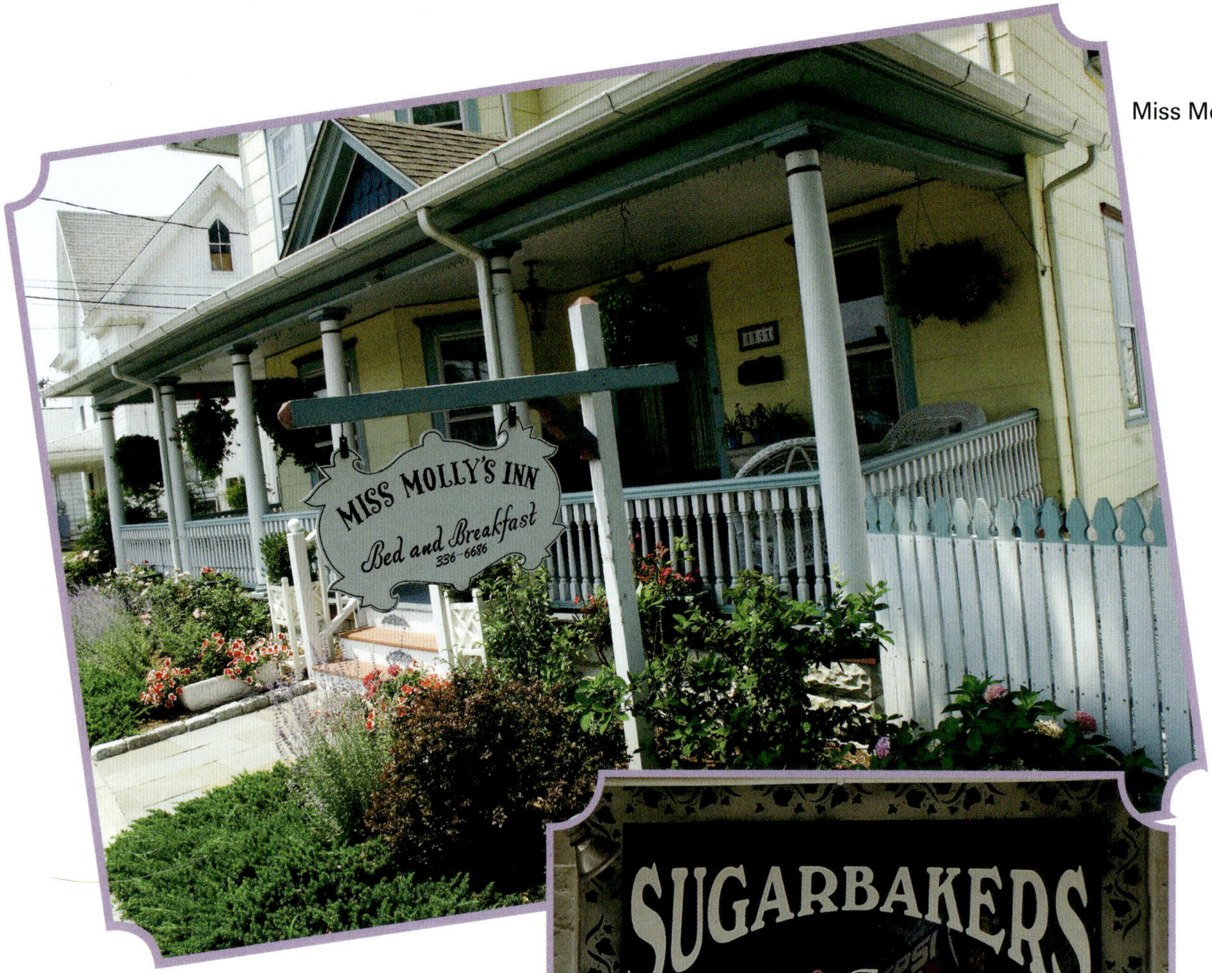

Miss Molly's Inn on Main Street.

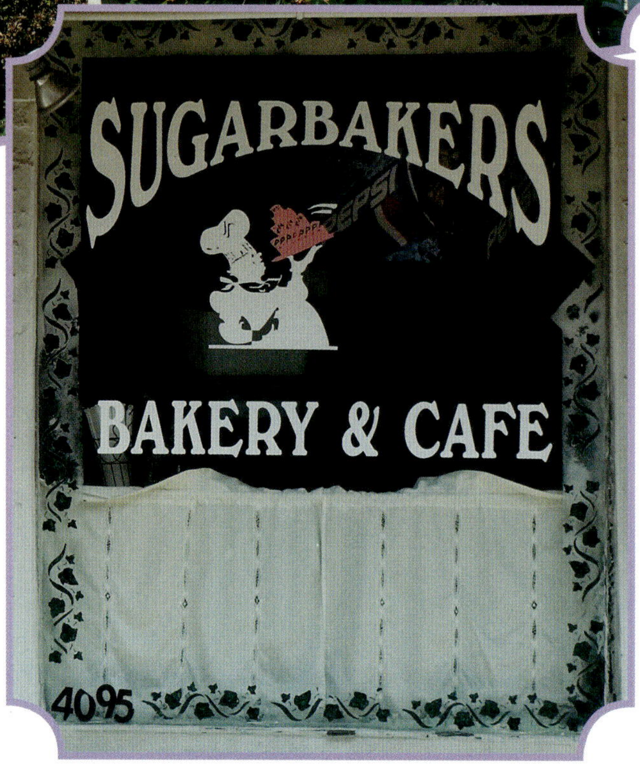

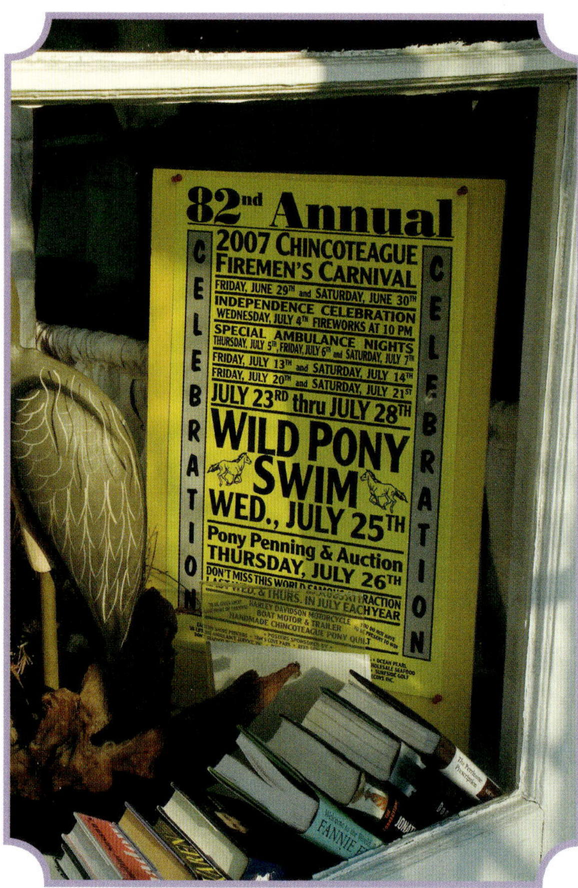

A downtown window on Main Street.

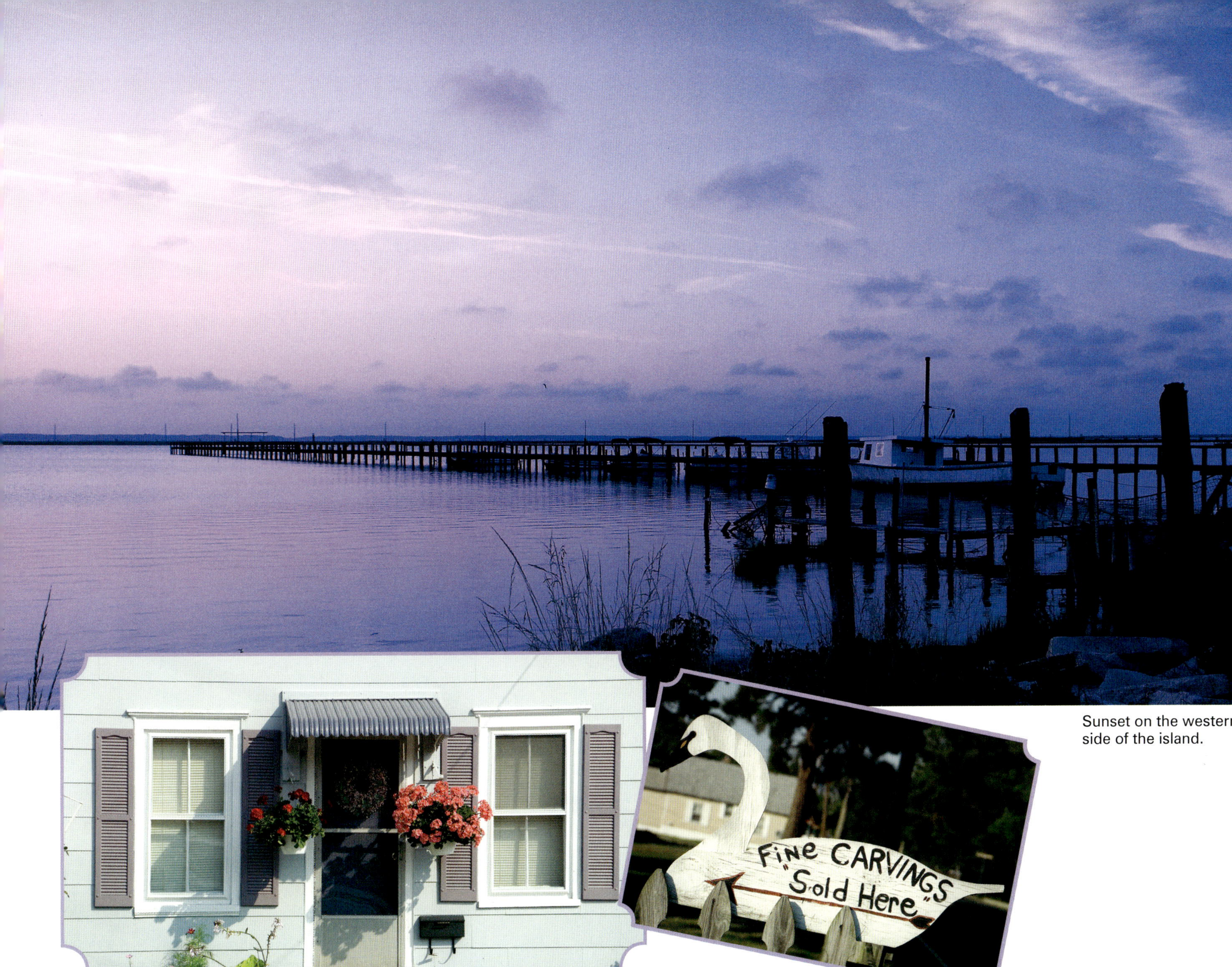

Sunset on the western side of the island.

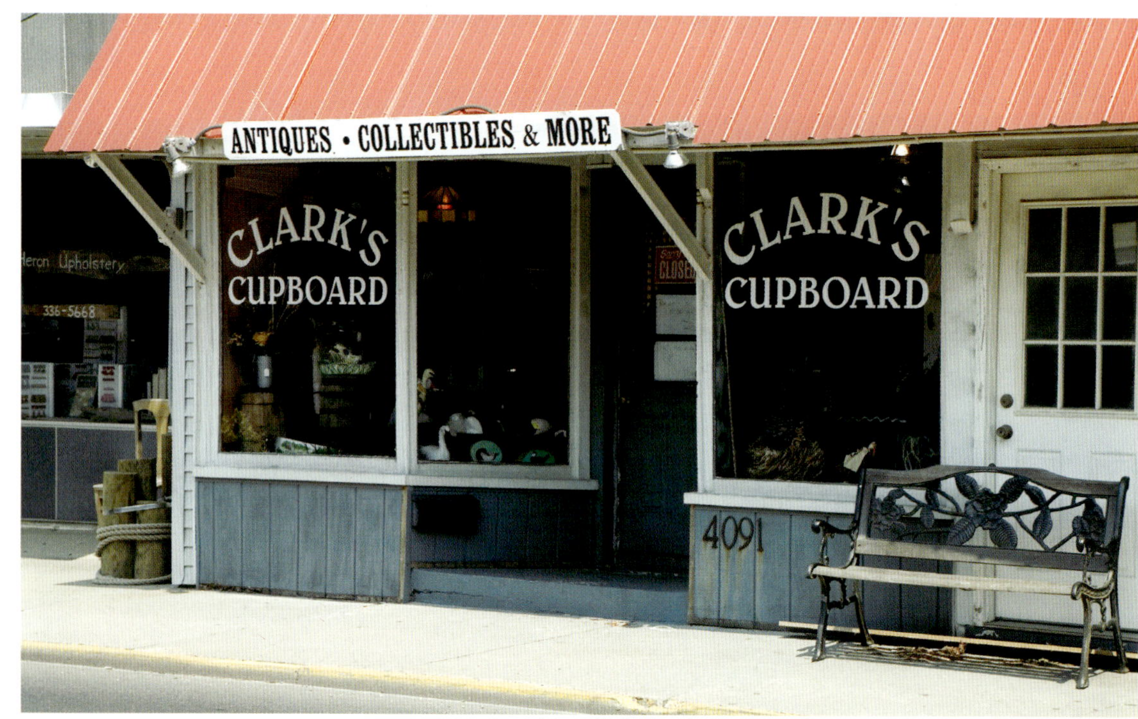

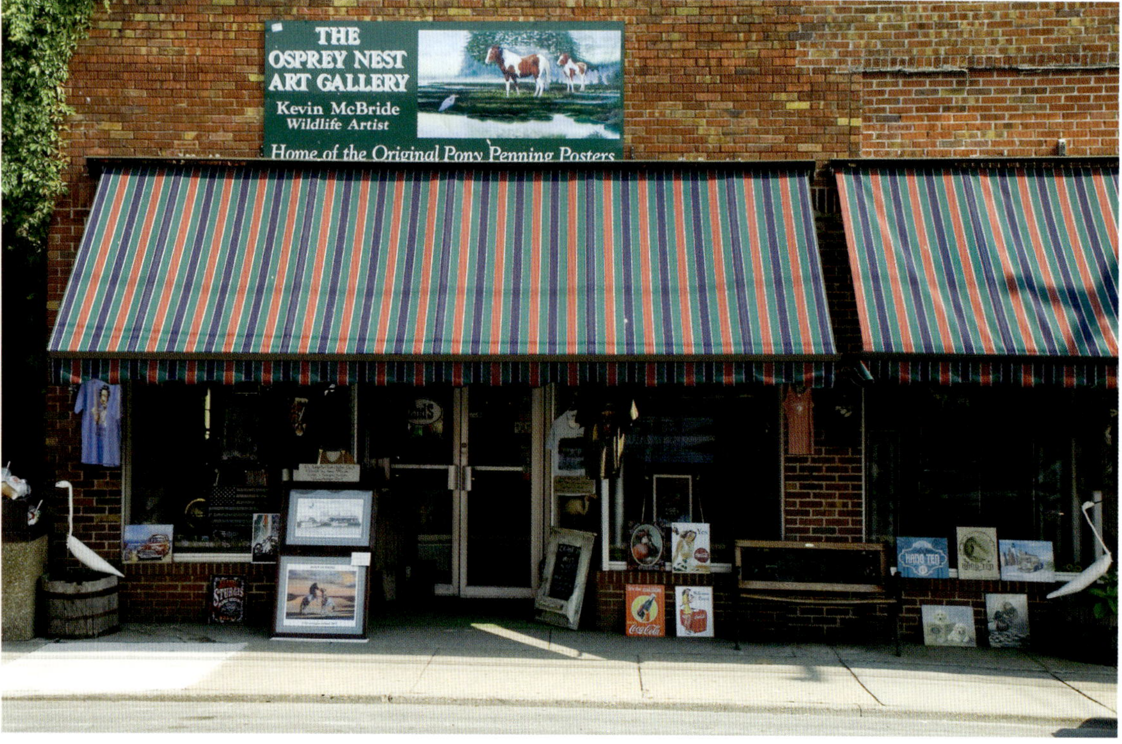

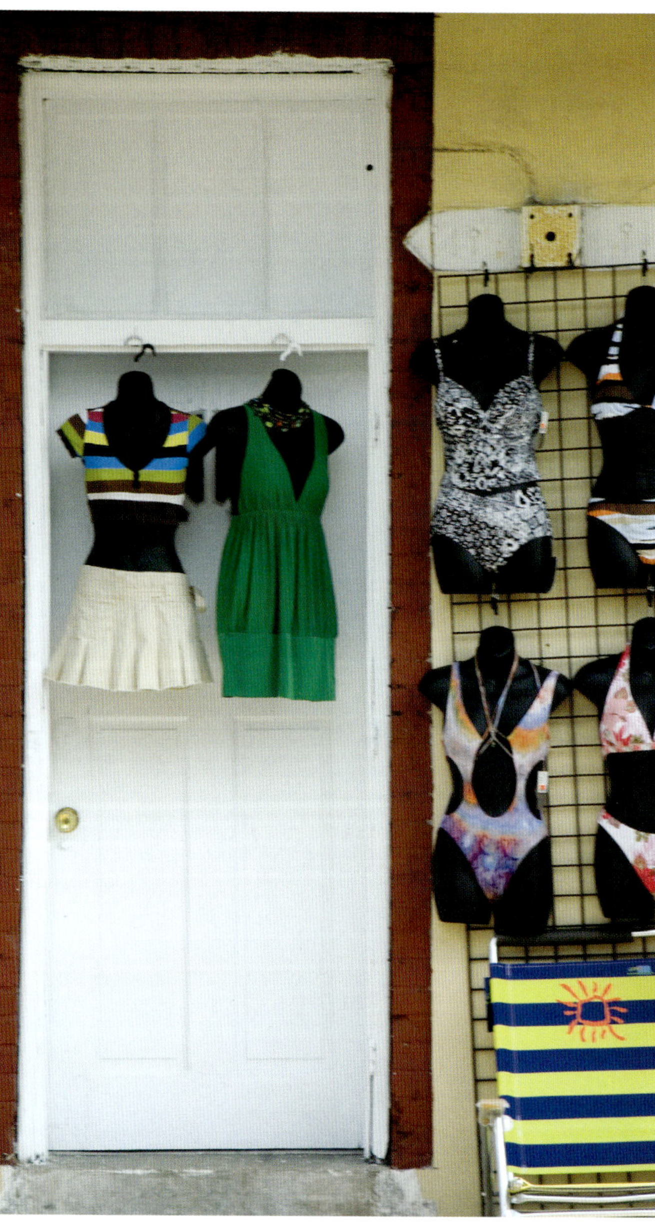

Downtown sidewalk clothing display.

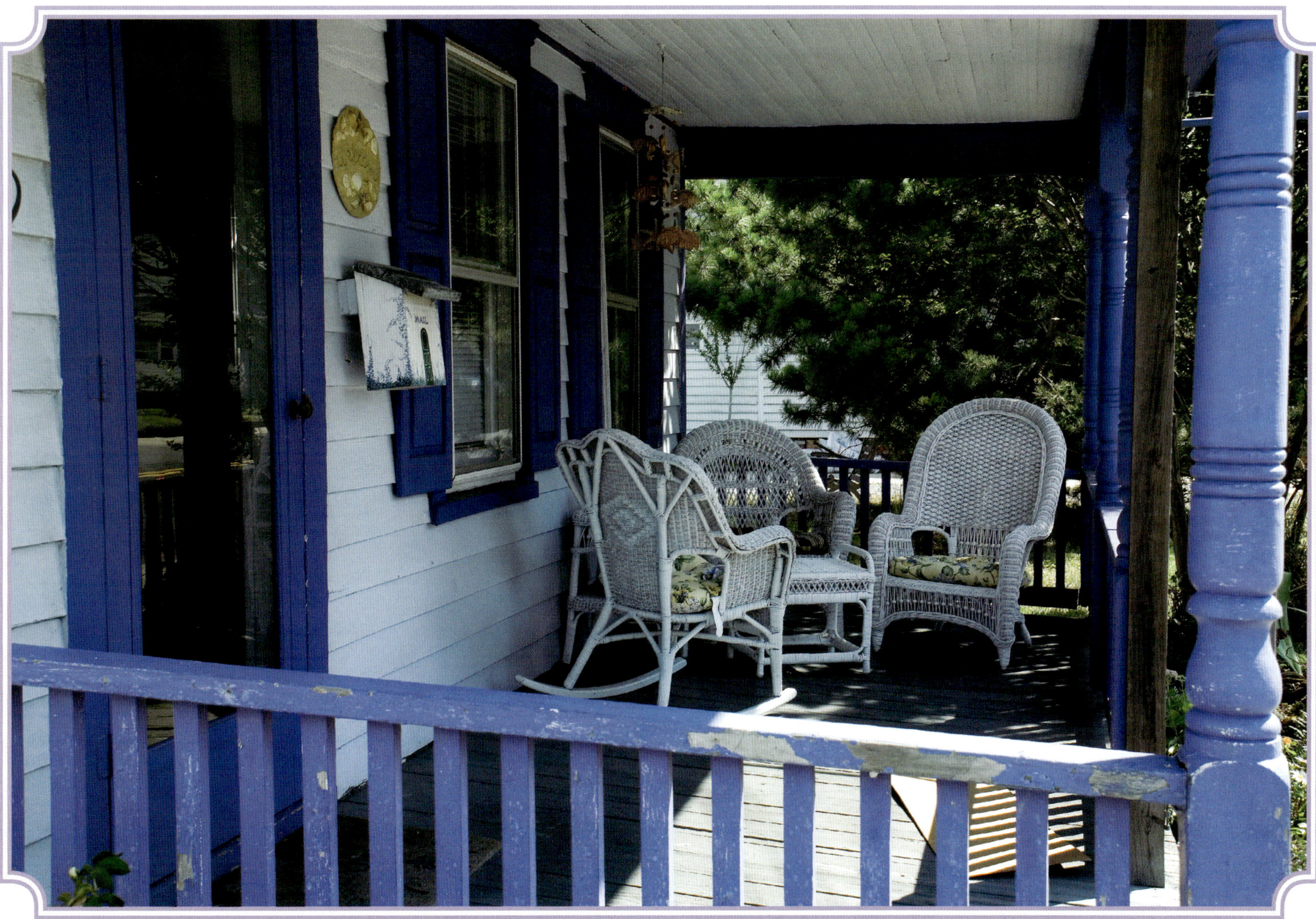

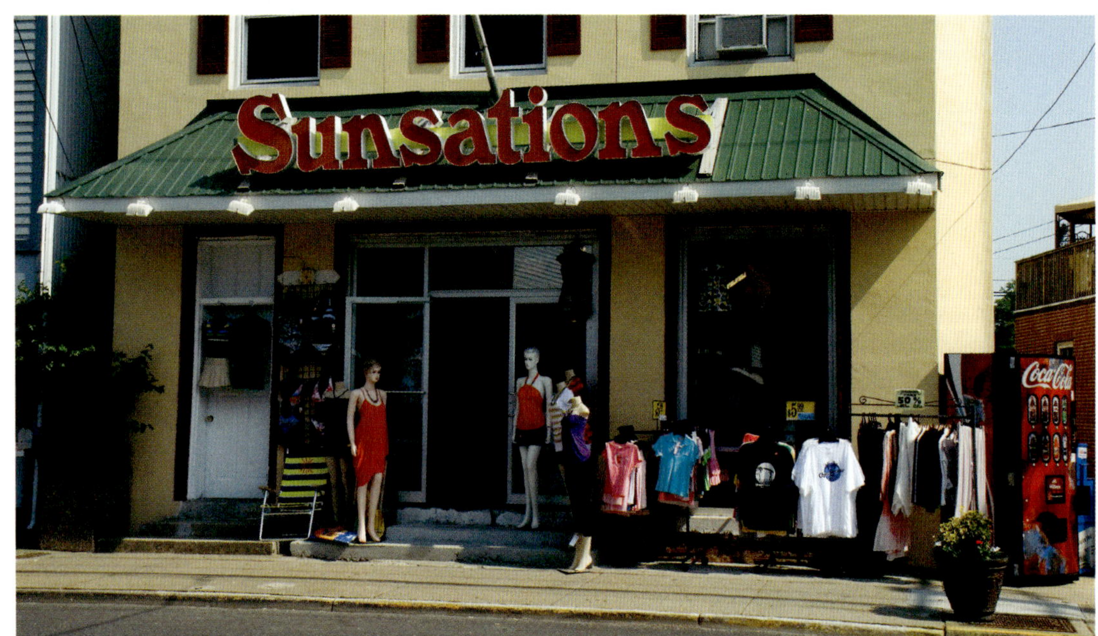

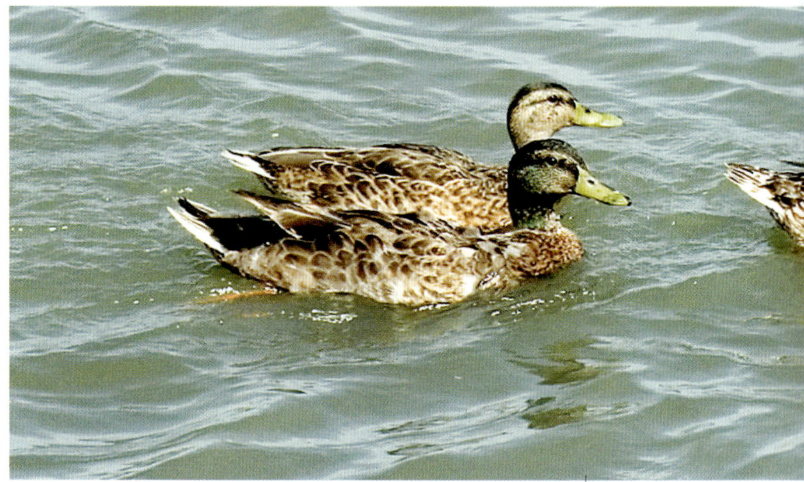

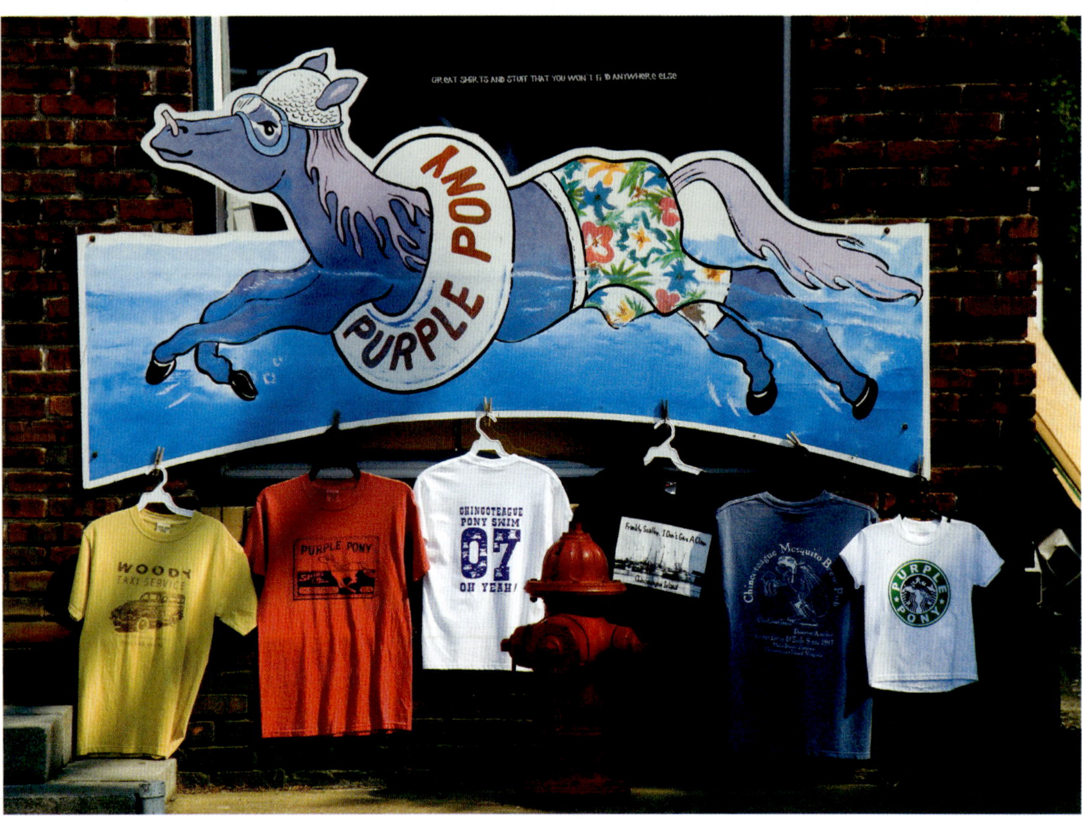

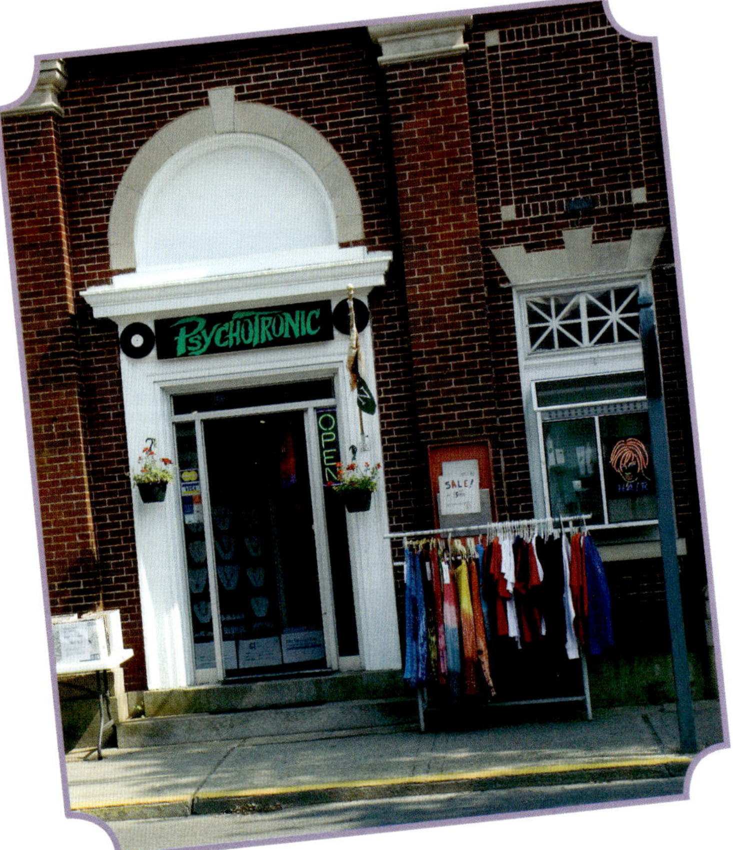

On Main Street.

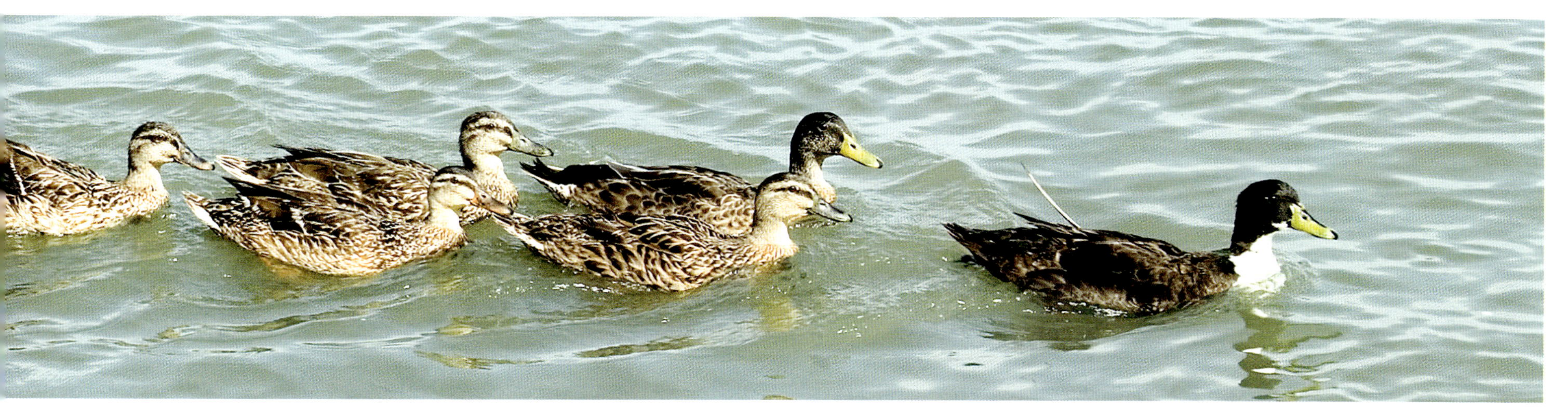

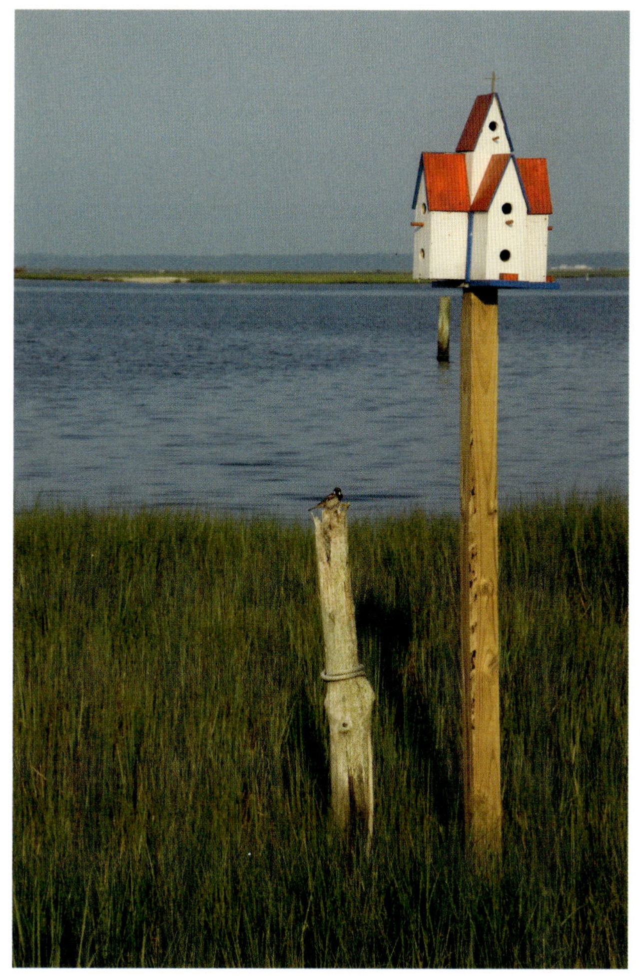

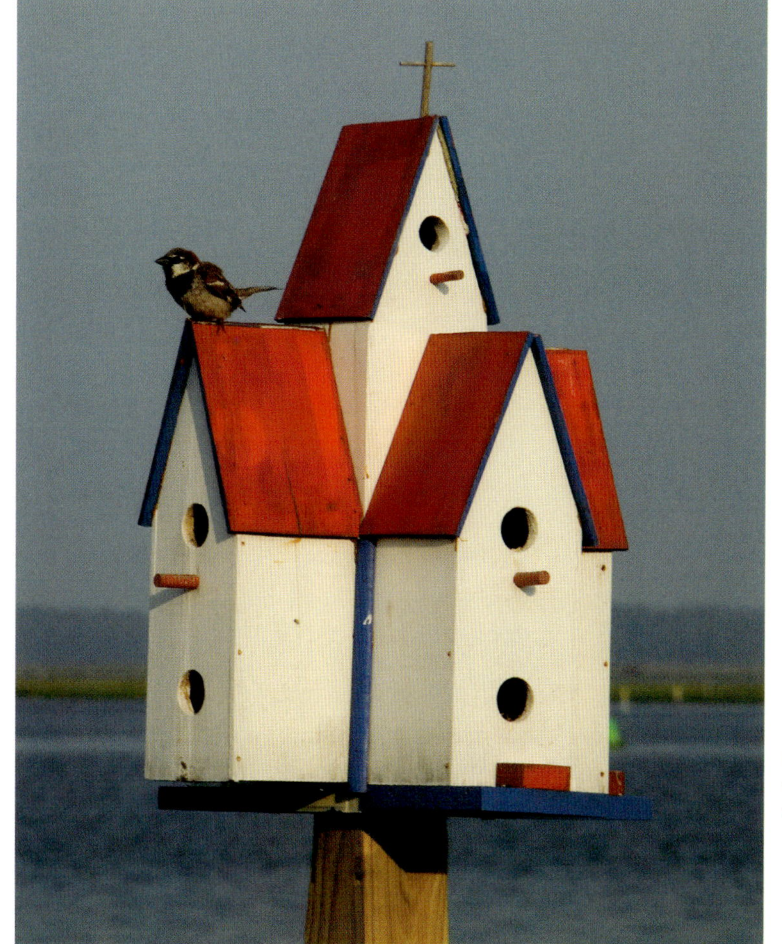

Early morning looking towards Chincoteague Channel.

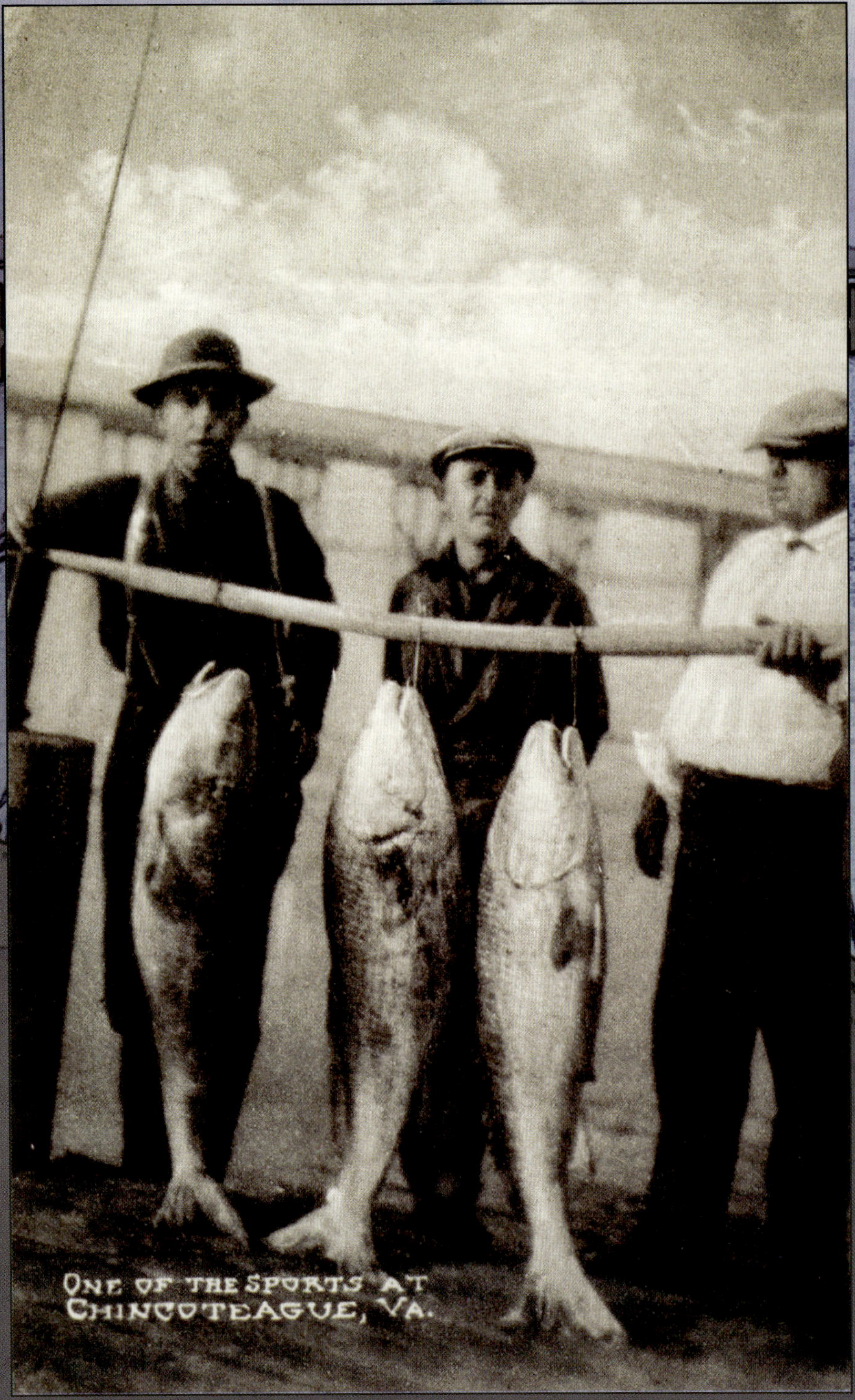

One of the sports at Chincoteague. Circa 1908.

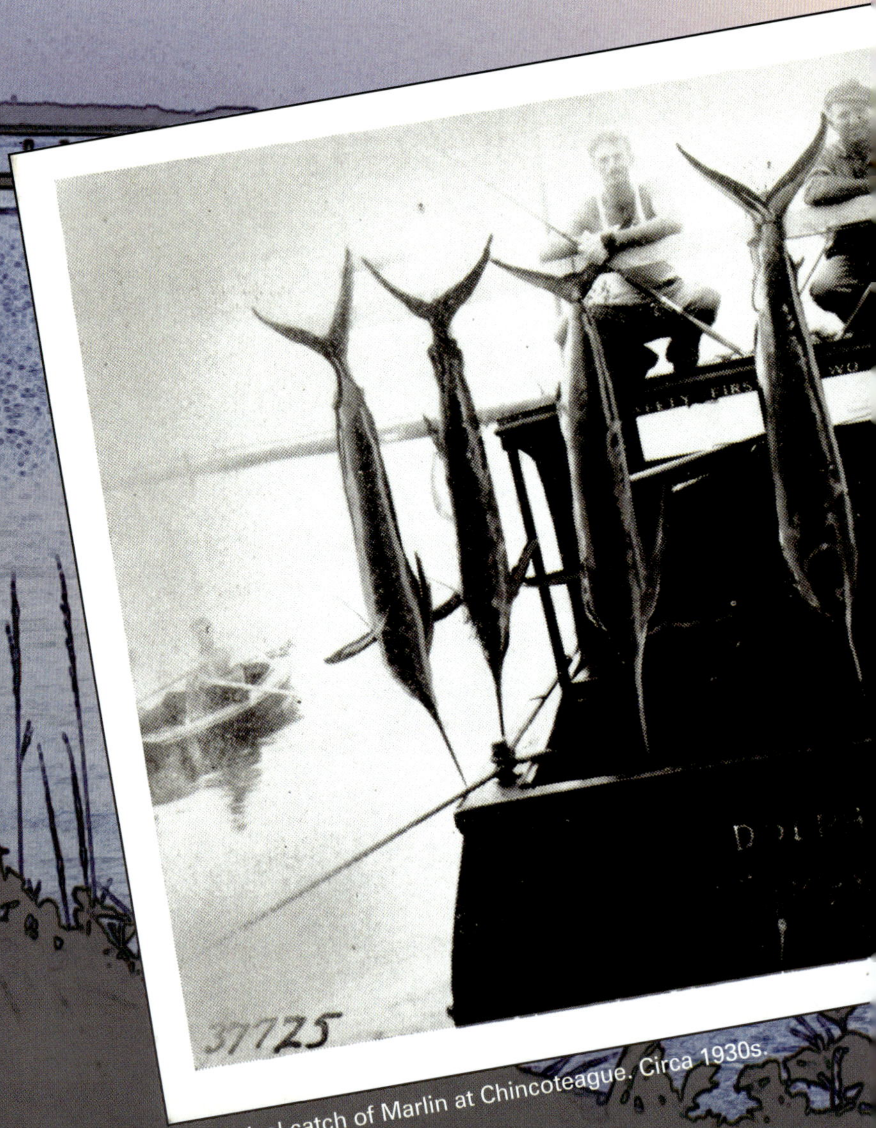

A typical catch of Marlin at Chincoteague. Circa 1930s.

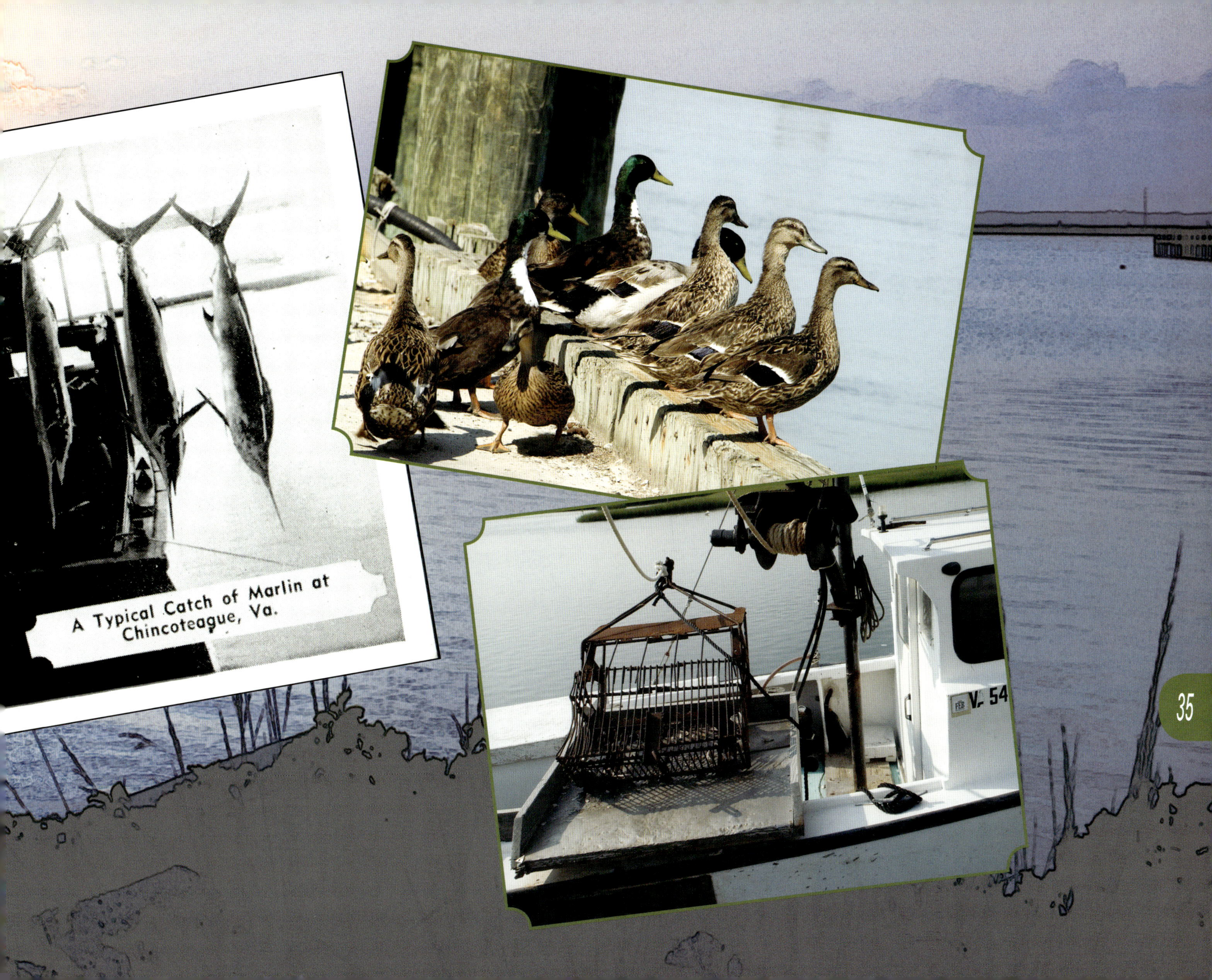

A Typical Catch of Marlin at
Chincoteague, Va.

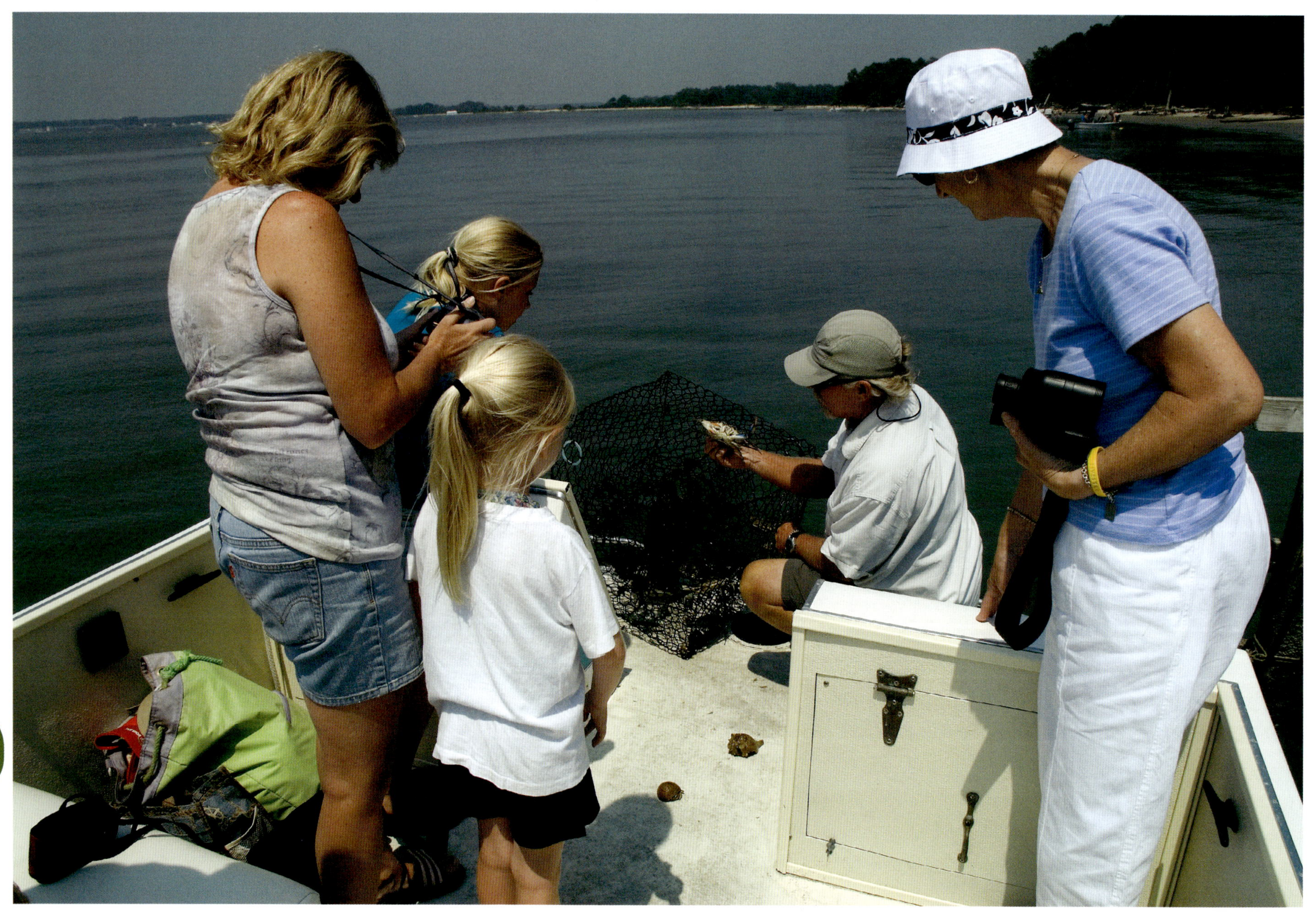

Crab Science 101 aboard
Chincoteague Cruises.

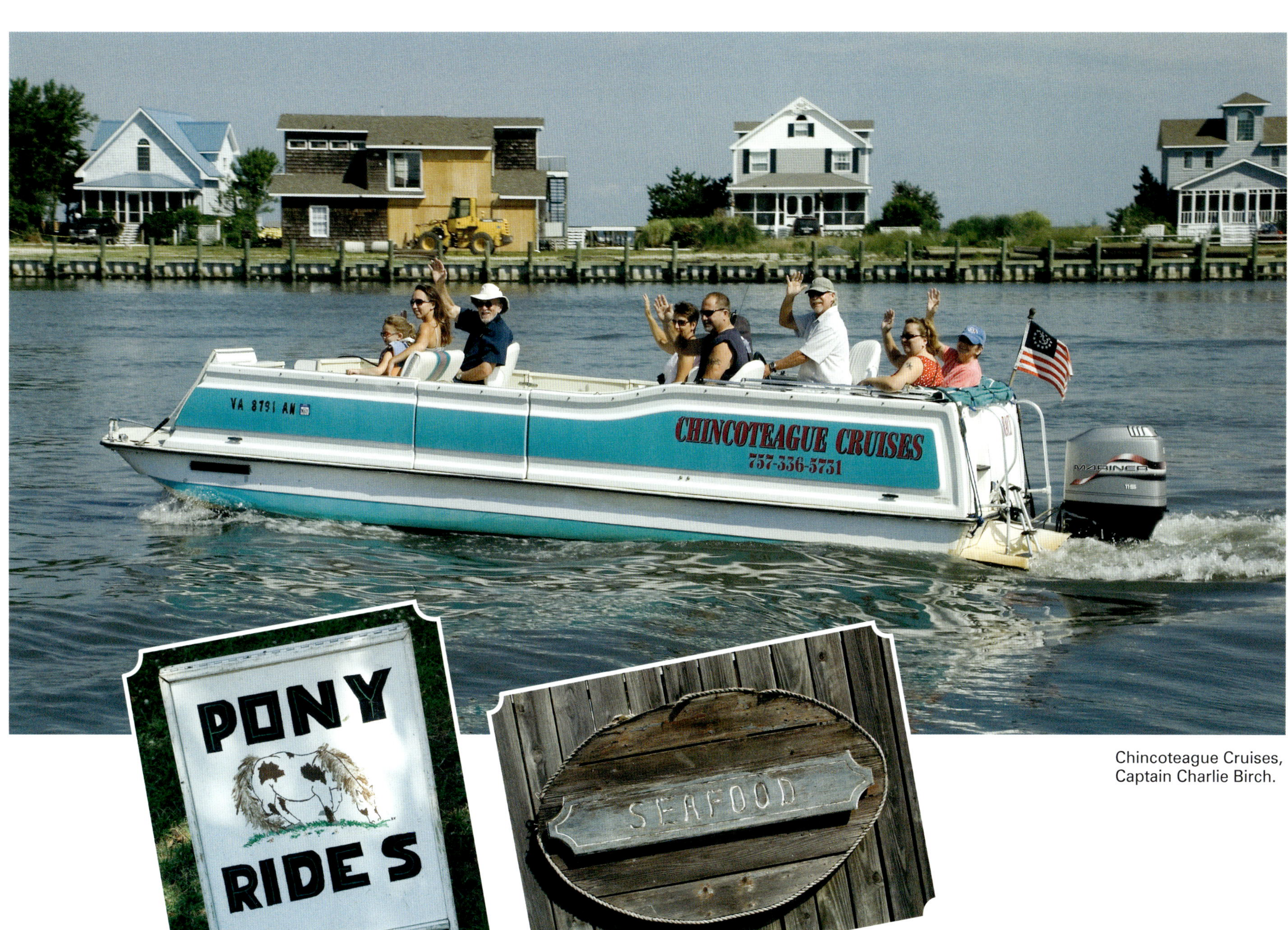

Chincoteague Cruises,
Captain Charlie Birch.

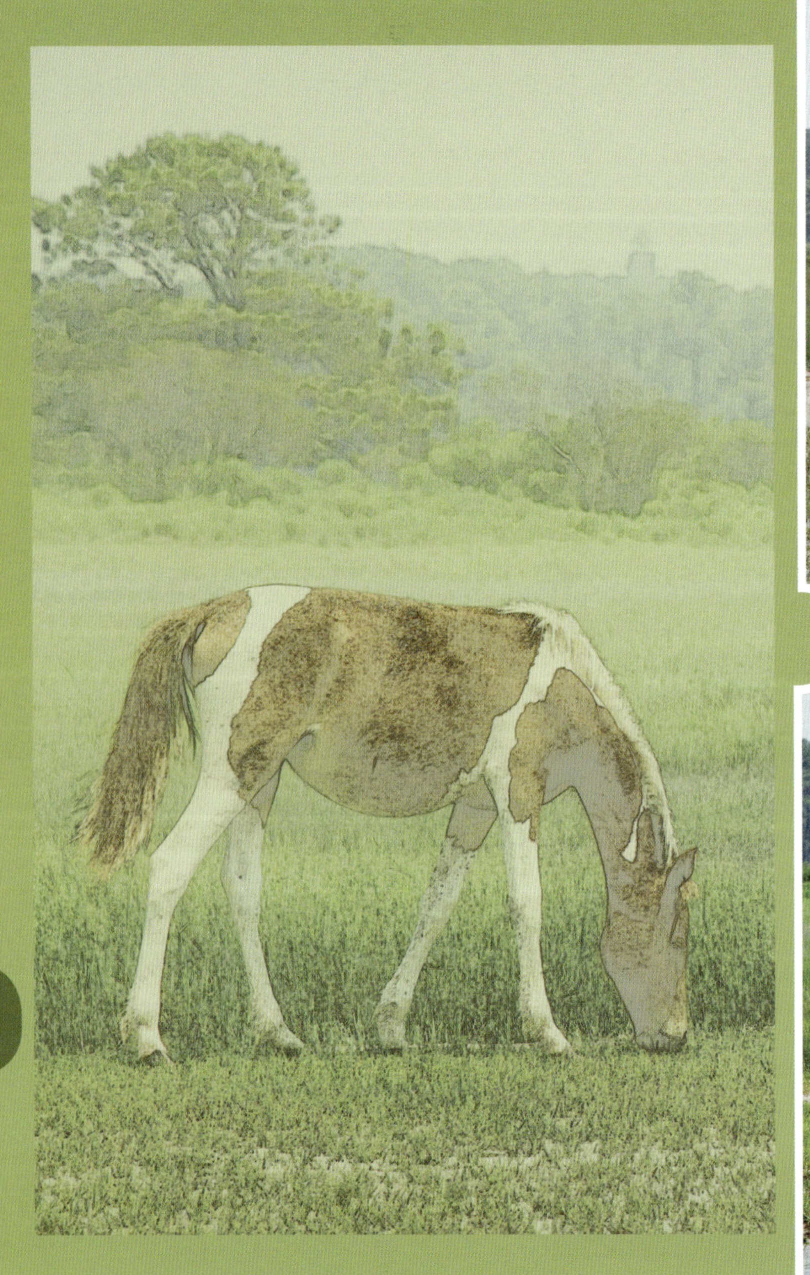

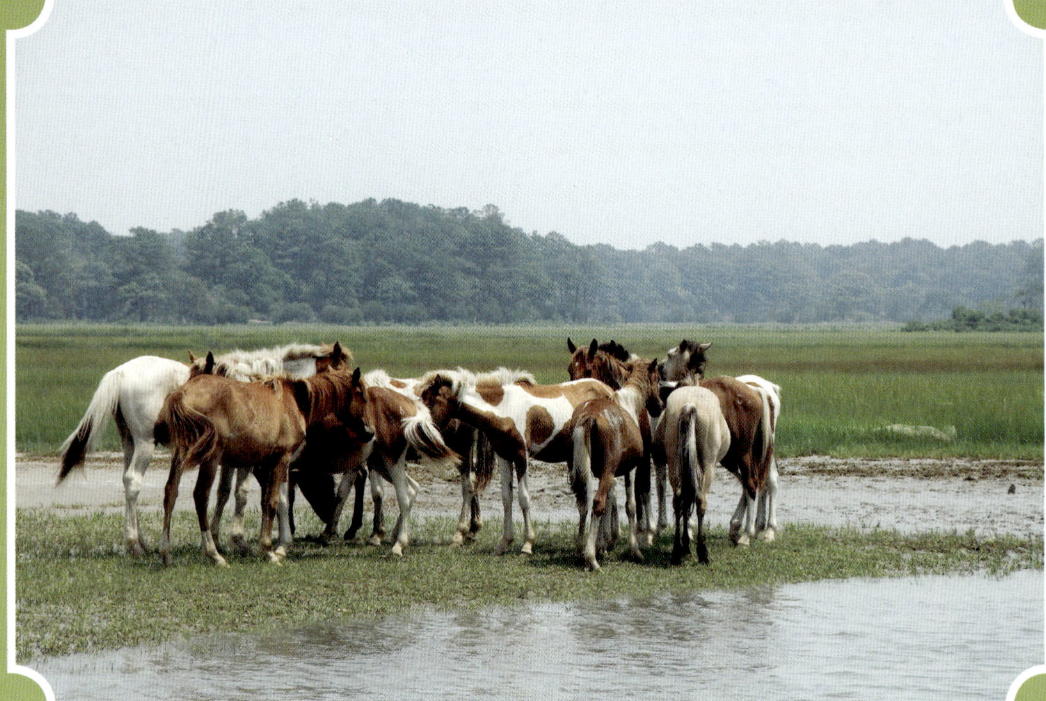

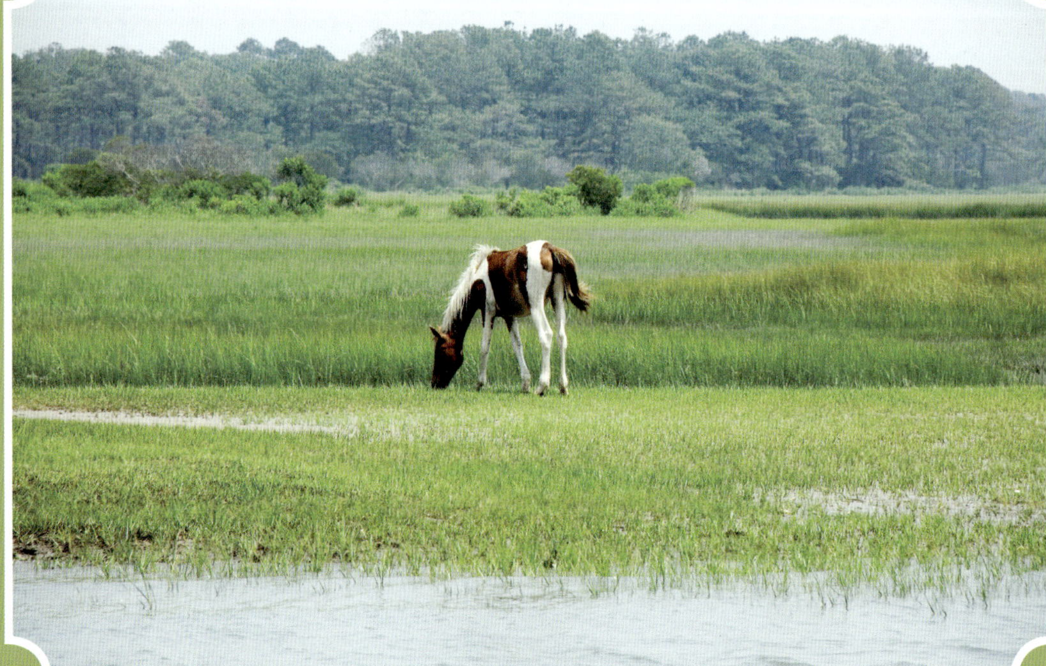

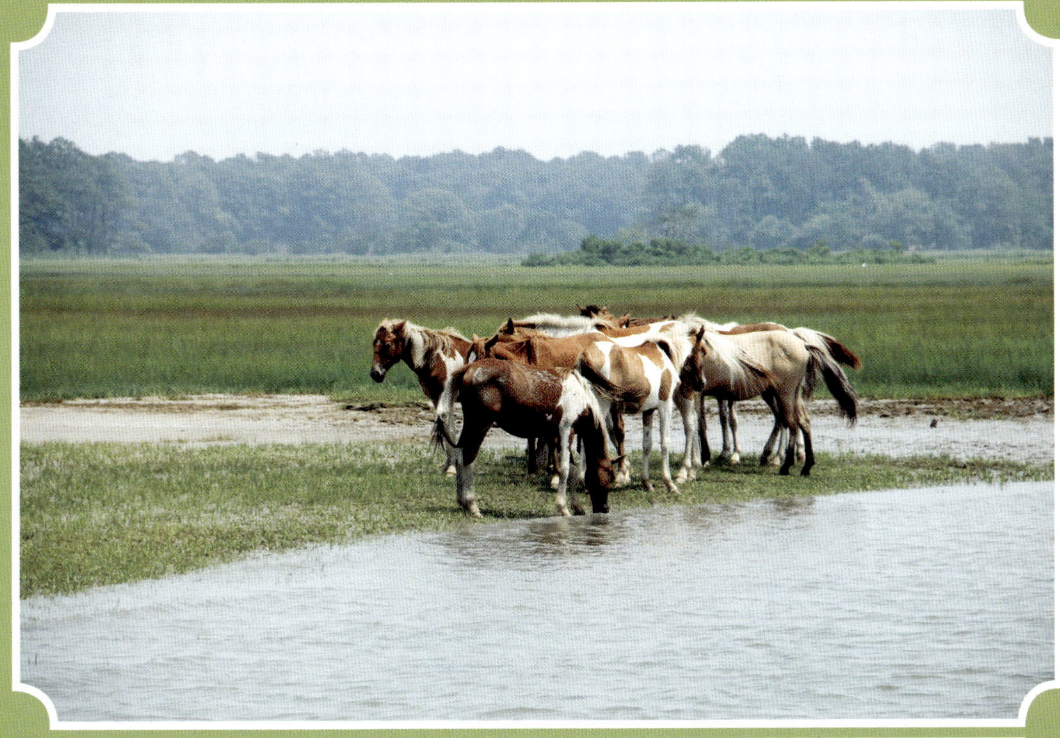

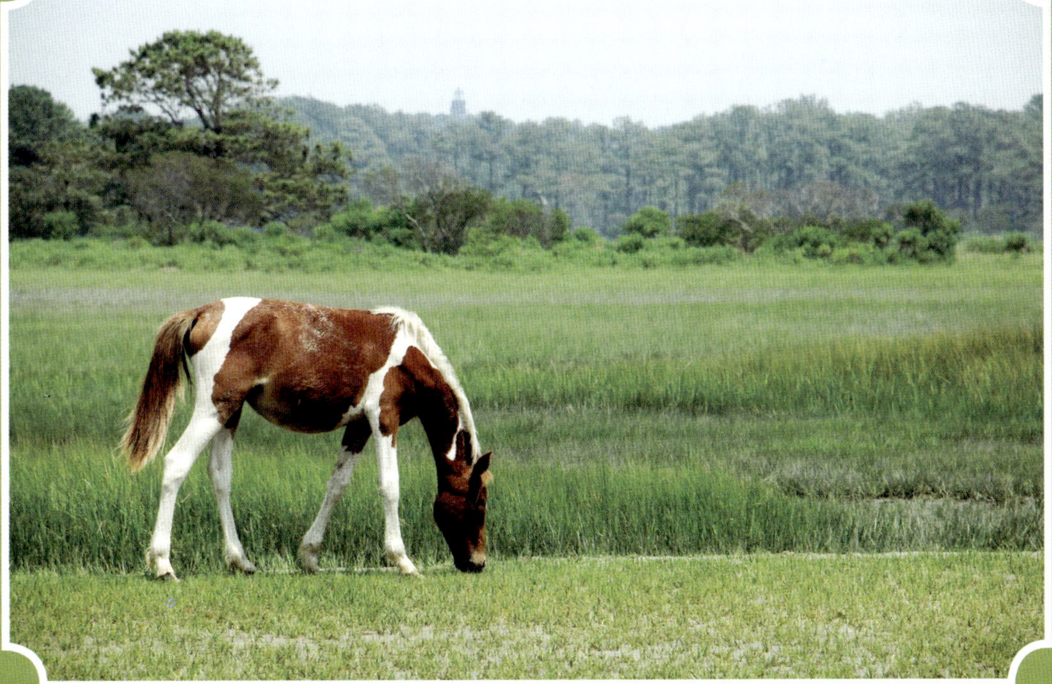

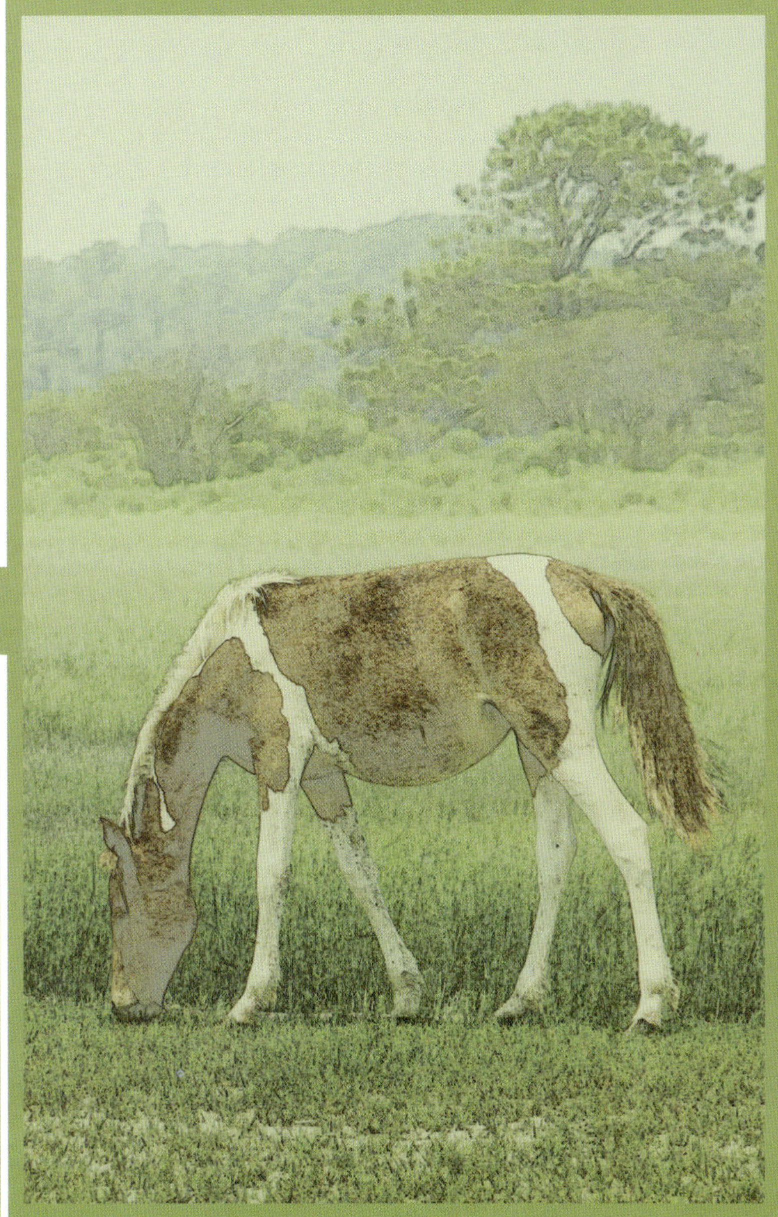

Wild ponies on Assateague.

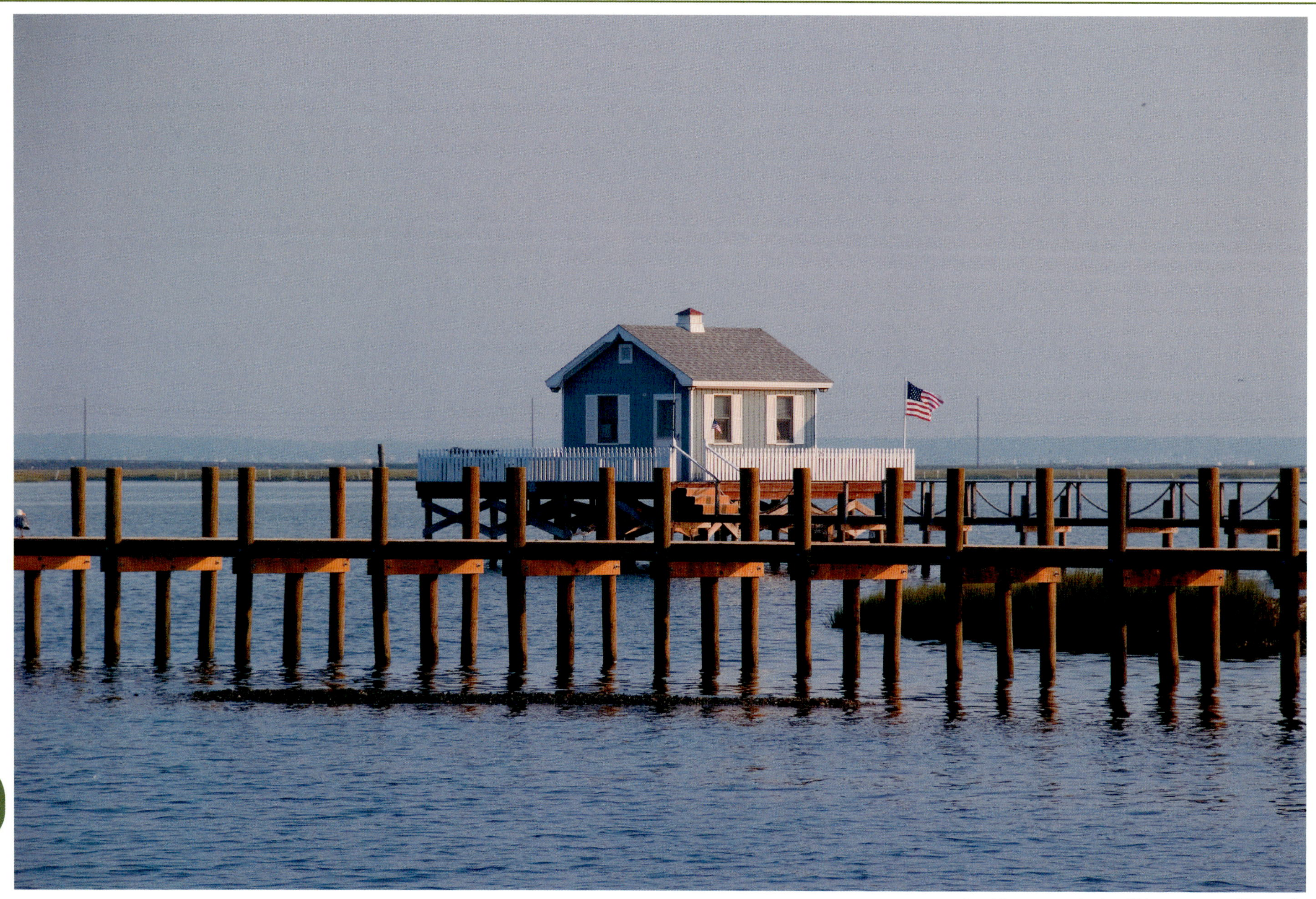

Looking towards the Chincoteague Channel.

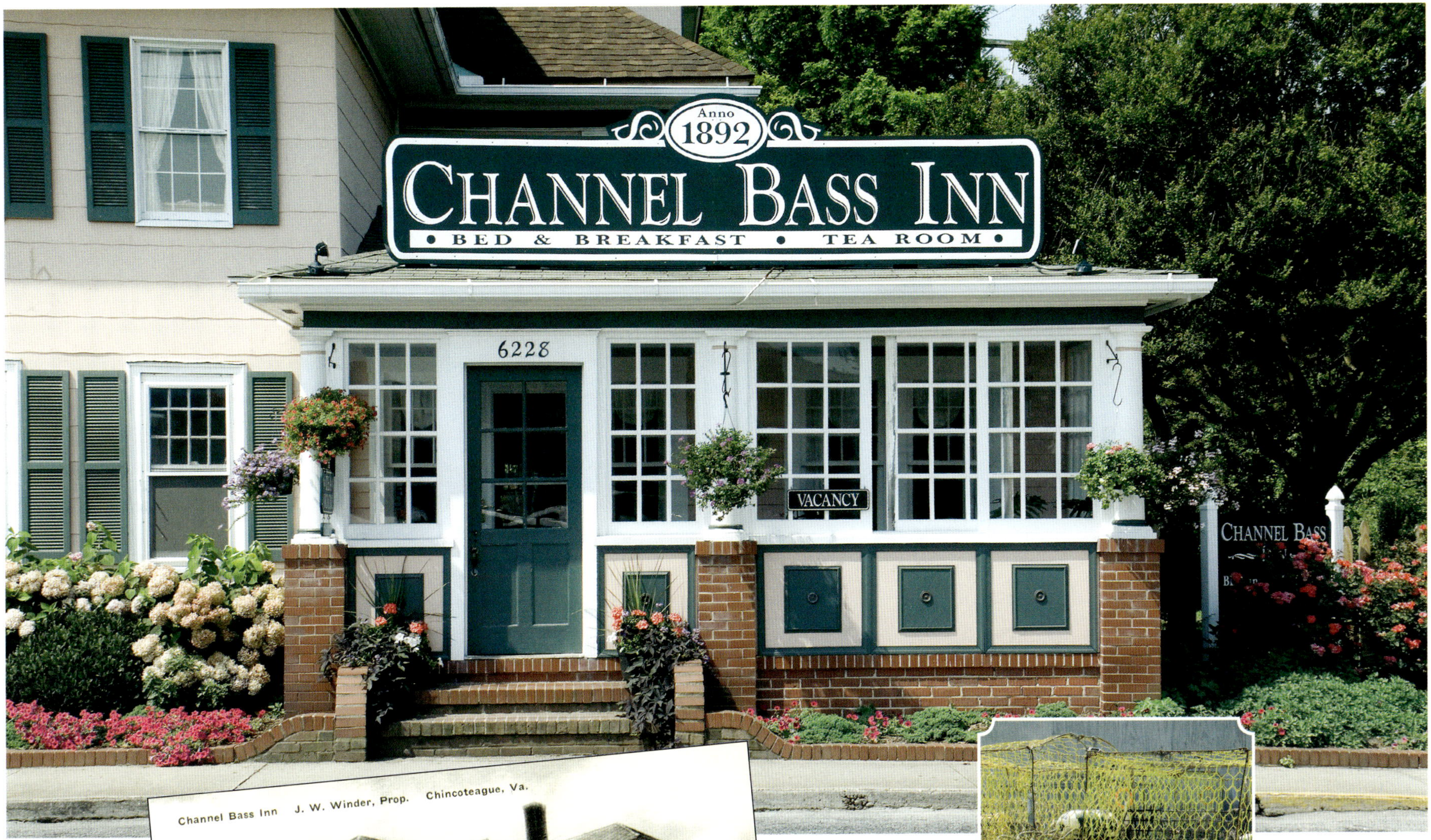

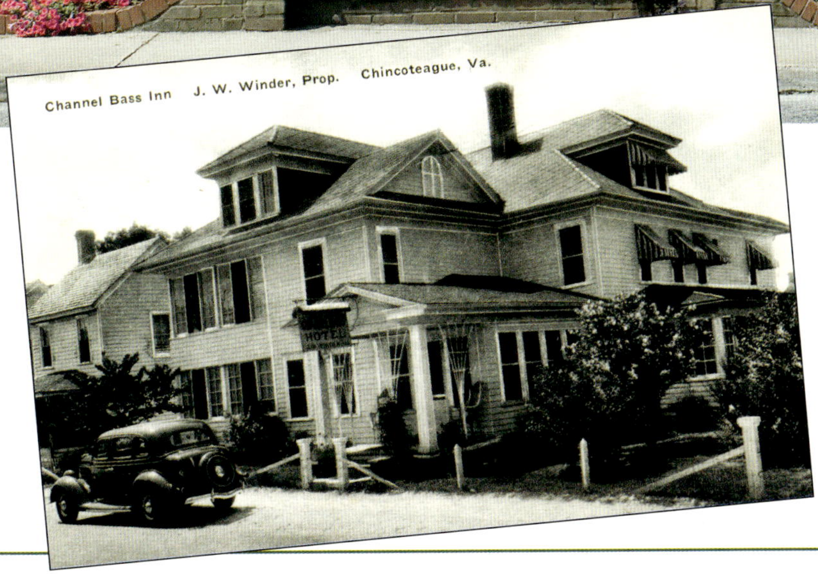

Channel Bass Inn   J. W. Winder, Prop.   Chincoteague, Va.

Channel Bass Inn.
Circa 1930s.

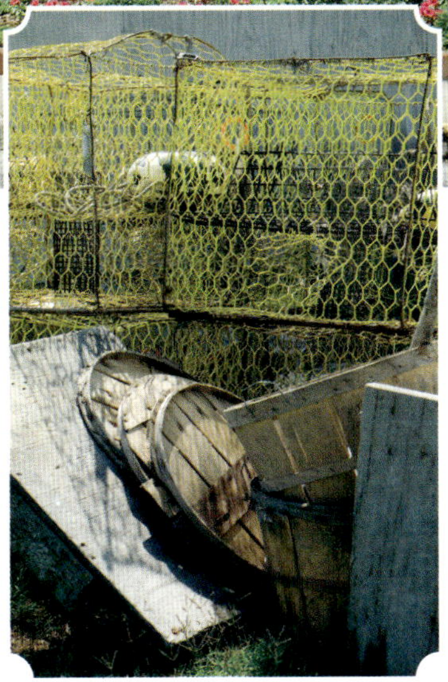

Crab pots

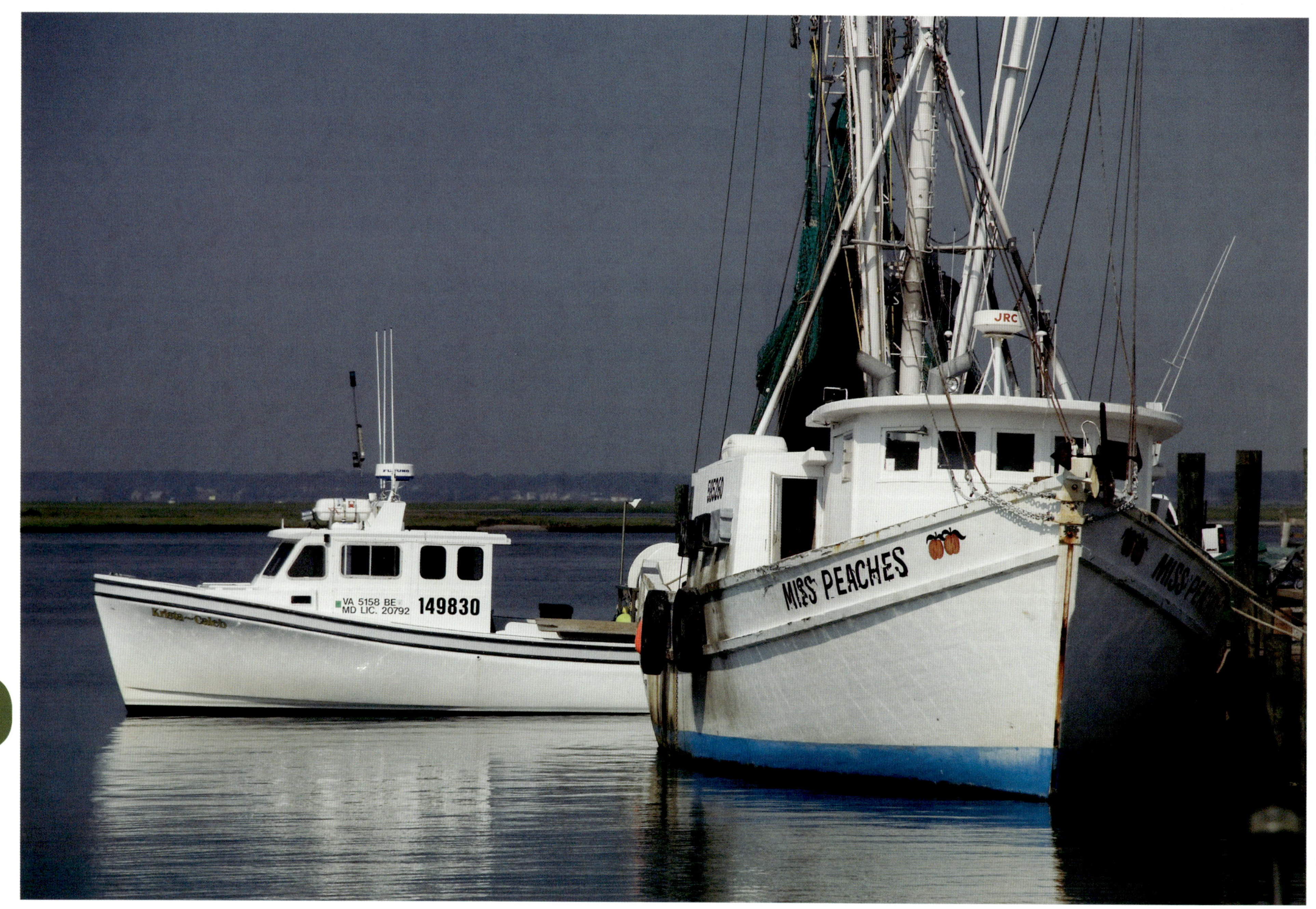

Curtis Merritt Harbor

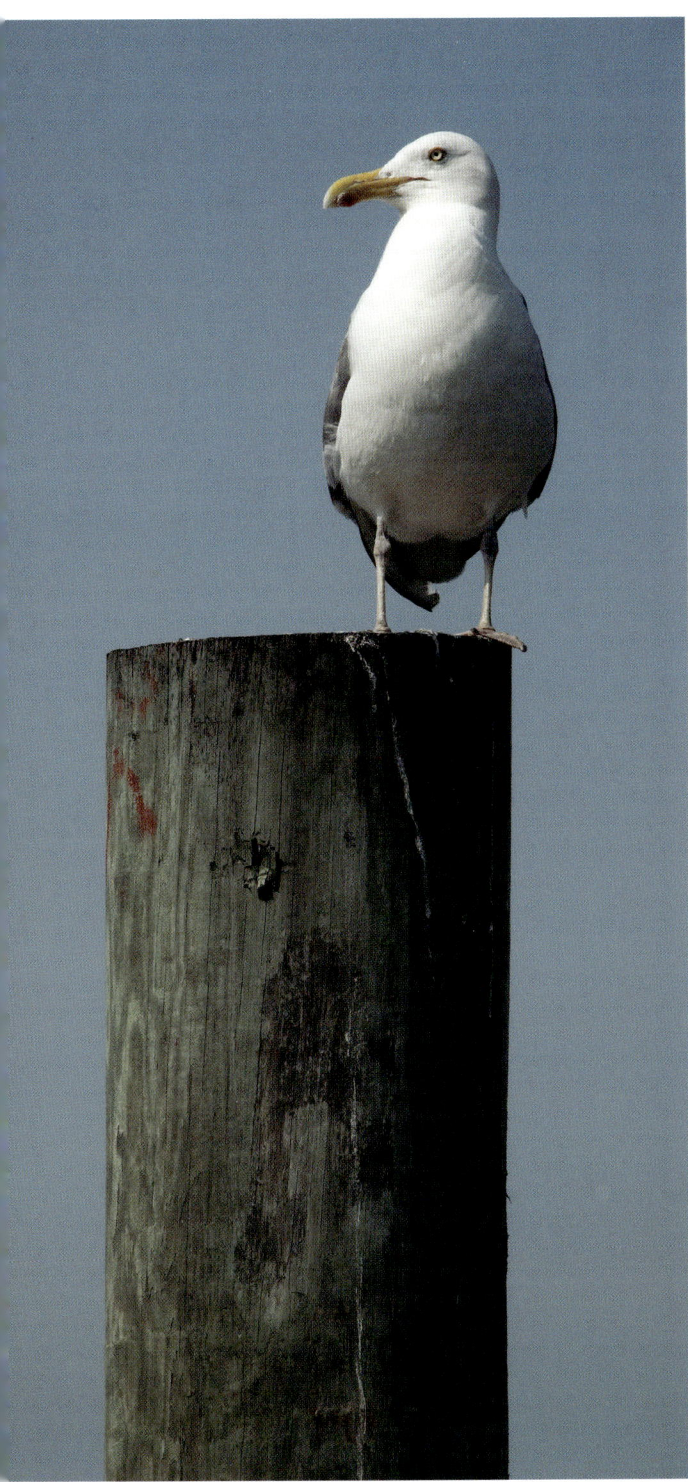

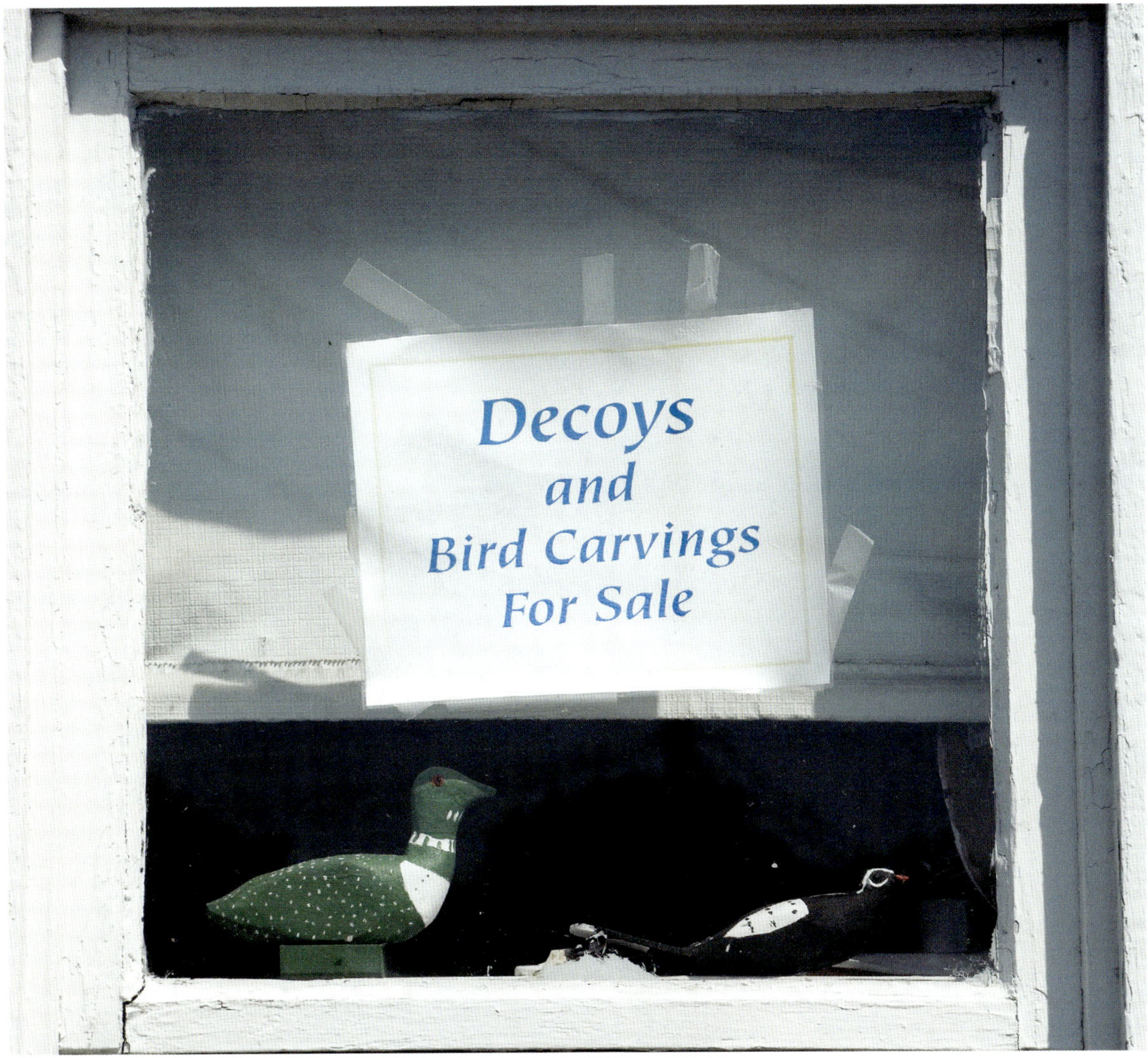

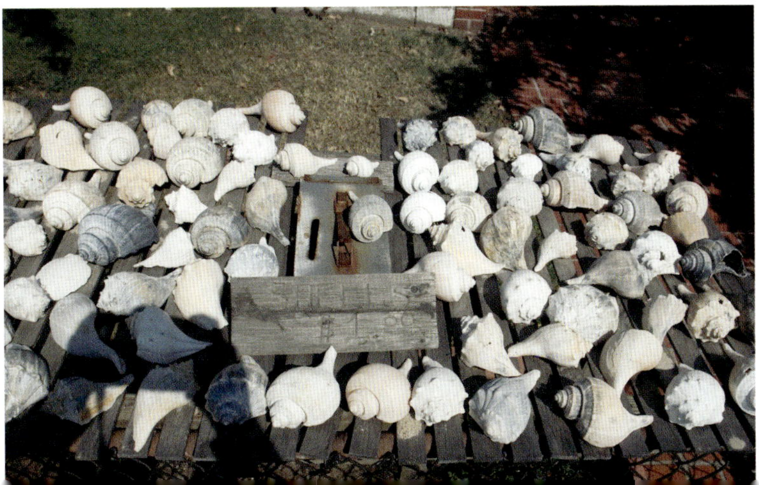

Shells for sale.

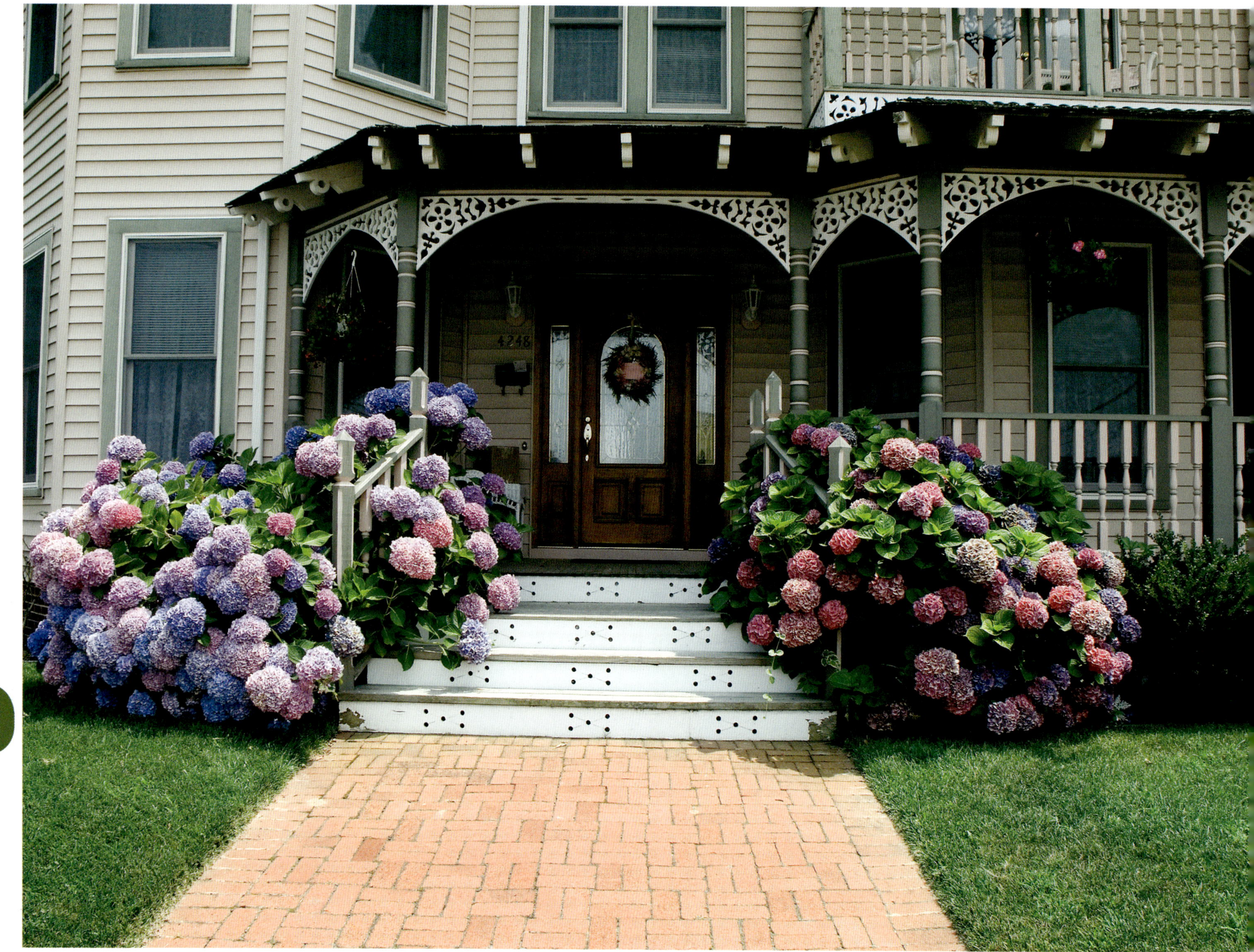

The Inn at Poplar Corner.

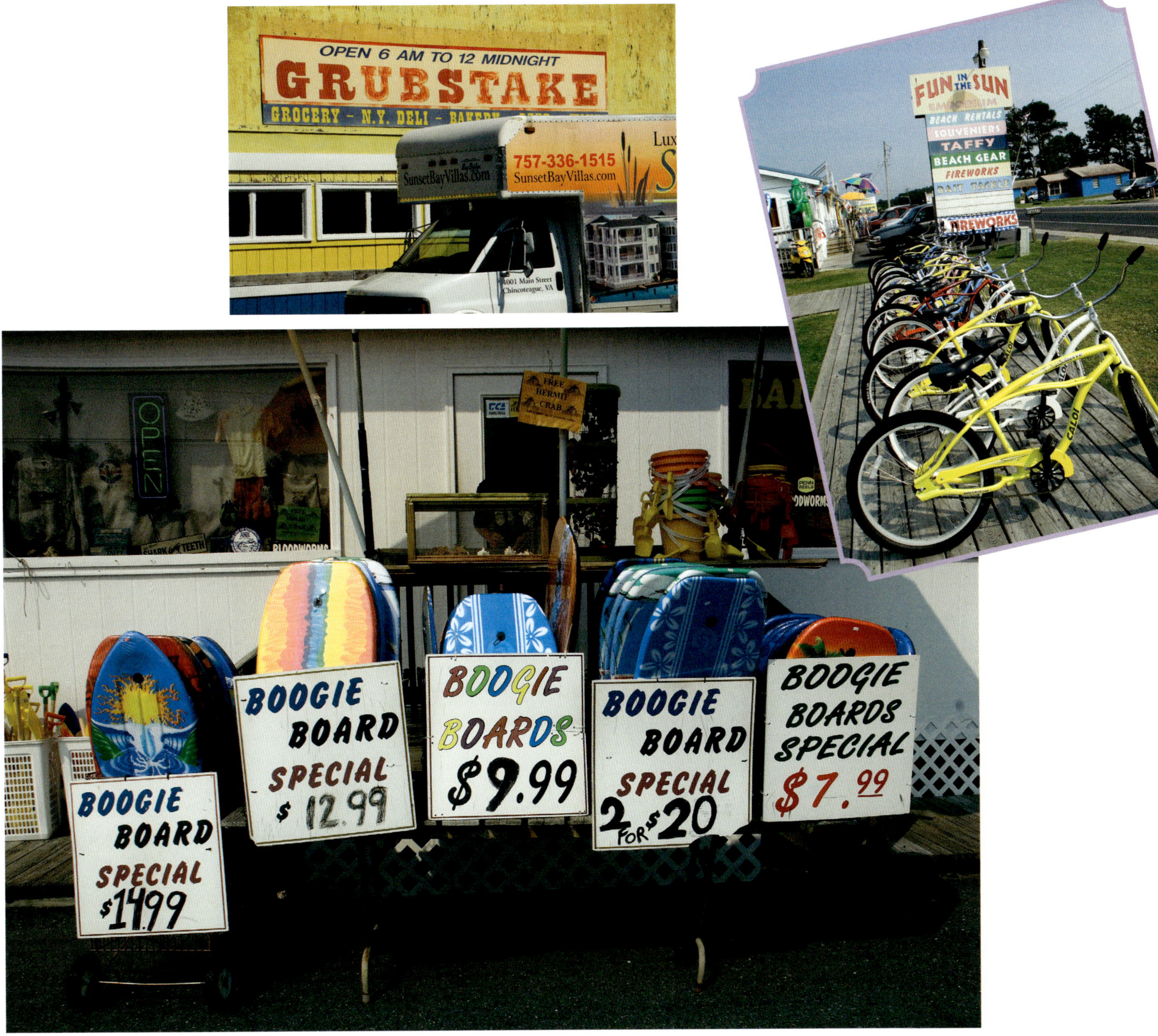

On Maddox Boulevard.

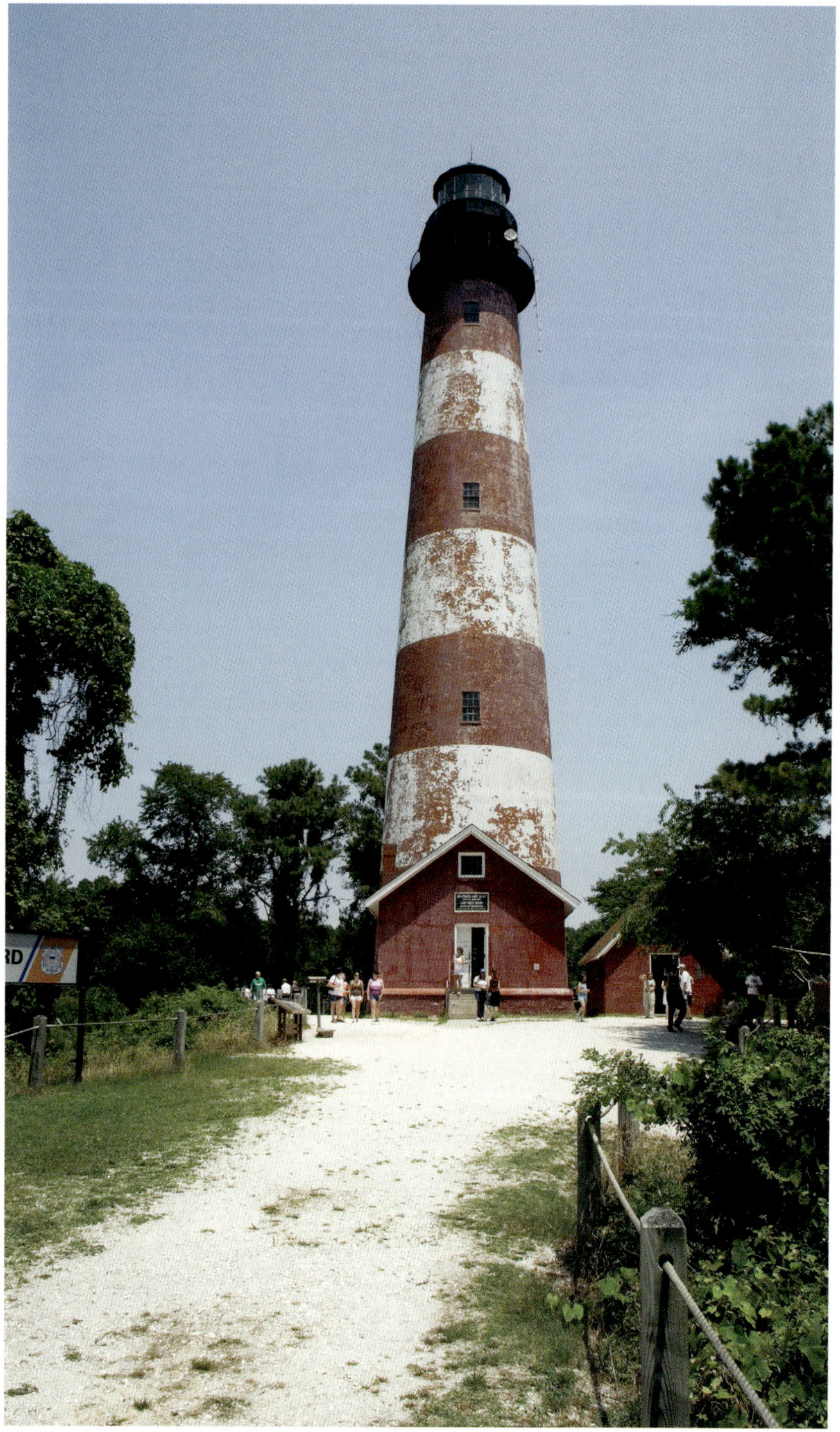

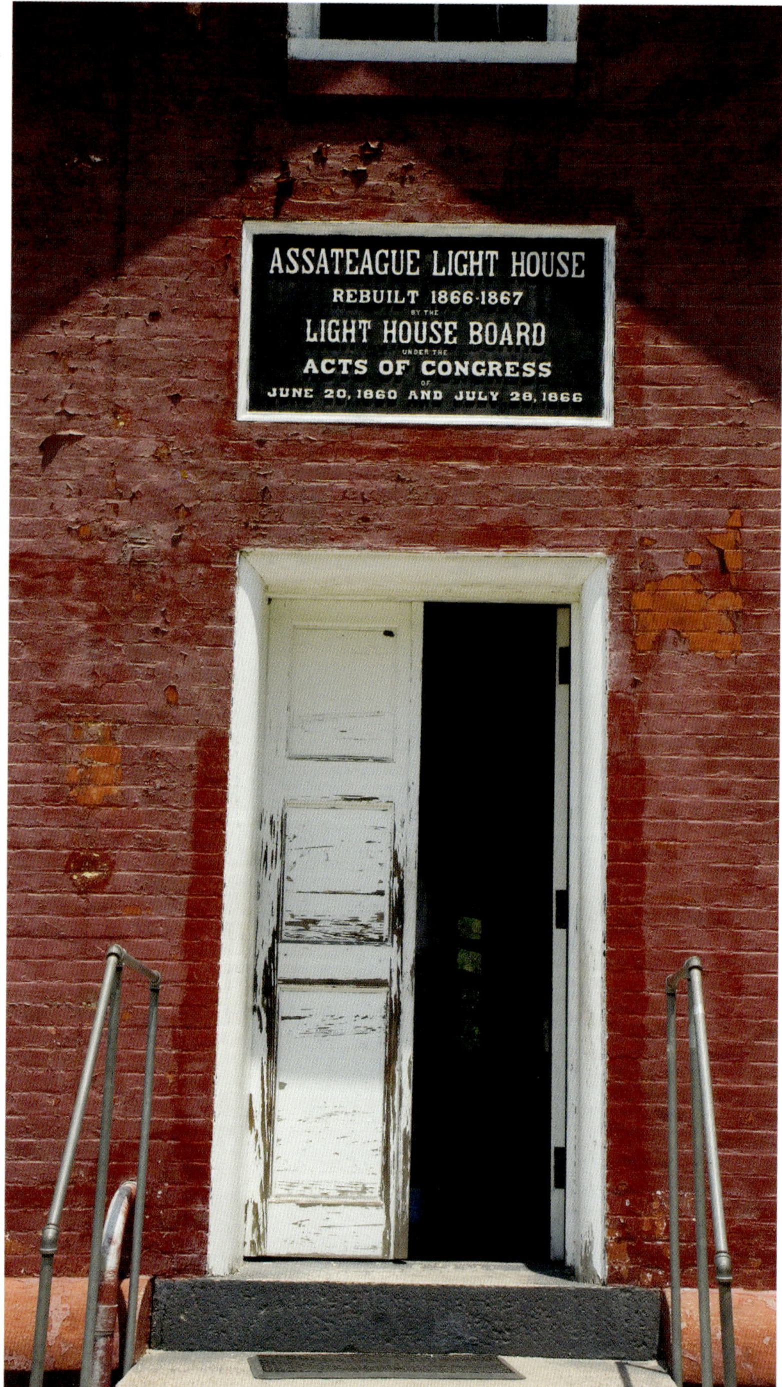

The 142 foot Assateague Light House.

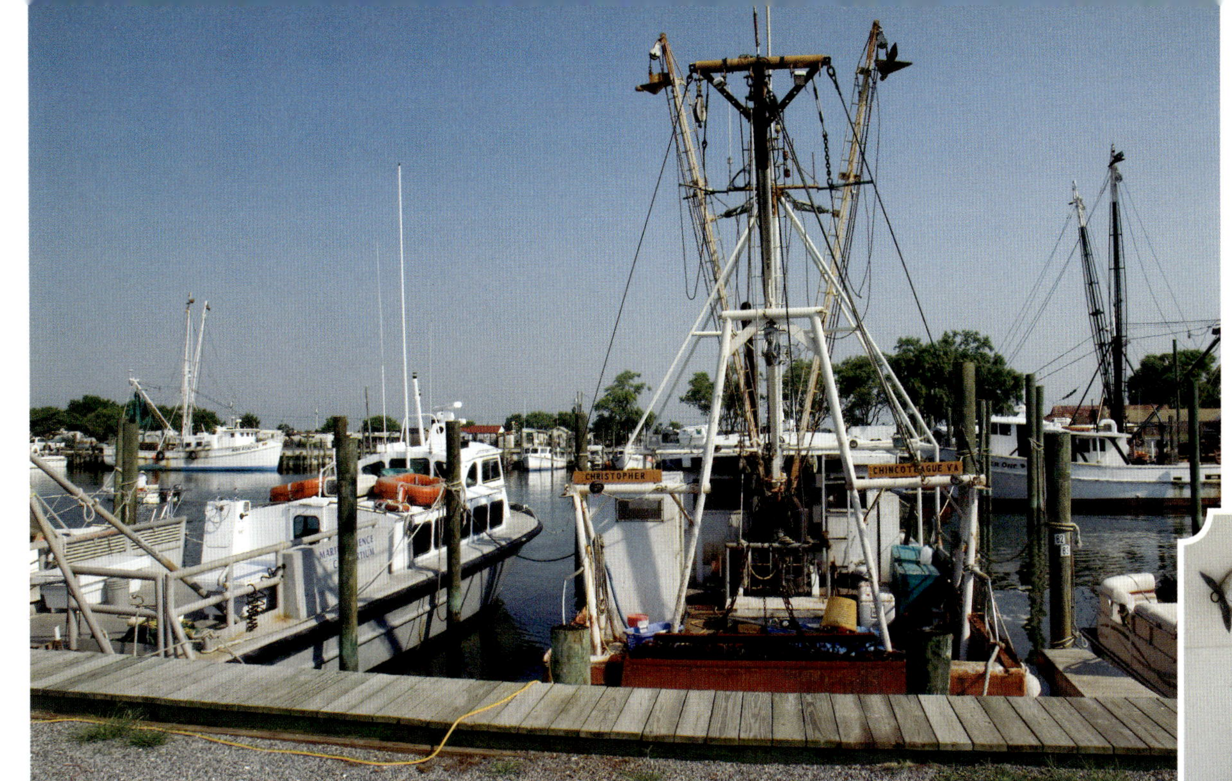

Curtiss Merritt Harbor

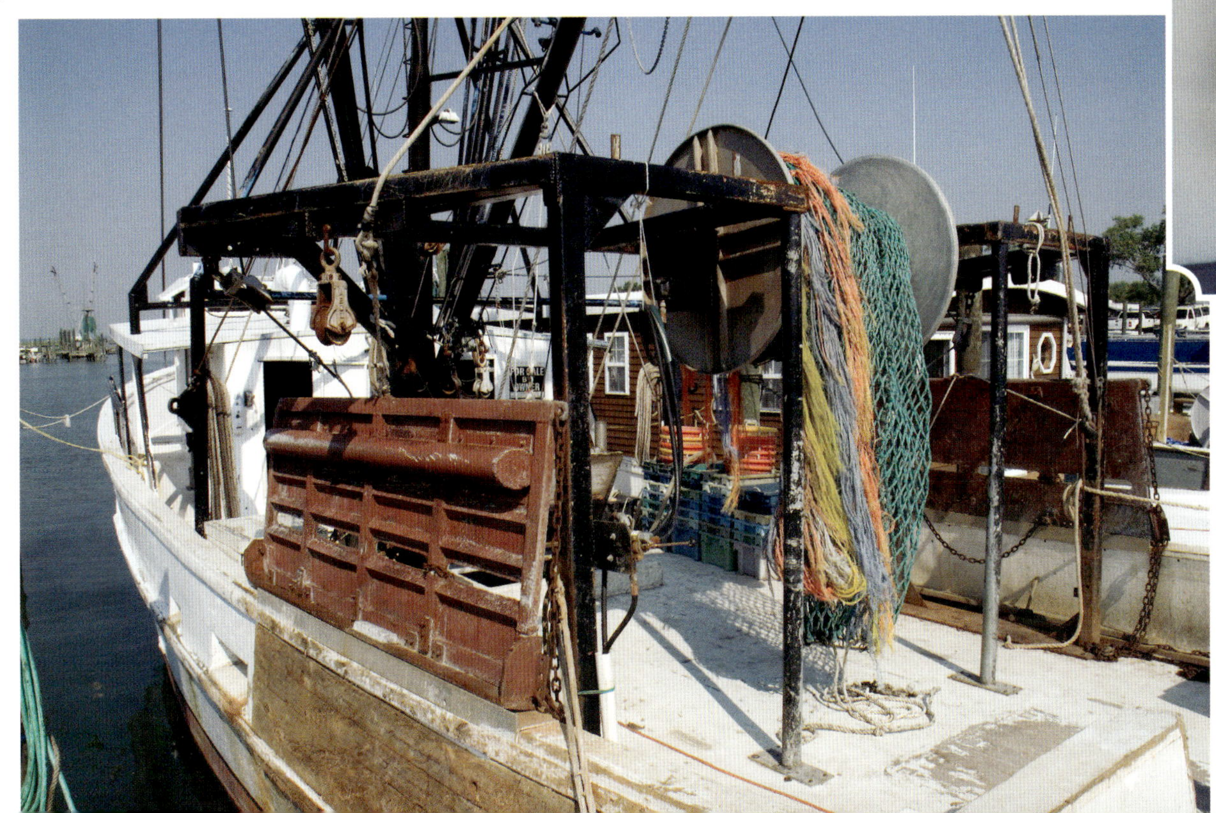

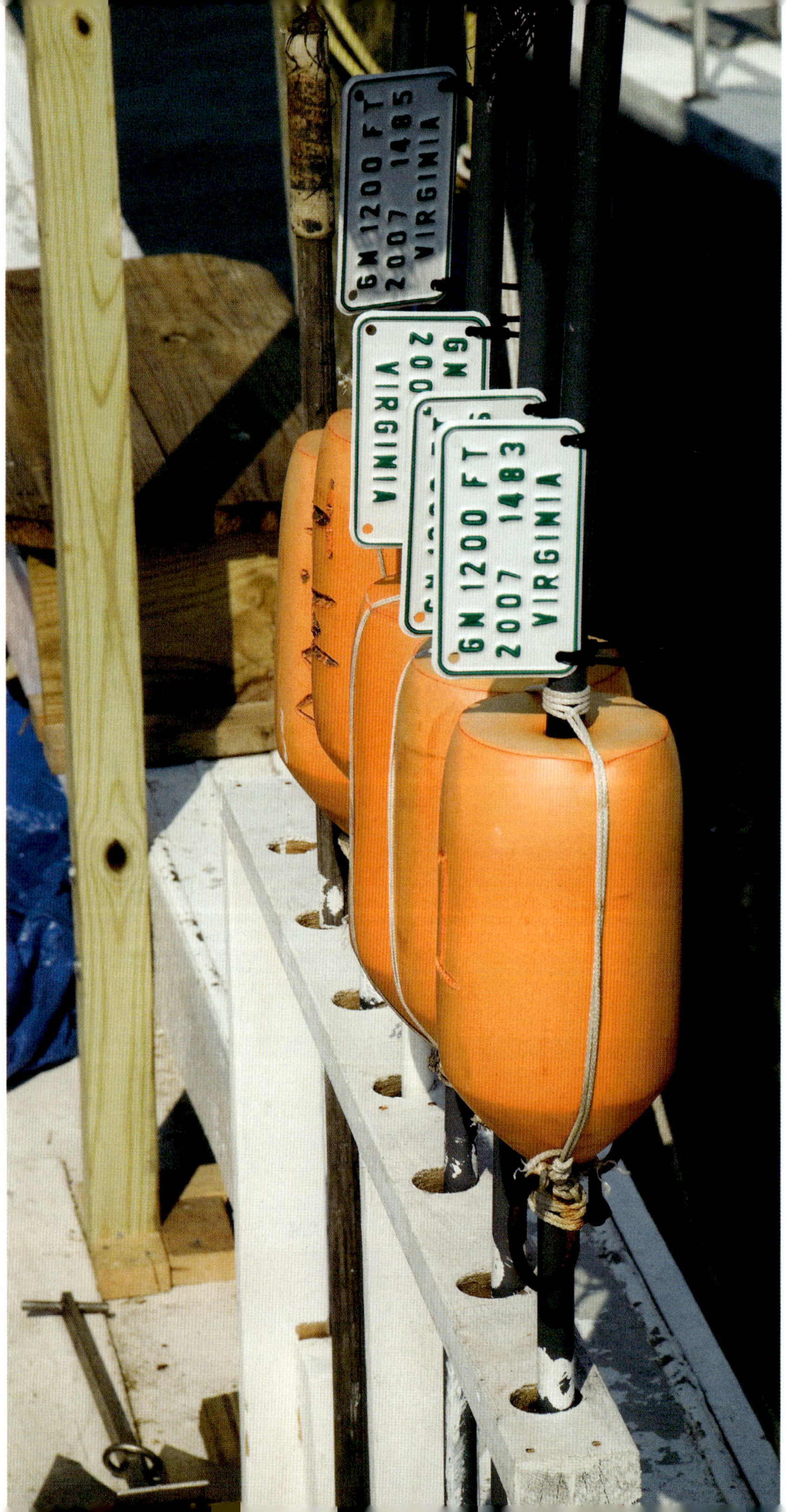
GN 1200 FT
2007 1485
VIRGINIA
GN 1200 FT
2007 1483
VIRGINIA

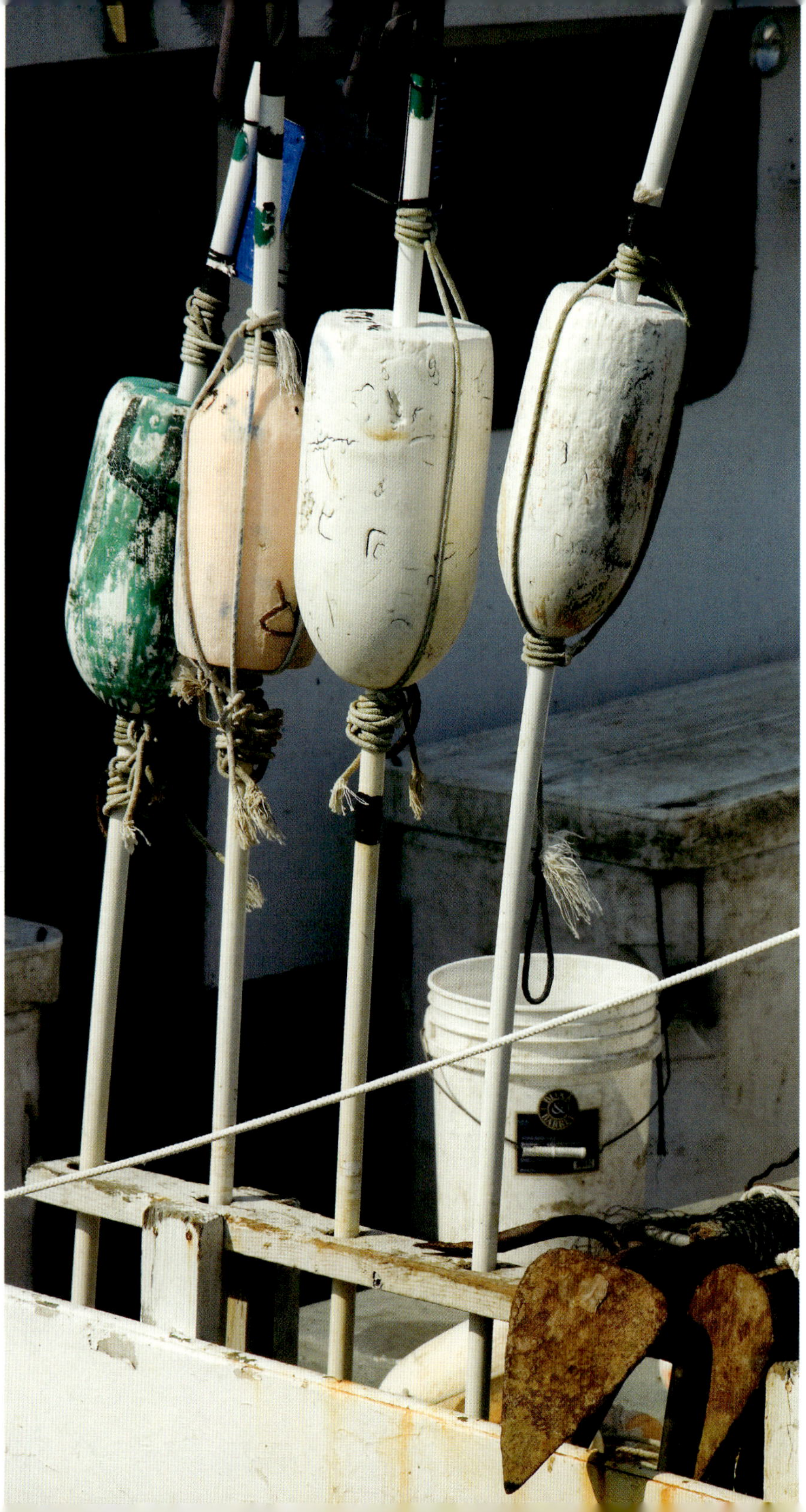

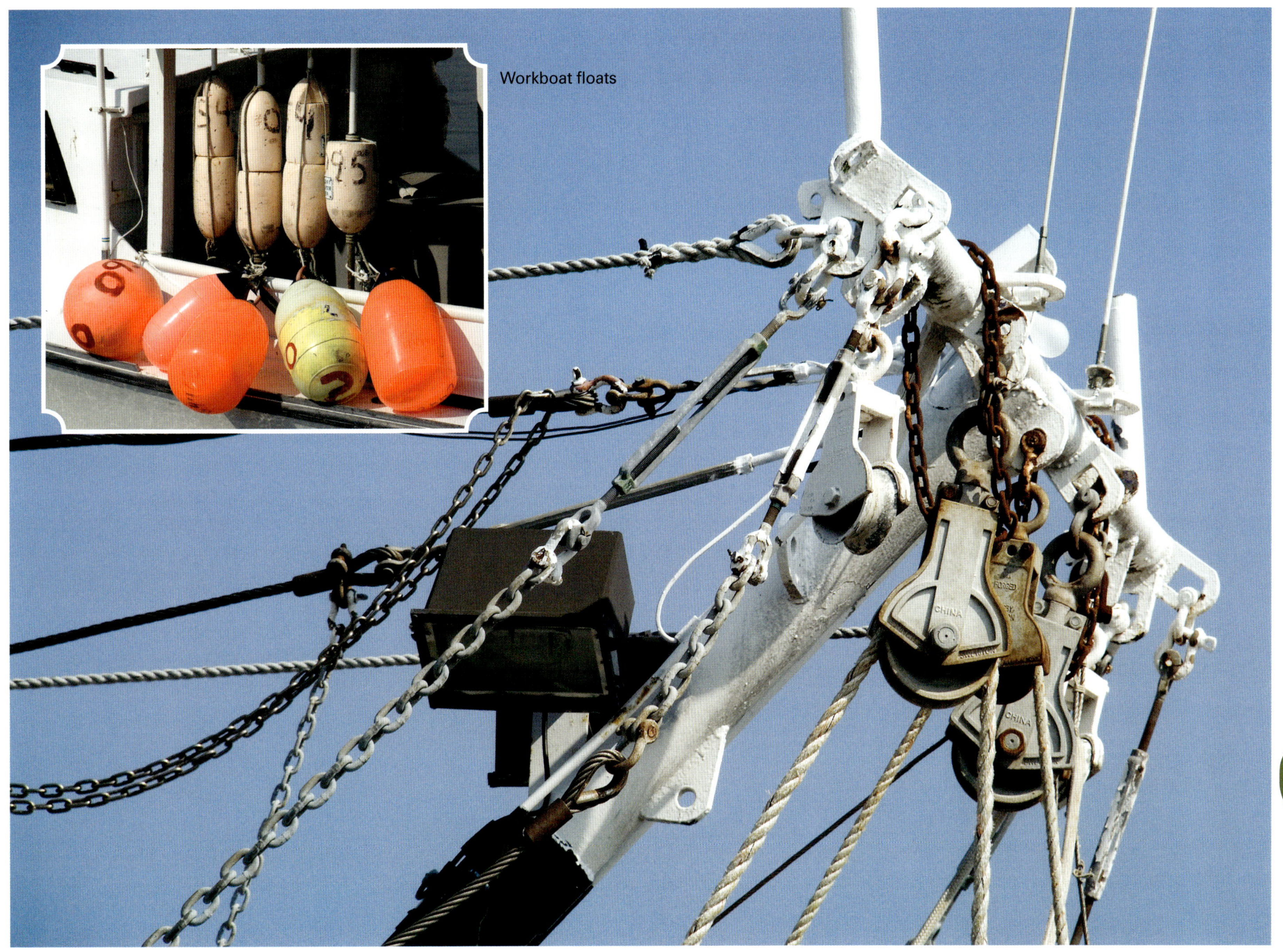

Workboat rigging

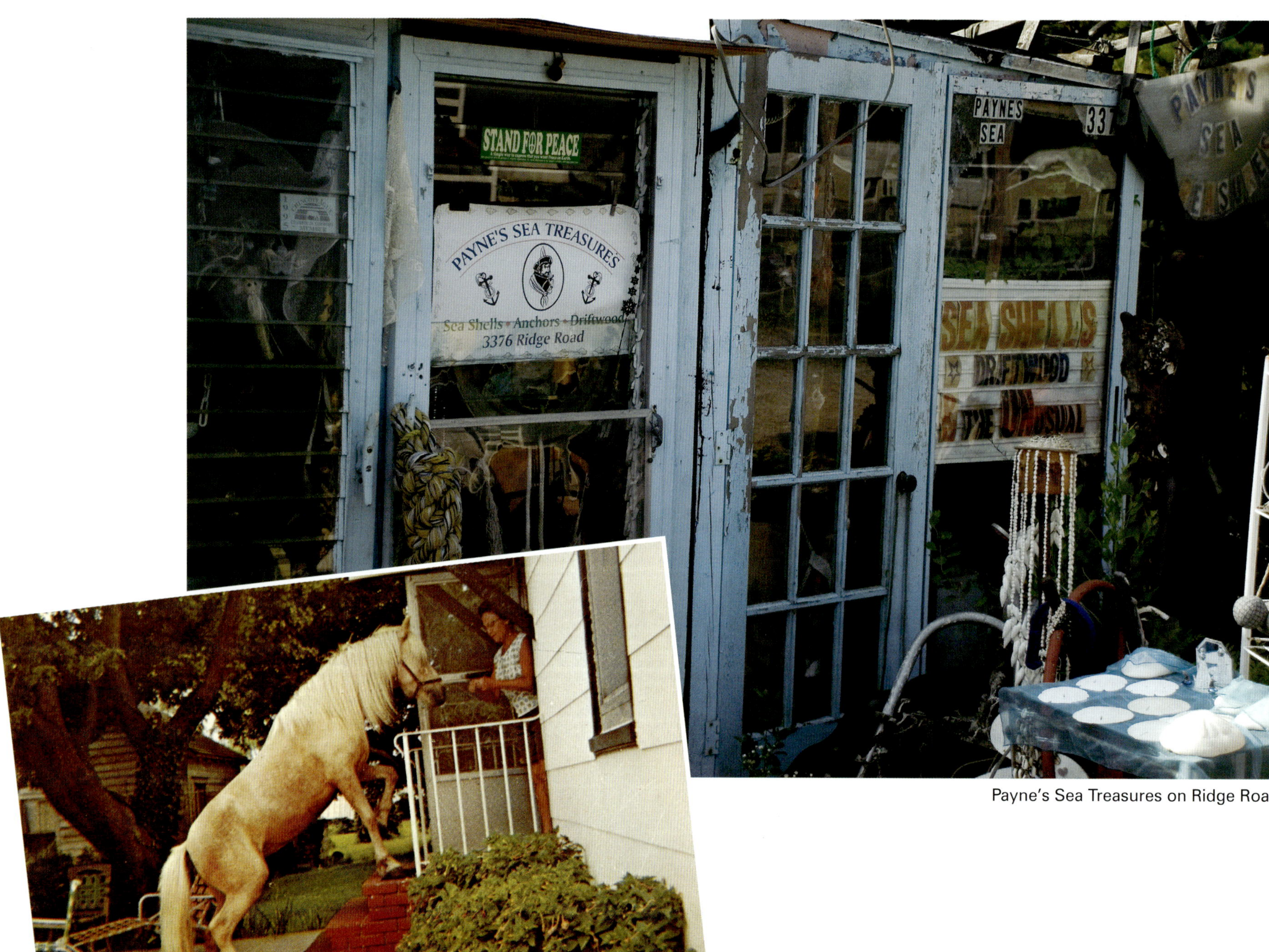

Payne's Sea Treasures on Ridge Road.

"Cloudy" calling at the backdoor for goodies. Circa 1960s.

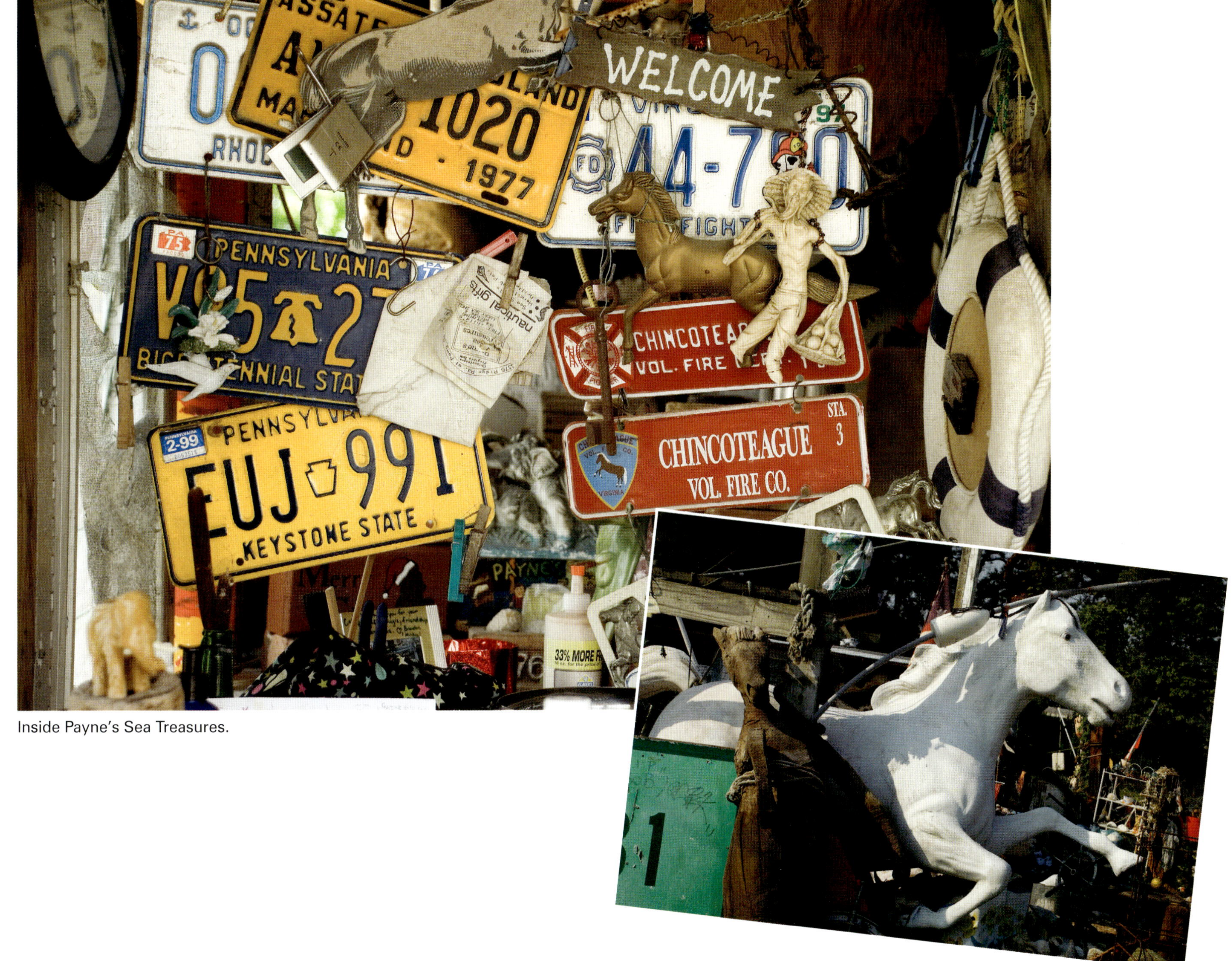
Inside Payne's Sea Treasures.

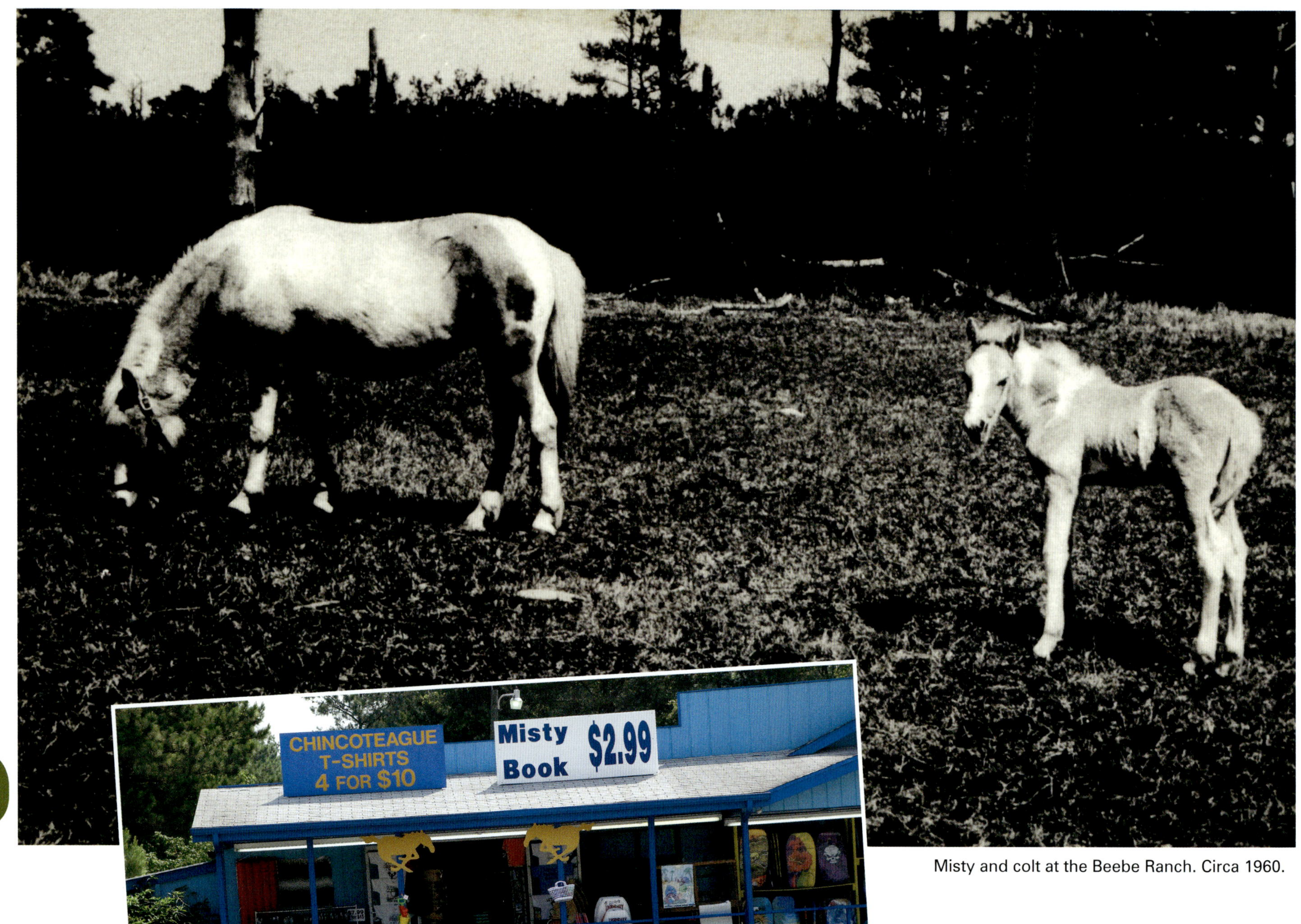

Misty and colt at the Beebe Ranch. Circa 1960.

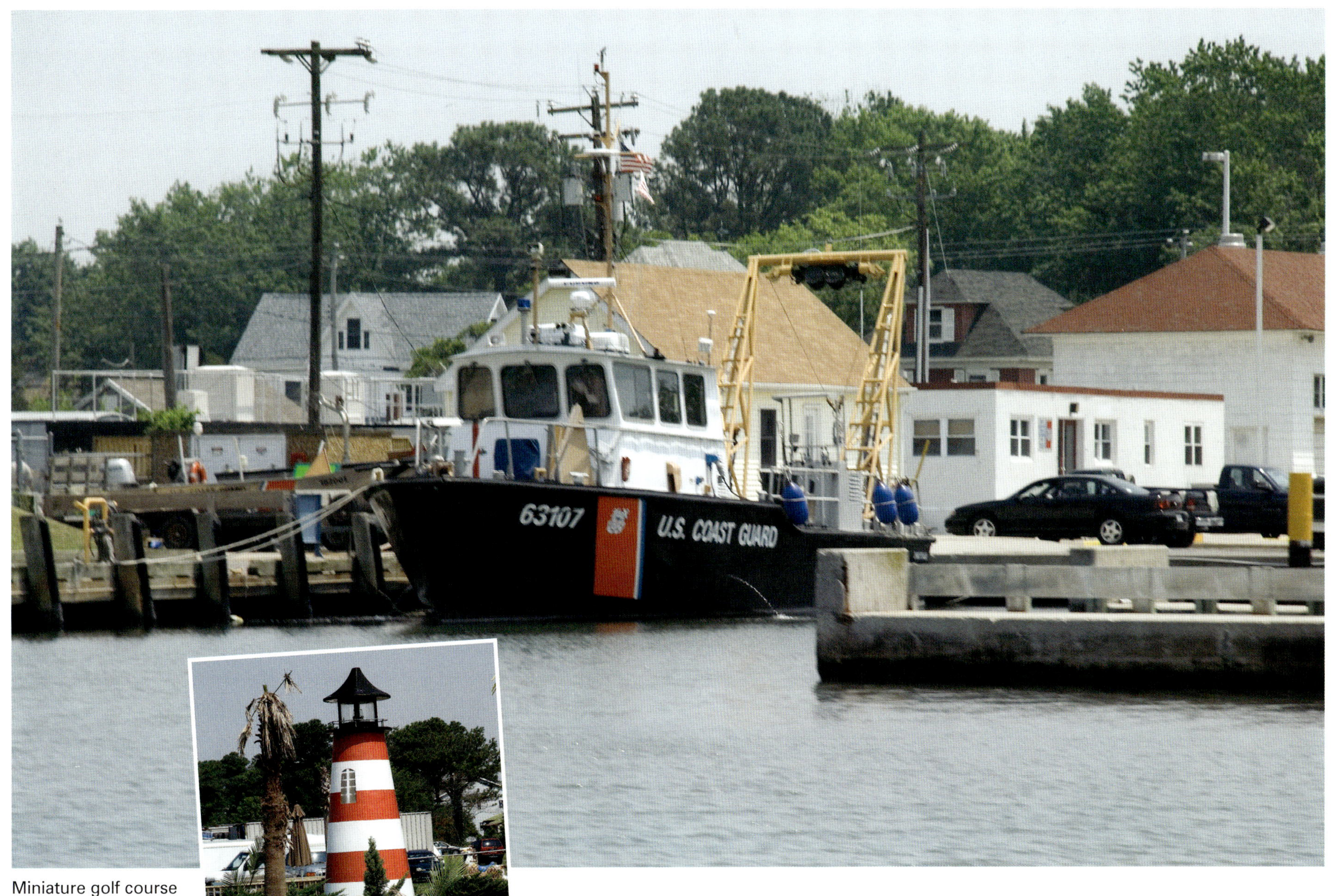

Miniature golf course
on Maddox Boulevard.

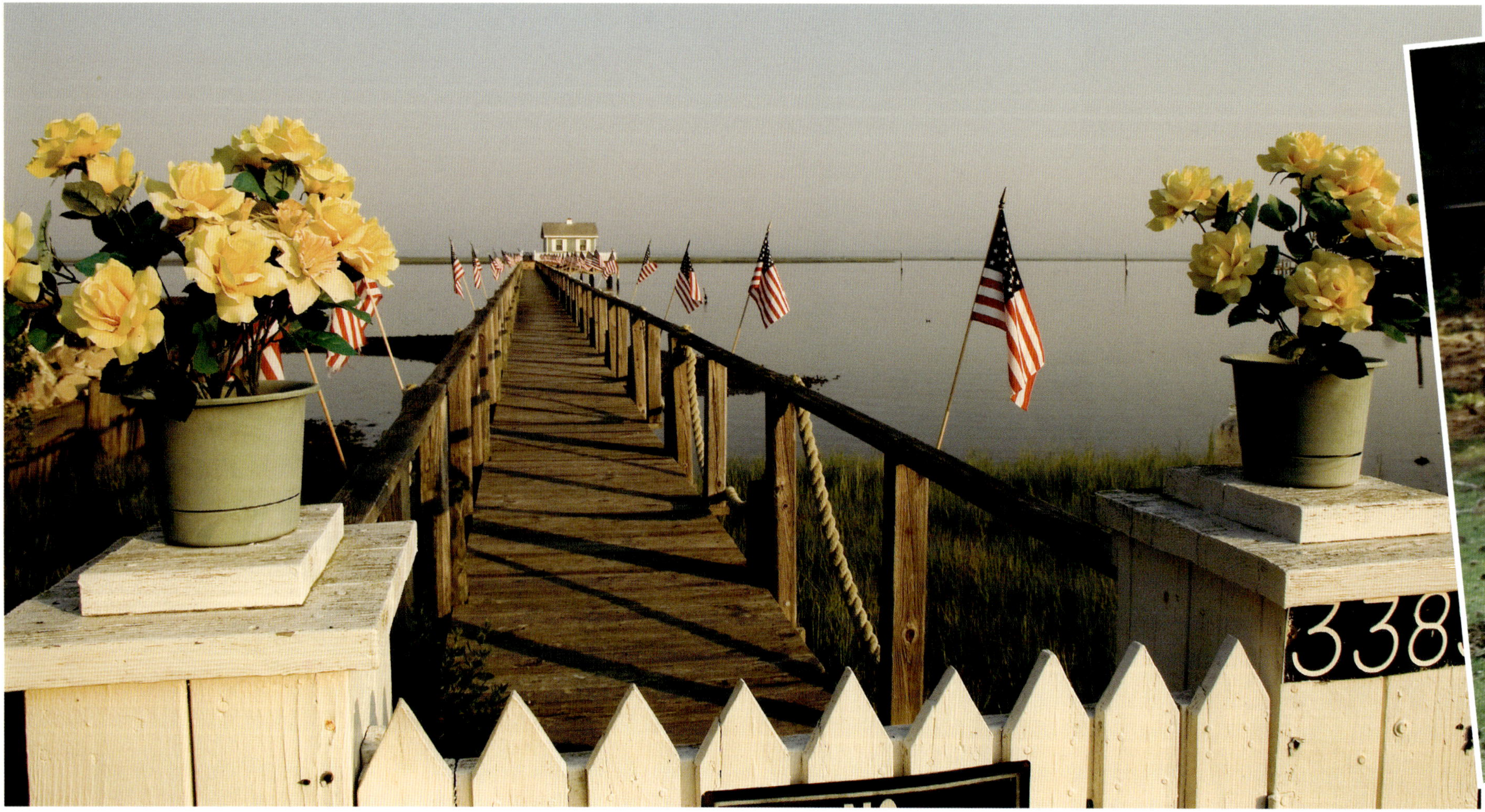

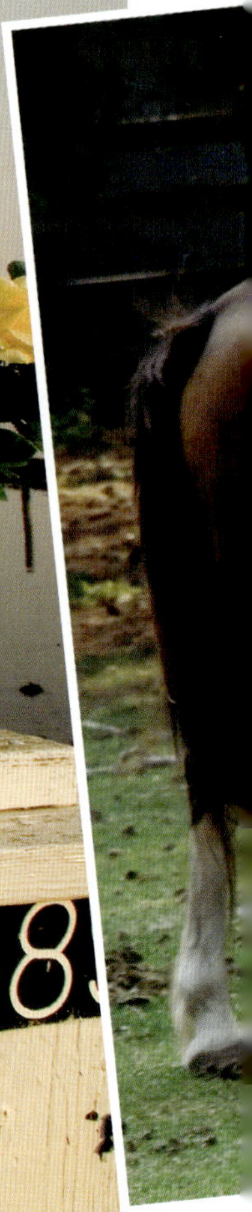

Early morning

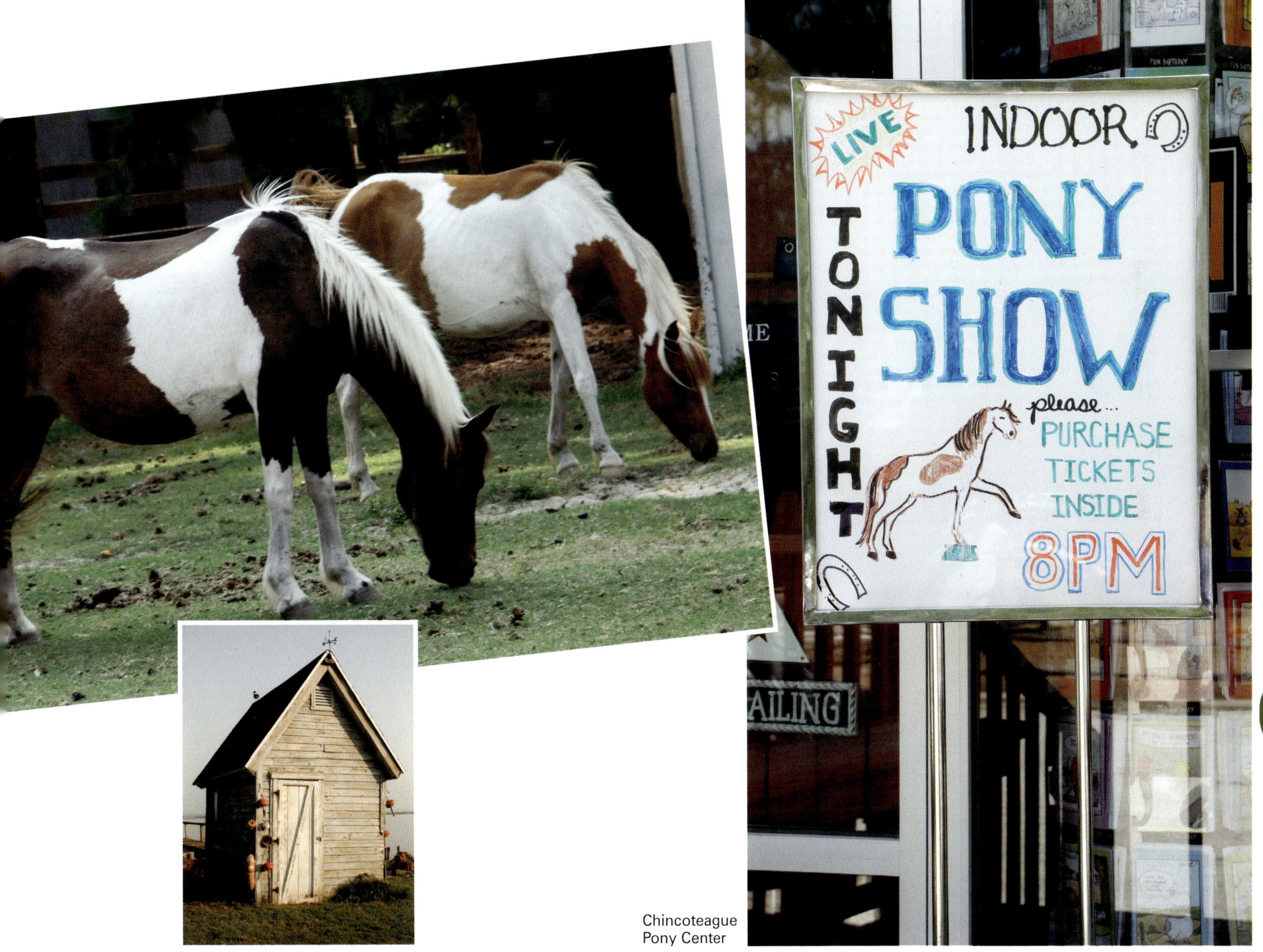

Chincoteague
Pony Center

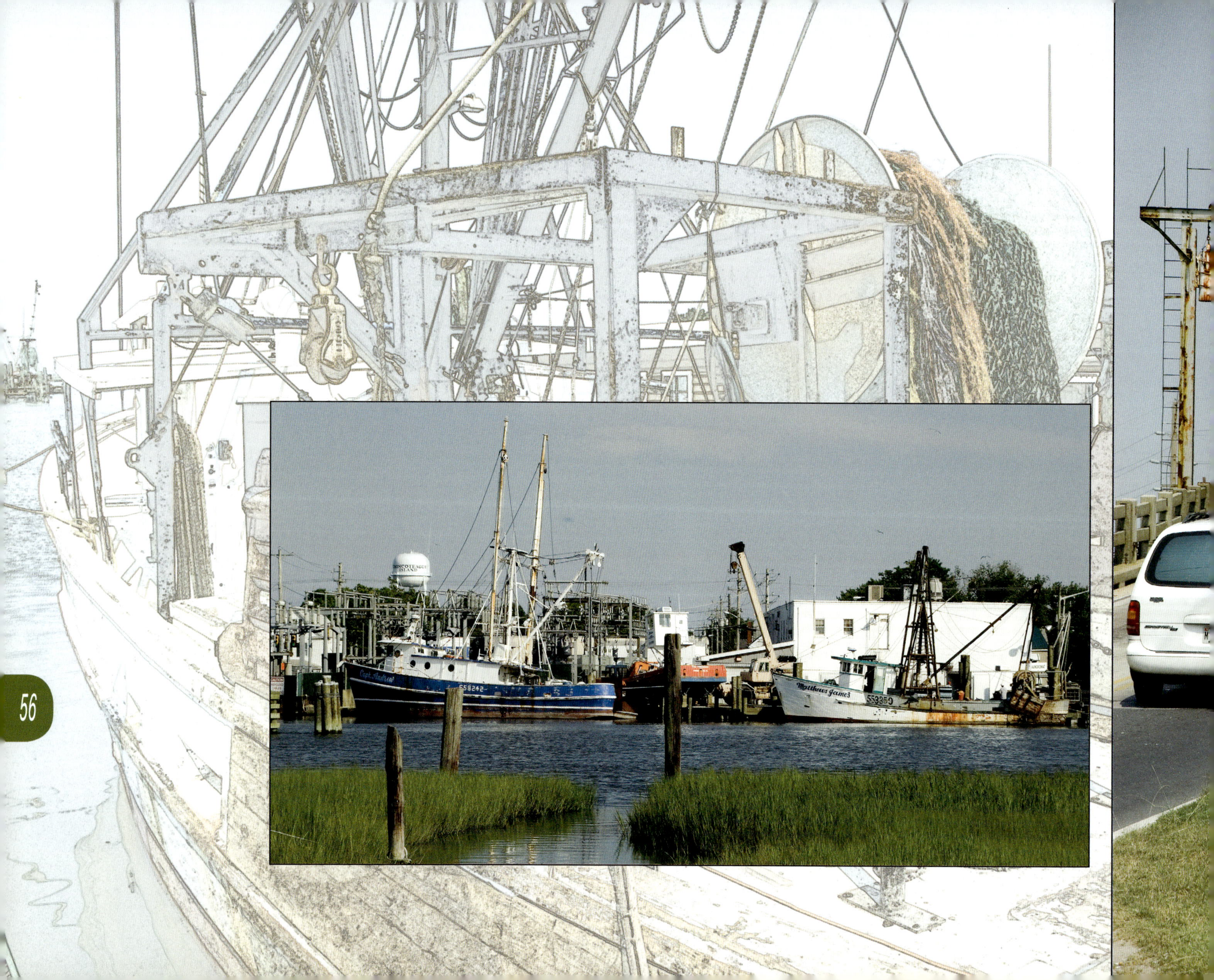

CHINCOTEAGUE ISLAND
Capt. Andrew
558242
Matthews James
553850

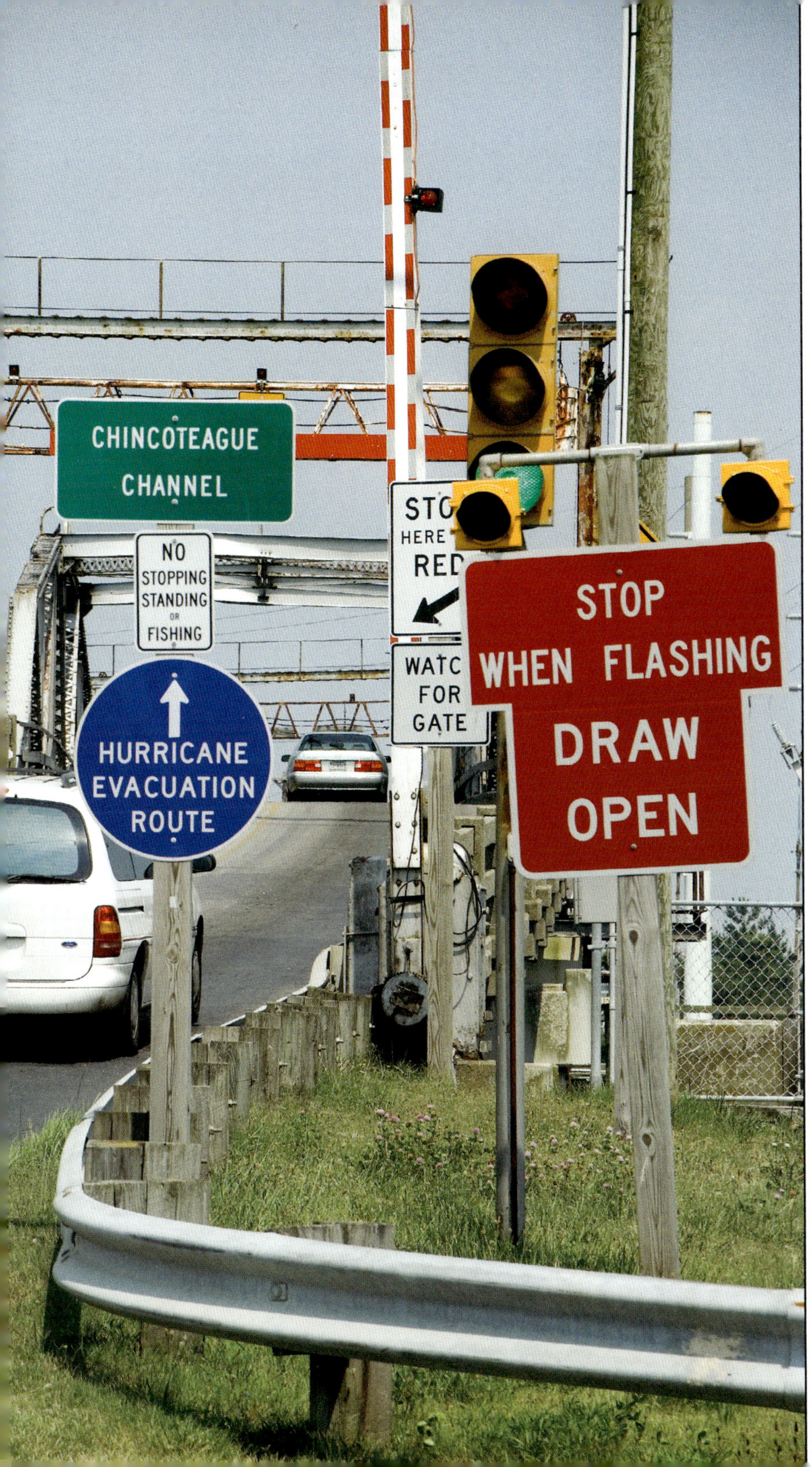

The swing bridge over Chincoteague Channel.

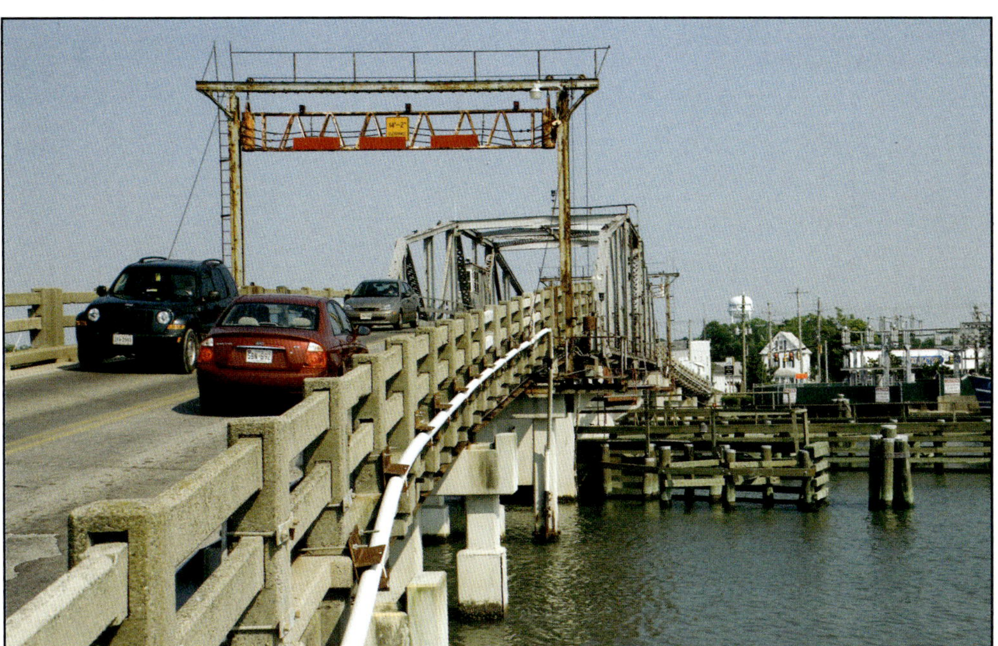

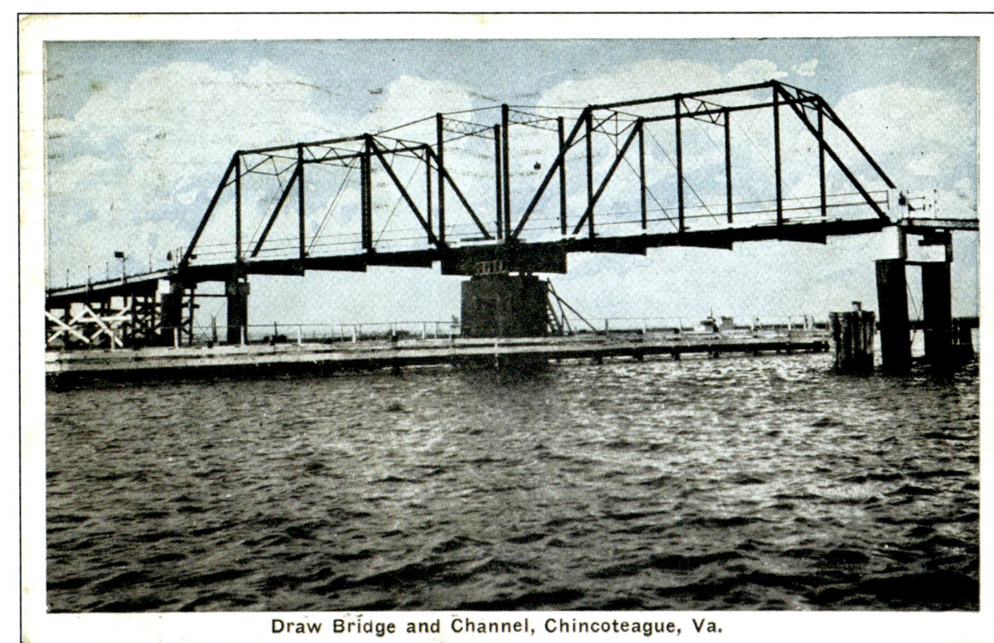

Draw Bridge and Channel. Postmarked 1932.

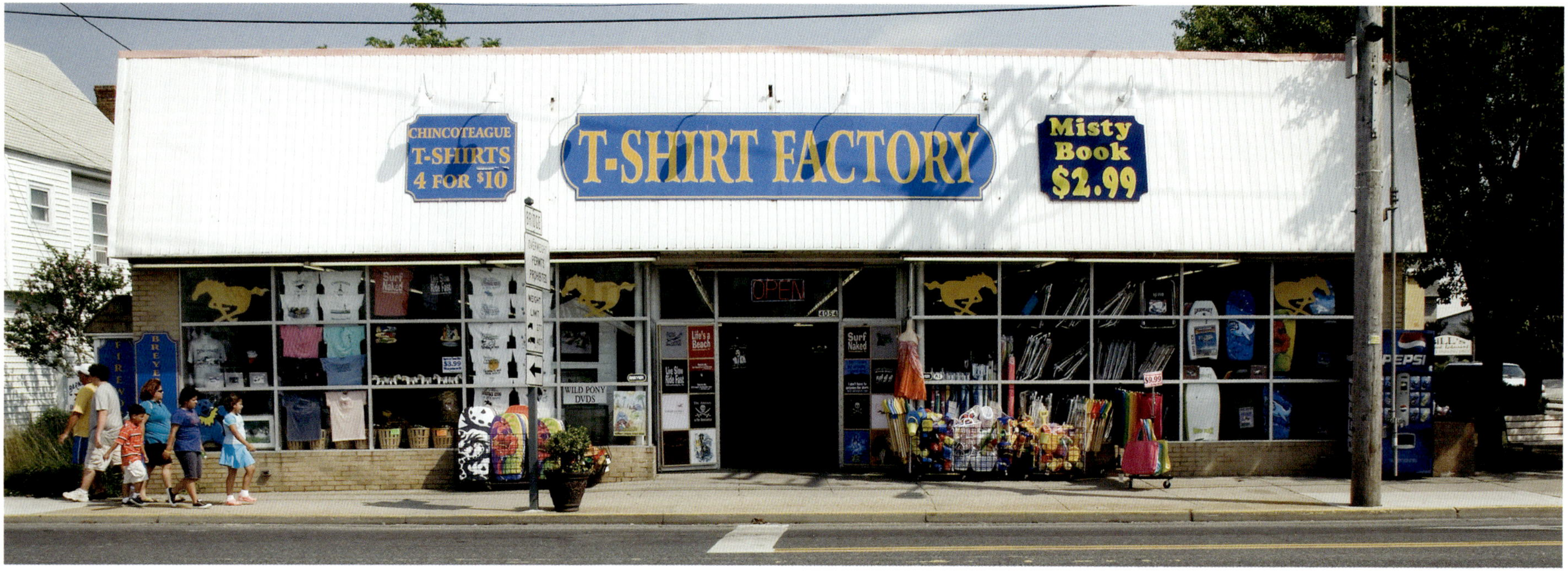

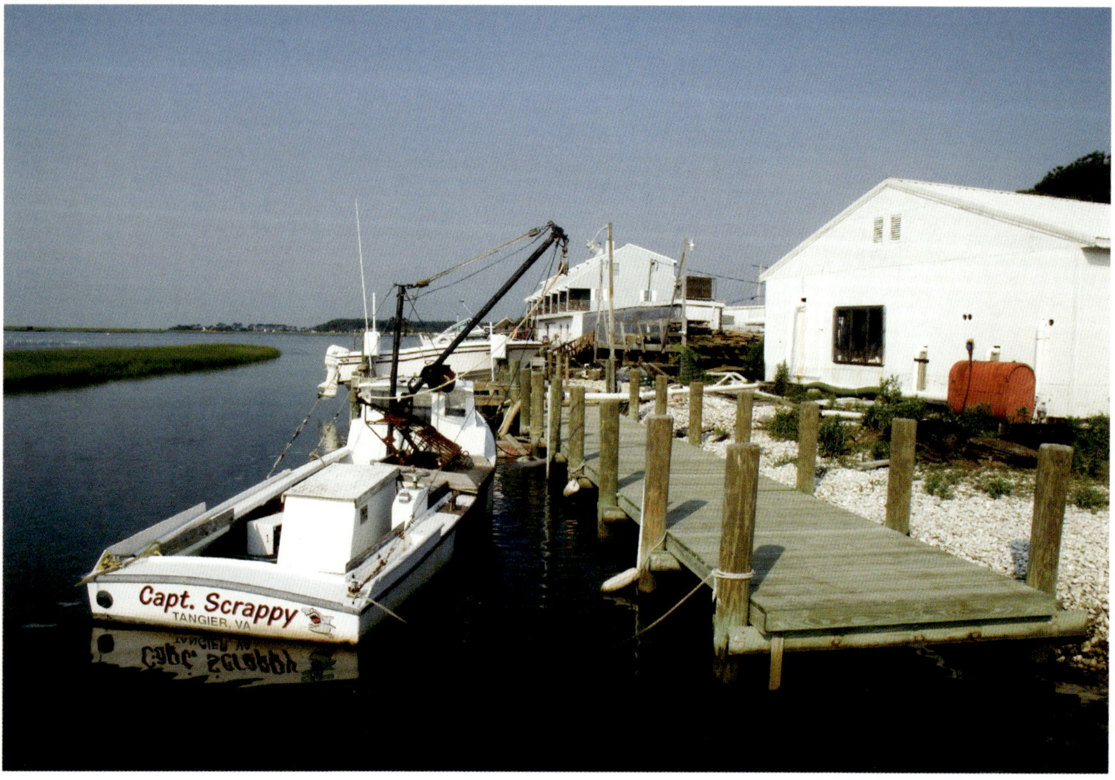

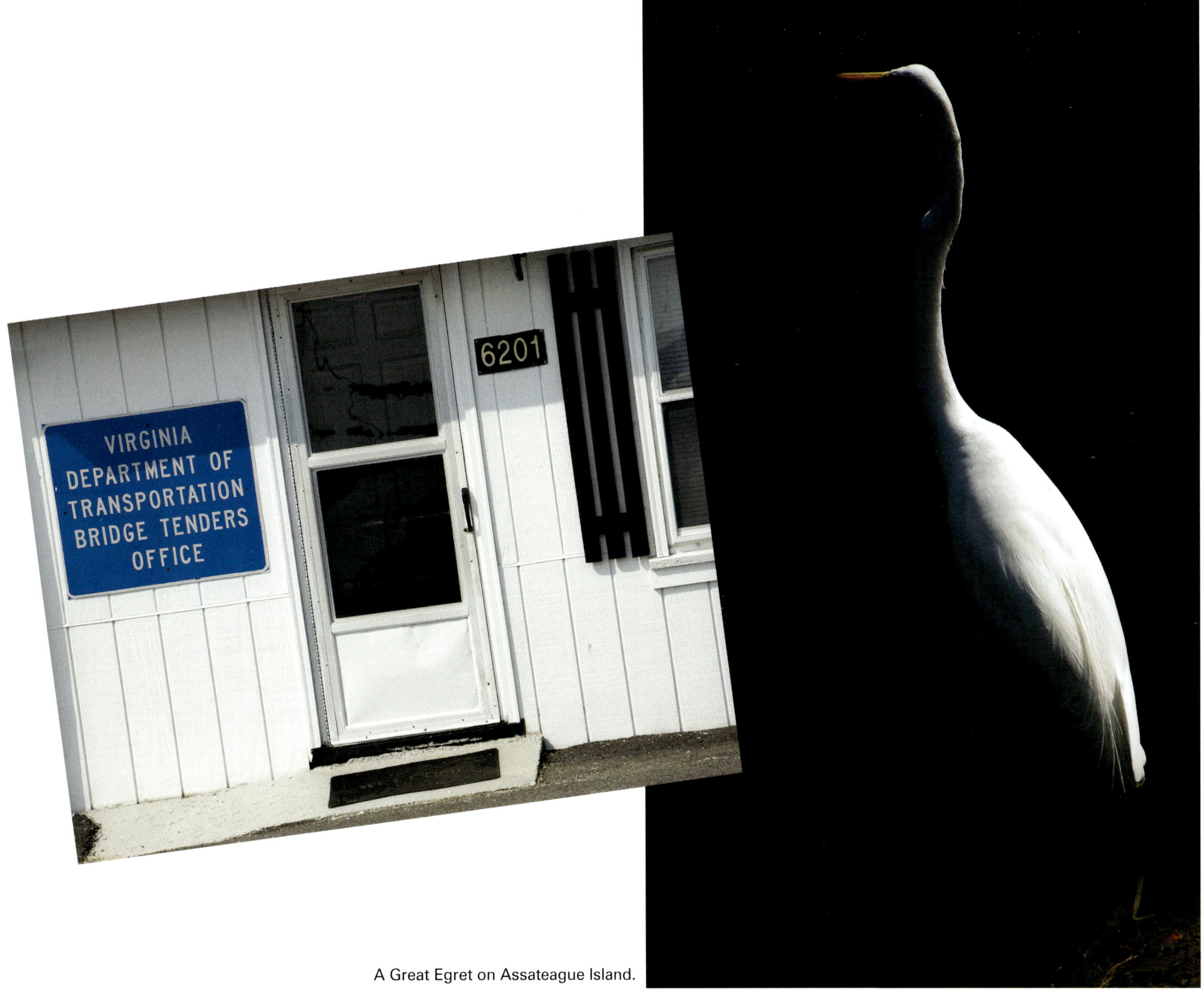

A Great Egret on Assateague Island.

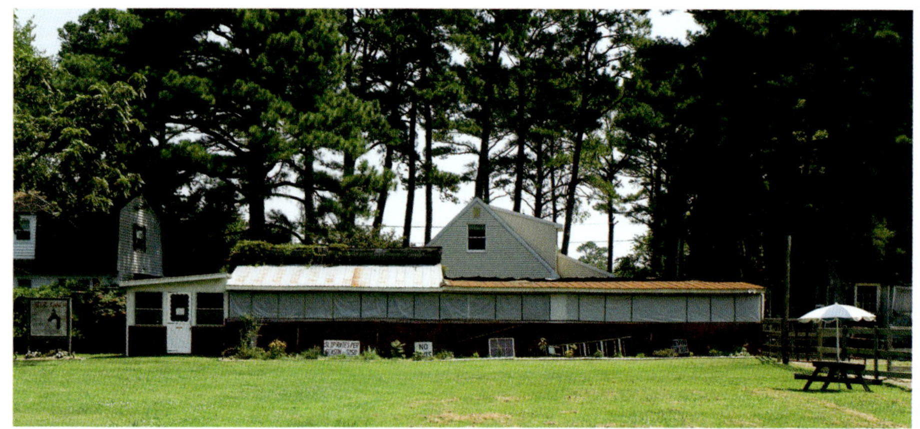
Horse stalls
on the Beebe
Ranch.

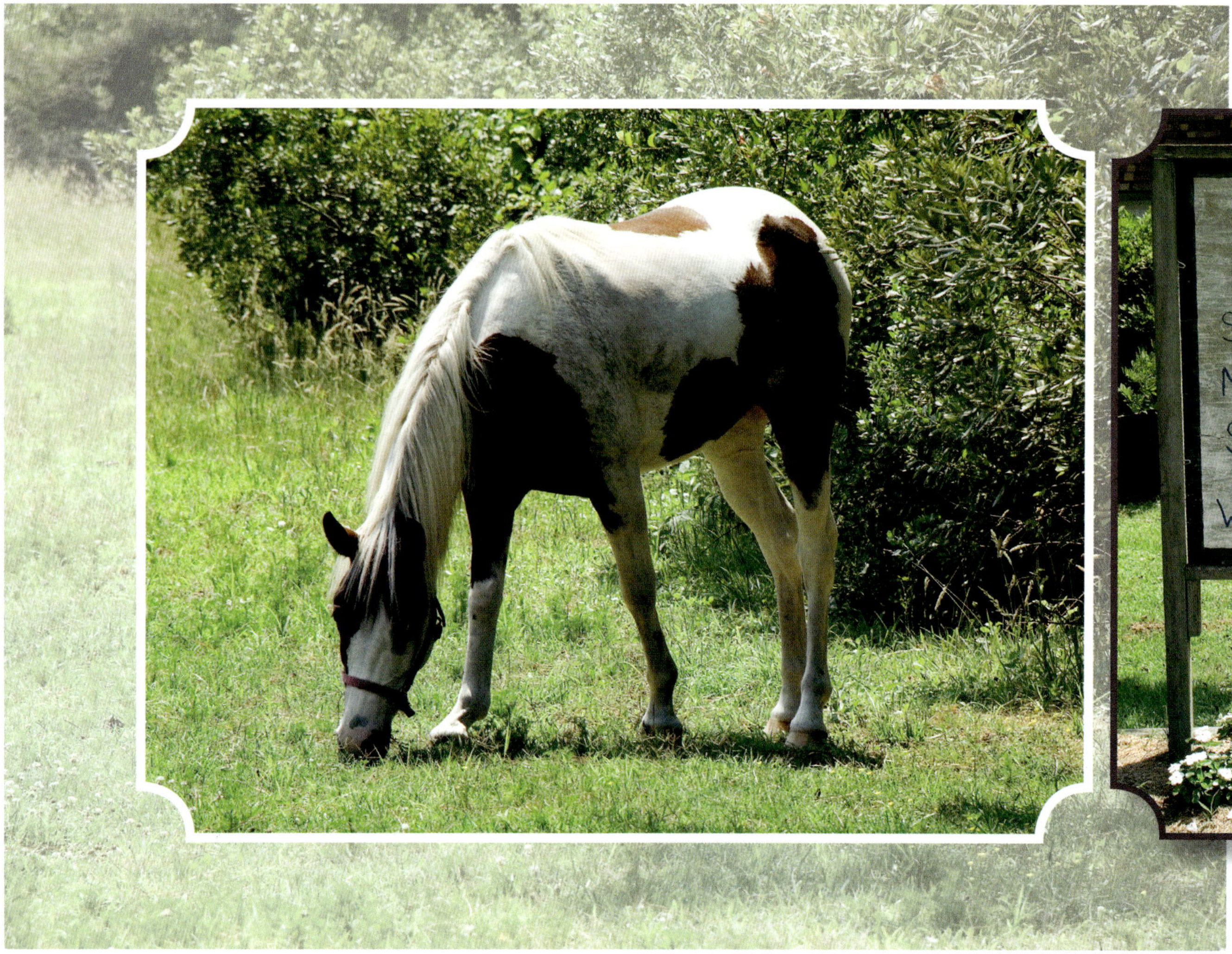

Beebe Ranch

Horse at Beebe Ranch.

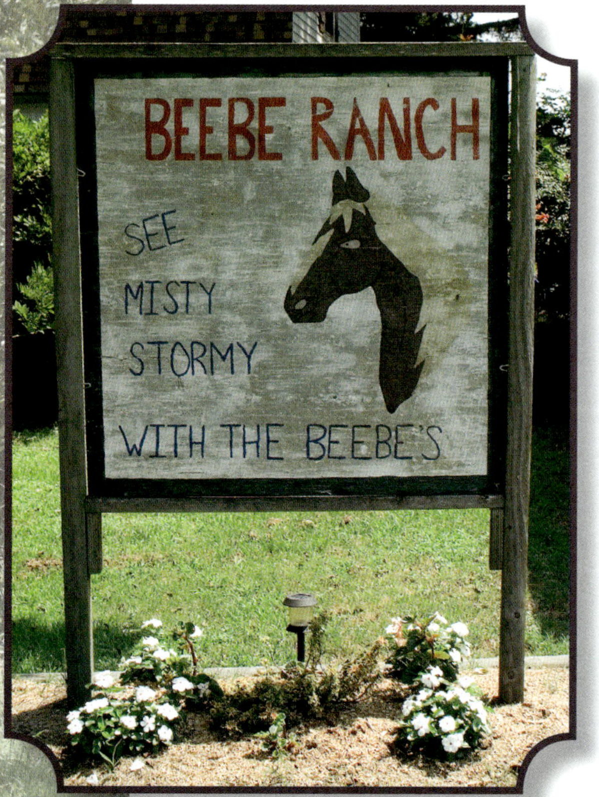

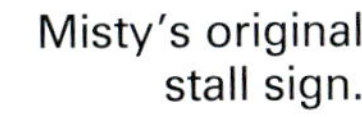

Misty's original stall sign.

The Beebe's kitchen where Misty waited out the Ash Wednesday Storm of 1962.

Misty and Stormy as they look today.

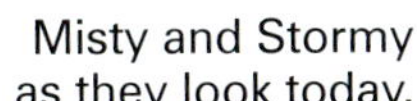

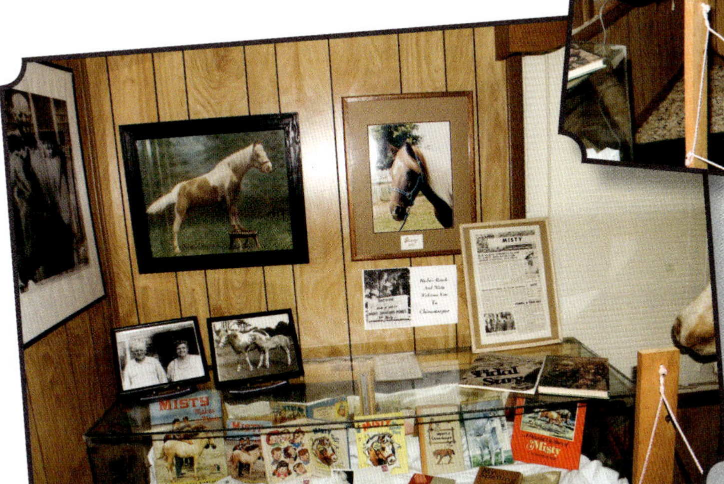

Misty memorabilia on display at the Beebe Ranch.

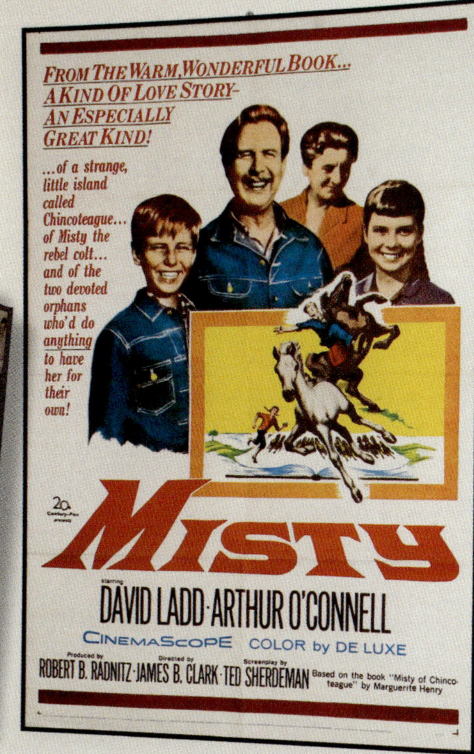

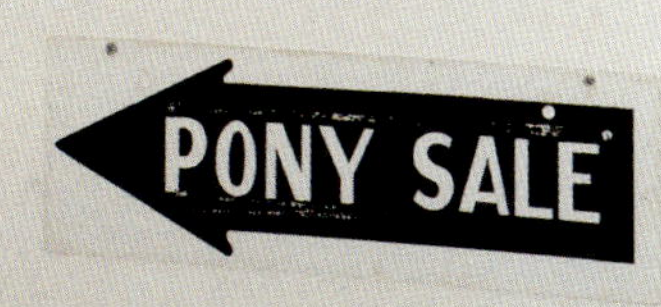

Theatre poster for the movie Misty on display at the Beebe Ranch.

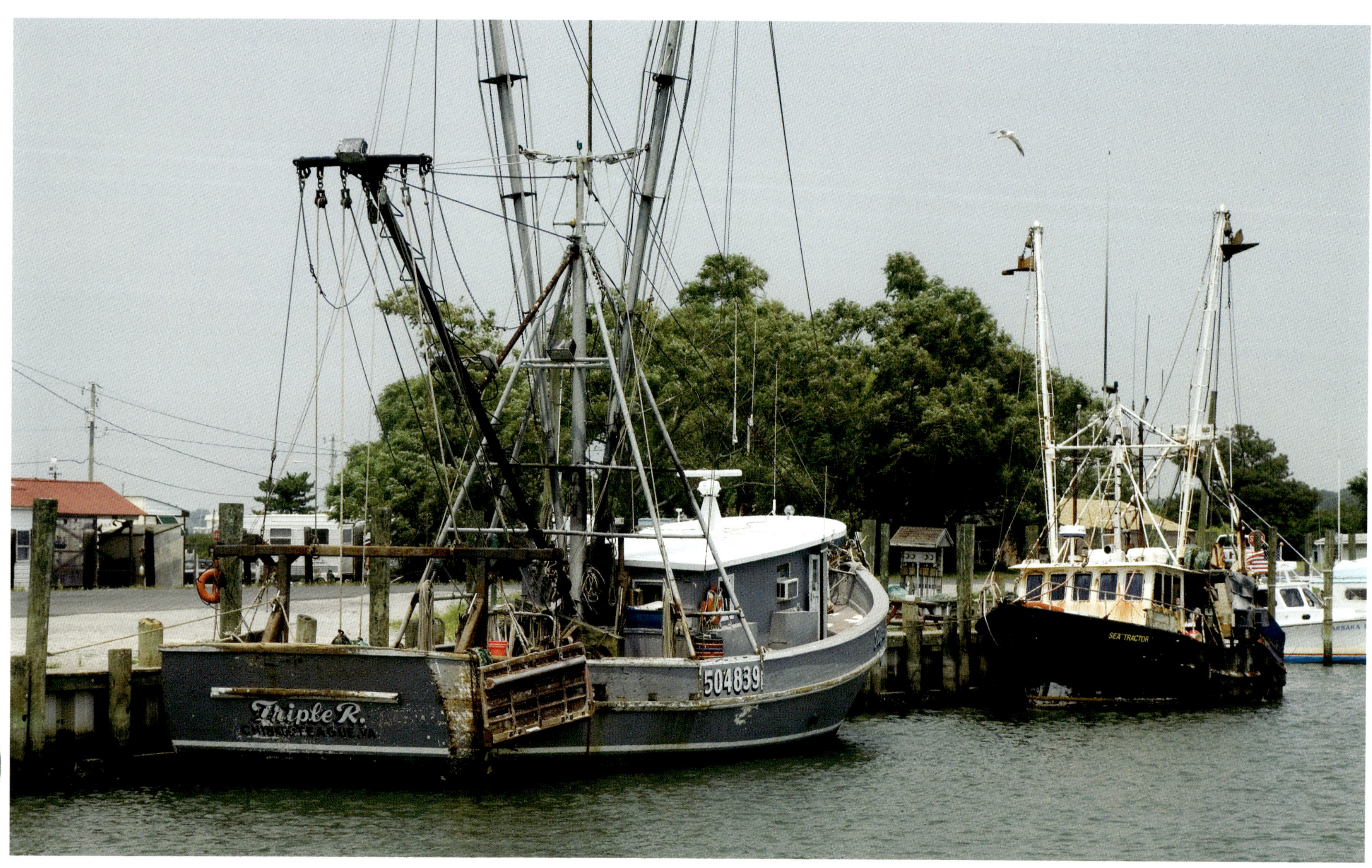
Triple R.
CHINCOTEAGUE VA
504839
SEA TRACTOR

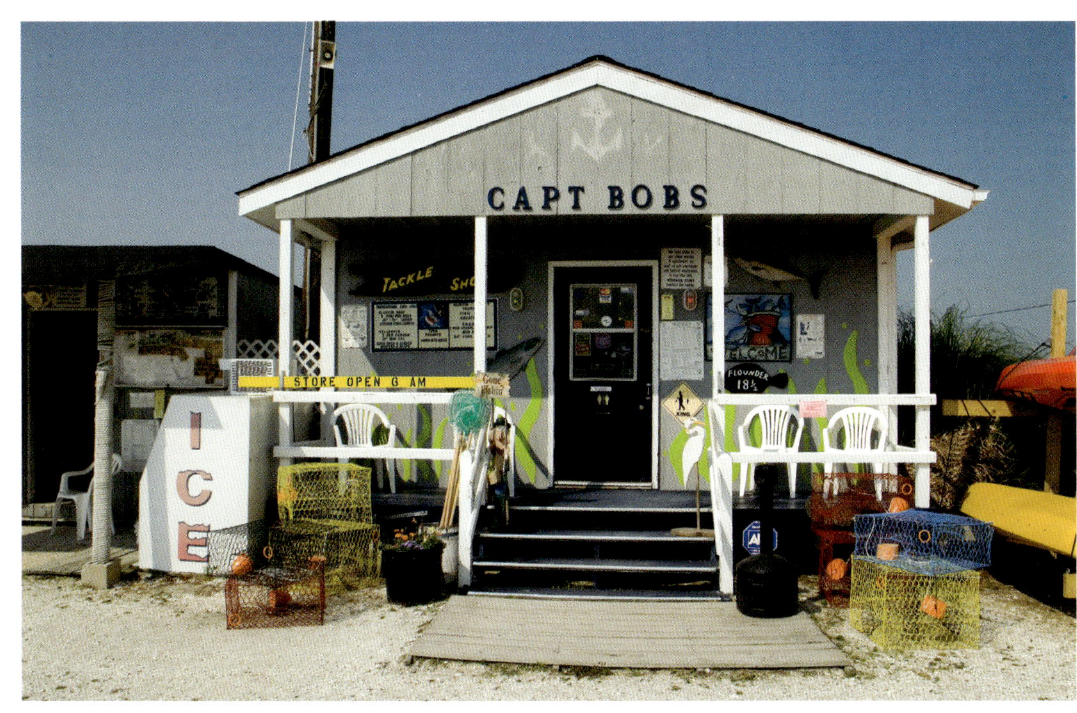

Captain Bob's

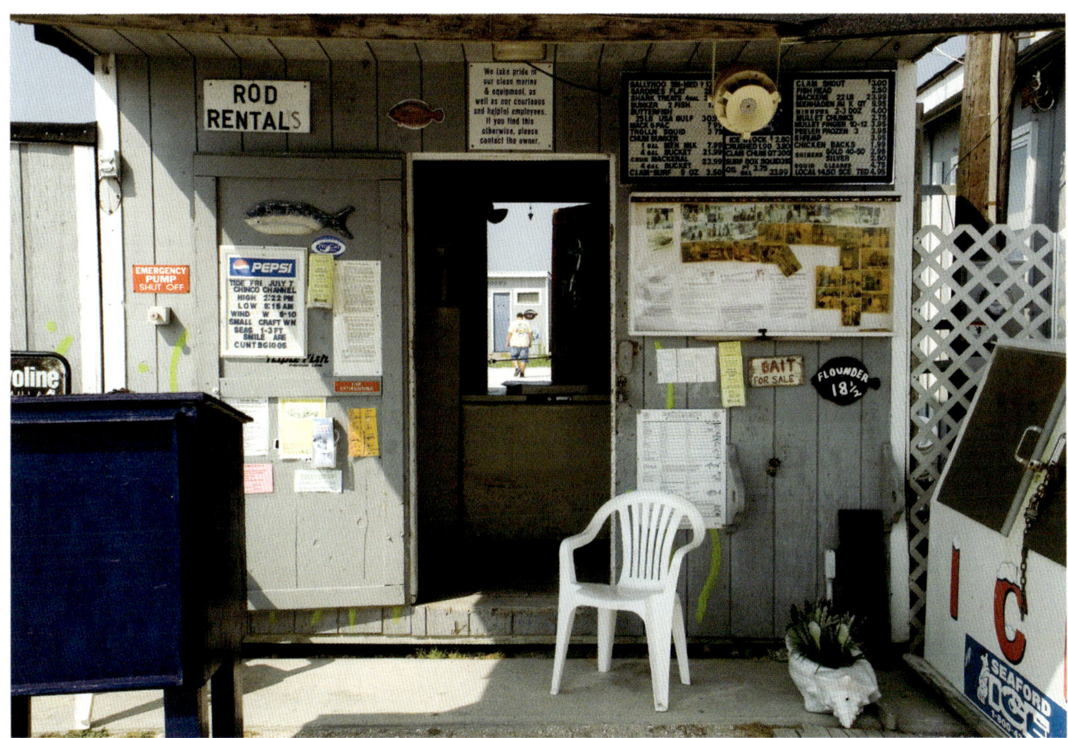

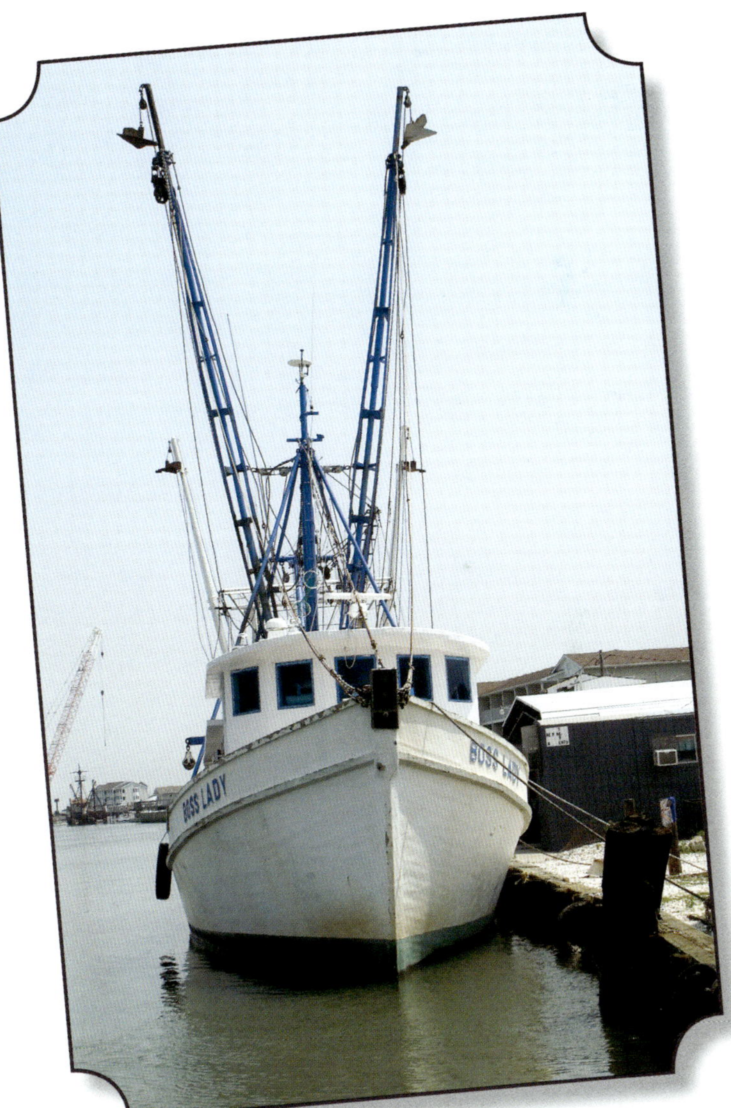

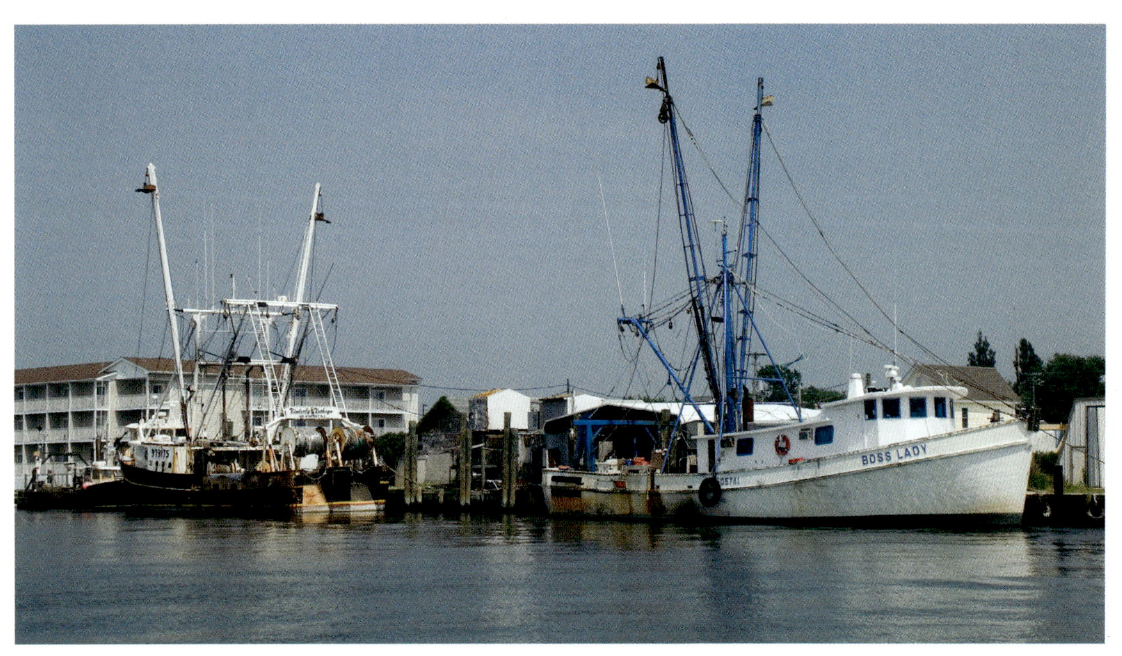

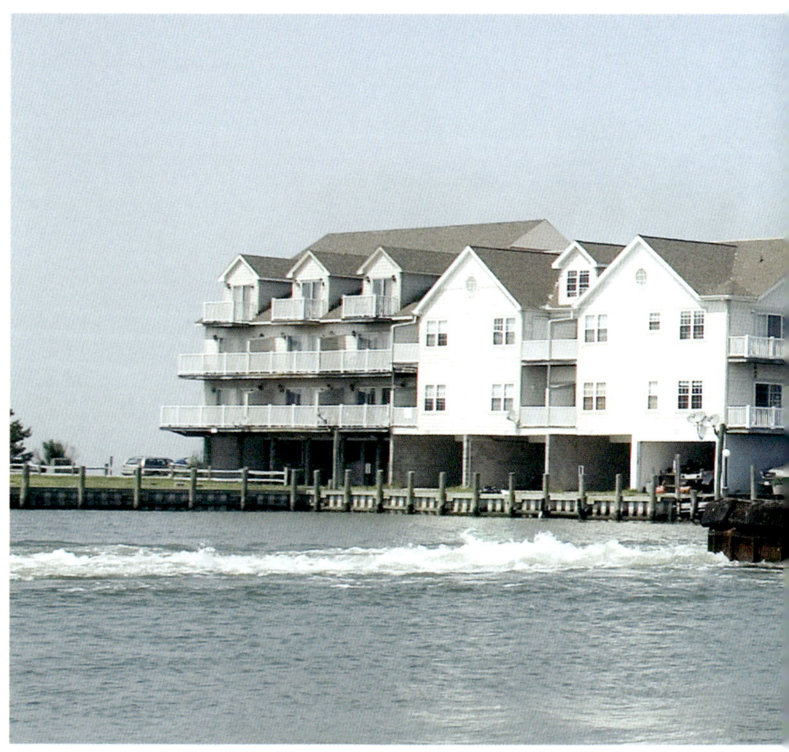

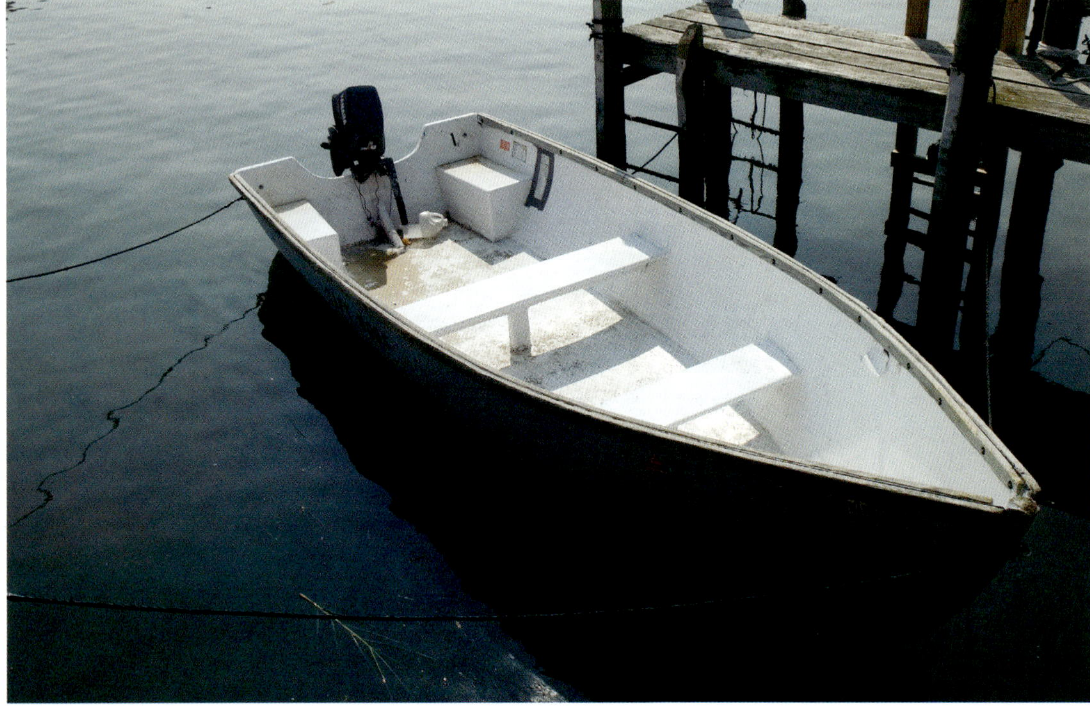

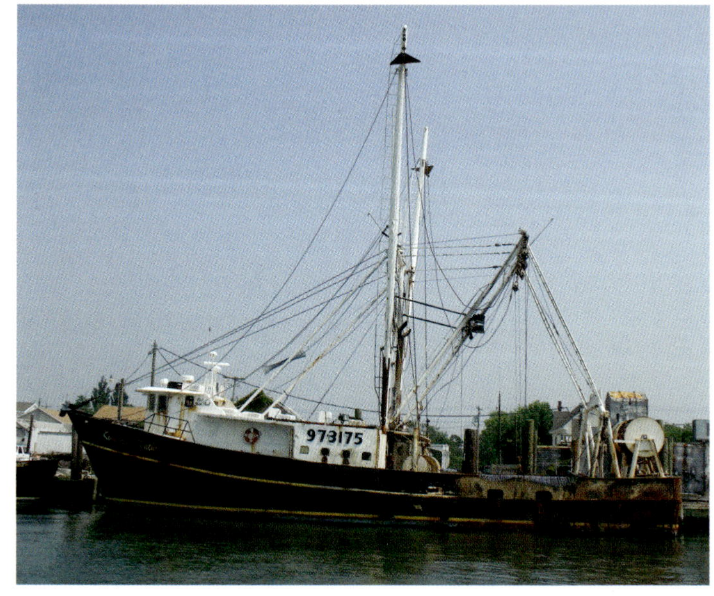

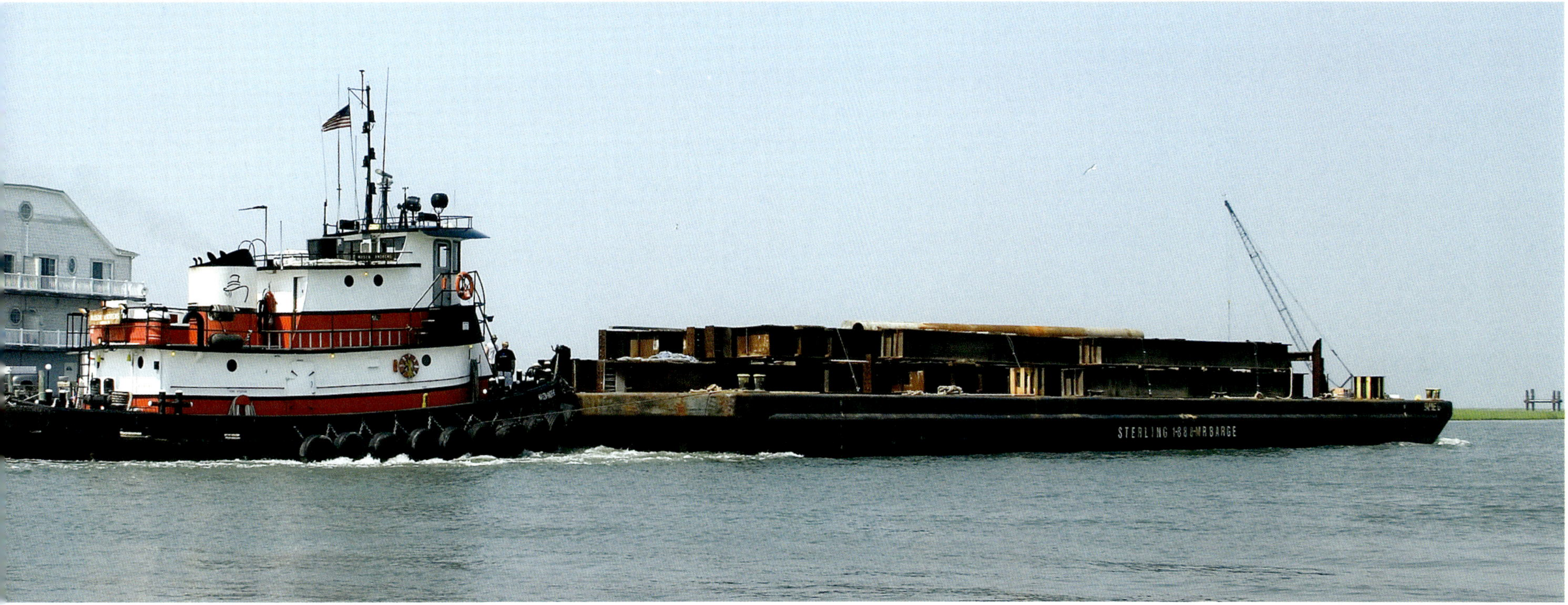

Bringing in steel beams for the new bridge under construction at the time of this writing over Black Narrows and Lewis Creek Channel. The bridge will be three-quarters of a mile long. The bridge is scheduled to be completed in November 2009.

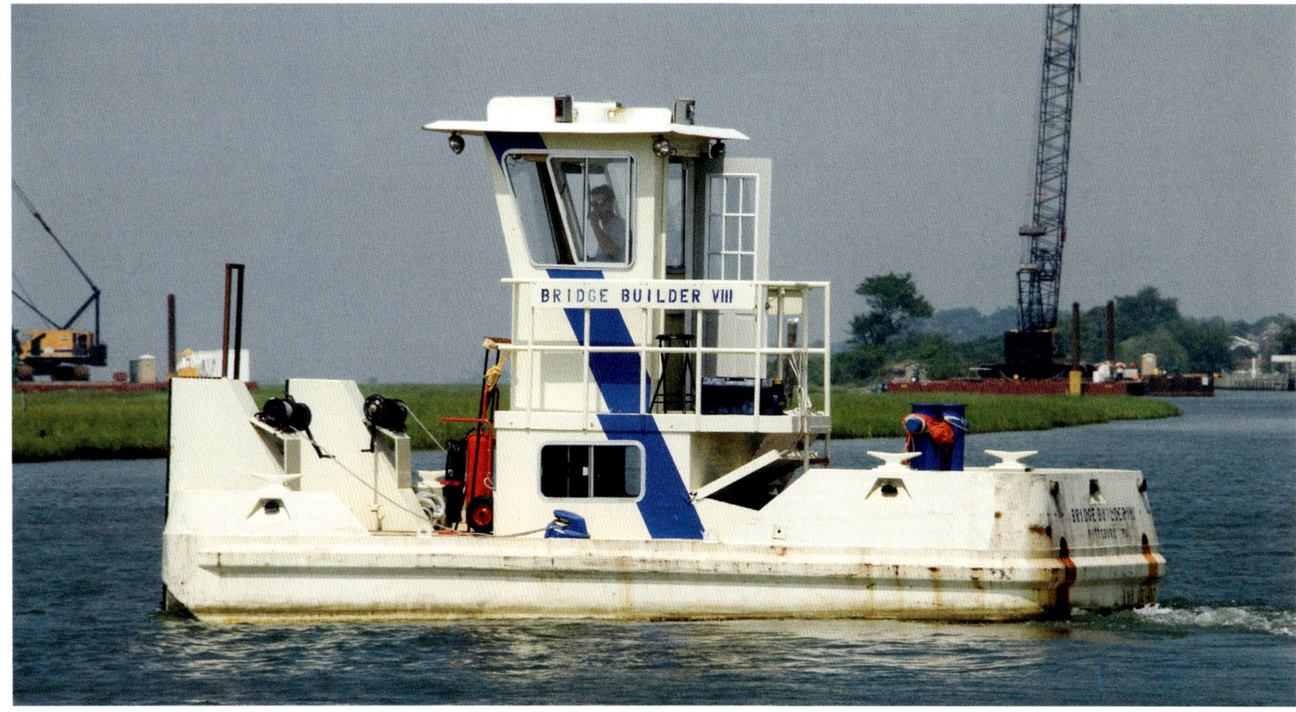

Bridge Builder VIII

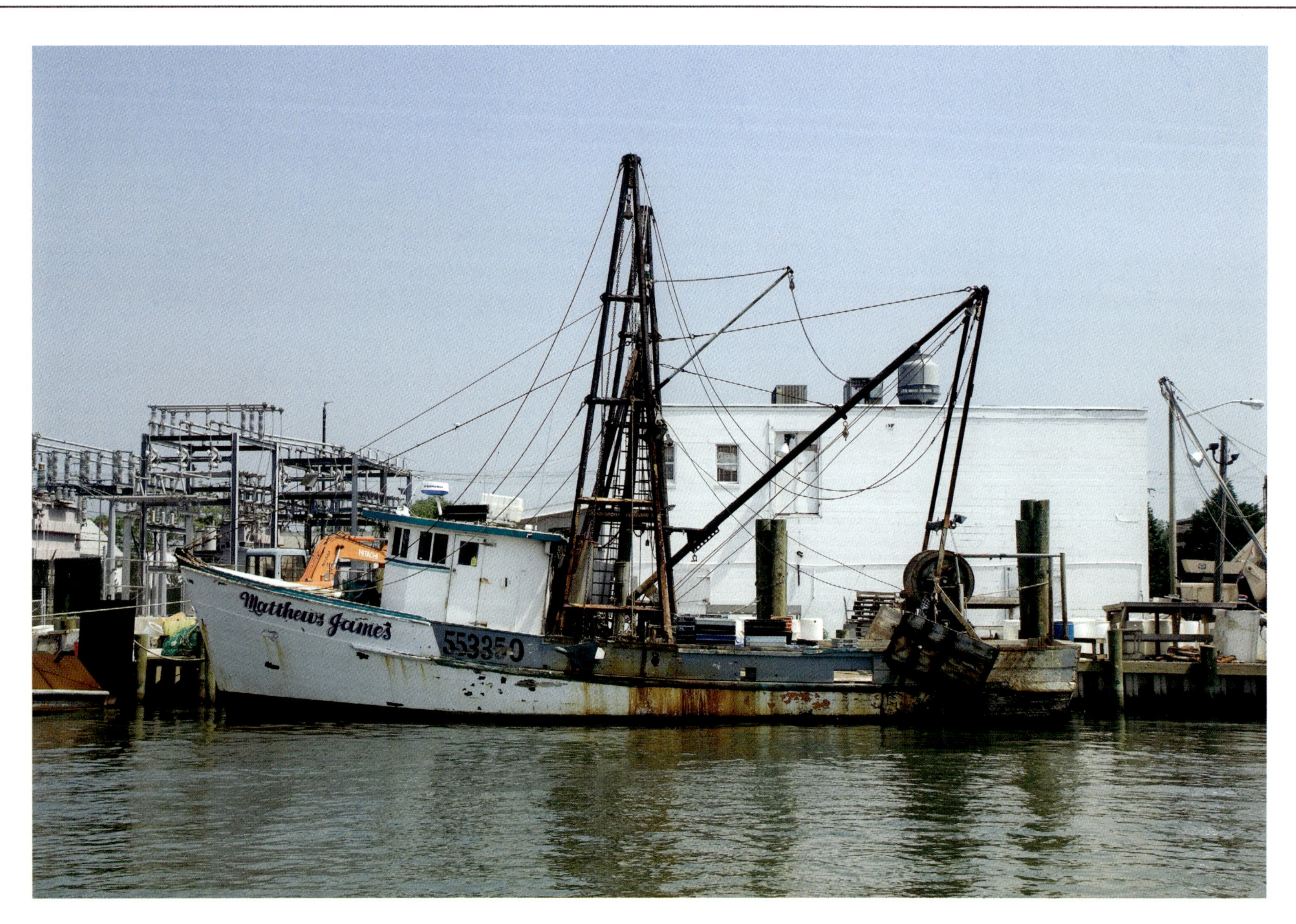

Matthews James
553350

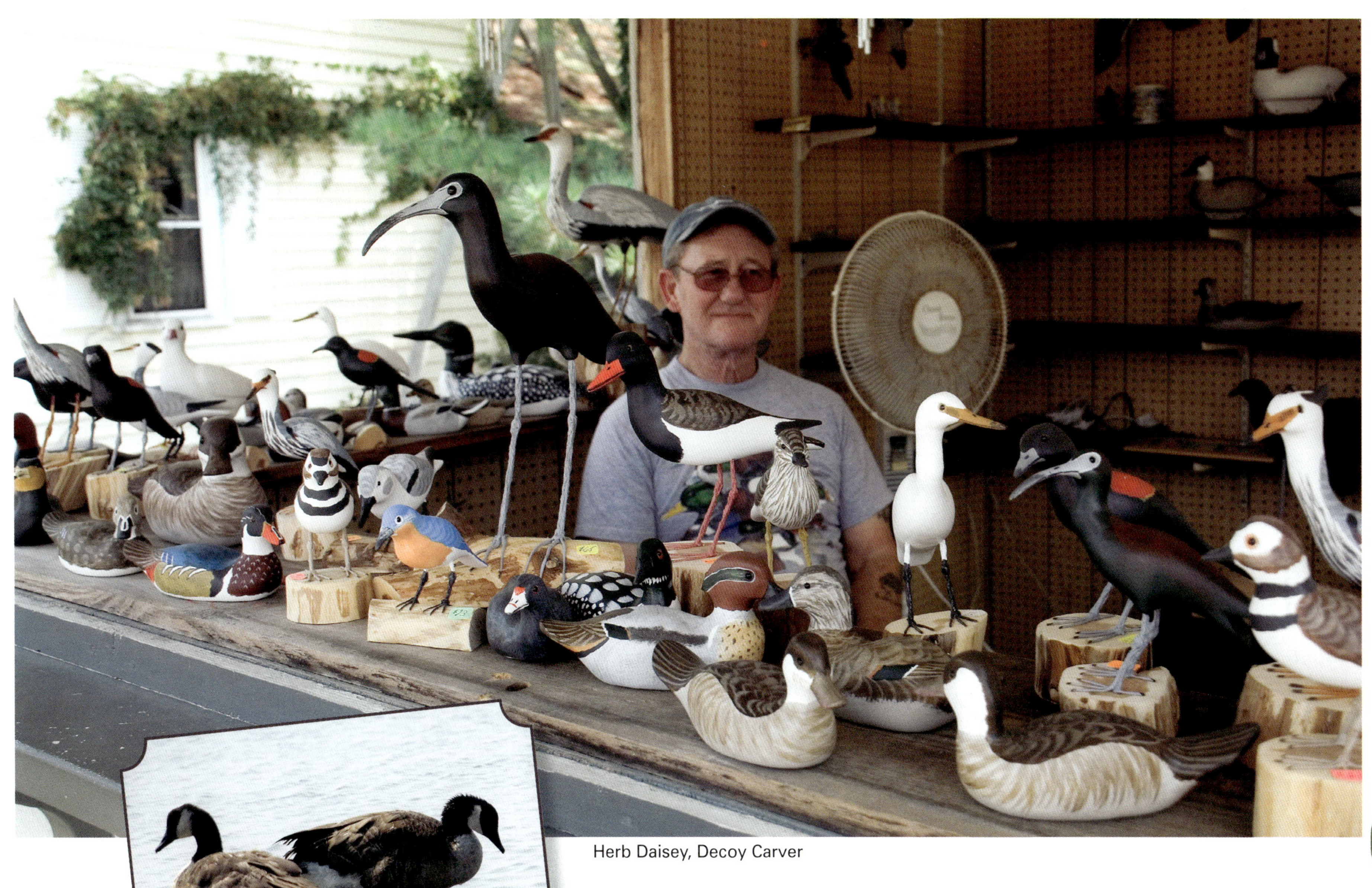

Herb Daisey, Decoy Carver

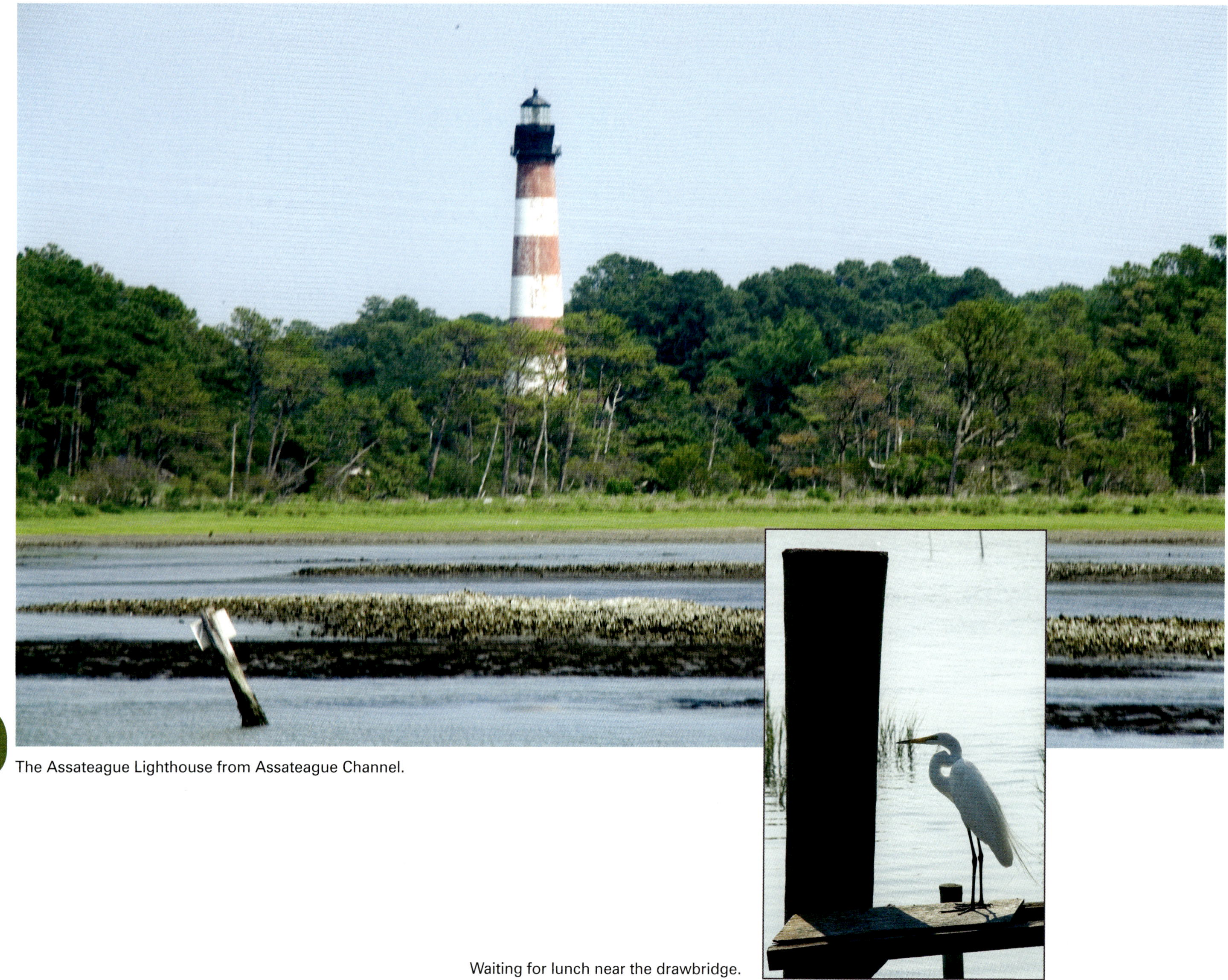

The Assateague Lighthouse from Assateague Channel.

Waiting for lunch near the drawbridge.

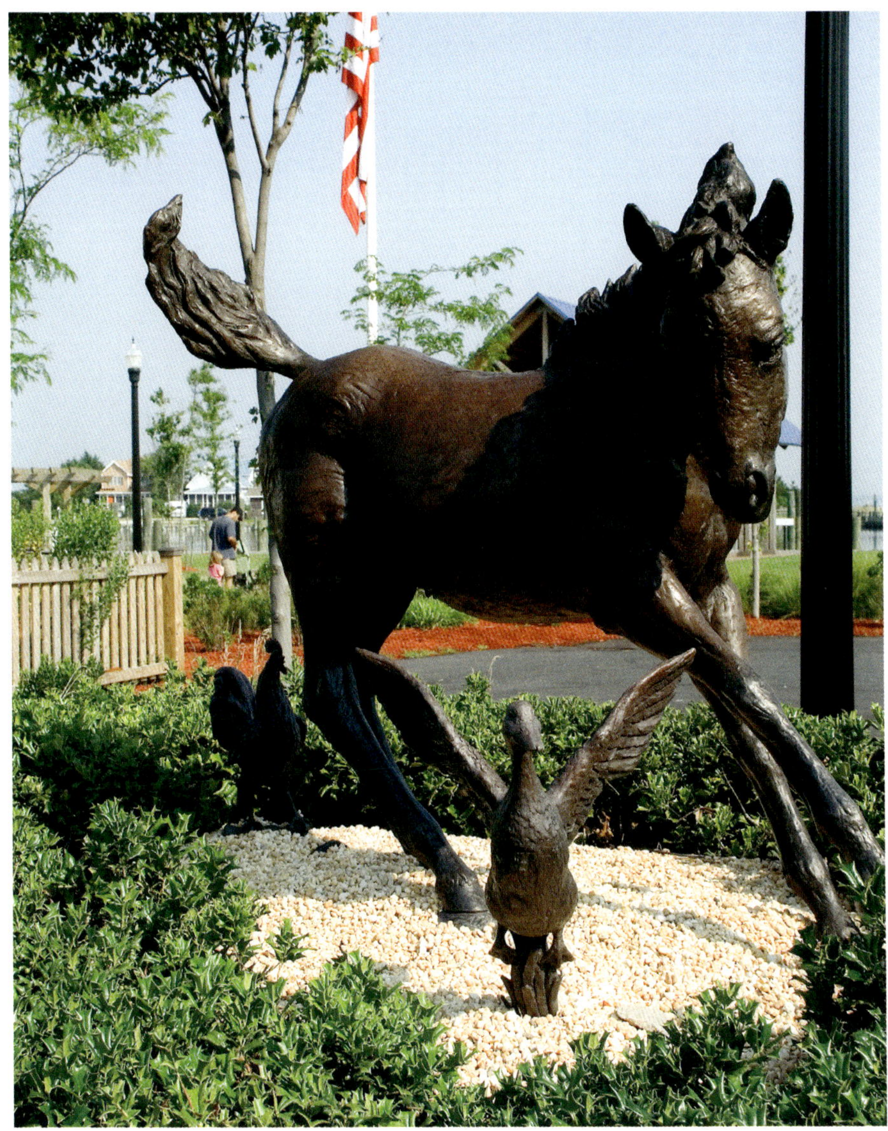
Misty of Chincoteague Statue on Main Street.

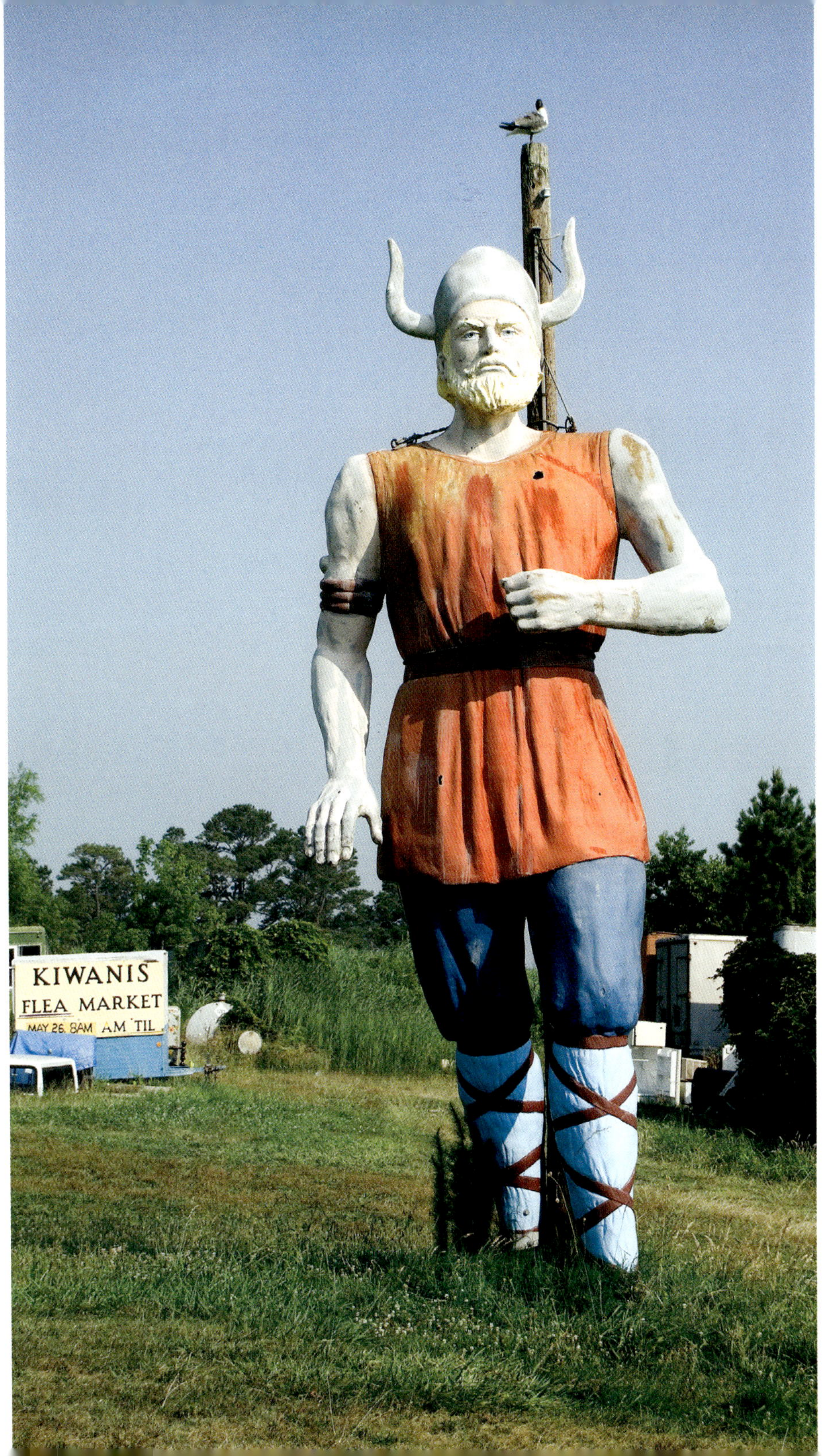

Kiwanis Flea Market lot on Ridge Road.

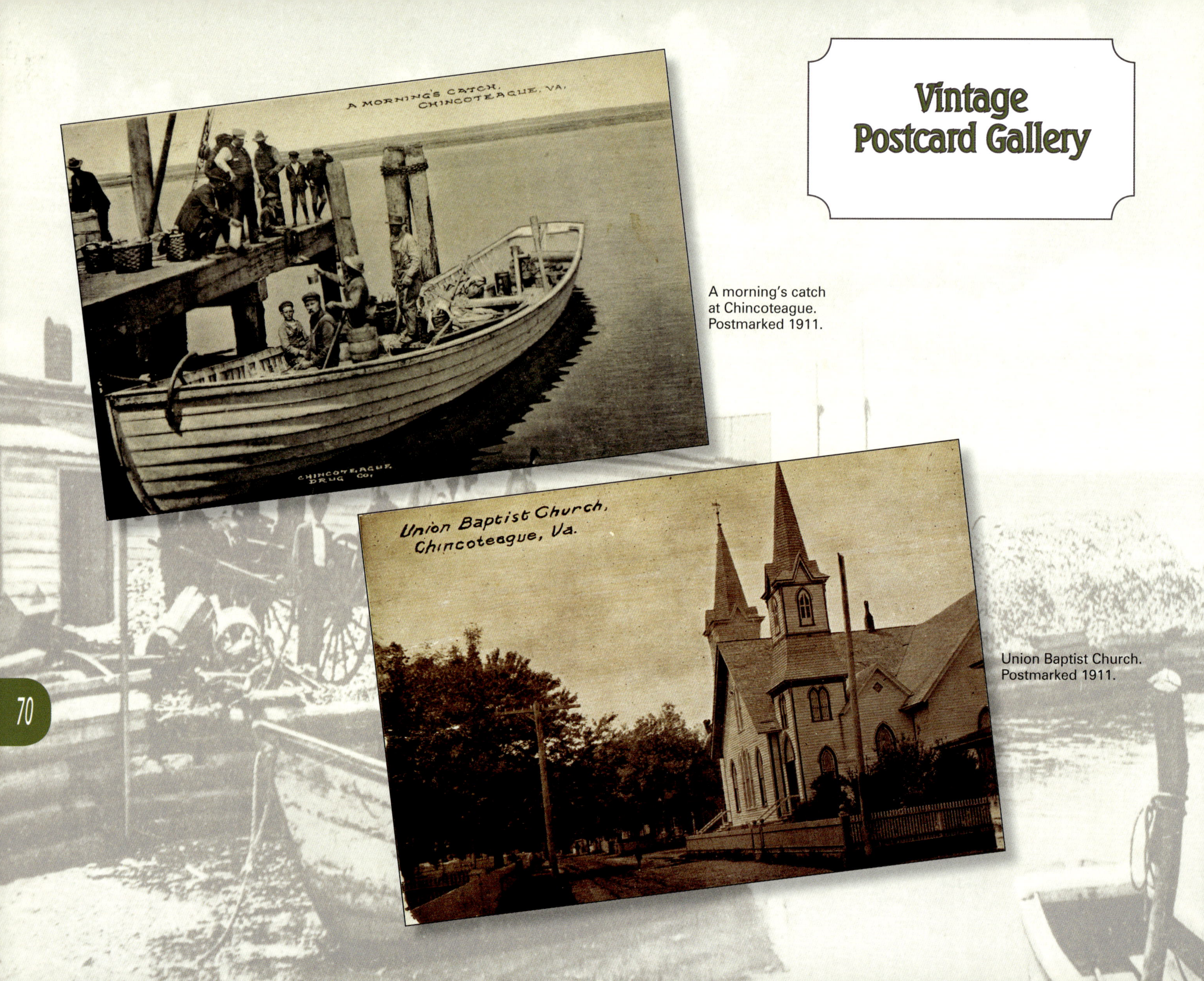

Vintage Postcard Gallery

A morning's catch
at Chincoteague.
Postmarked 1911.

Union Baptist Church.
Postmarked 1911.

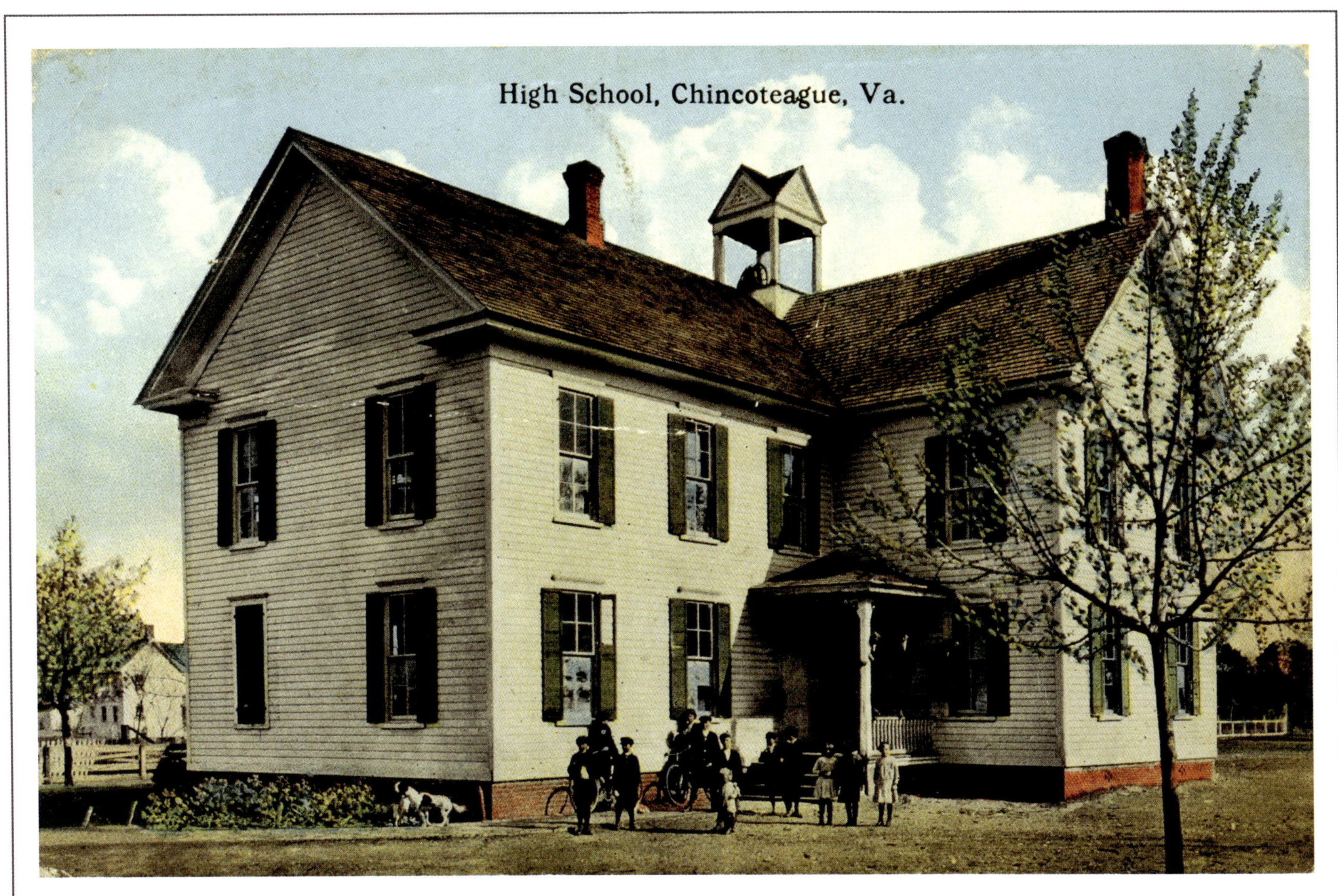

The High School, Chincoteague. Postmarked 1915.

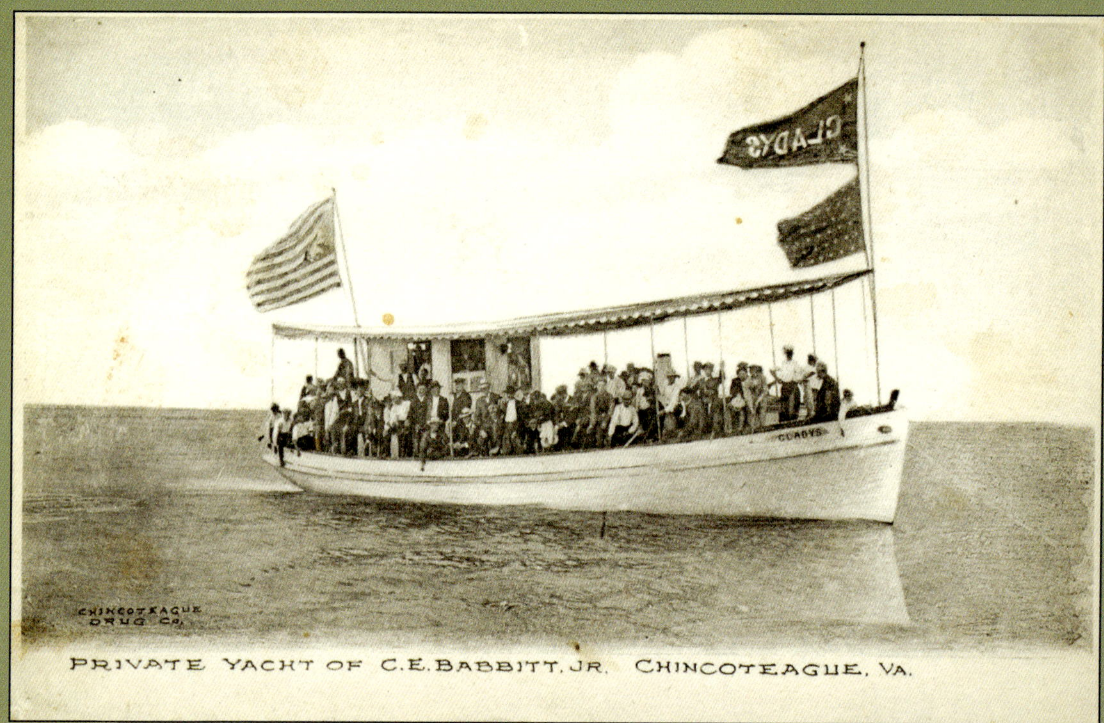

Private yacht of C. E. Babbitt, Jr. Postmarked 1908.

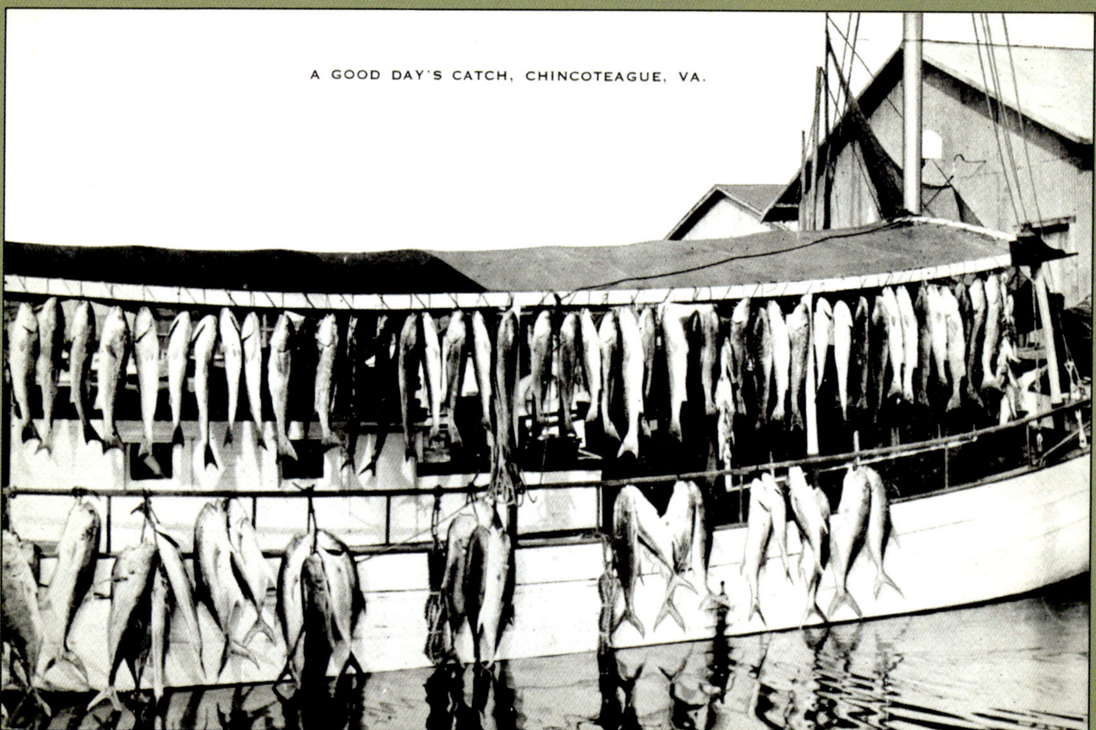

A good day's catch at Chincoteague. Circa 1940s.

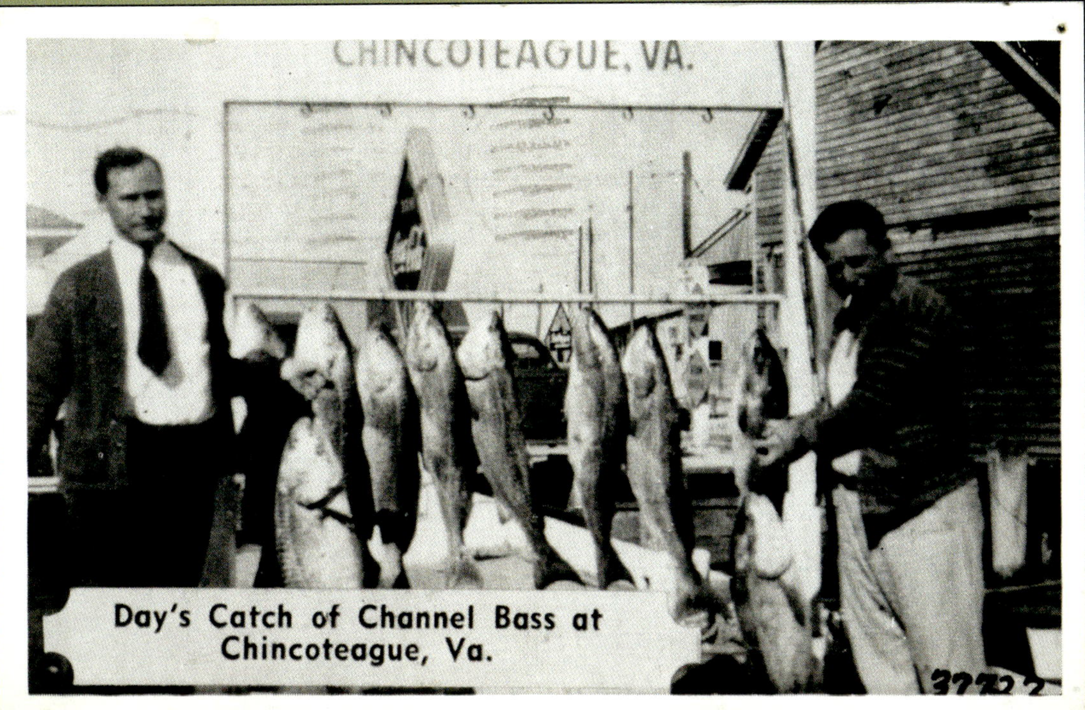

Day's catch of Channel Bass at Chincoteague. Postmarked 1949.

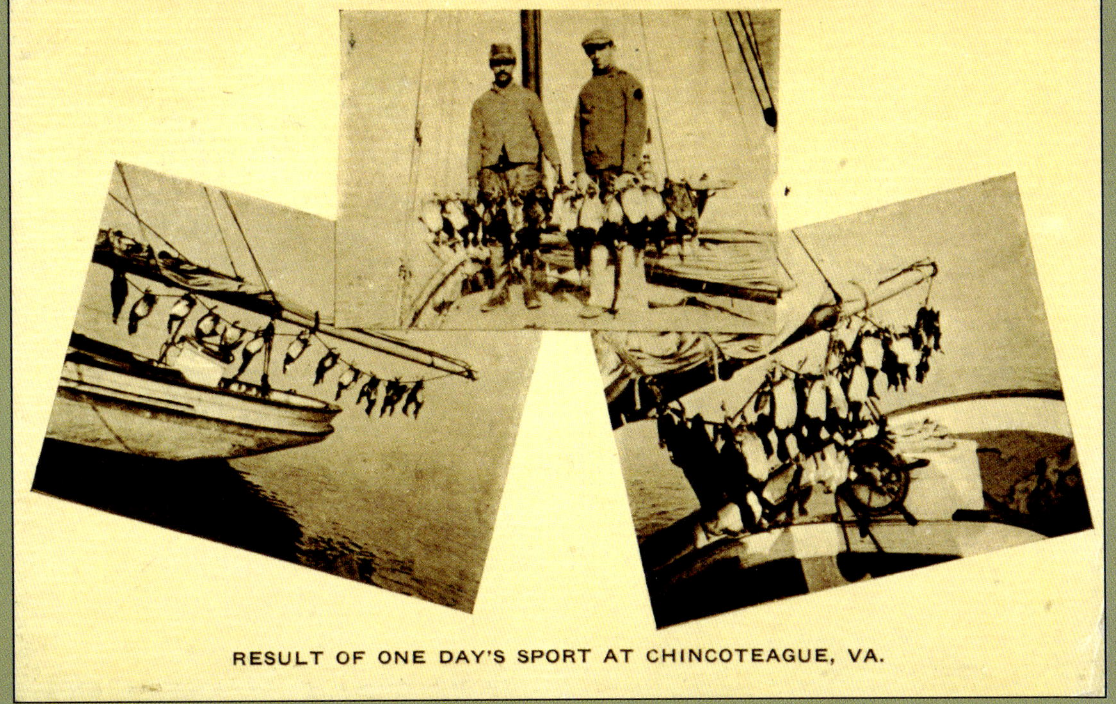

Result of one day's sport (duck hunting) at Chincoteague. Postmarked 1913.

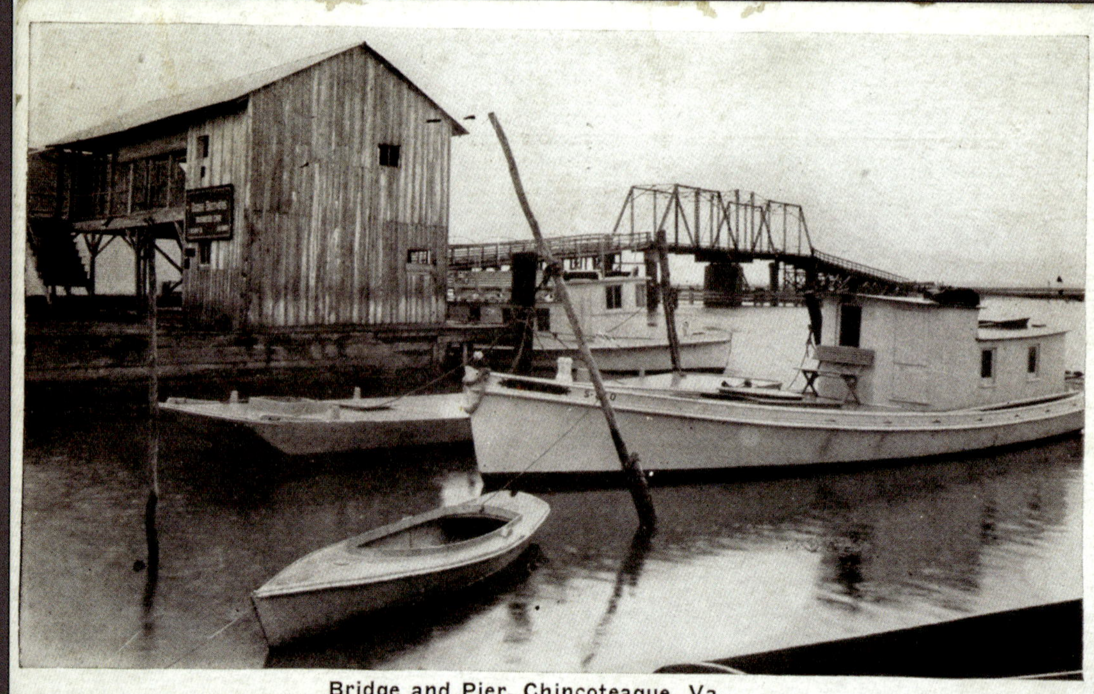

Bridge and pier. Message on the backside reads: "This is a great oyster place down here. All you see is oysters and oysters and more oysters." Postmarked 1923.

Bridge and Pier, Chincoteague, Va.

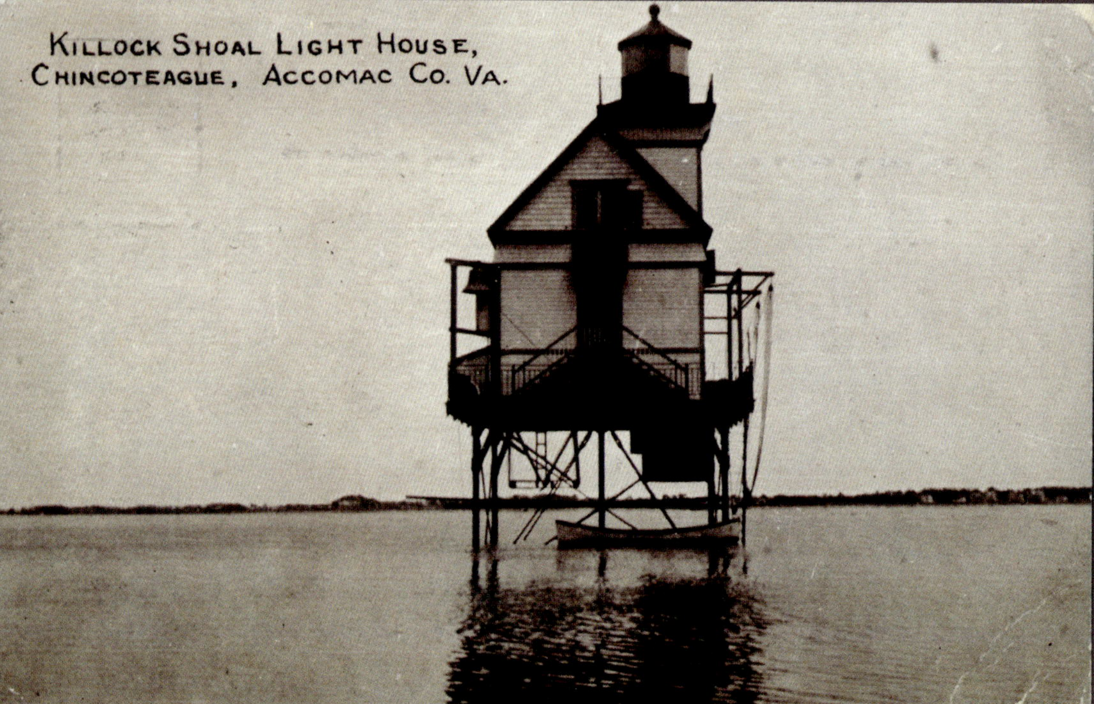

Killock (Killick) Shoal Light House, Chincoteague, Accomac (Accomack) County, Virginia. The lighthouse was built in 1886. Postmarked 1910.

74

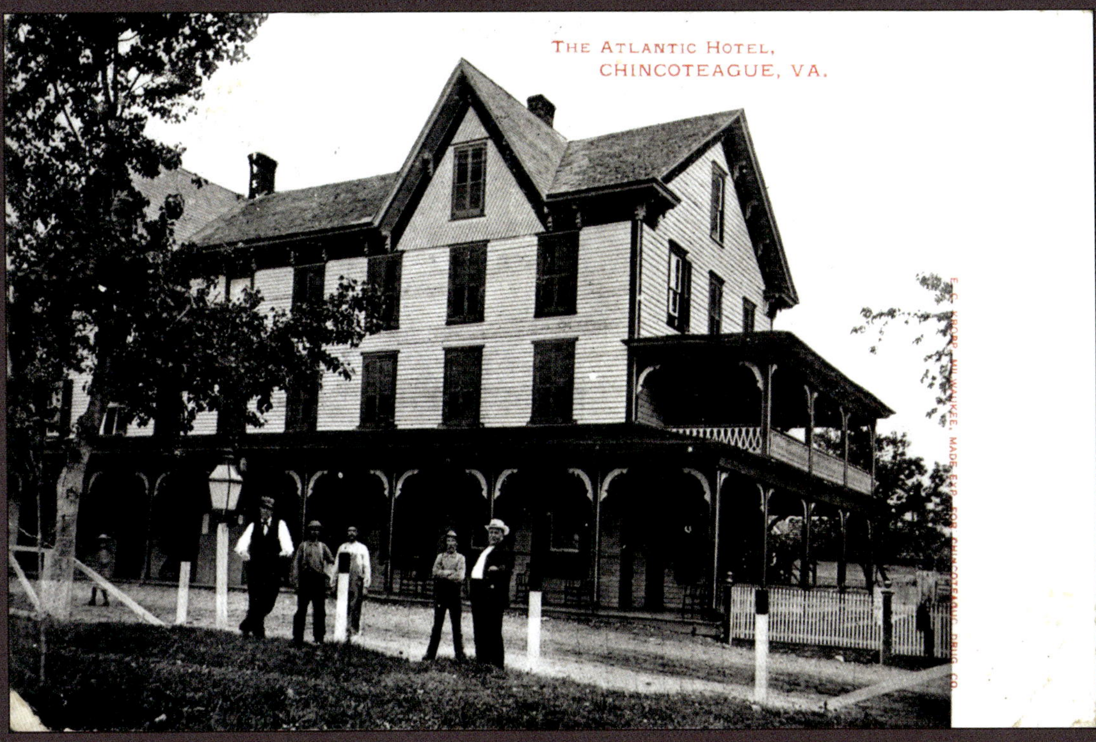

The Atlantic Hotel on Chincoteague. Postmarked 1906.

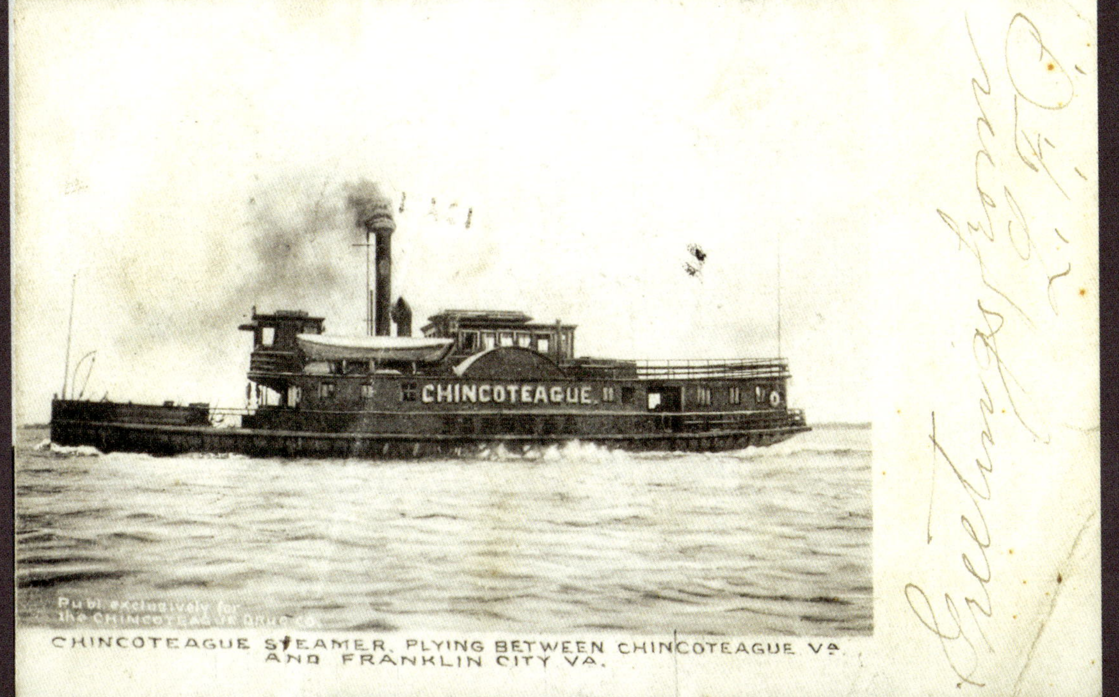

Chincoteague steamer plying between Chincoteague and Franklin City, Virginia. Postmarked 1907.

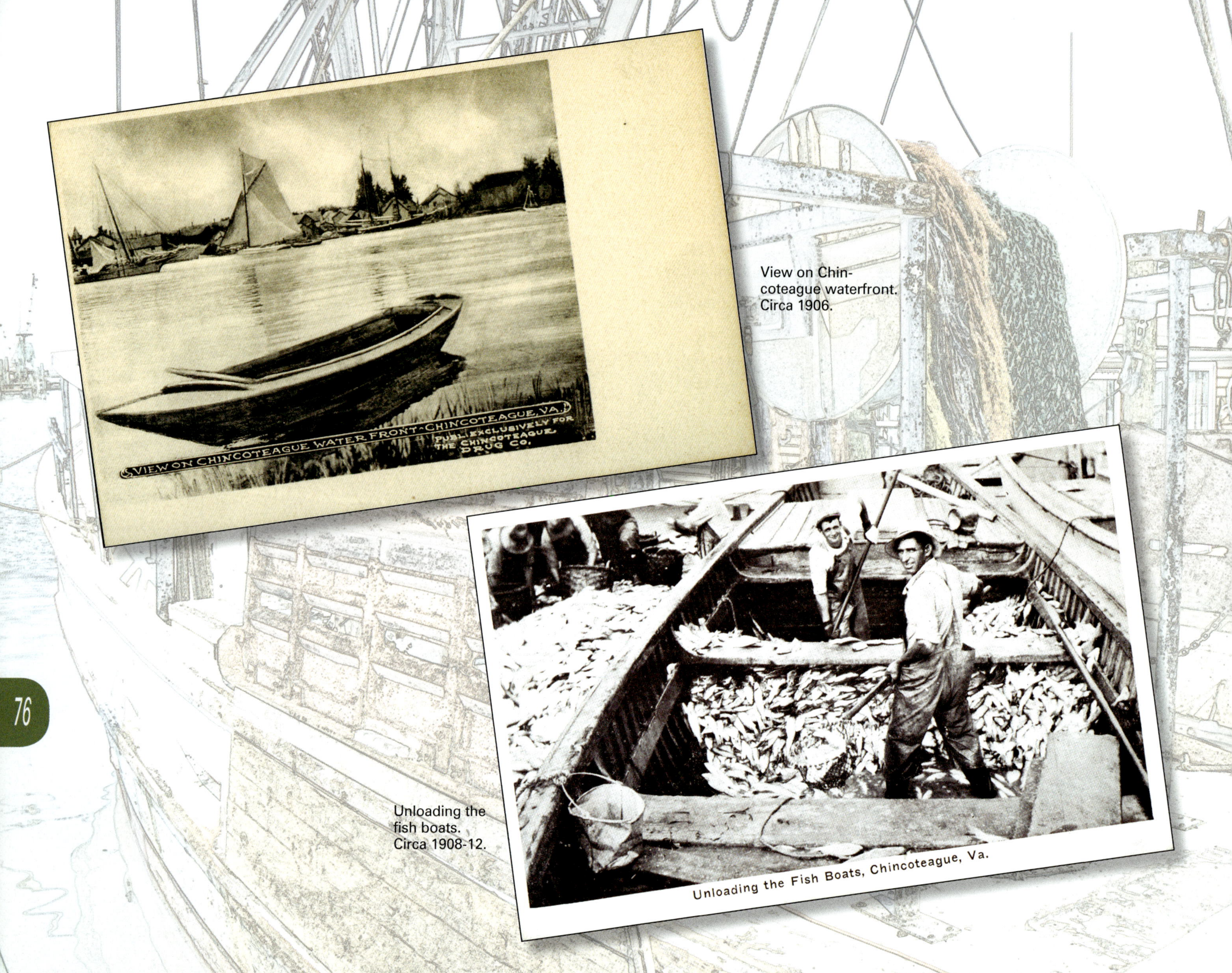

View on Chin-
coteague waterfront.
Circa 1906.

Unloading the
fish boats.
Circa 1908-12.

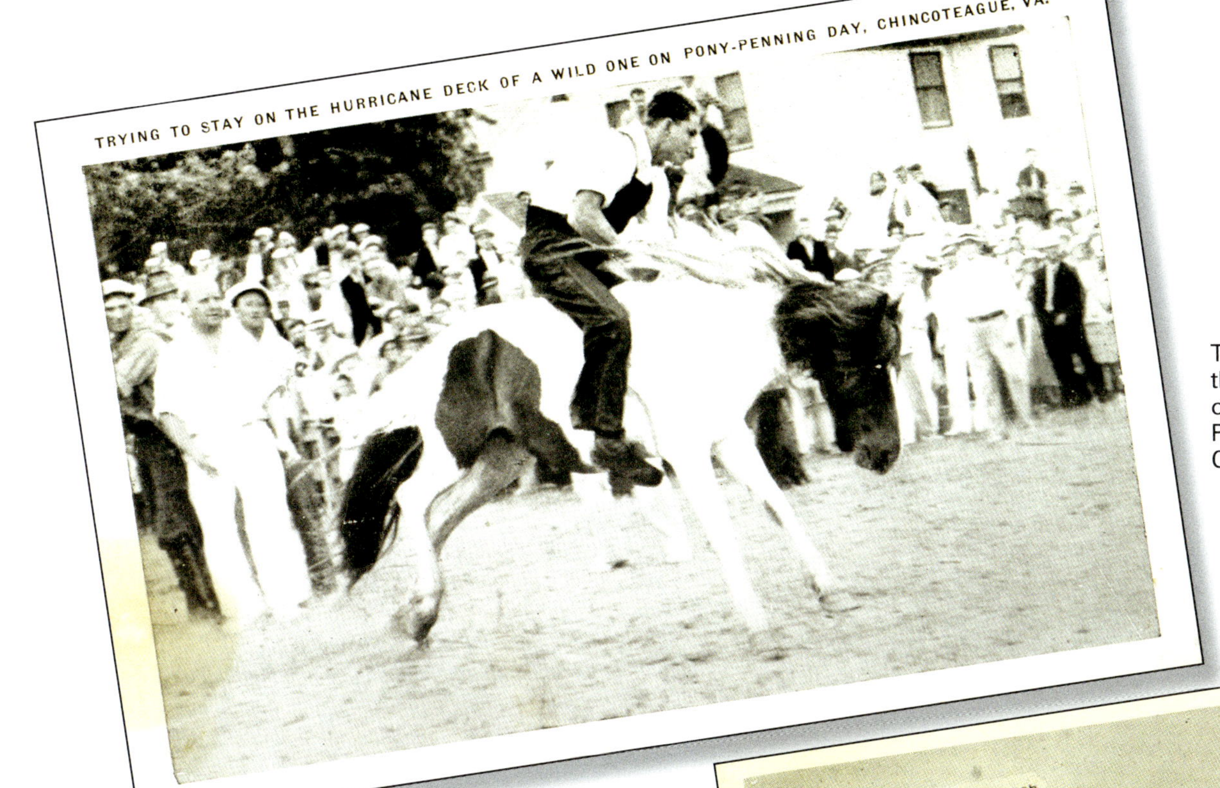

Trying to stay on the hurricane deck of a wild one on Pony Penning day. Circa 1950s.

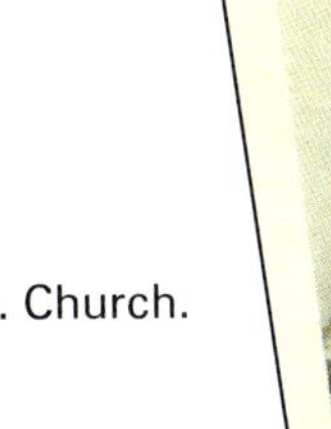

Christ's M. E. Church. Circa 1940s.

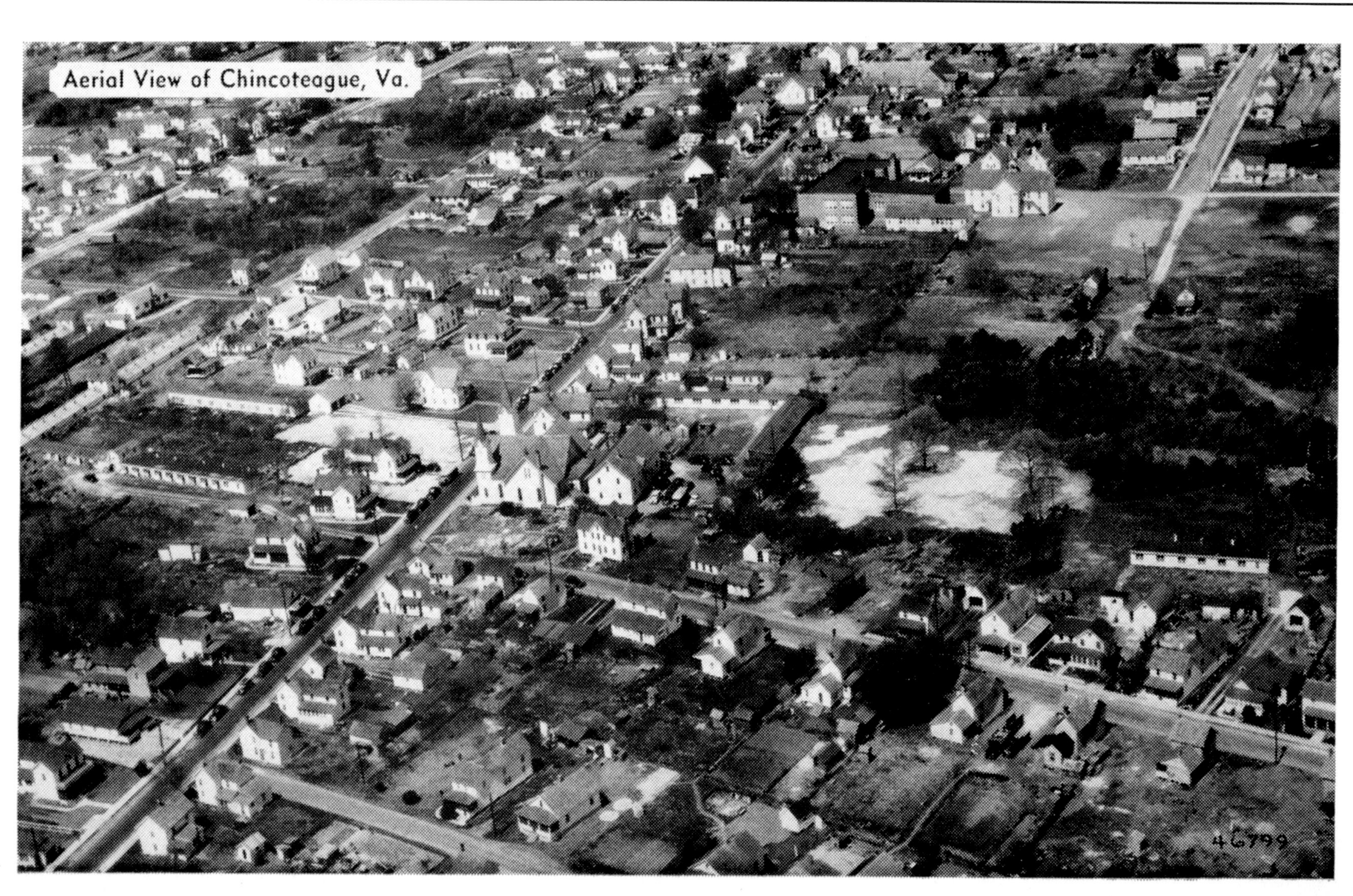

Aerial view of Chincoteague.
Circa 1940s.

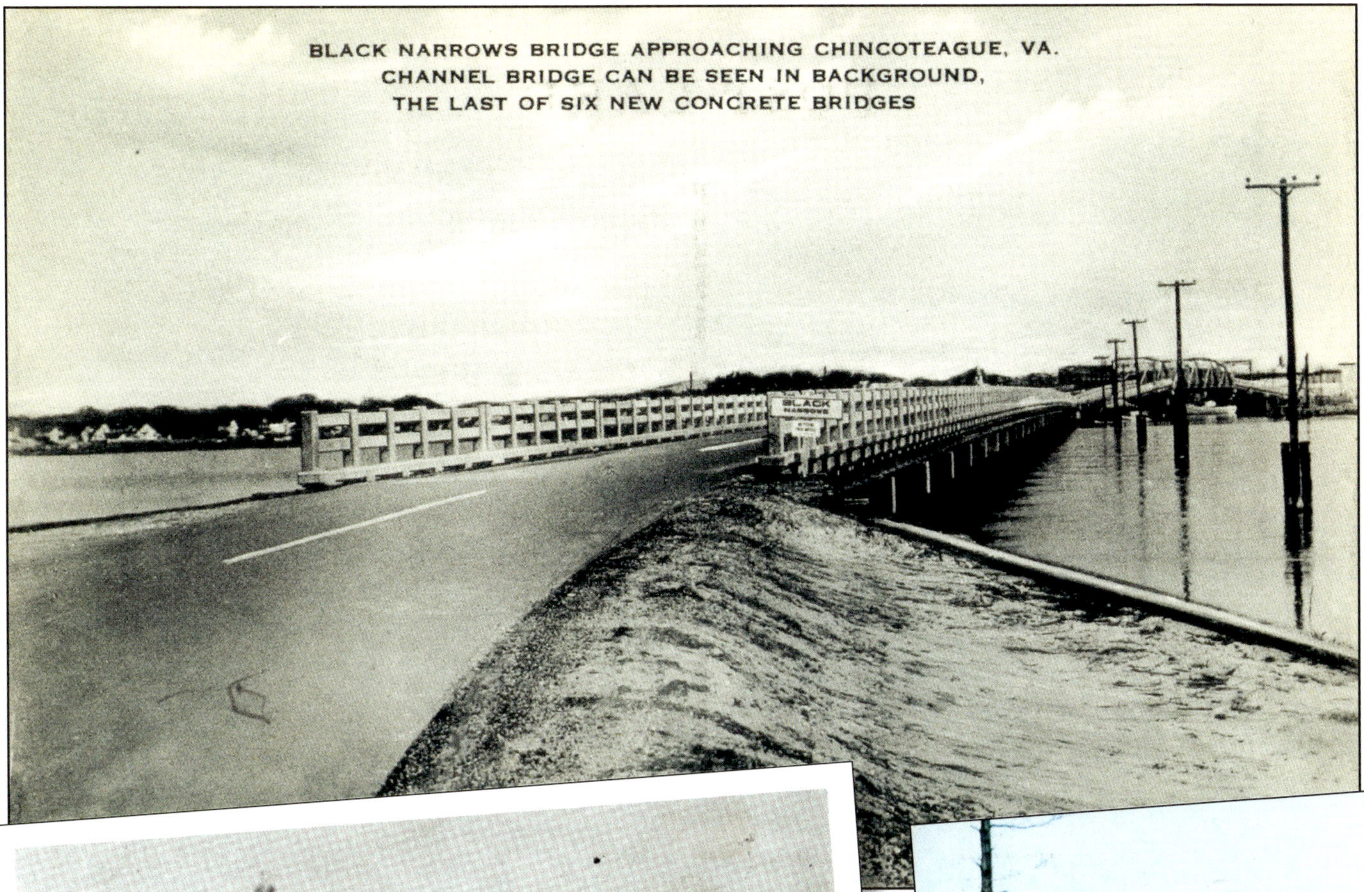

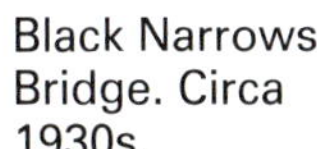

Black Narrows Bridge. Circa 1930s.

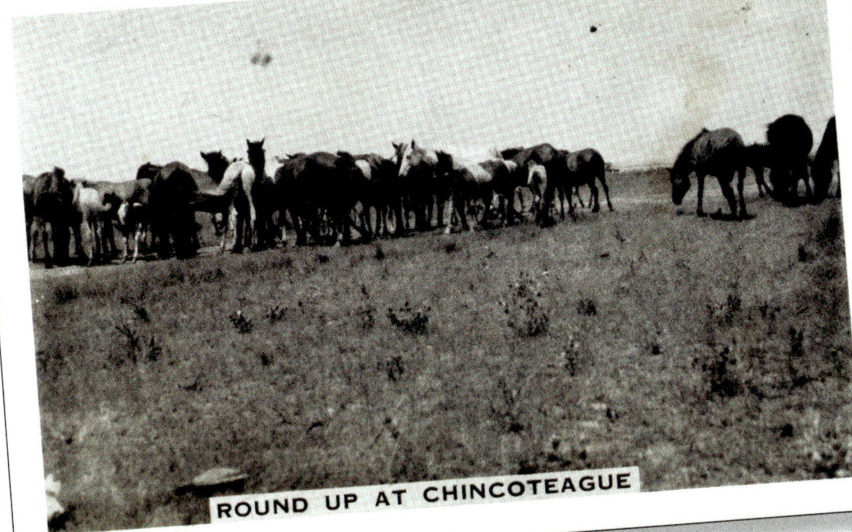

Round up at Chincoteague. Circa 1950s.

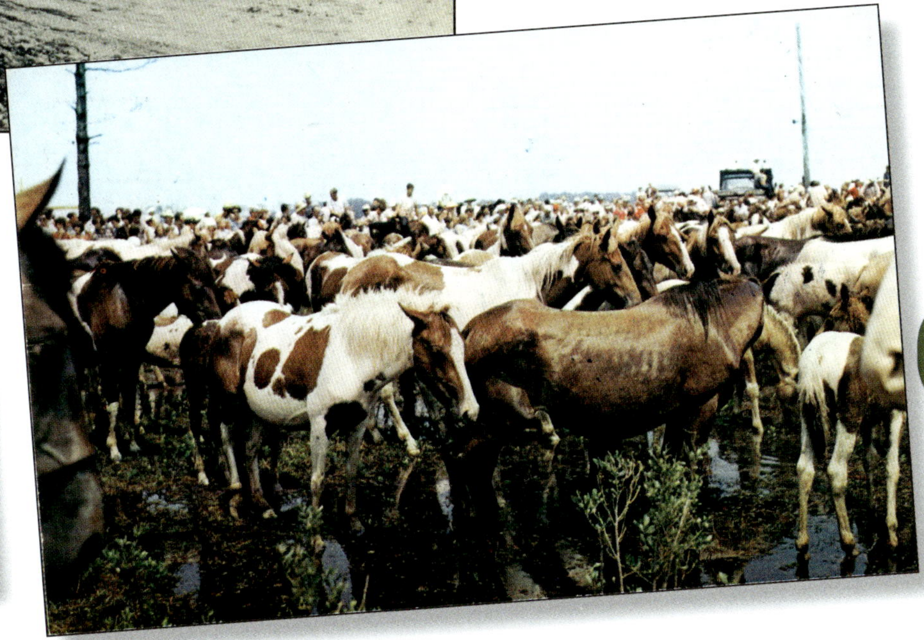

Ponies resting after swimming the channel. Circa 1960s.

Ponies being driven down Main Street to the corrals at the carnival grounds. Circa 1940s.

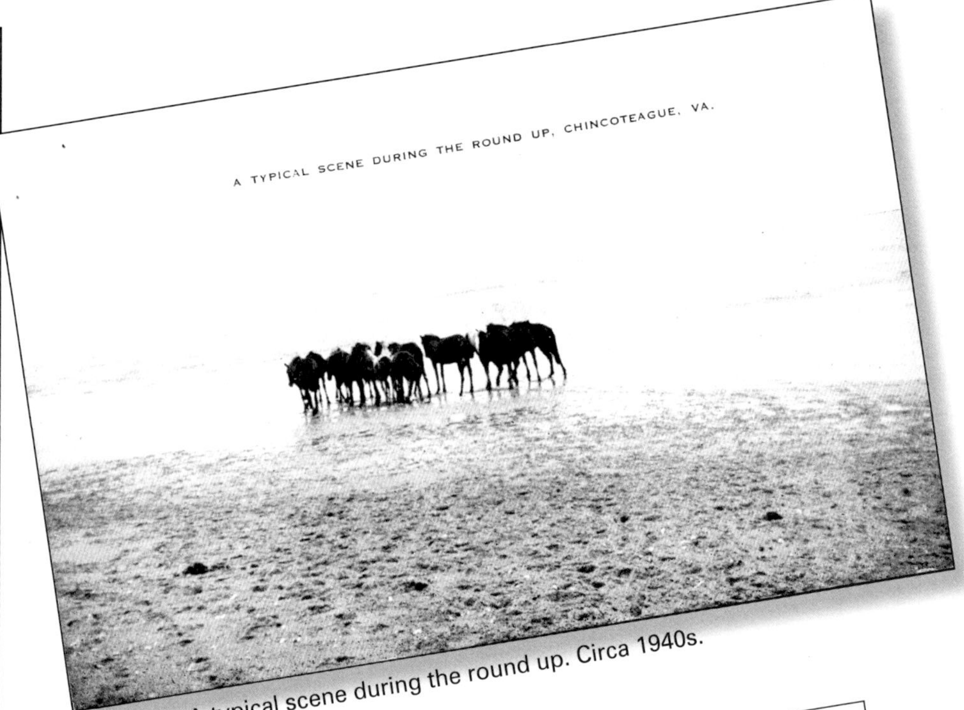

A typical scene during the round up. Circa 1940s.

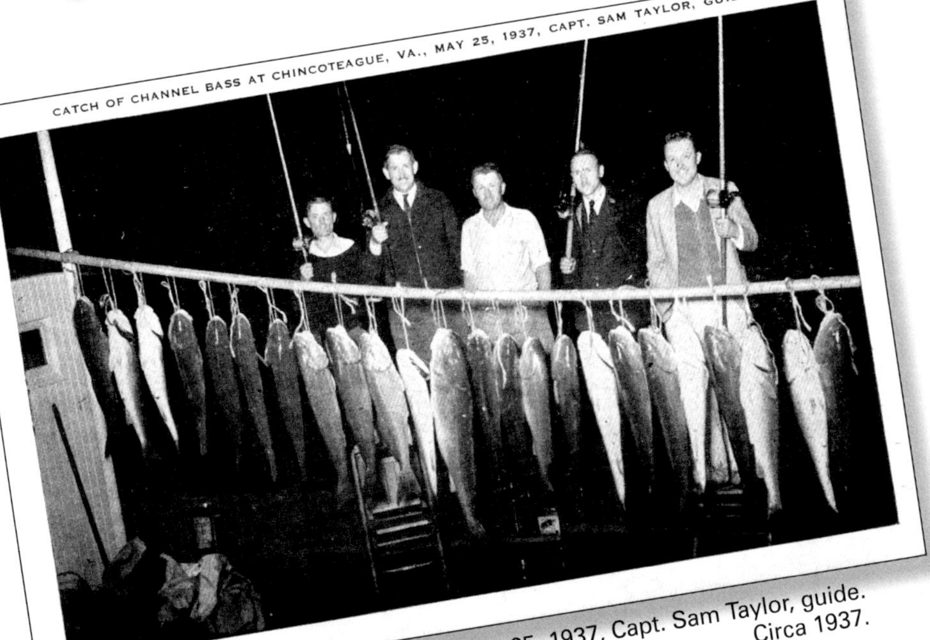

A catch of Channel Bass, May 25, 1937, Capt. Sam Taylor, guide. Circa 1937.

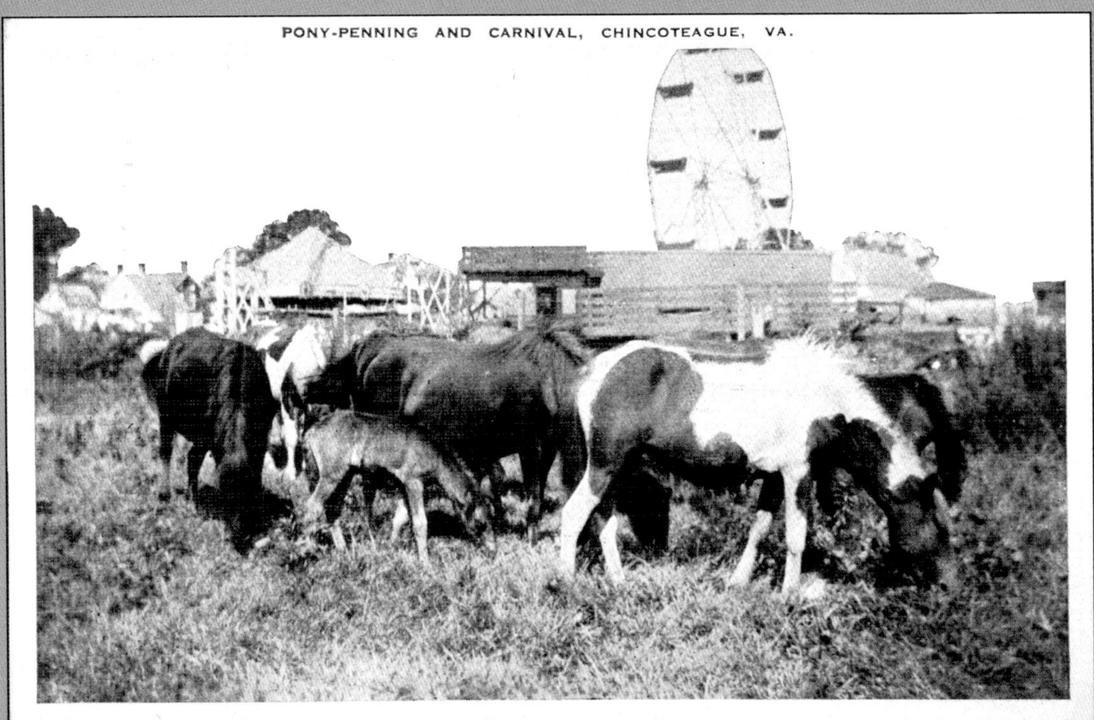

Pony Penning and carnival.
Postmarked 1938.

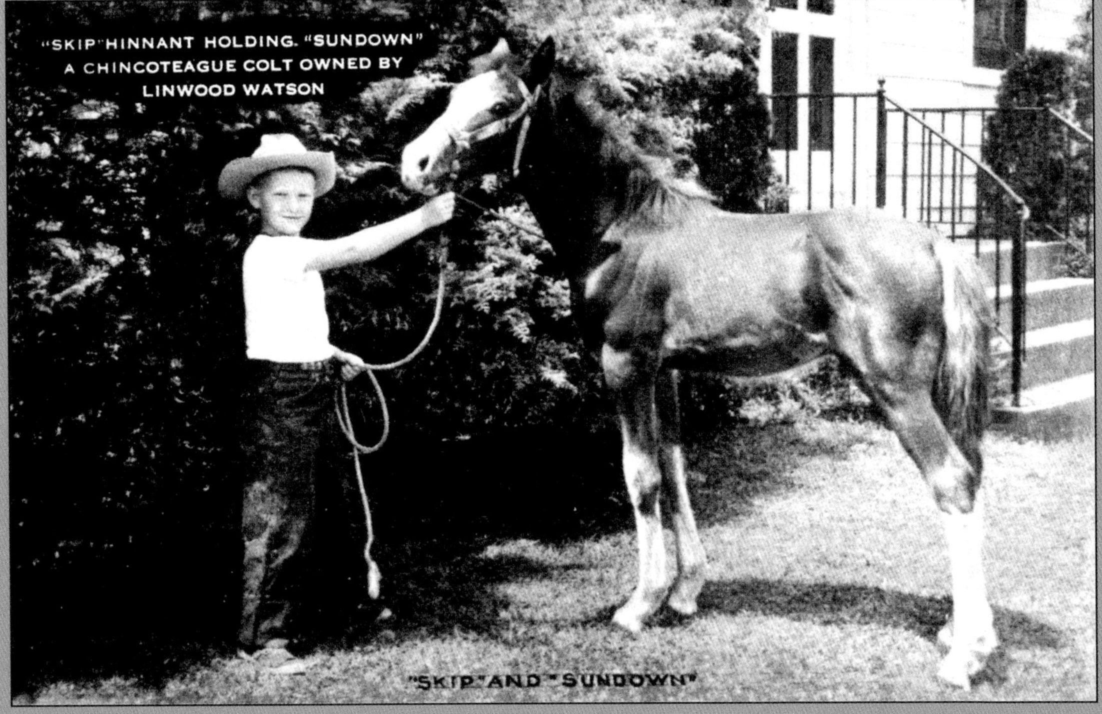

Skip and Sundown.
Circa 1940s.

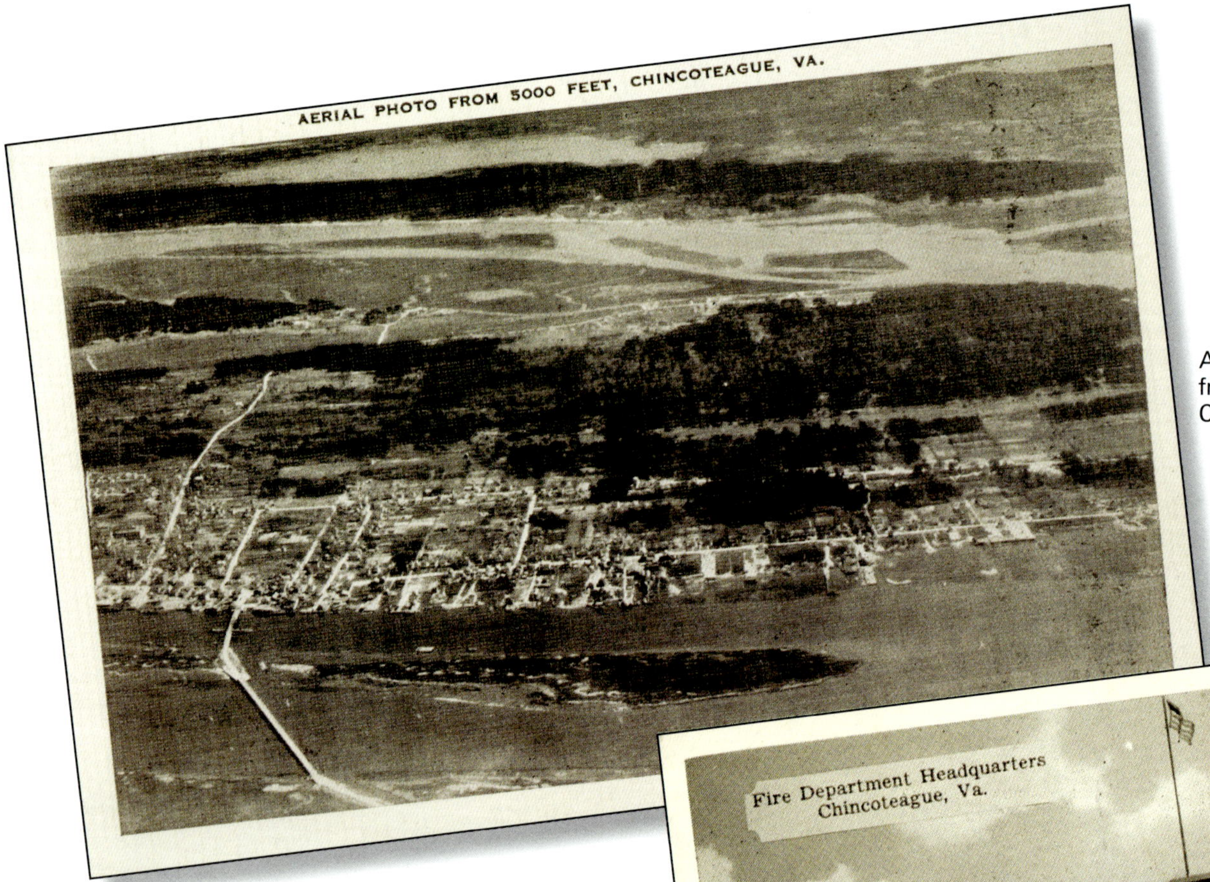

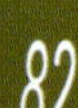

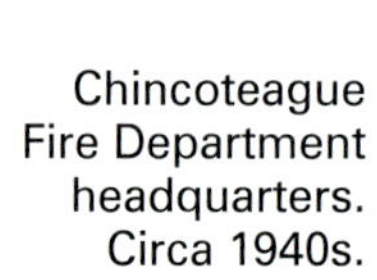

Aerial view
from 5000 feet.
Circa 1940s.

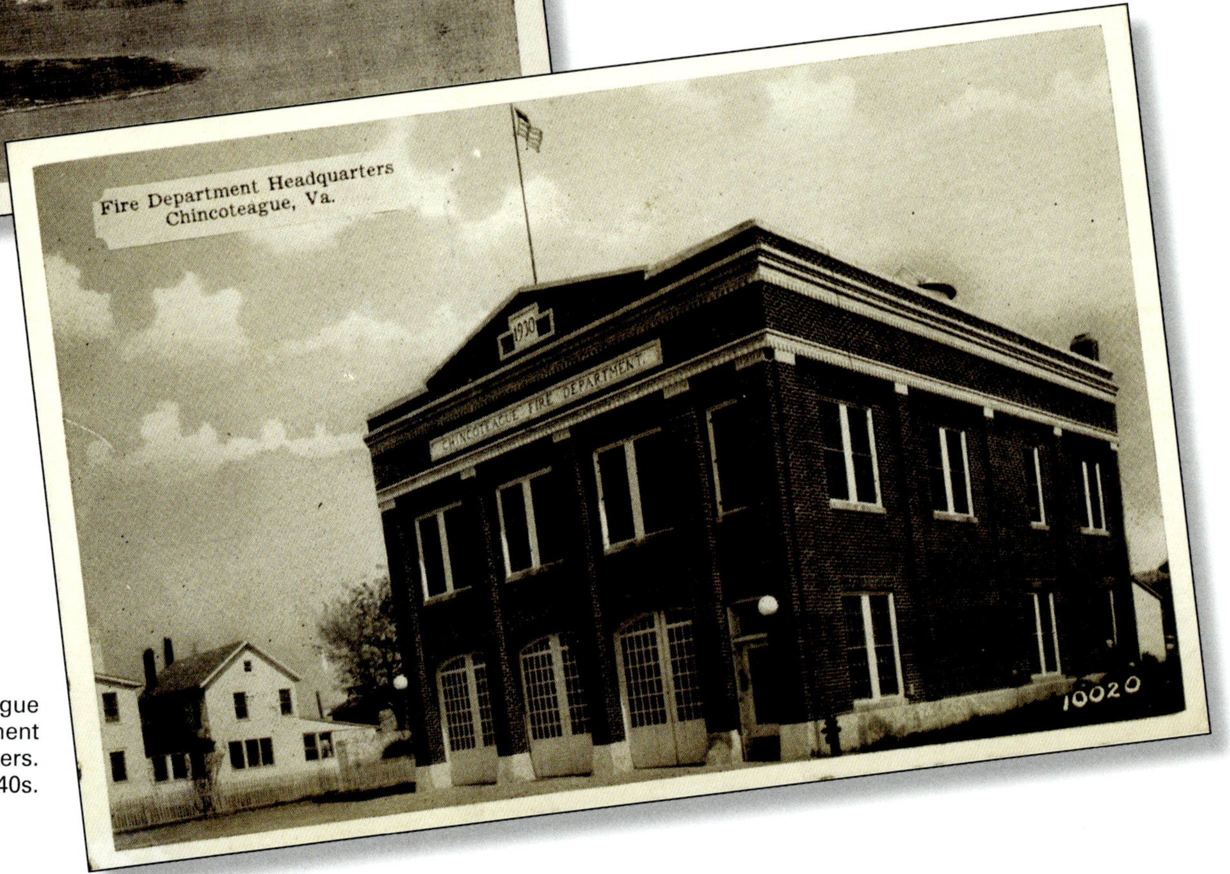

Chincoteague
Fire Department
headquarters.
Circa 1940s.

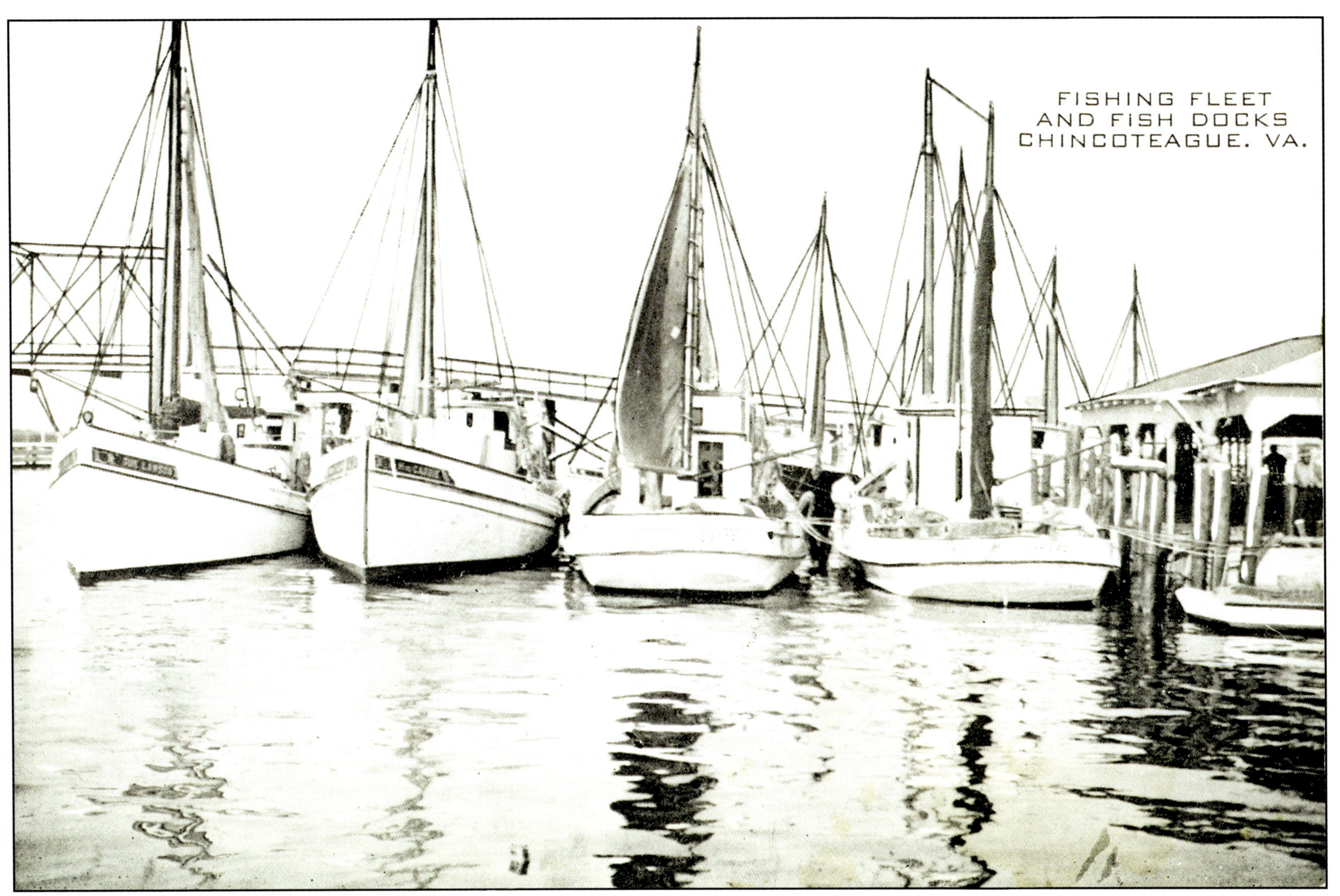

Fishing fleet and fish docks. Circa 1940s.

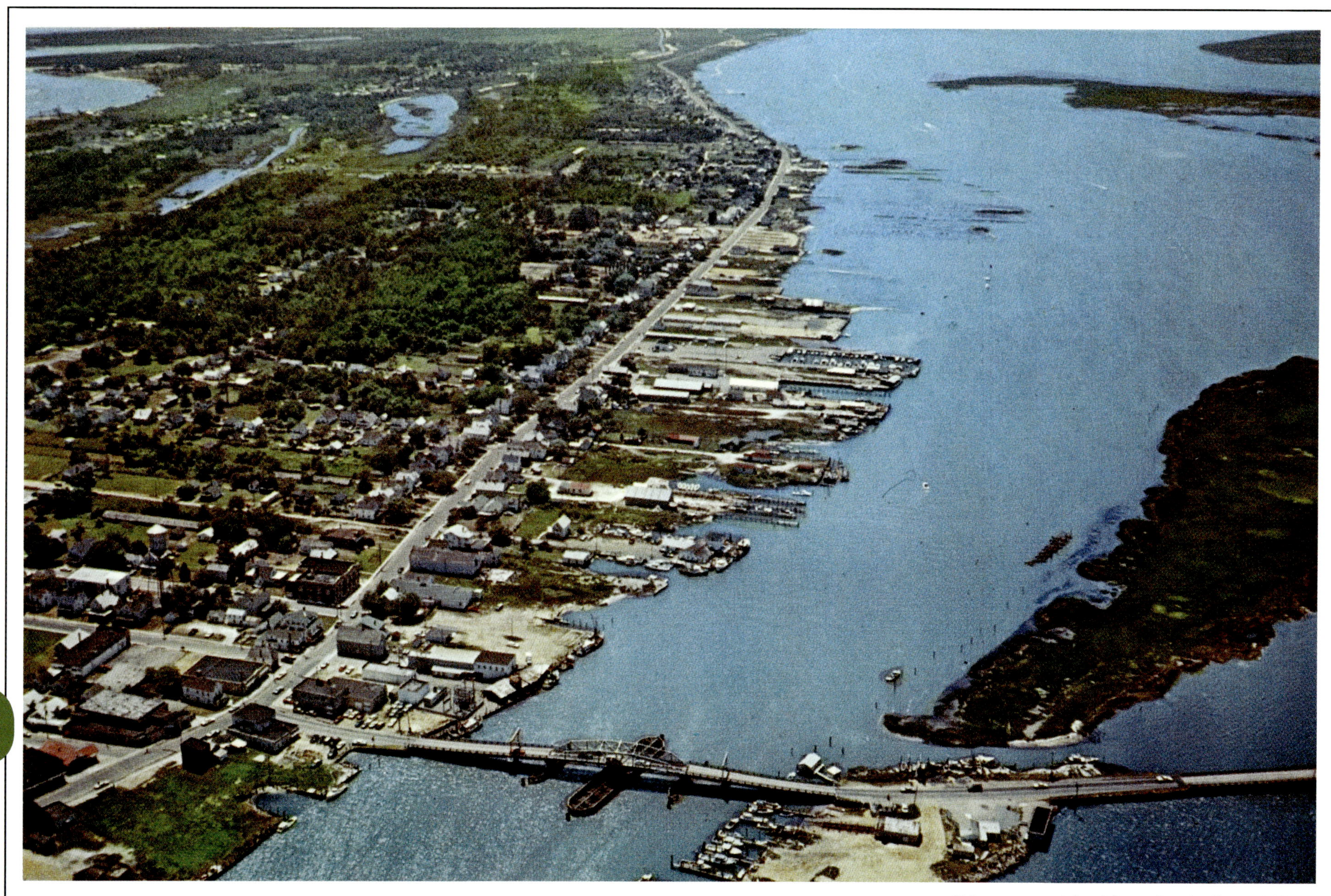

Chincoteague Island from the air. Circa 1960s.

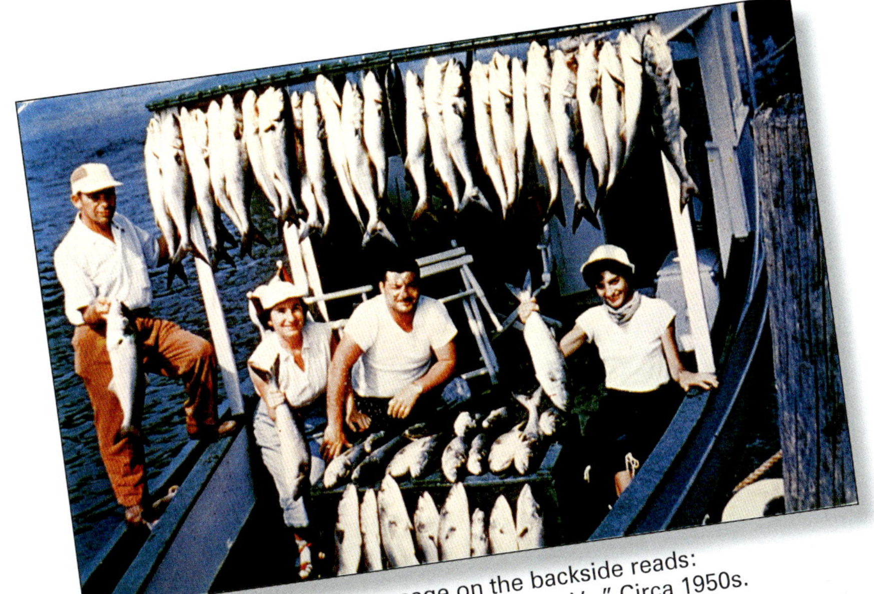

Fishing party. Printed message on the backside reads: "Fishing is always good at Chincoteague, Va." Circa 1950s.

Chincoteague Carnival Grounds. Circa 1960s.

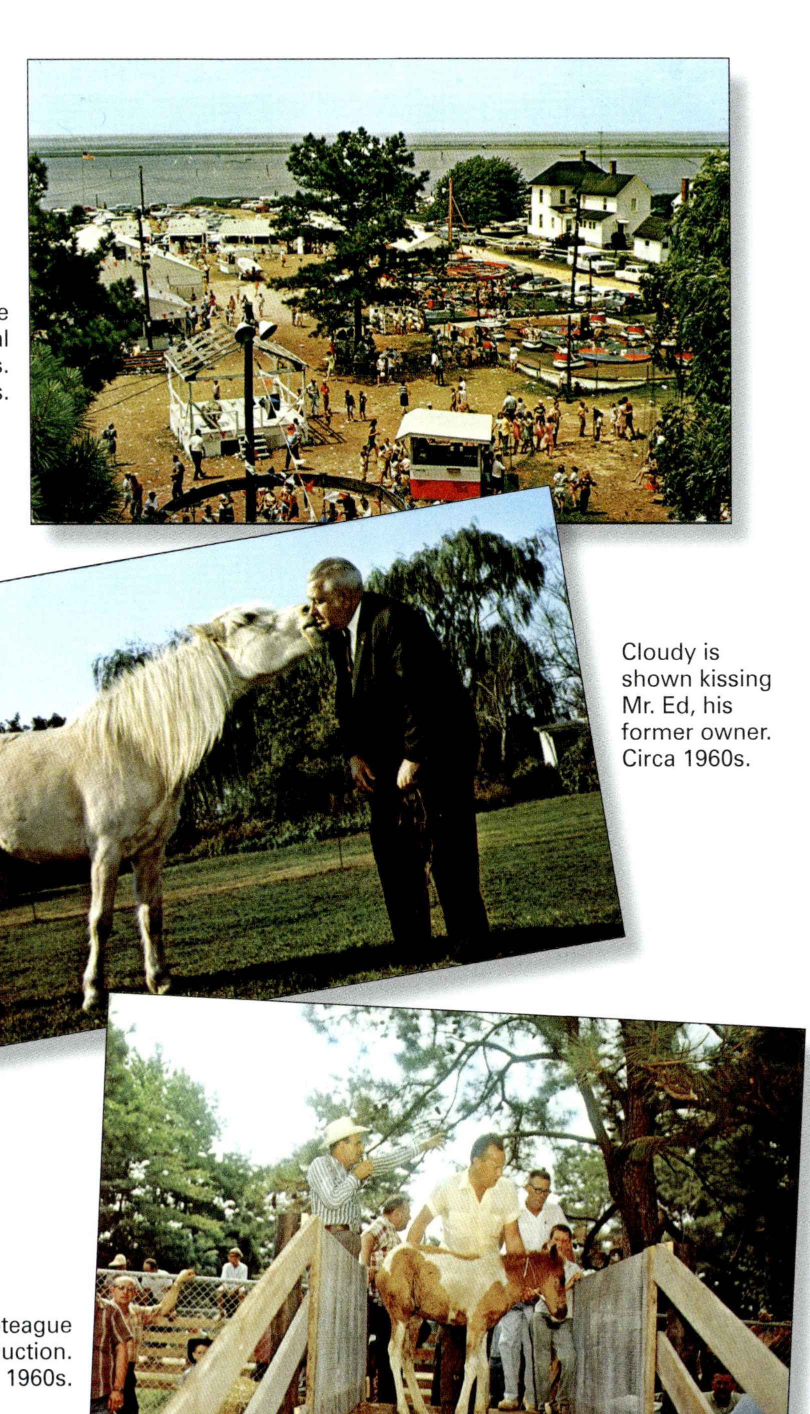

Cloudy is shown kissing Mr. Ed, his former owner. Circa 1960s.

Mr. Miles Hancock, decoy carver. Circa 1960s.

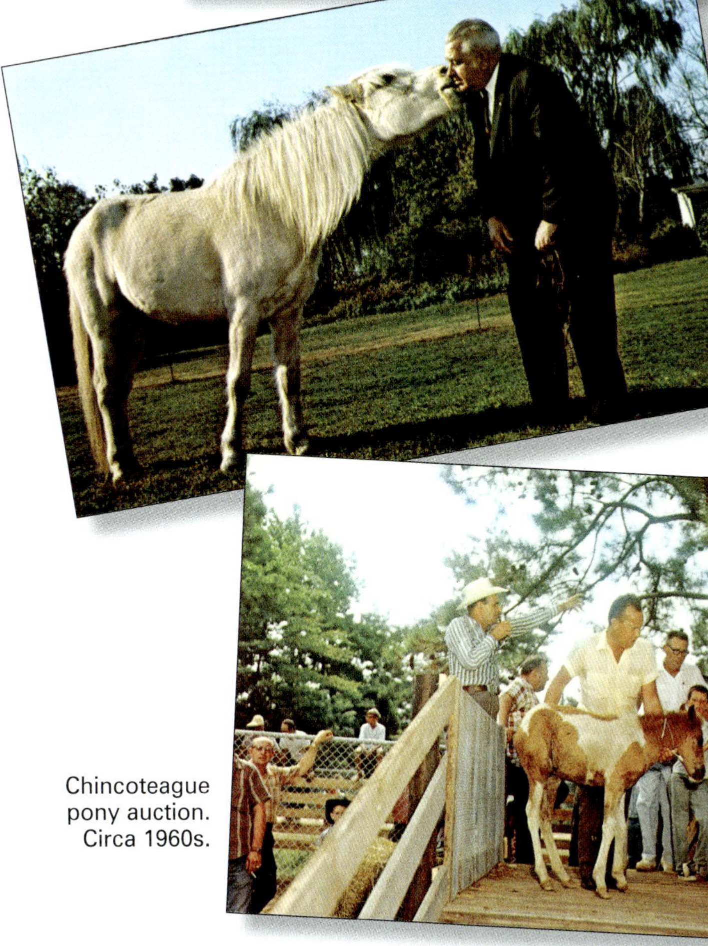

Chincoteague pony auction. Circa 1960s.

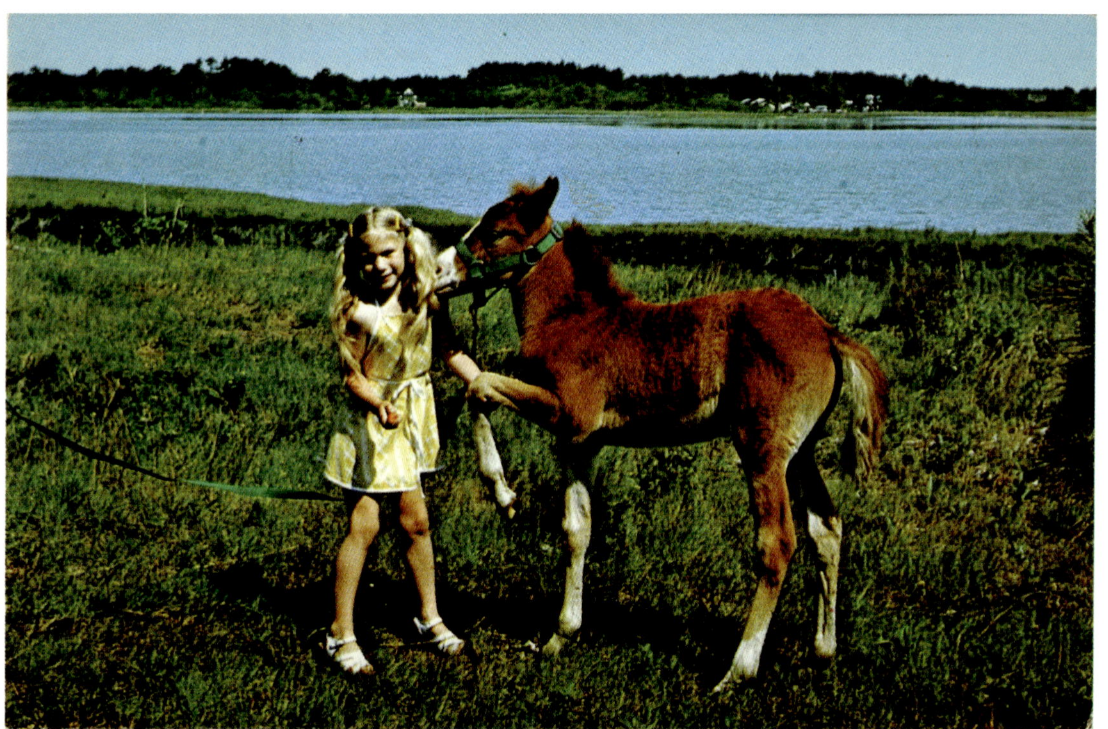

Printed message on the backside reads: "Sunshine, a Chincoteague wild pony colt, greets her little mistress, Louella Cole of Chincoteague with a friendly hoof." Circa 1960s.

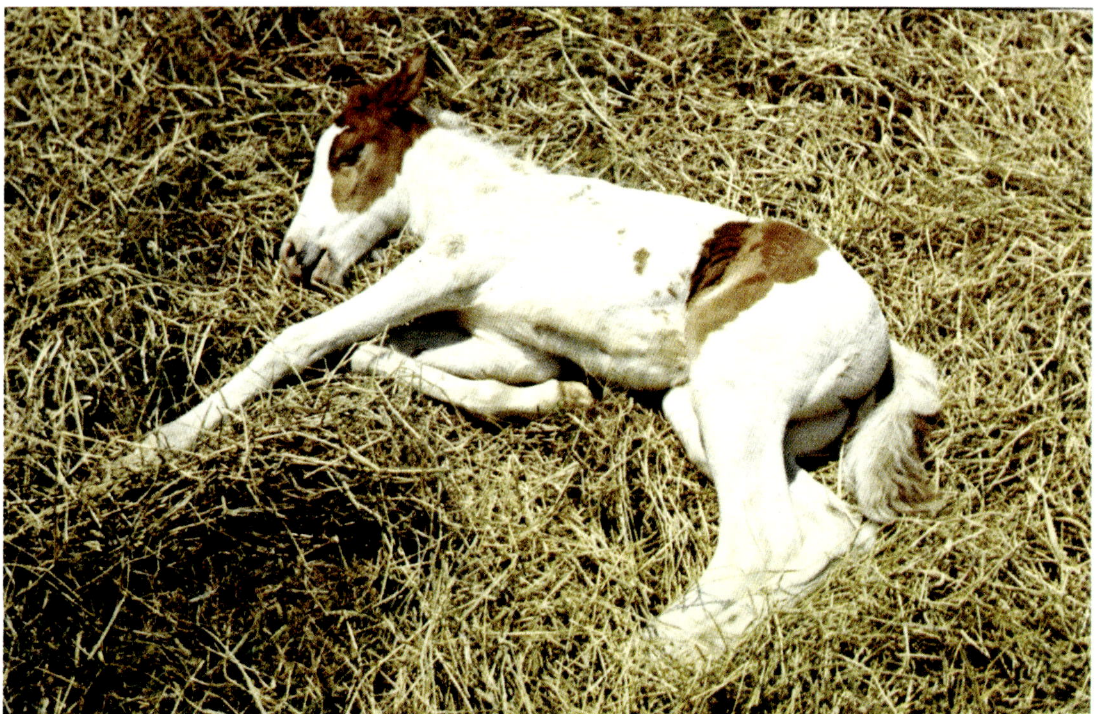

Printed message on the backside reads: "Nap time for a Chincoteague wild pony colt." Circa 1960s.

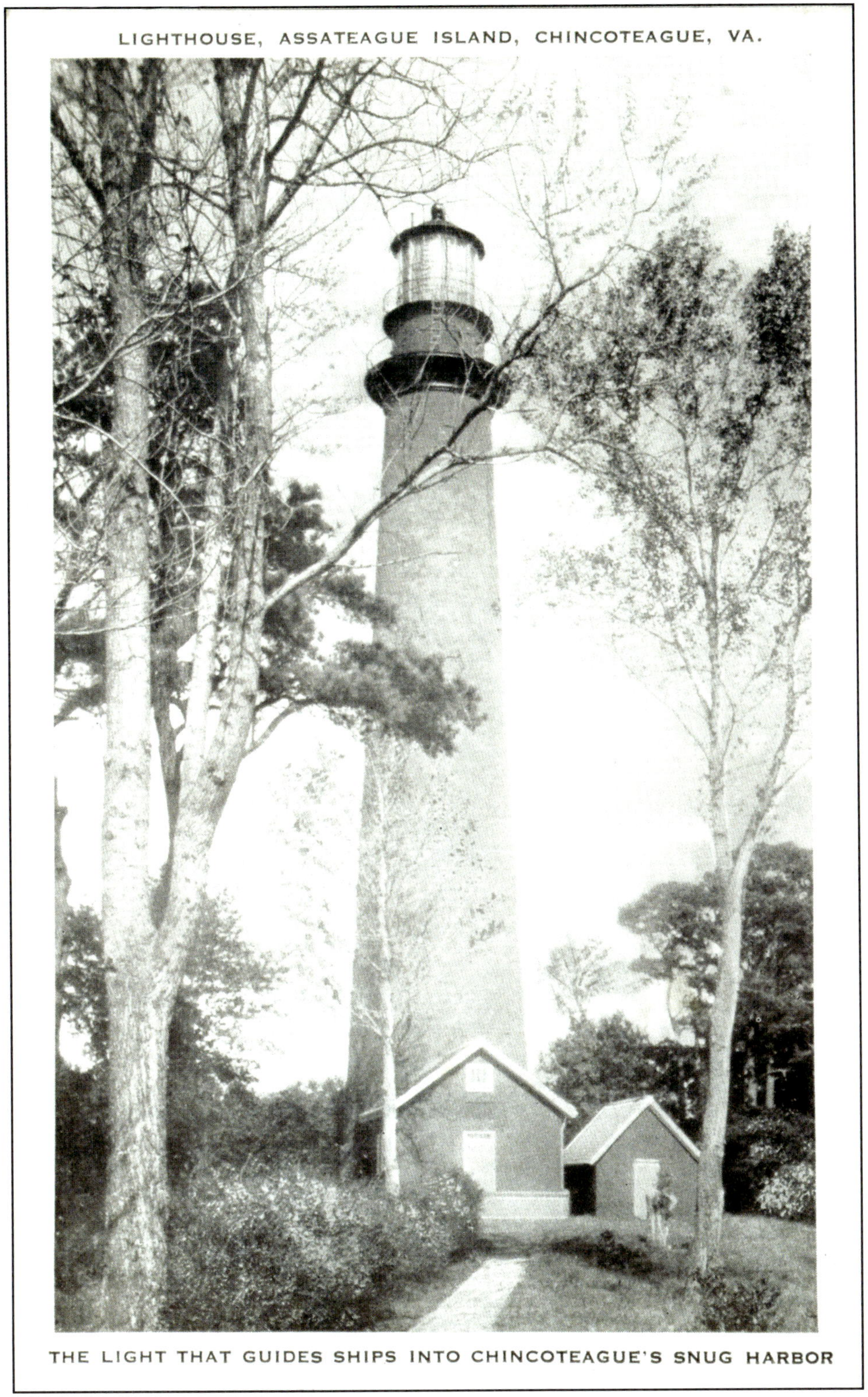

The light that guides ships into Chincoteague's snug harbor. Circa 1940s.

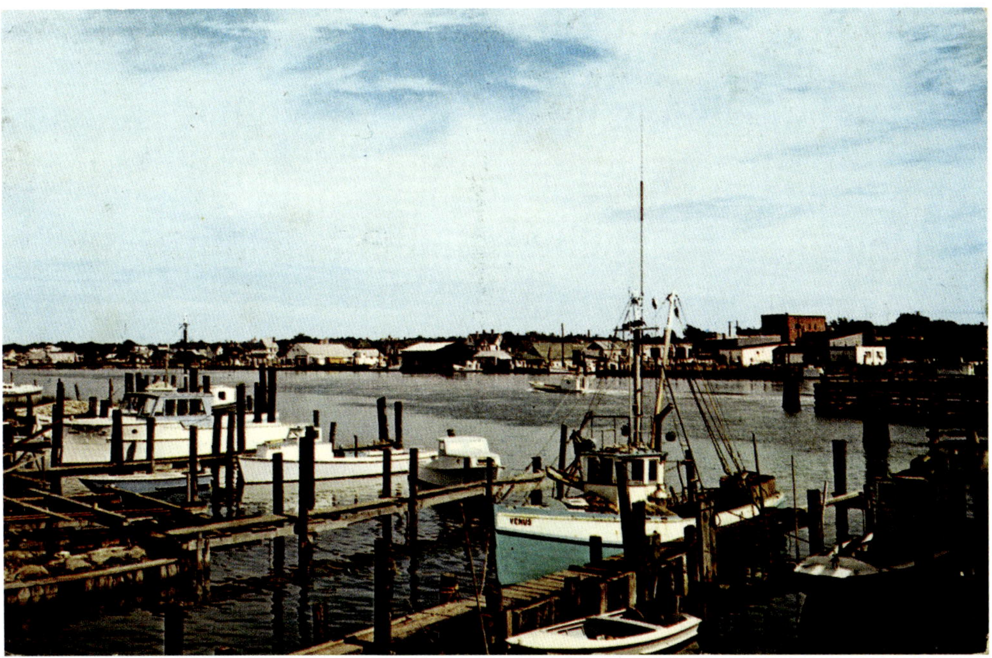

Printed message on the backside reads: "Chincoteague Harbor." Circa 1960s.

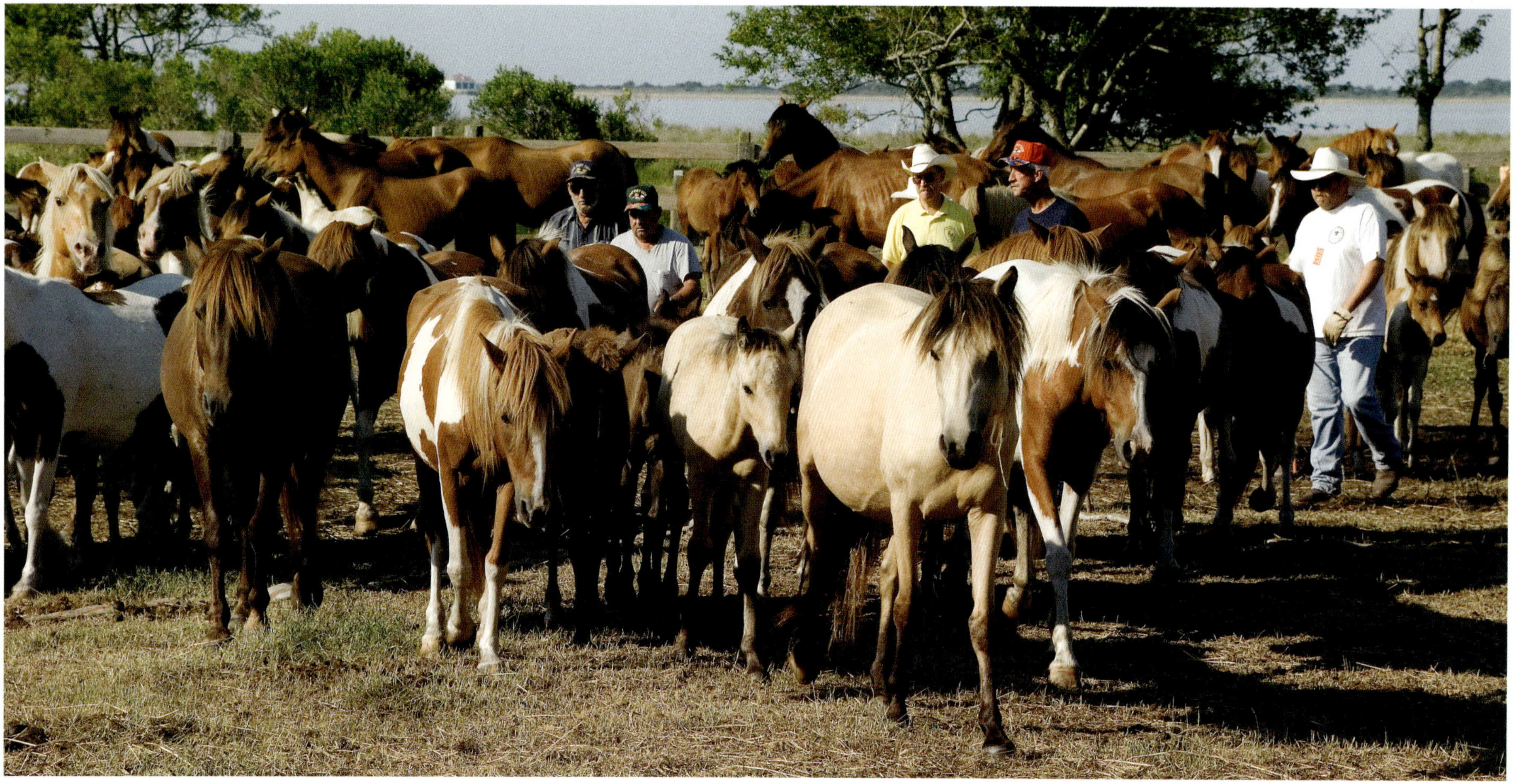

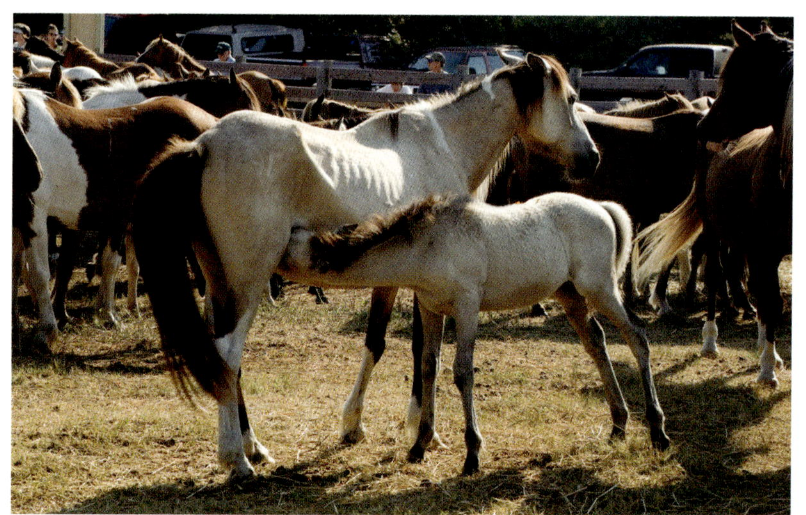

Chincoteague's Pony Swim and Auction

The rounded up ponies on Assateague the day before the swim.

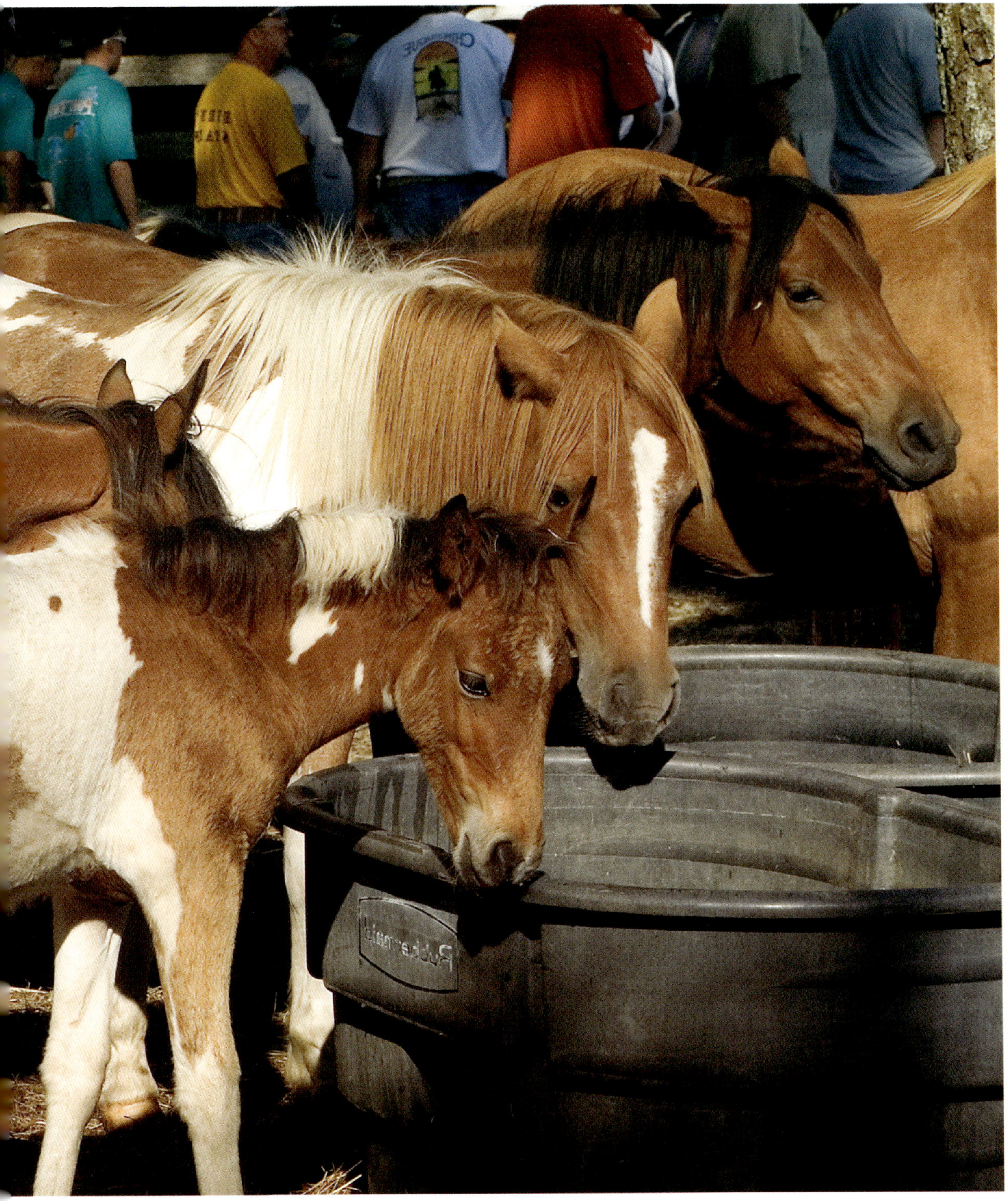

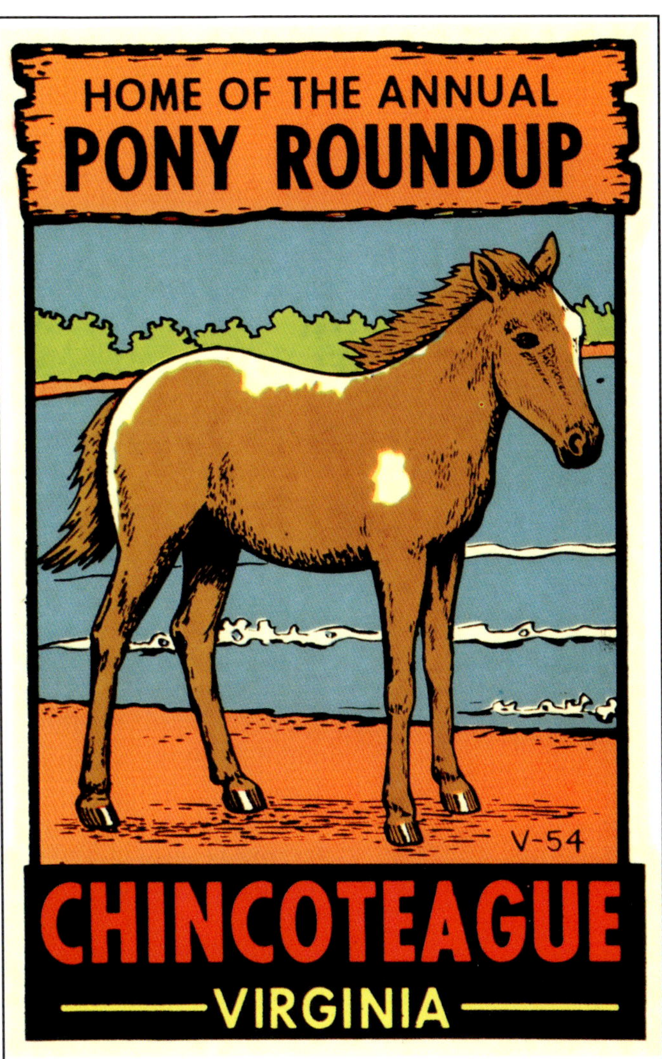

HOME OF THE ANNUAL
PONY ROUNDUP
V-54
CHINCOTEAGUE
VIRGINIA

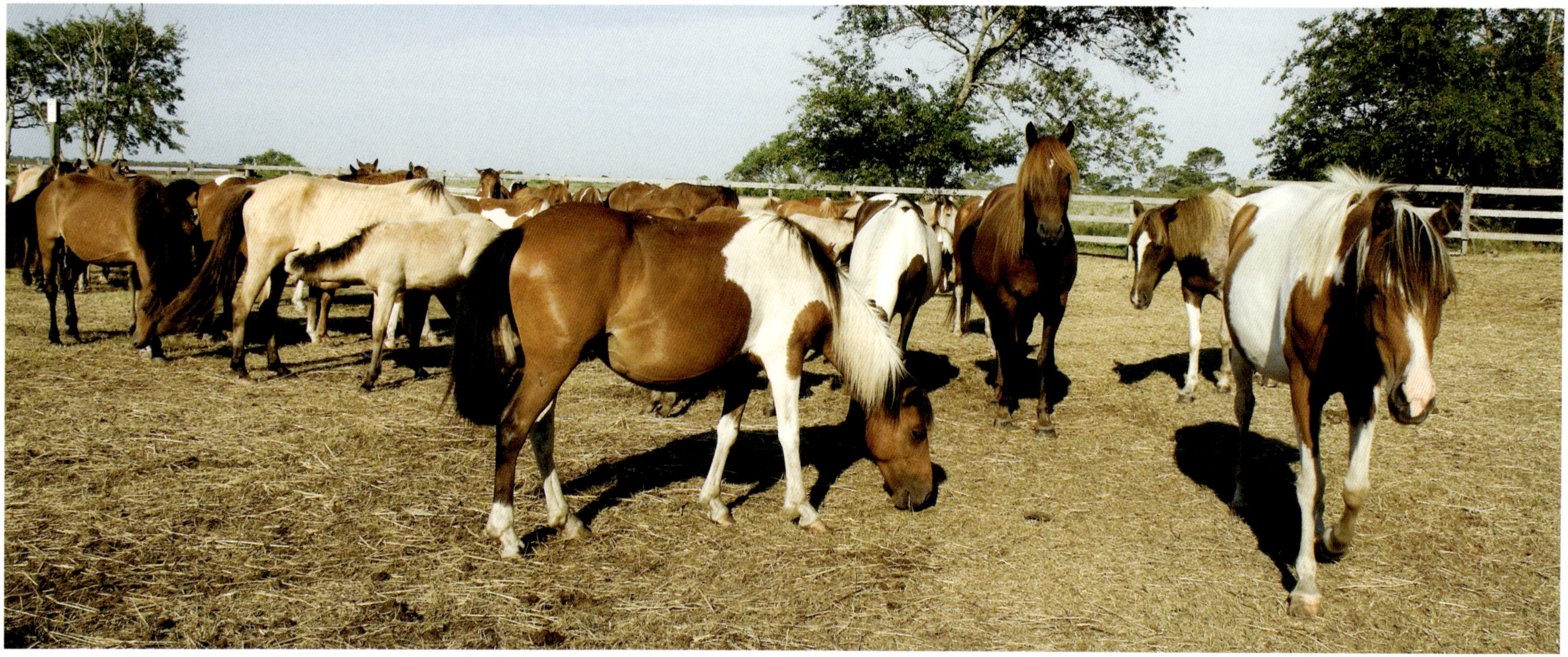

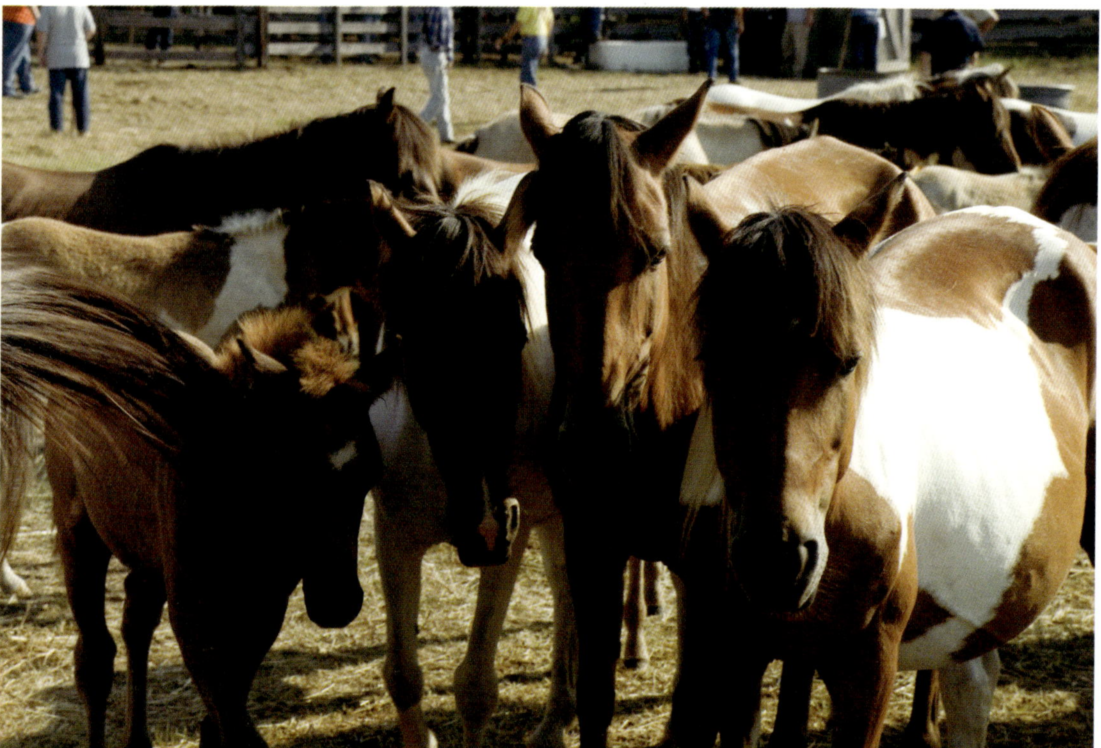

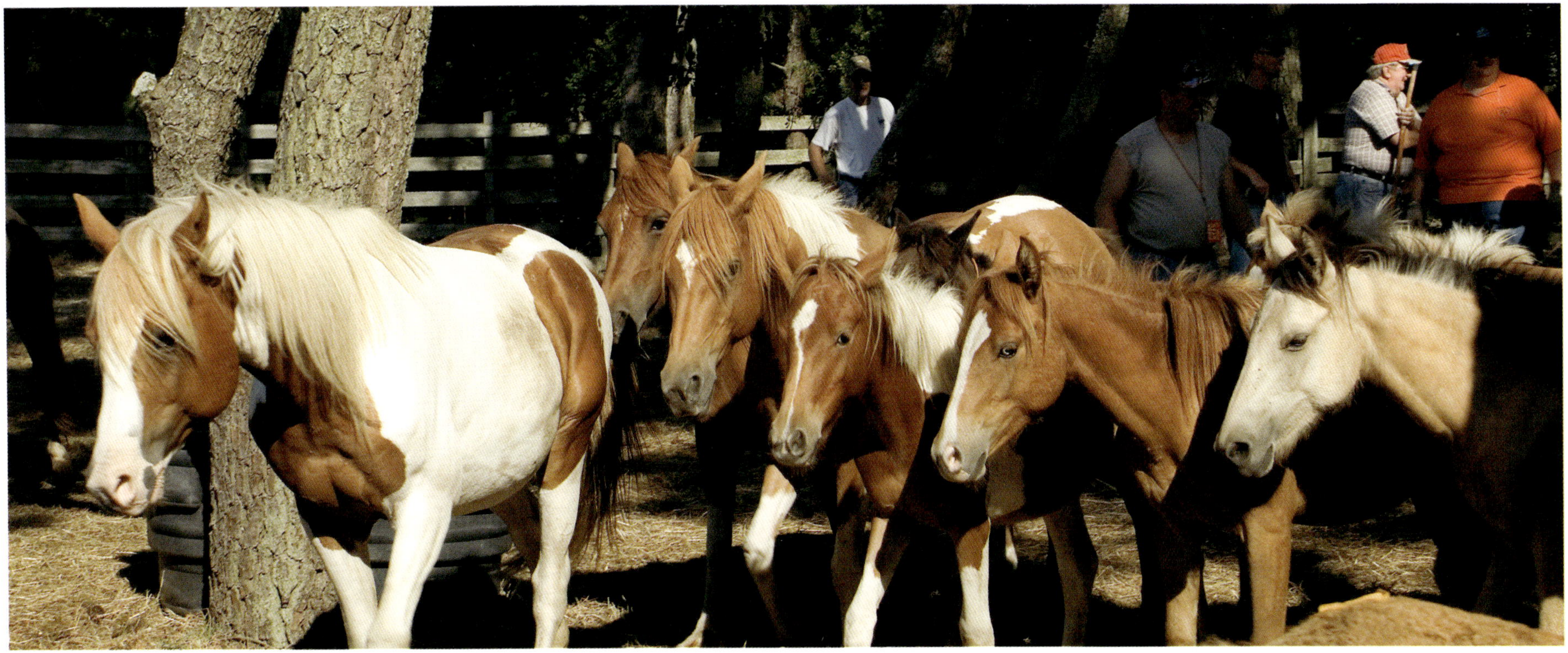

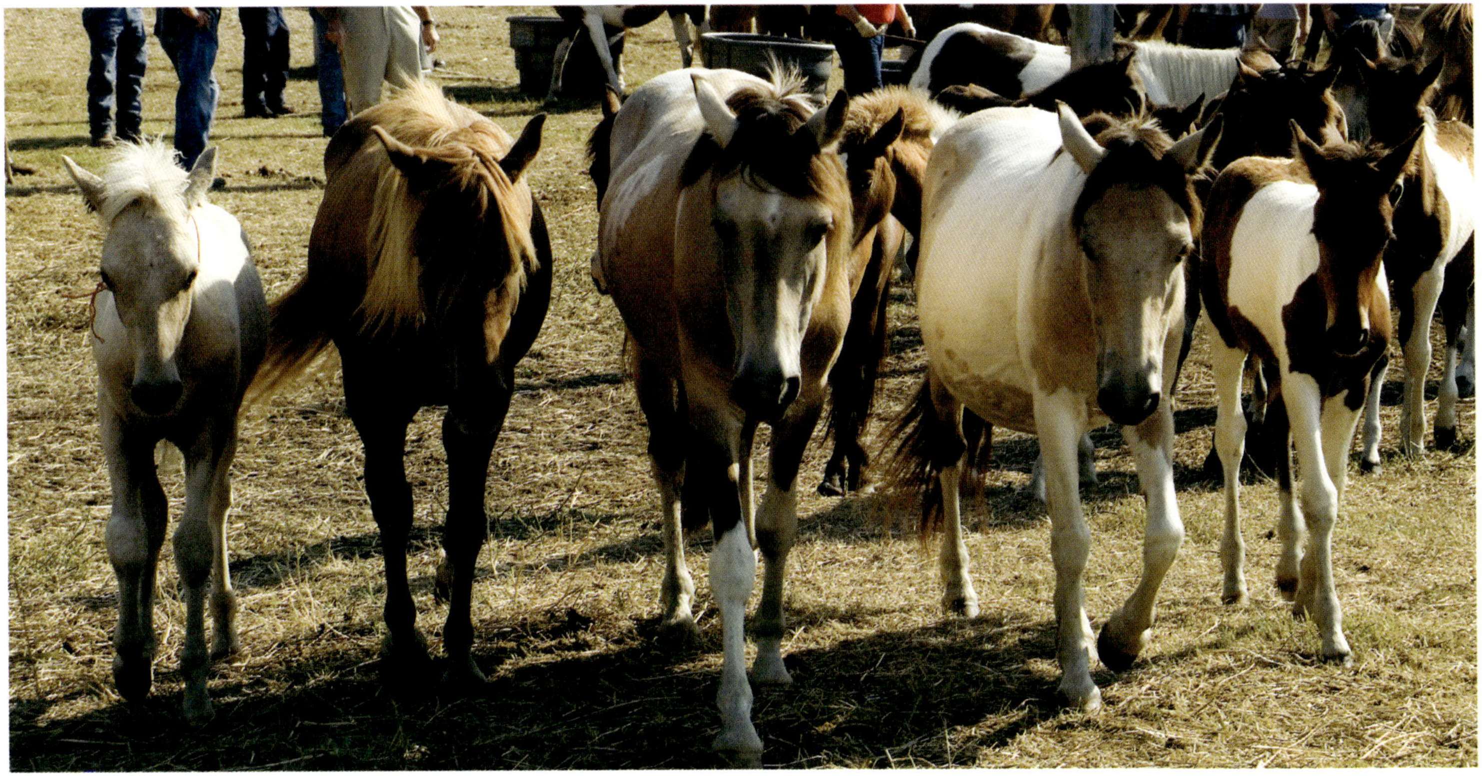

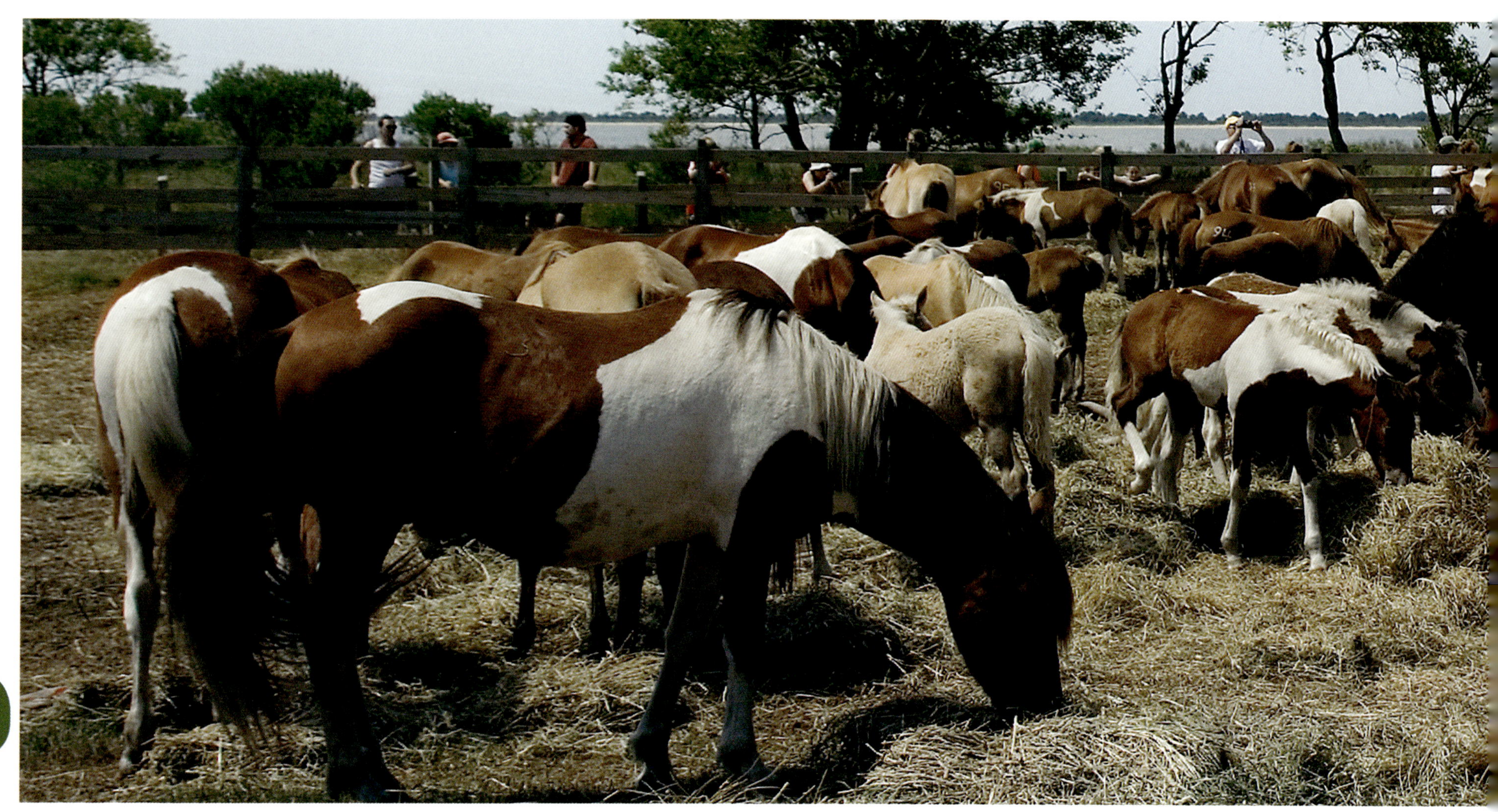

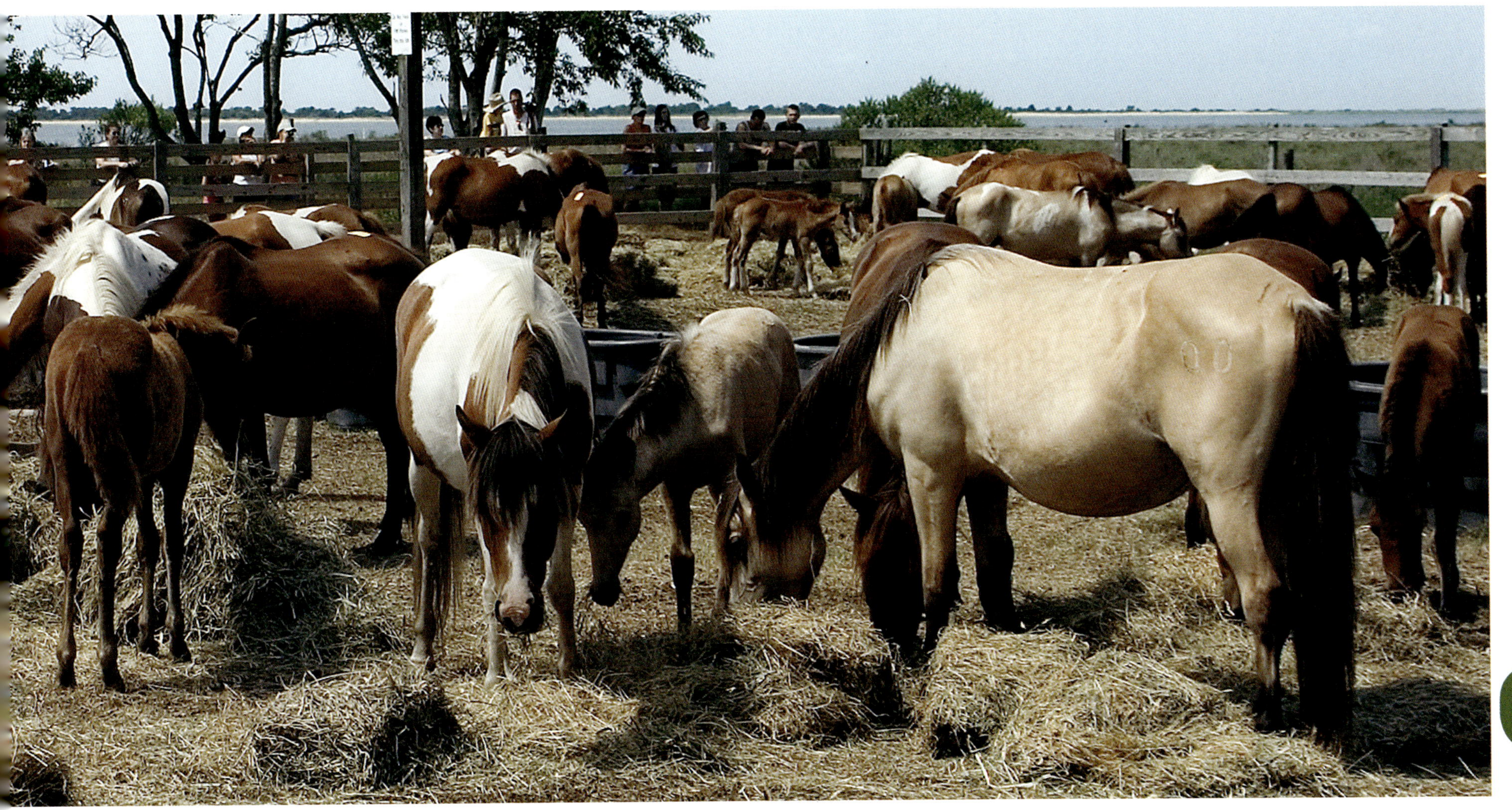

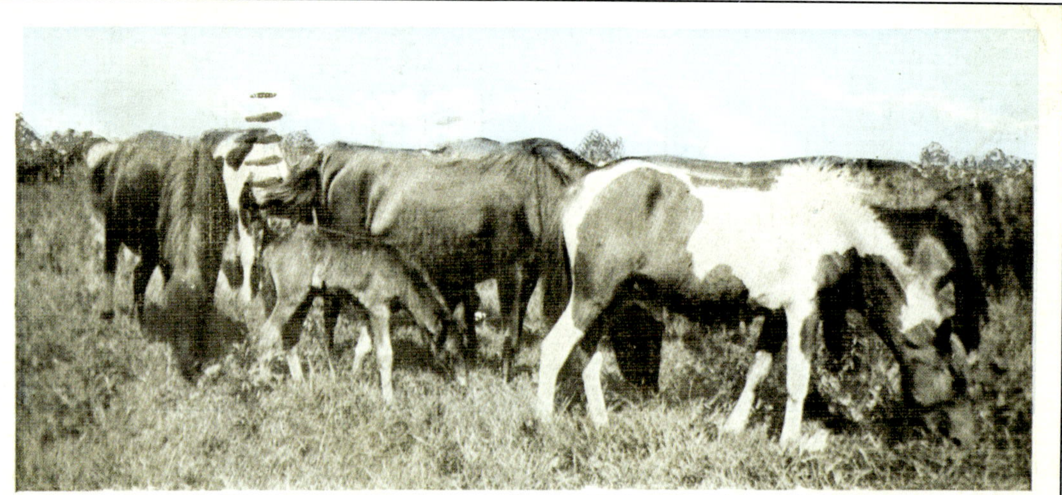

Nature made Chincoteague an Island, surrounding it with channels and bays filled with game fish from early Spring to late Fall. These waters furnish the world famous "Chincoteague" Oysters and Clams.

The Island is about seven miles long, each end marshlands offer roaming grounds for the wild ponies. These ponies roam at will eating the salt grass and myrtle bushes. They are rounded up and sold the last Thursday in July, "Pony-Penning" day. Thousands of visitors witness the biggest "Wild West Show of the East" every year.

Chincoteague is connected to mainland by good roads, is very modern in every way. Good hotels, Theatre—Churches—Western Union and Telephone connections, a nice place to visit, a grand place to spend your vacation.

Thousands of visitors witness the biggest "Wild West Show of the East" every year. Printed message on the backside reads: "Pony penning is held each year on the picturesque island the last Thursday in July. A ten-day carnival is held to add to the traditional pageant." Postmarked 1938.

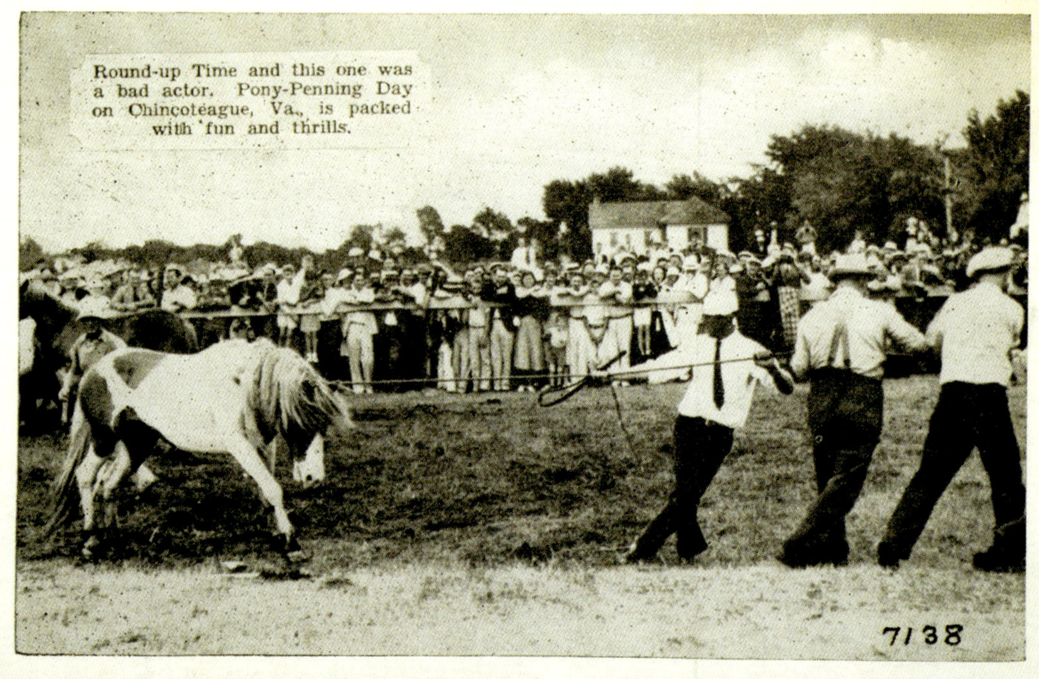

Round-up time and this one was a bad actor. Circa 1930s.

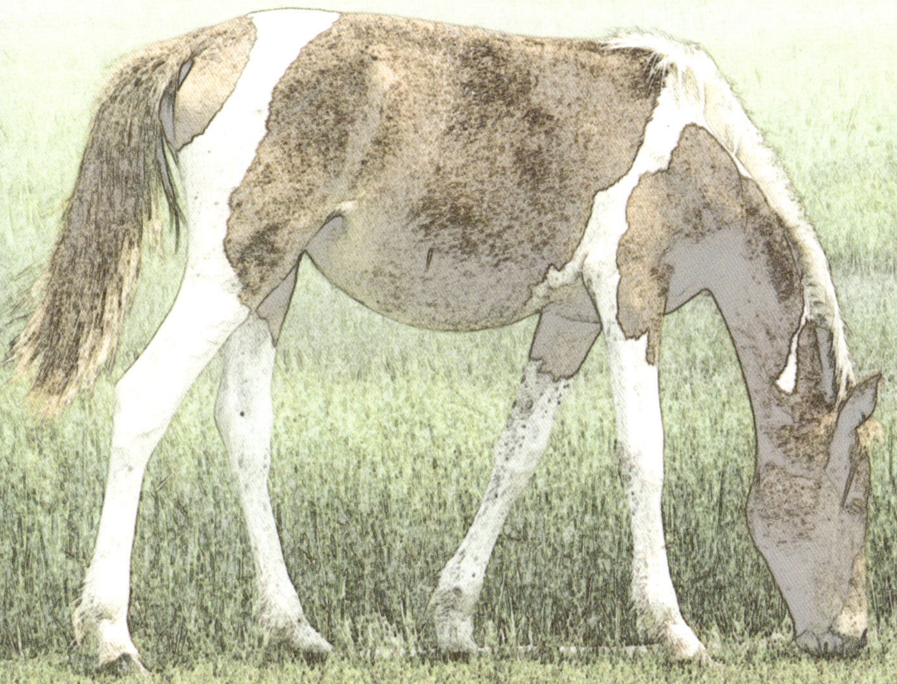

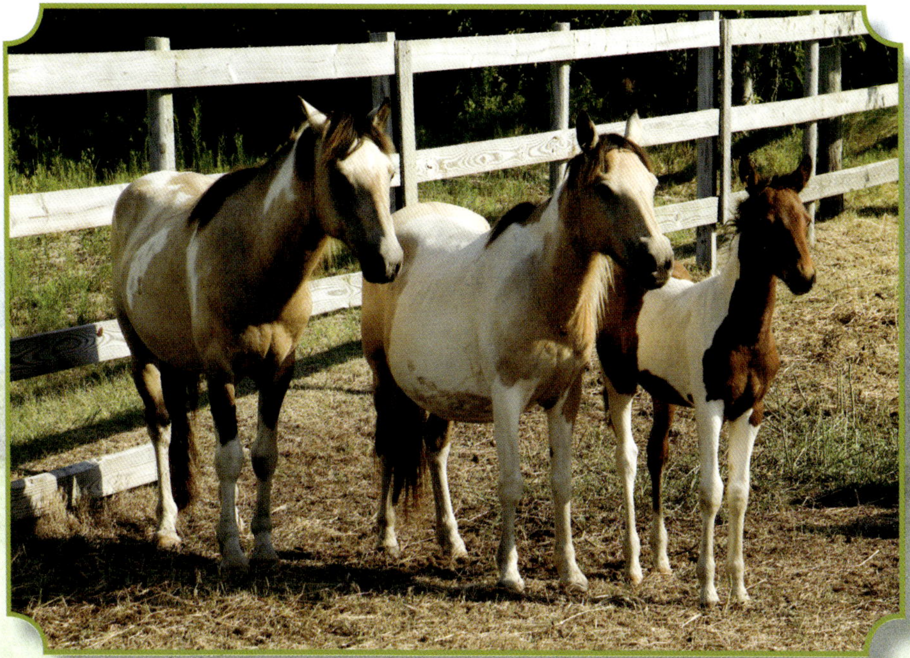

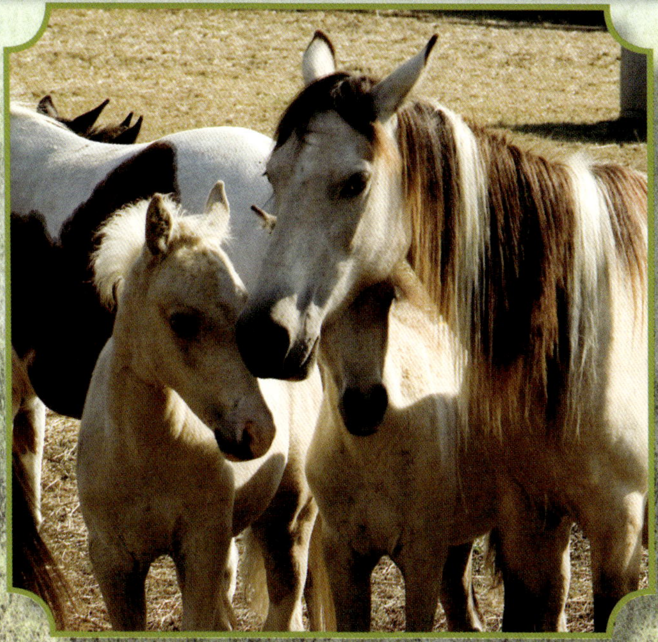

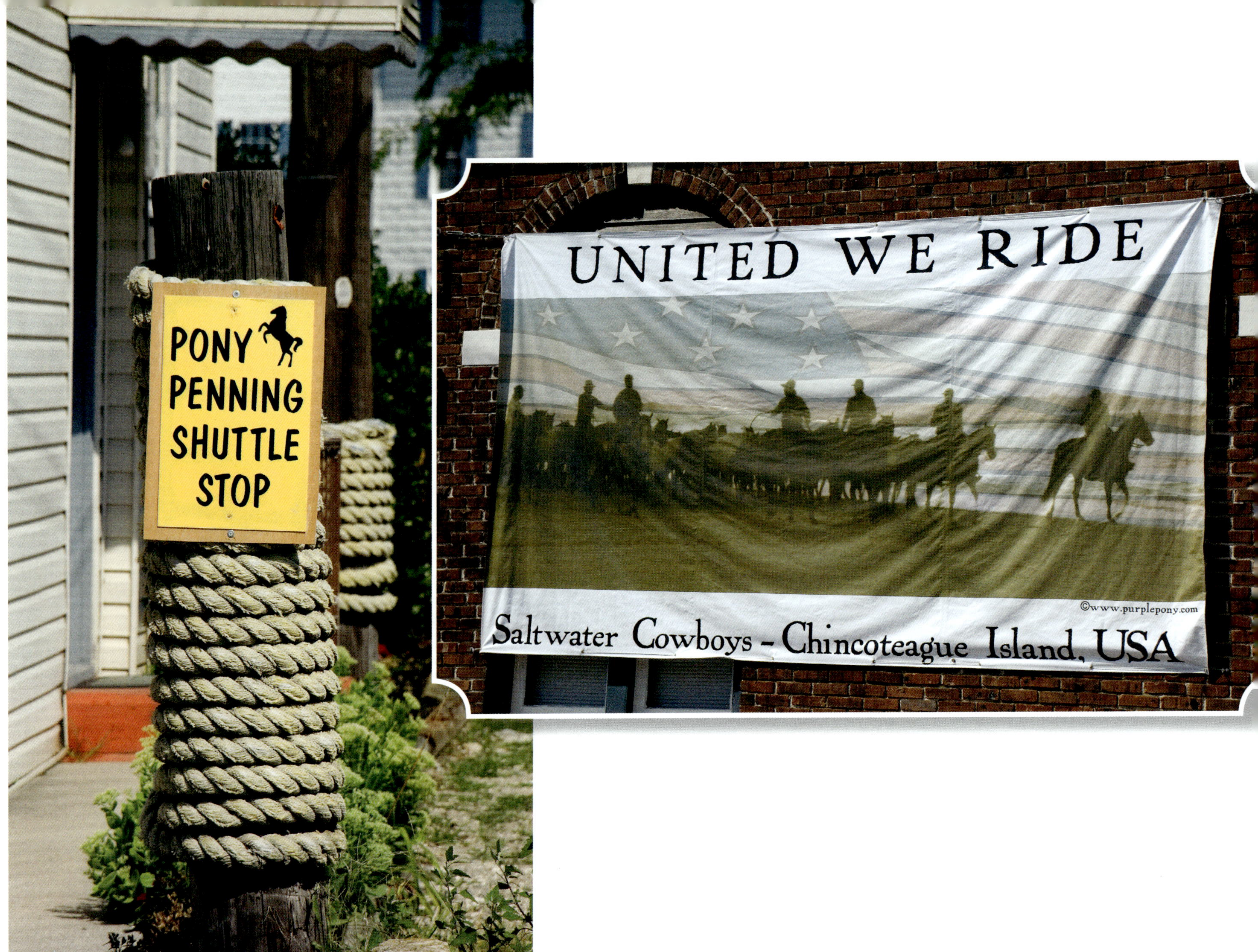
PONY
PENNING
SHUTTLE
STOP
UNITED WE RIDE
©www.purplepony.com
Saltwater Cowboys - Chincoteague Island, USA

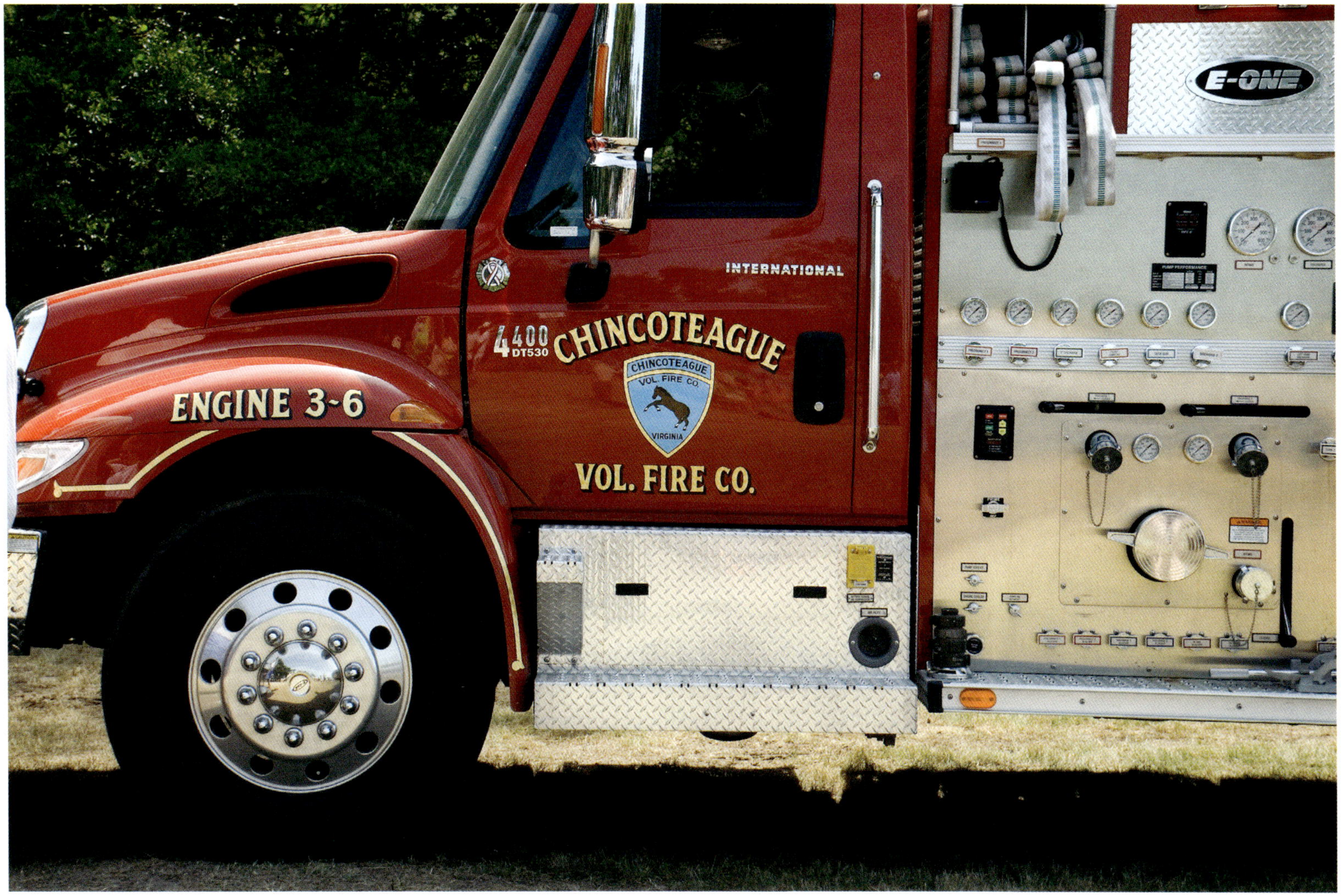

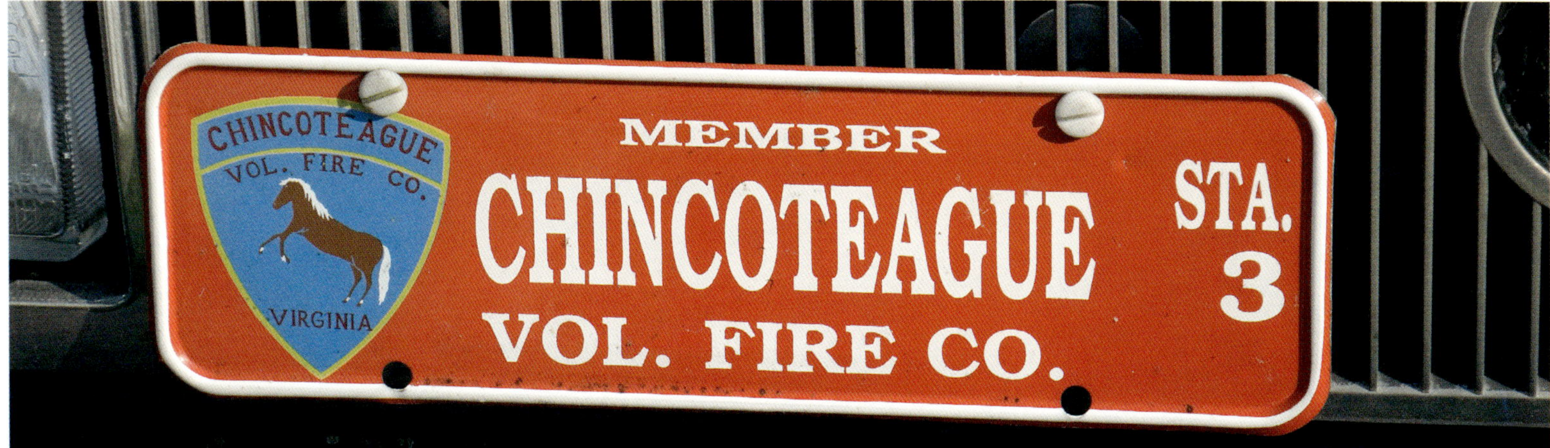
CHINCOTEAGUE
VOL. FIRE CO.
VIRGINIA
MEMBER
CHINCOTEAGUE
VOL. FIRE CO.
STA.
3

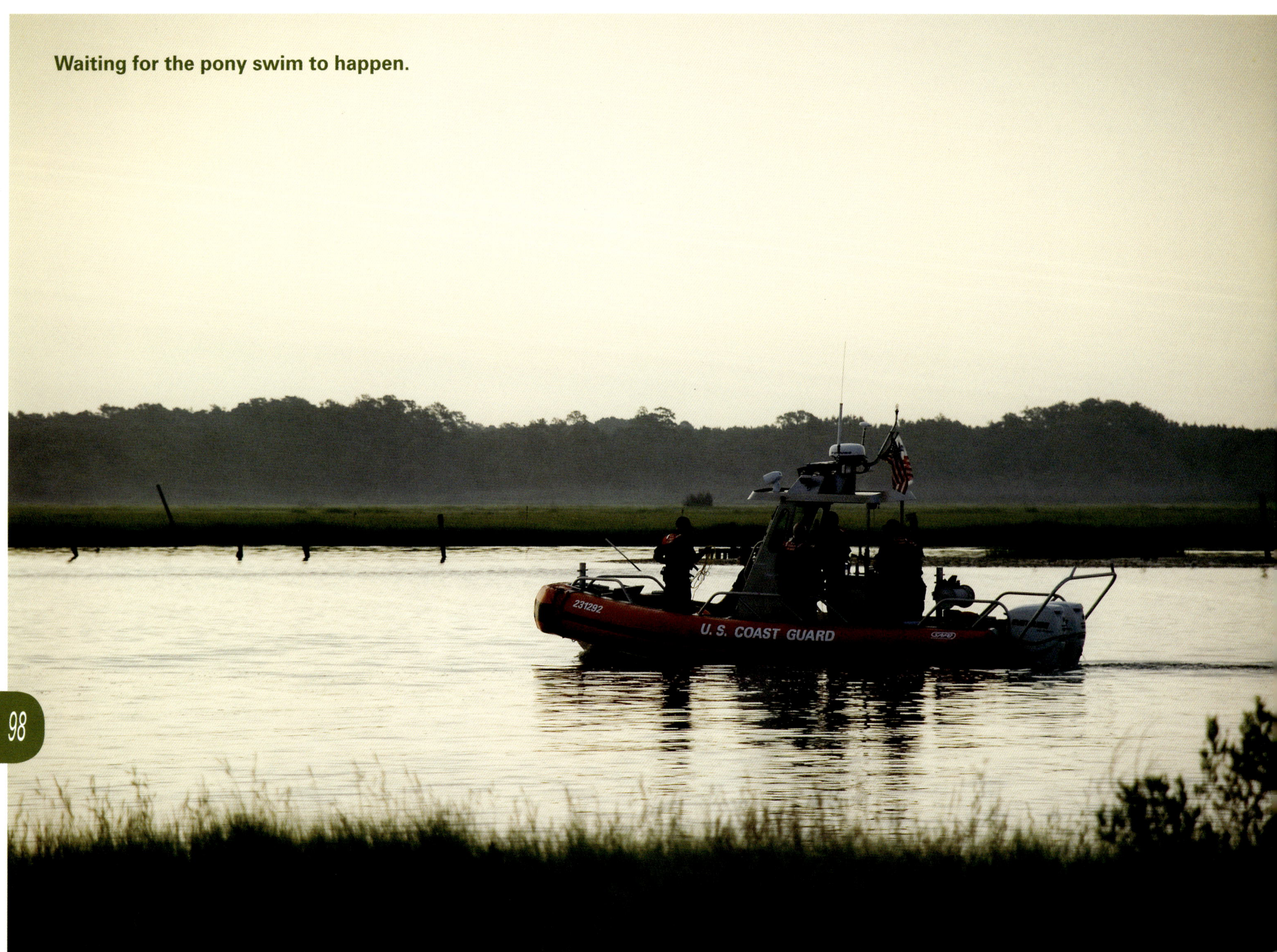

Waiting for the pony swim to happen.

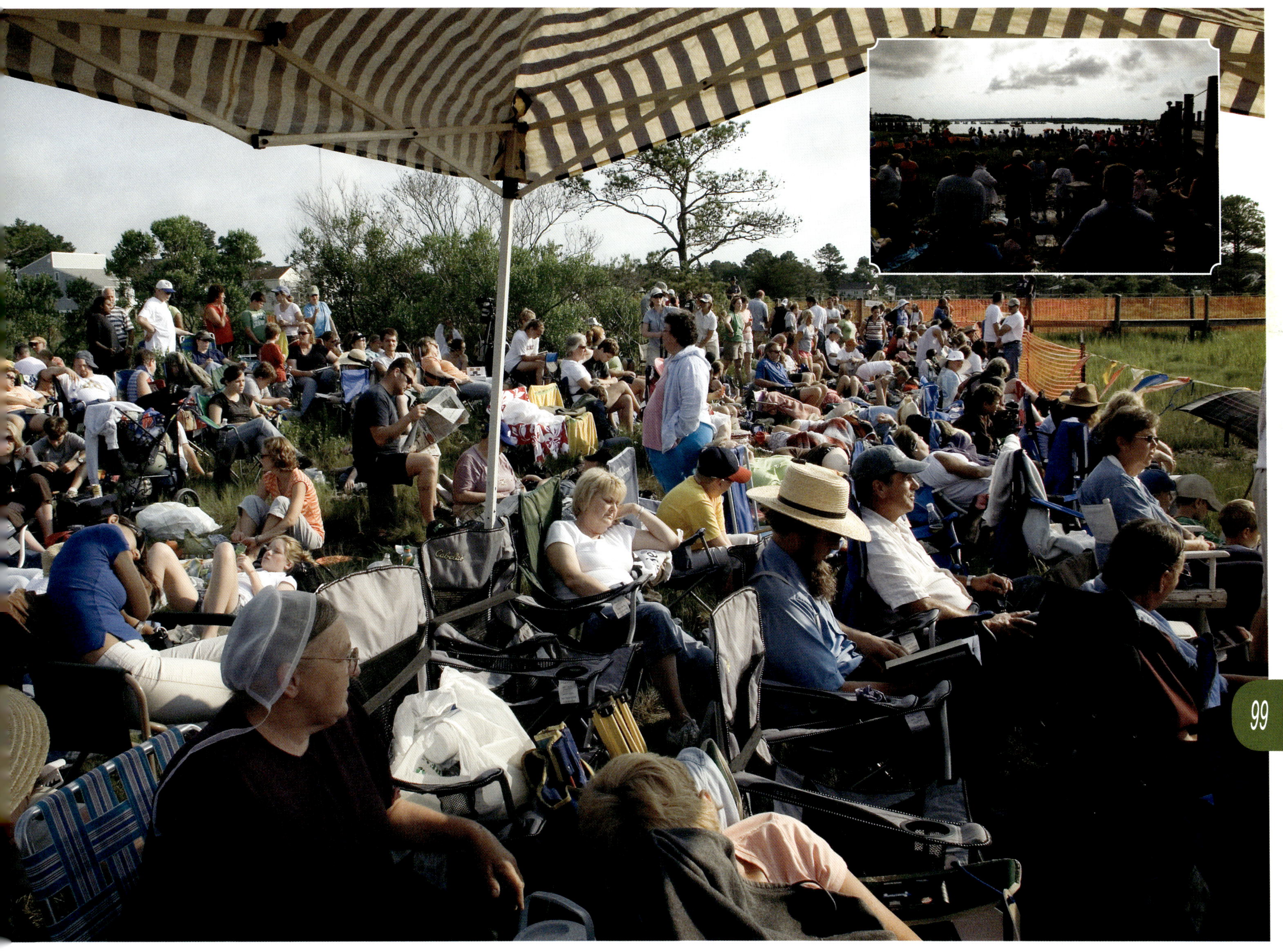

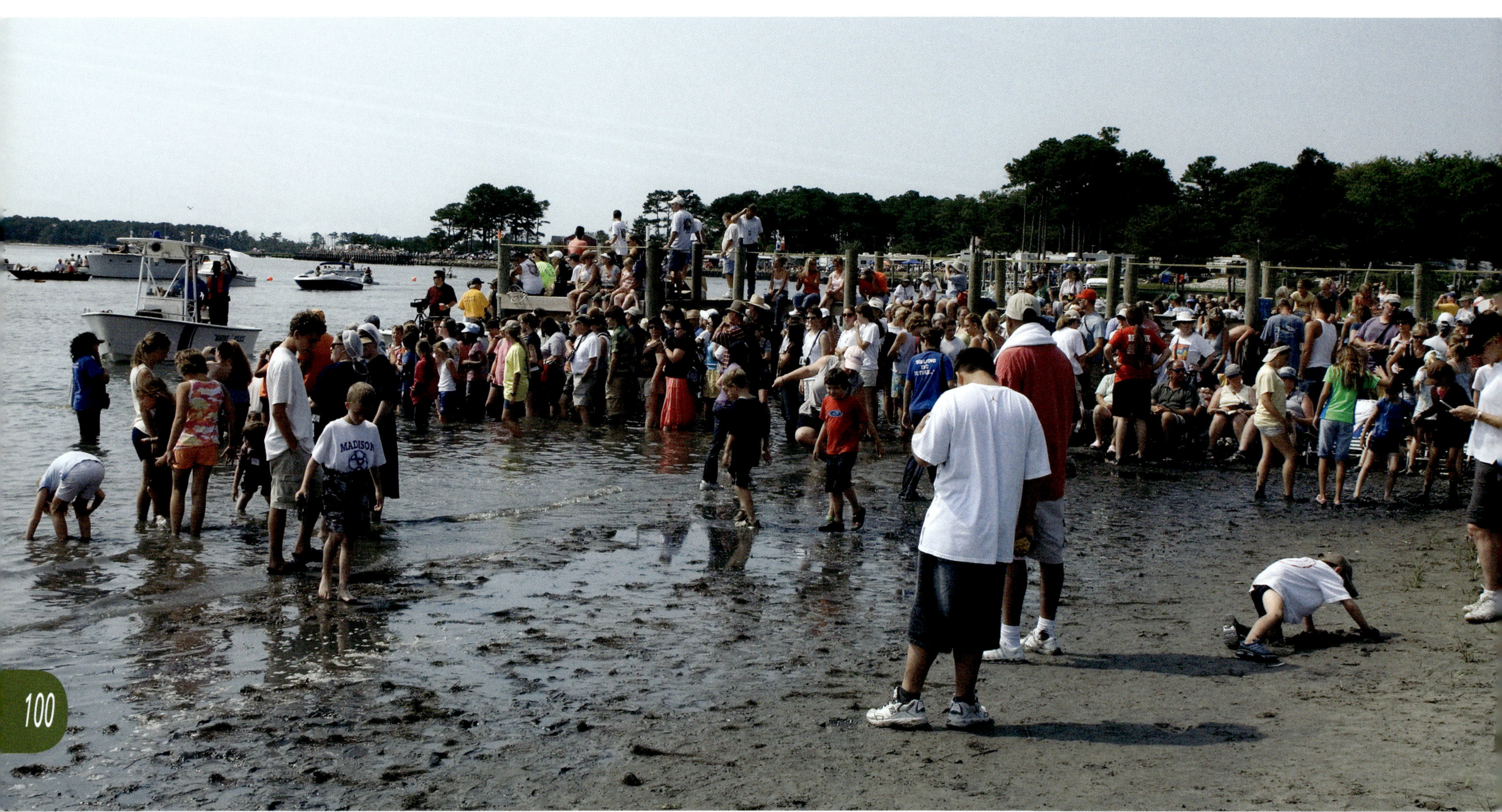

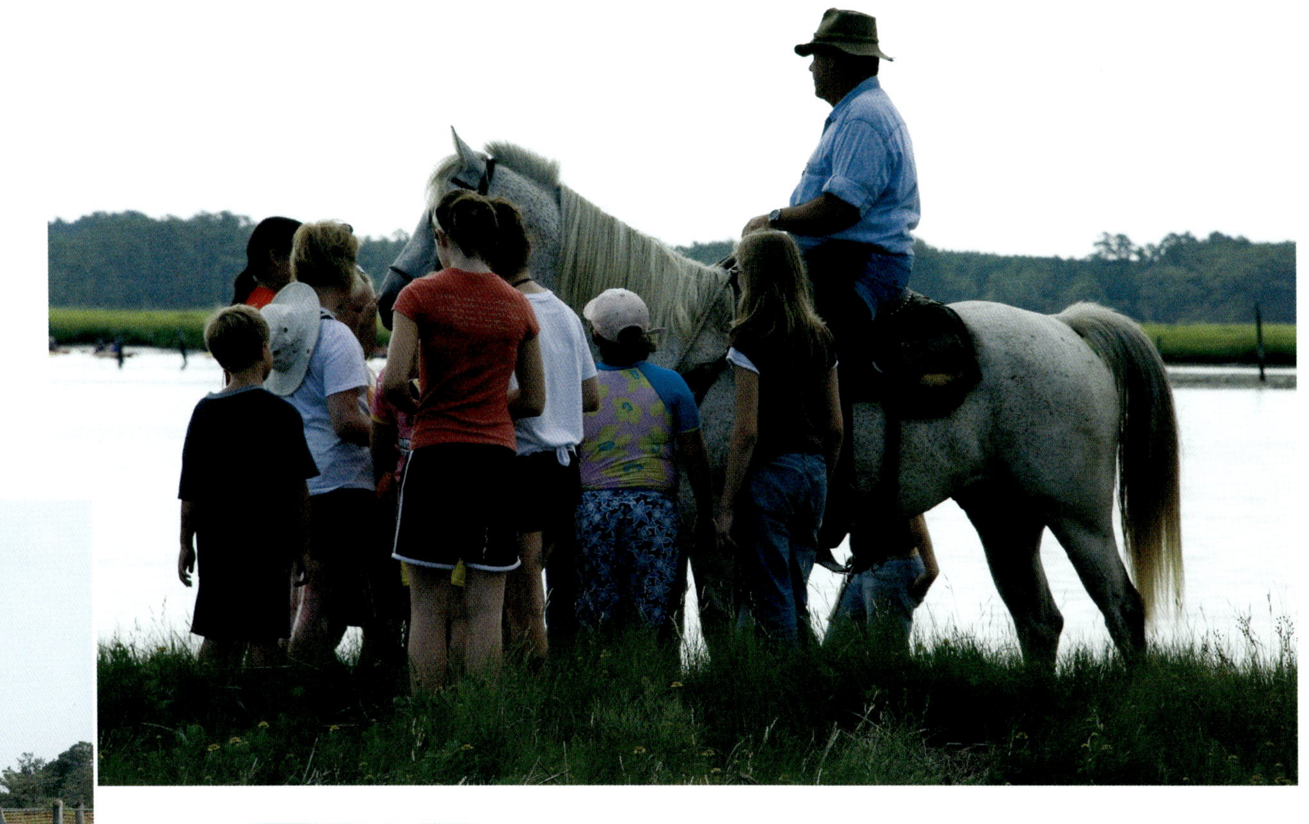

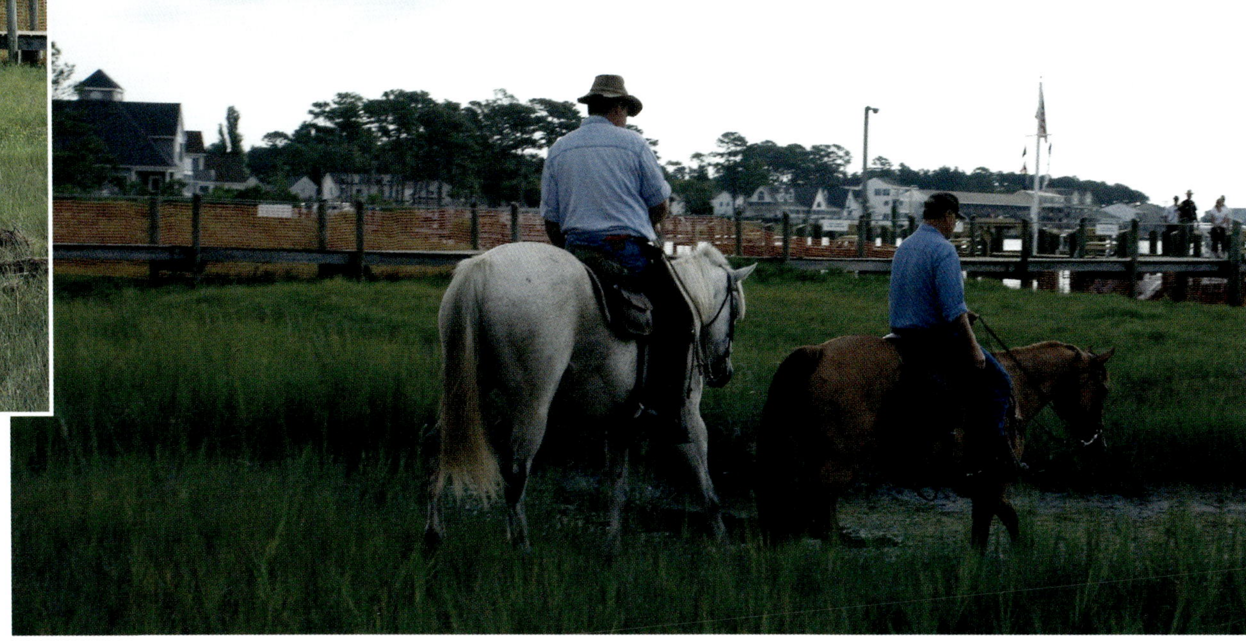

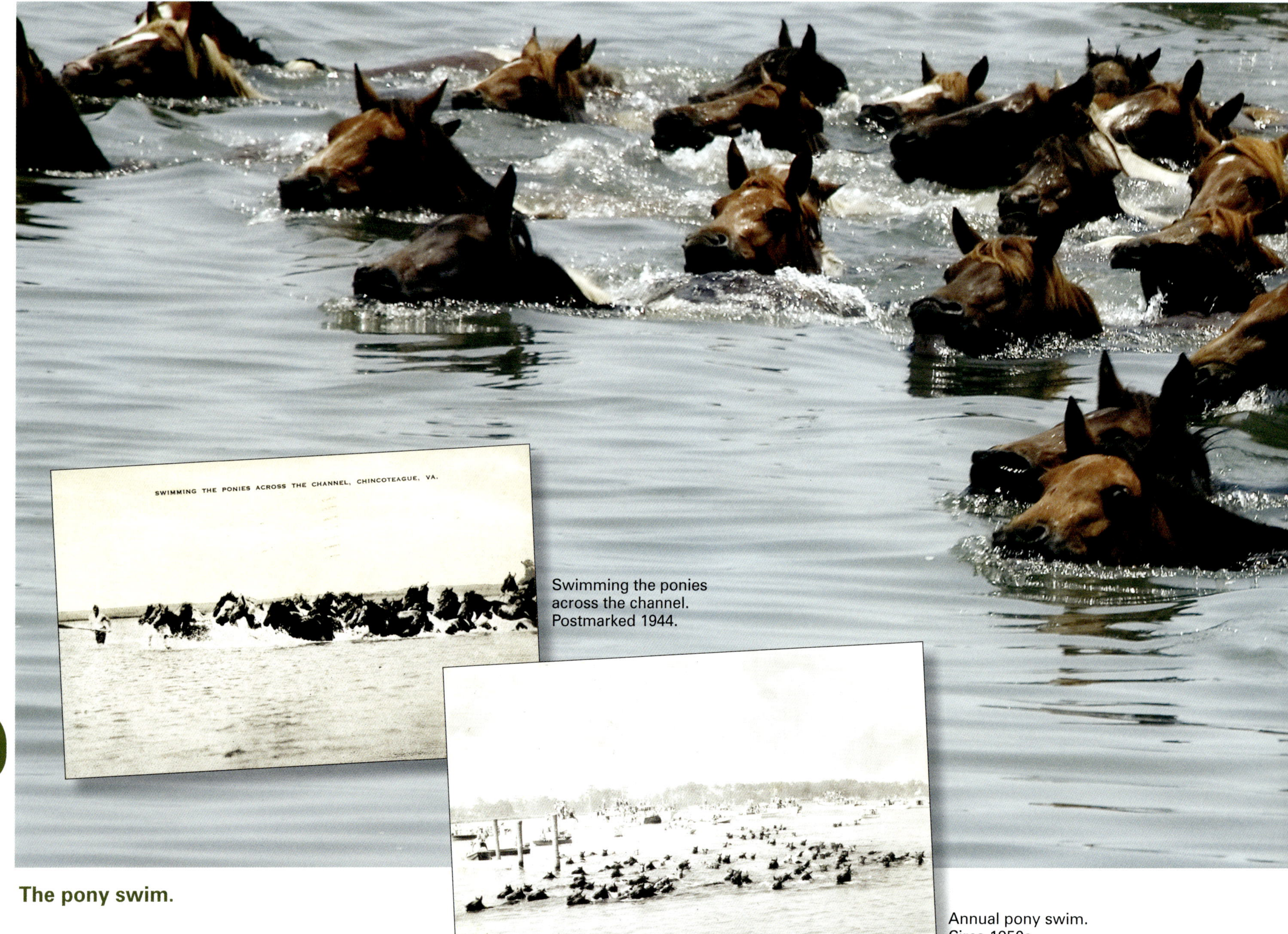

Swimming the ponies
across the channel.
Postmarked 1944.

Annual pony swim.
Circa 1950s.

The pony swim.

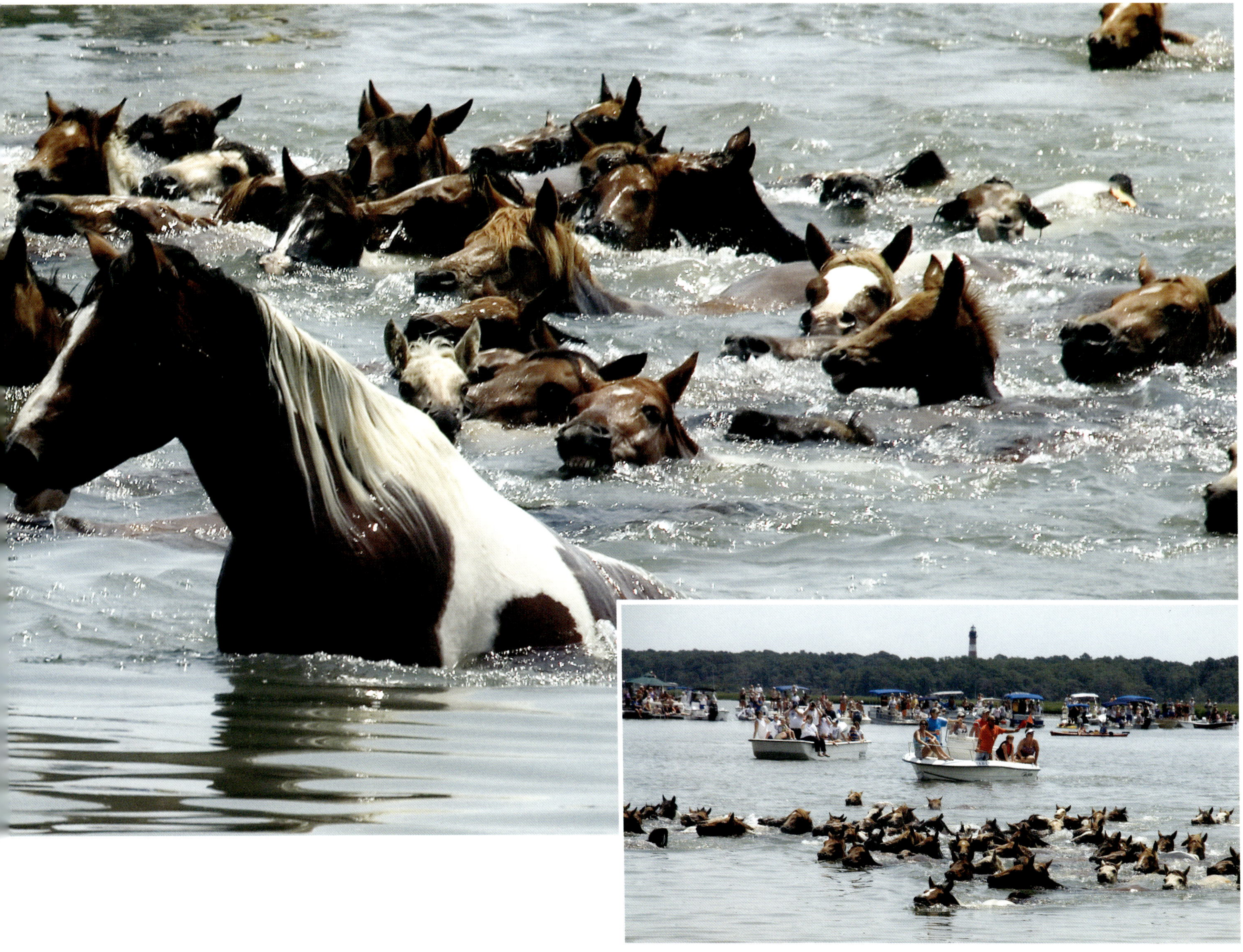

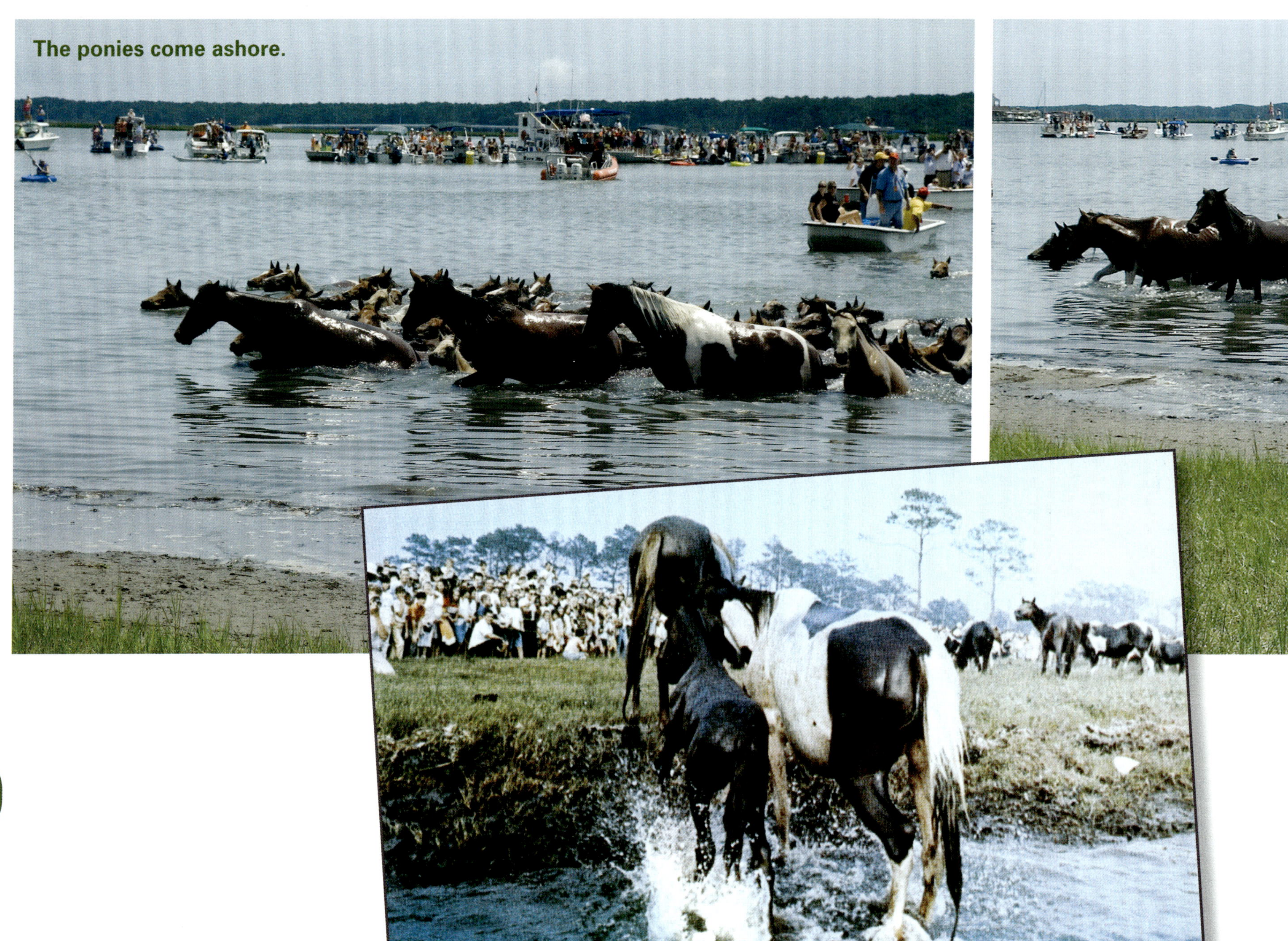

Pony Swim.
Circa 1960s.

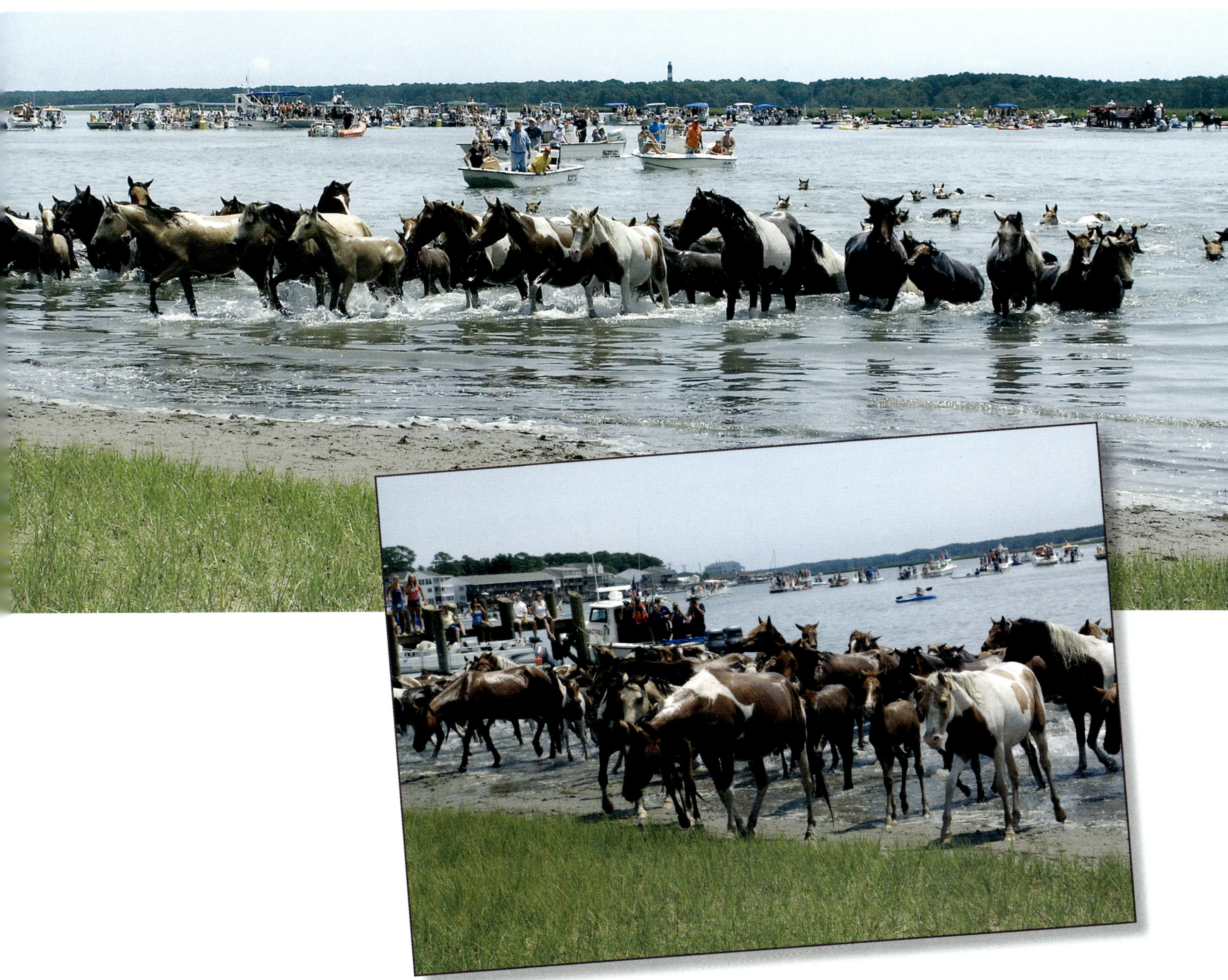

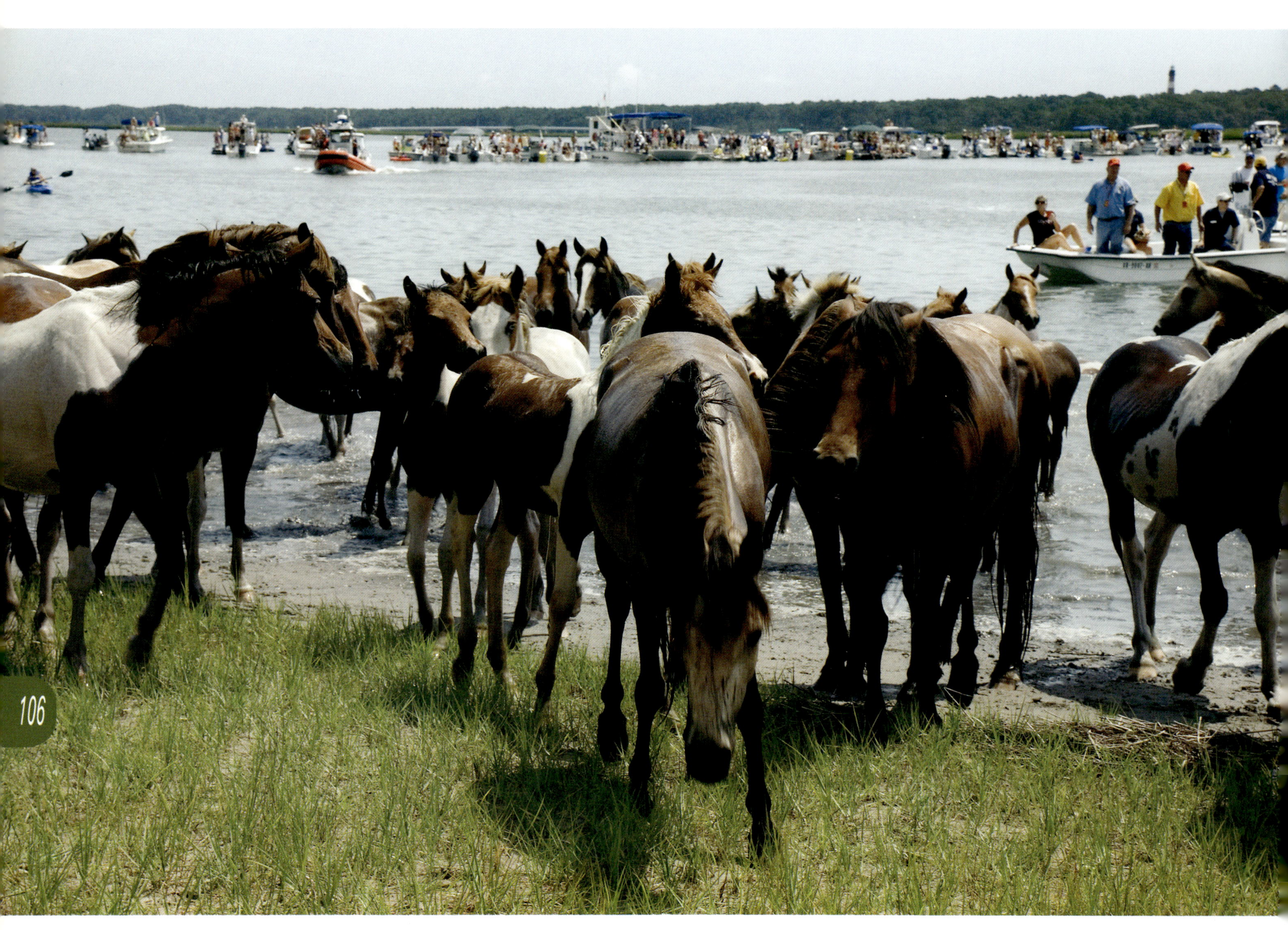

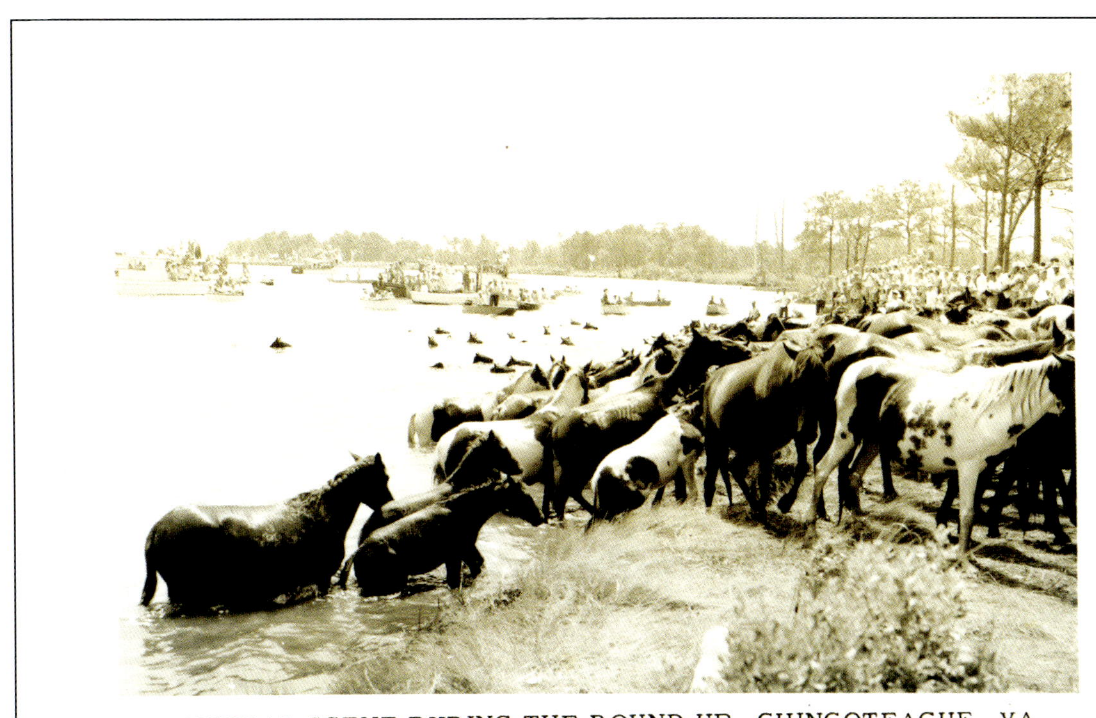

A TYPICAL SCENE DURING THE ROUND UP, CHINCOTEAGUE, VA.

A typical scene during round up. Postmarked 1954.

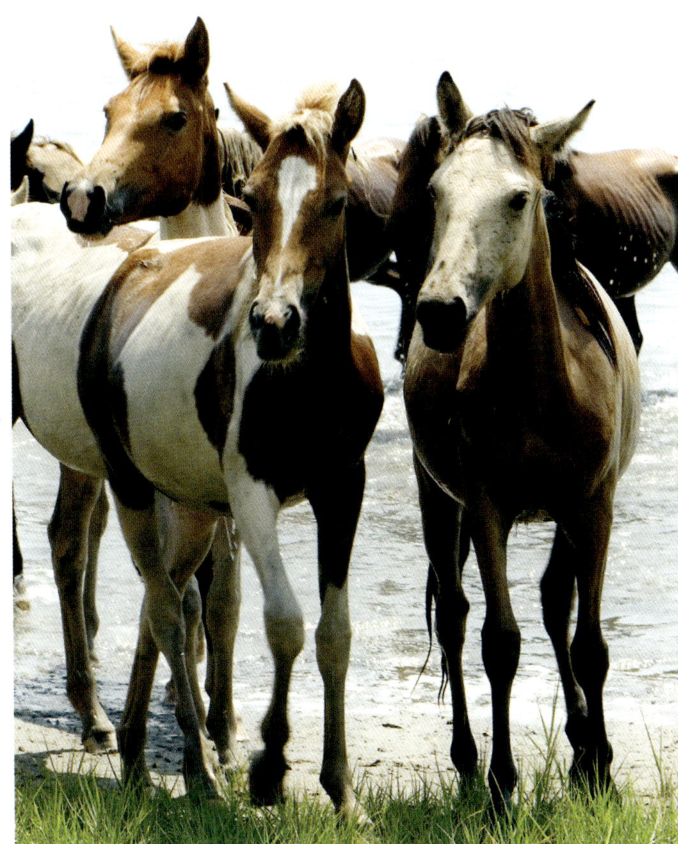

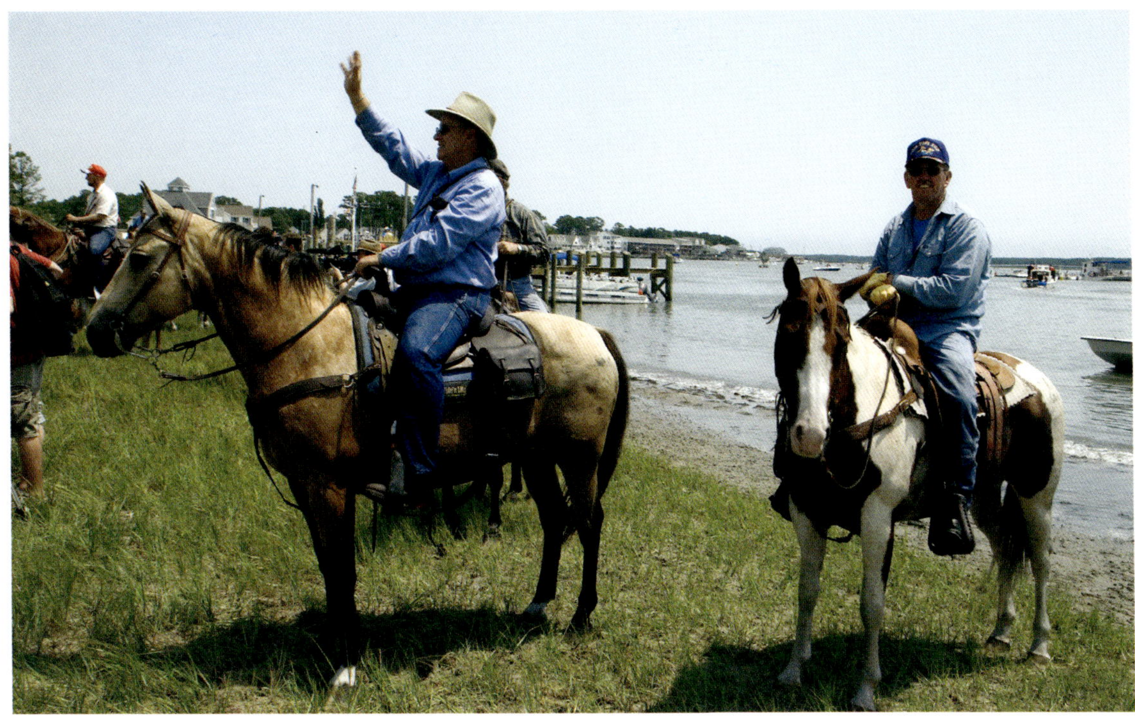

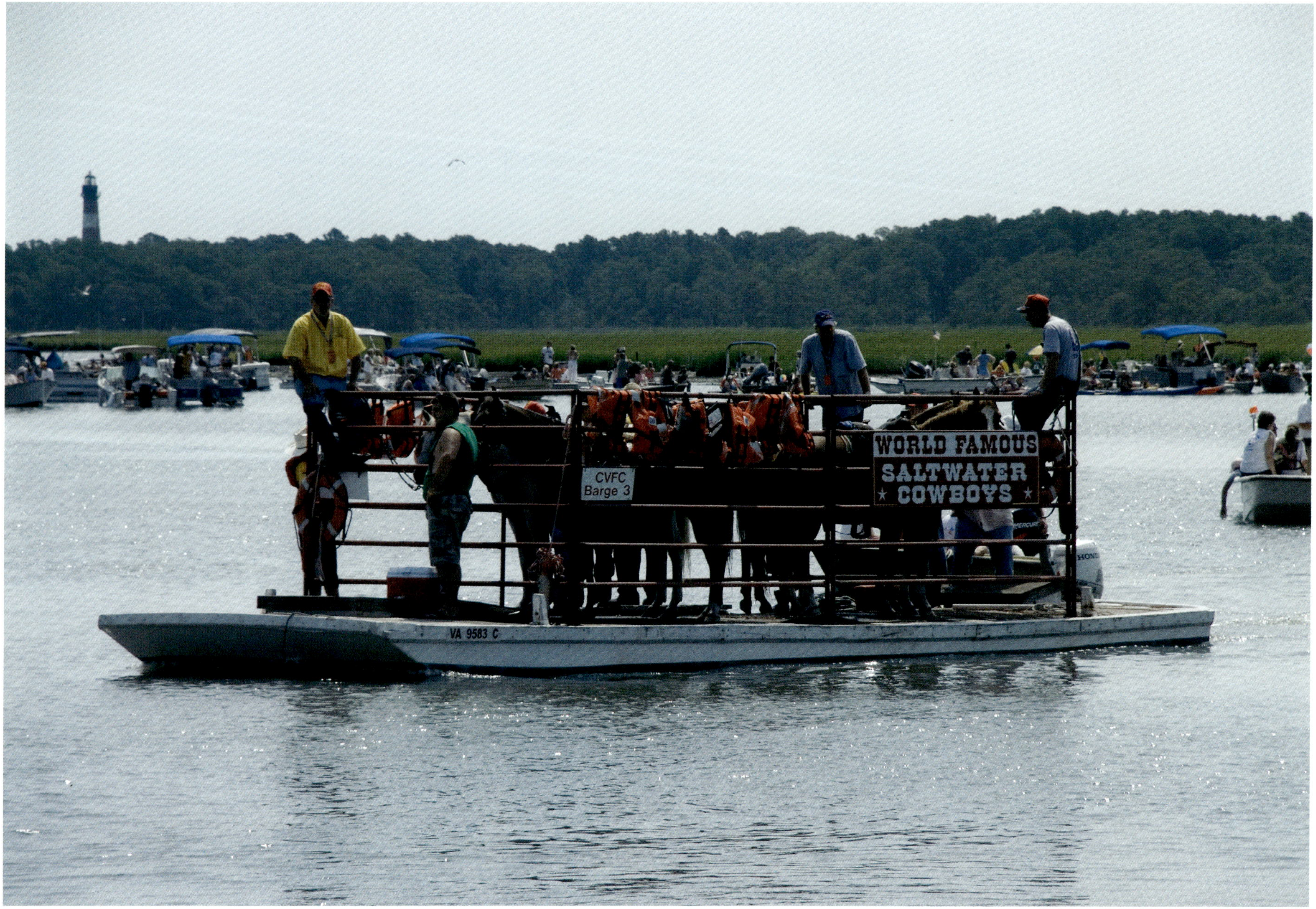

WORLD FAMOUS
SALTWATER
★ COWBOYS ★
CVFC
Barge 3
VA 9583 C

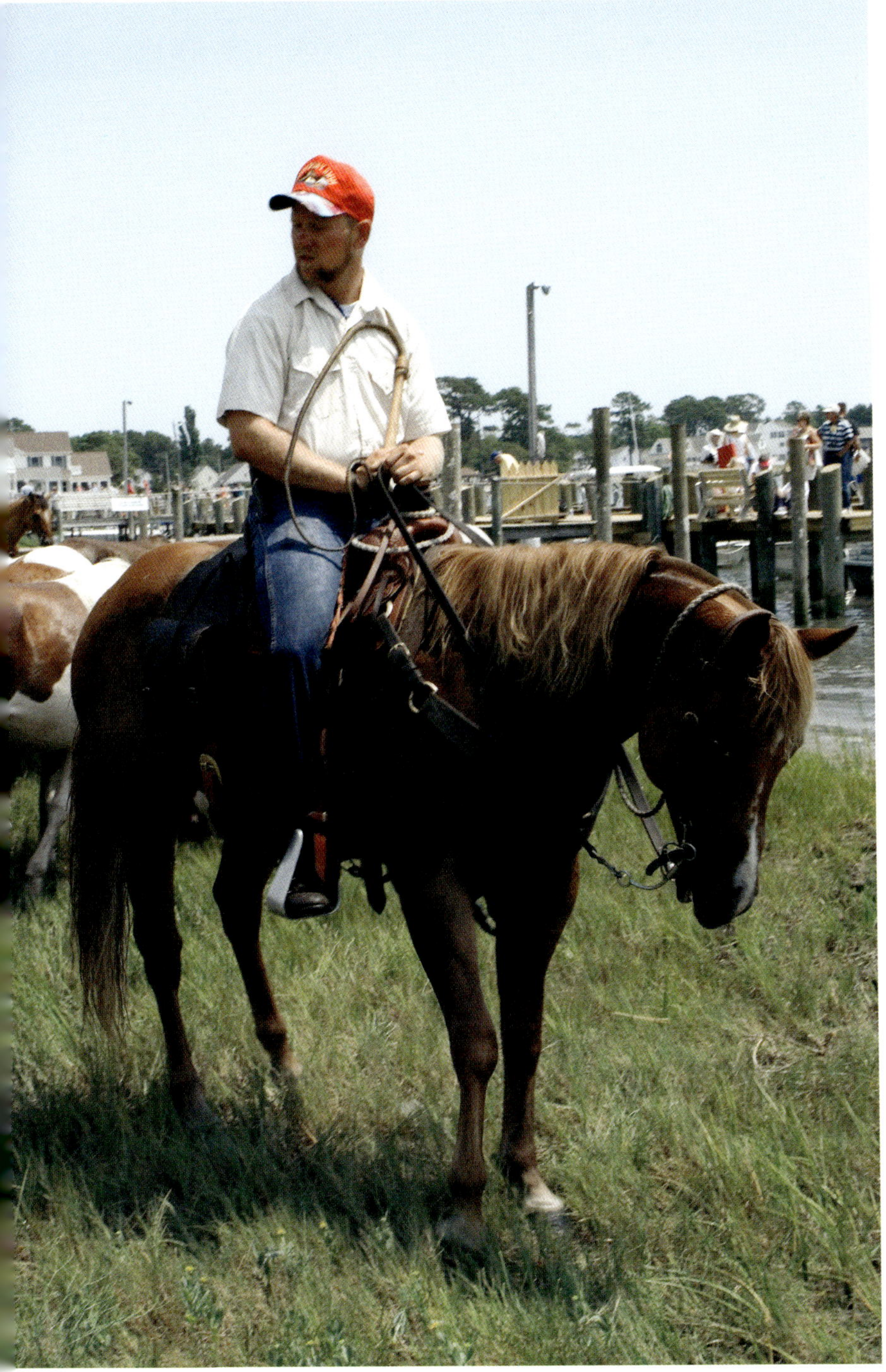

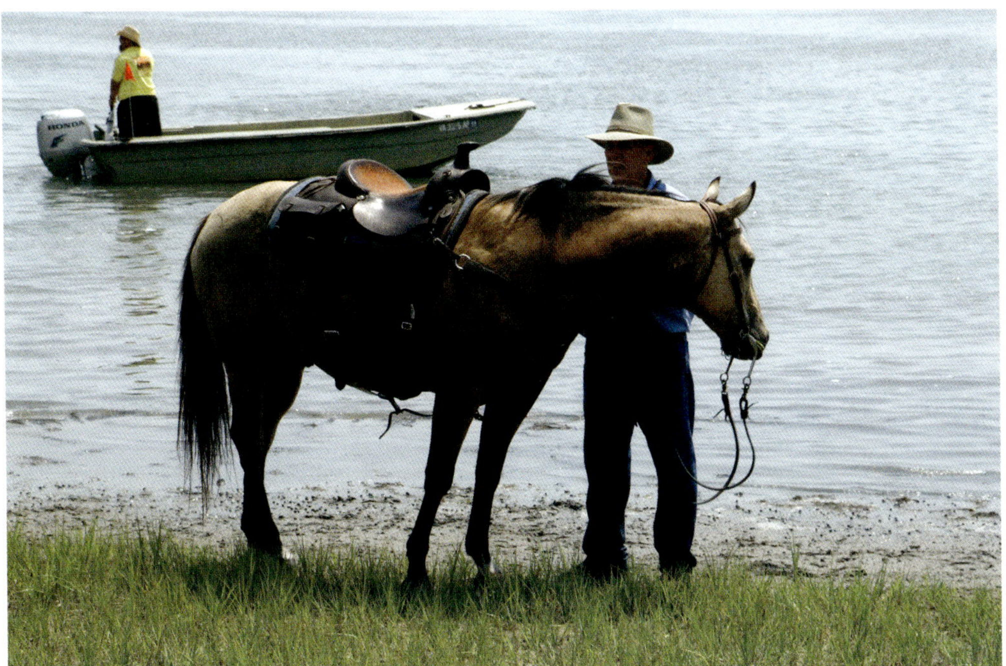

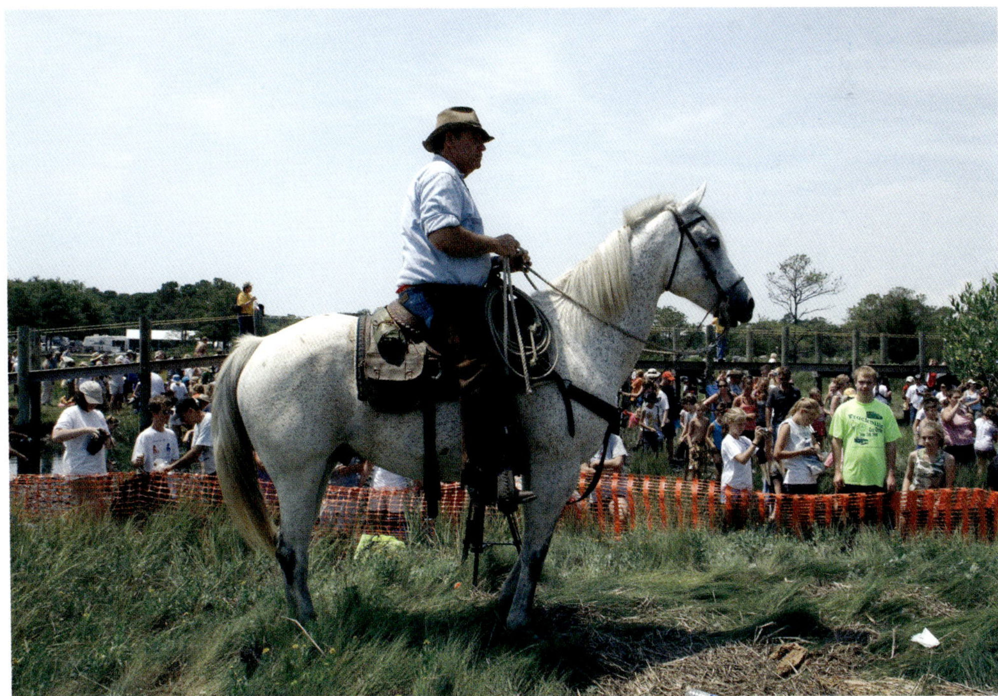

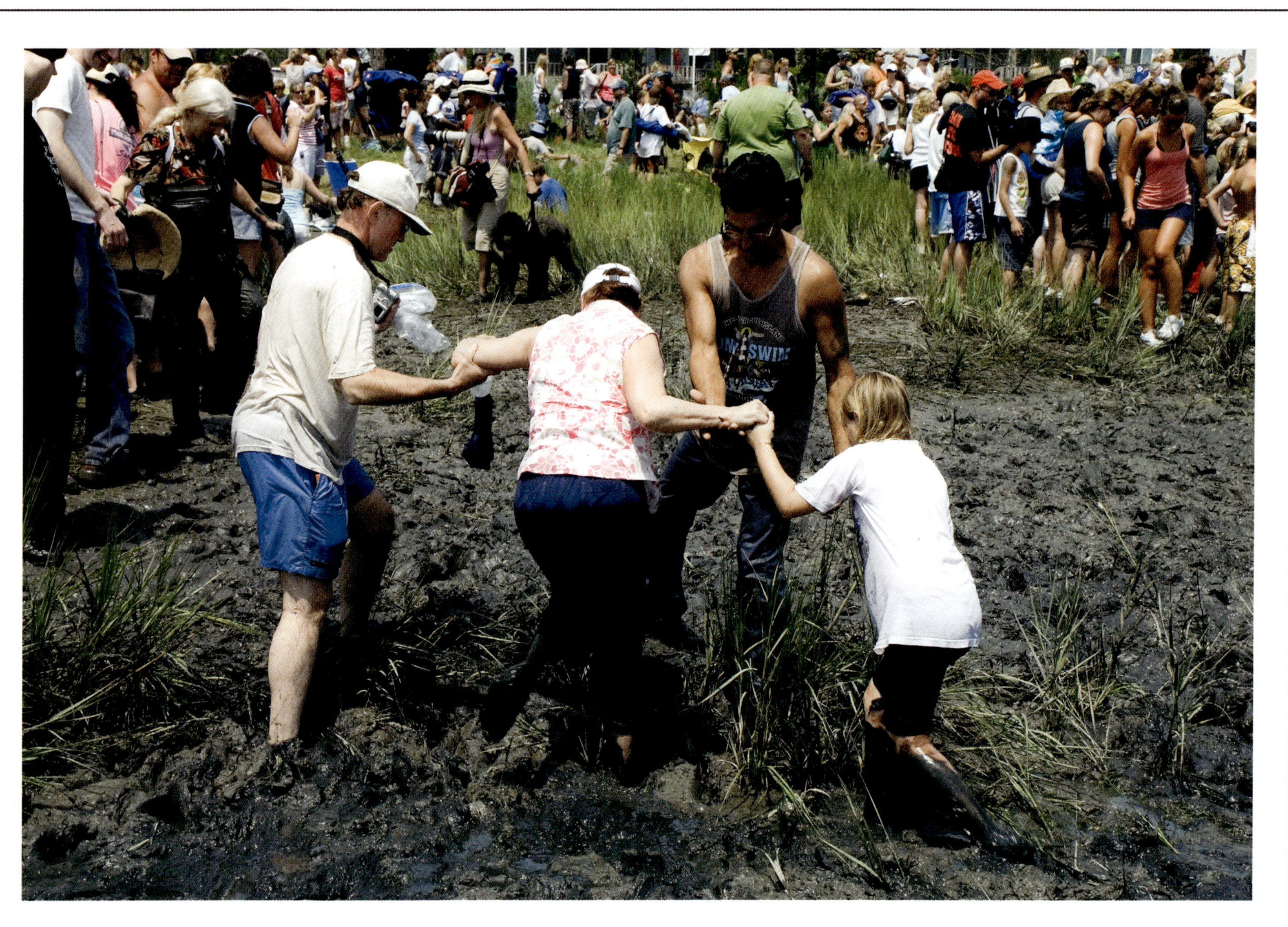

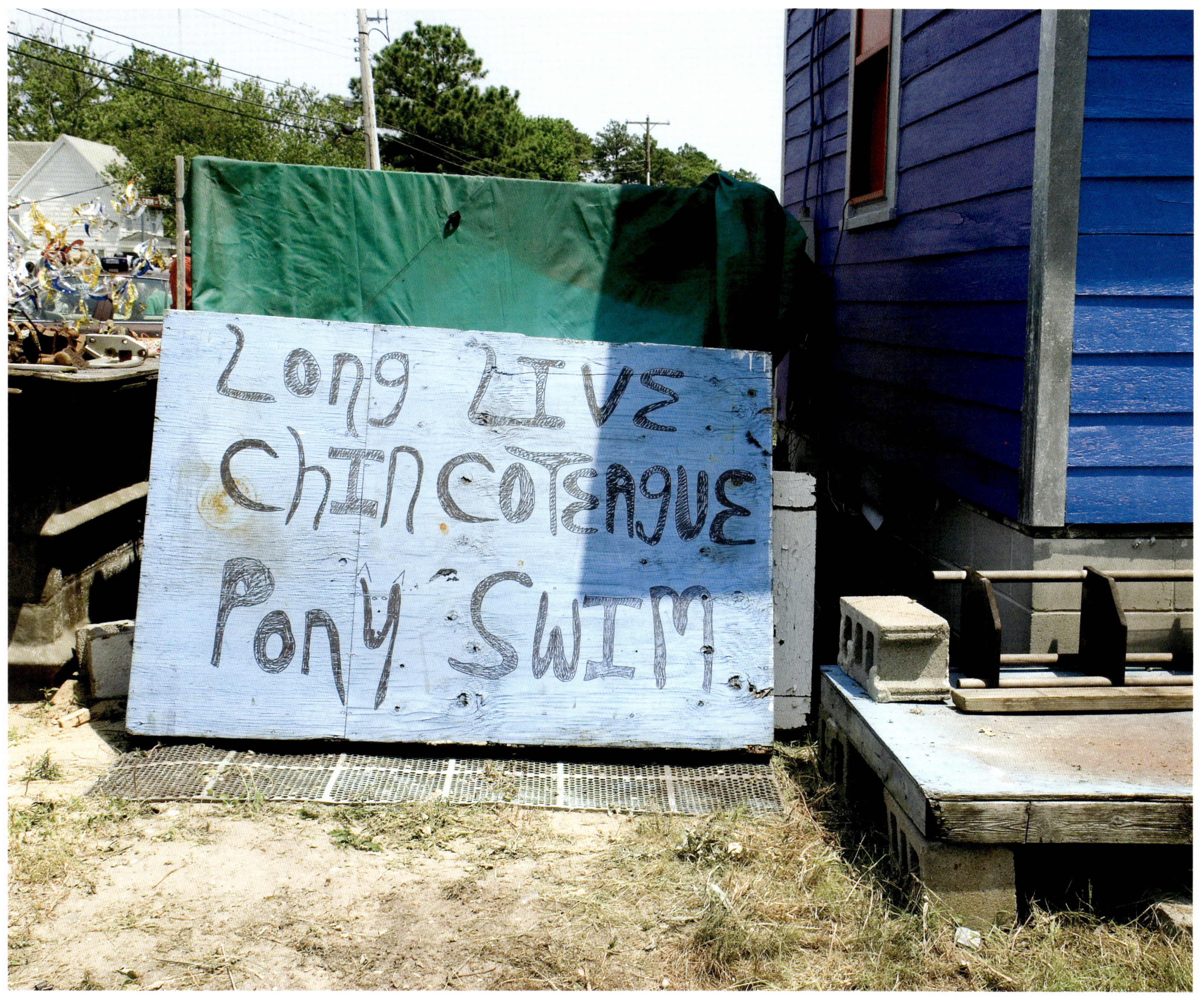

Long Live
Chincoteague
Pony Swim

Ponies being paraded down Main Street
to the carnival grounds.

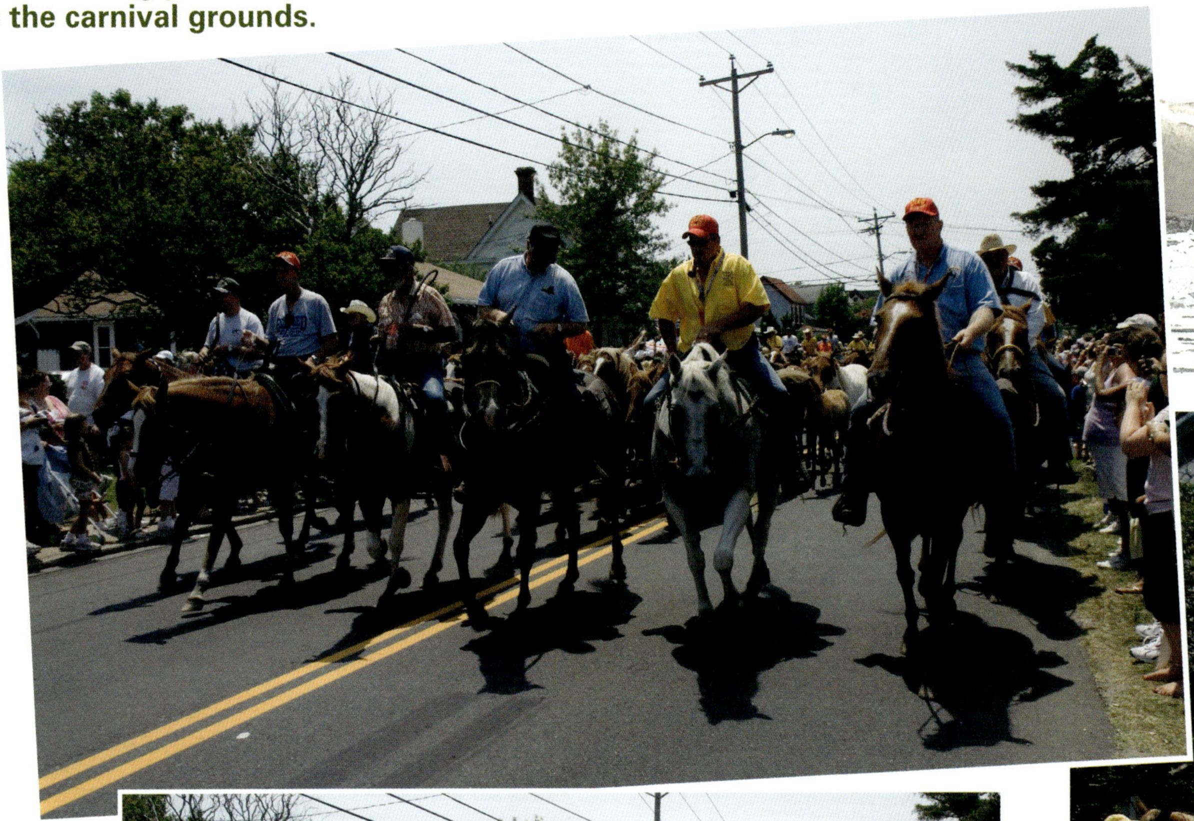

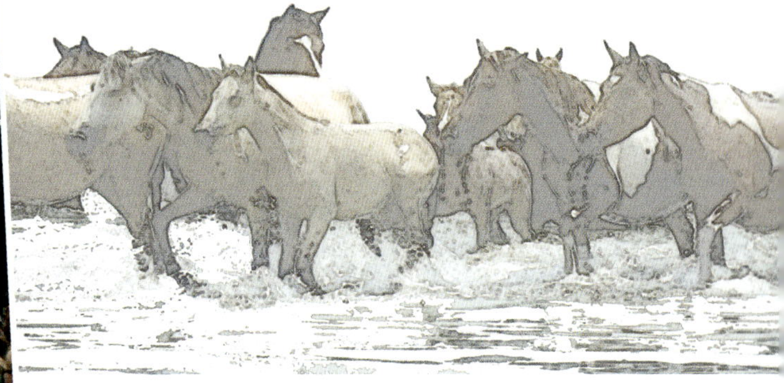

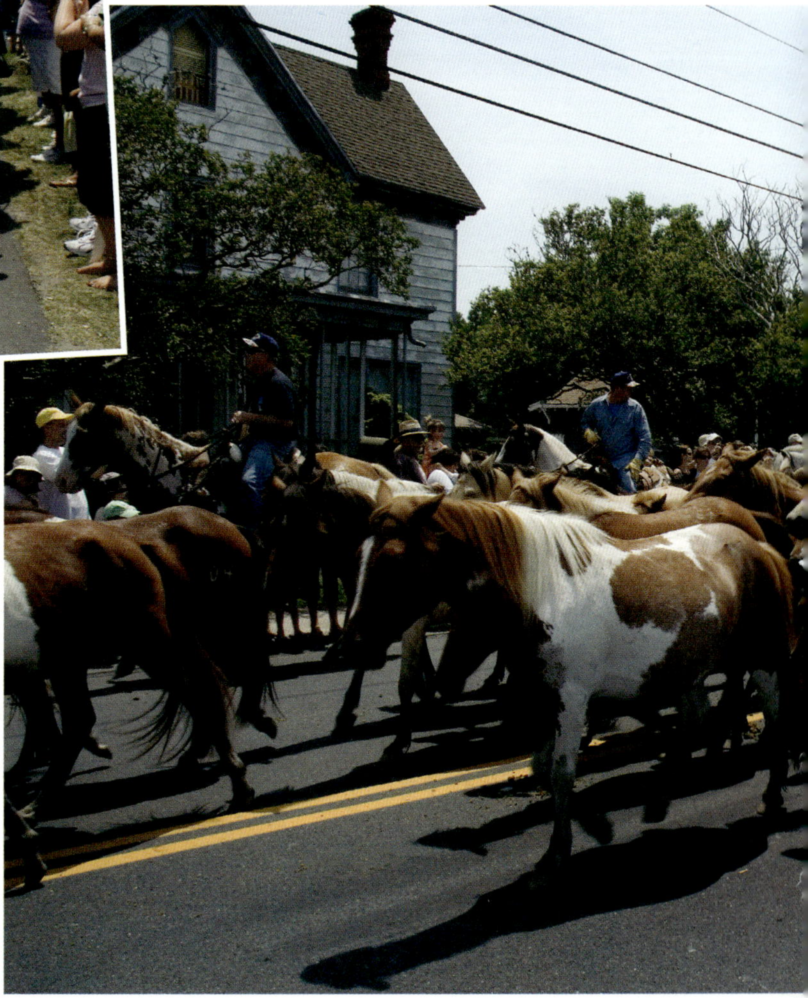

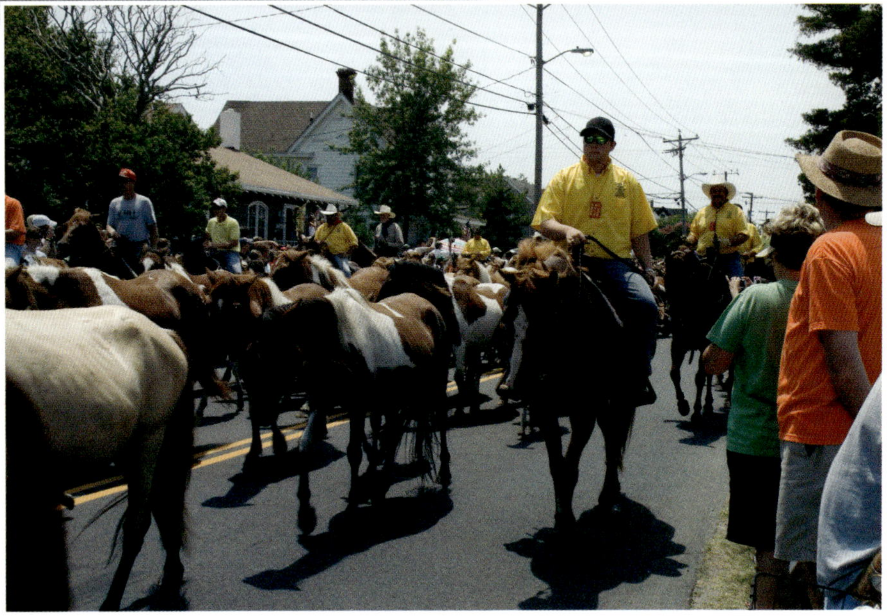

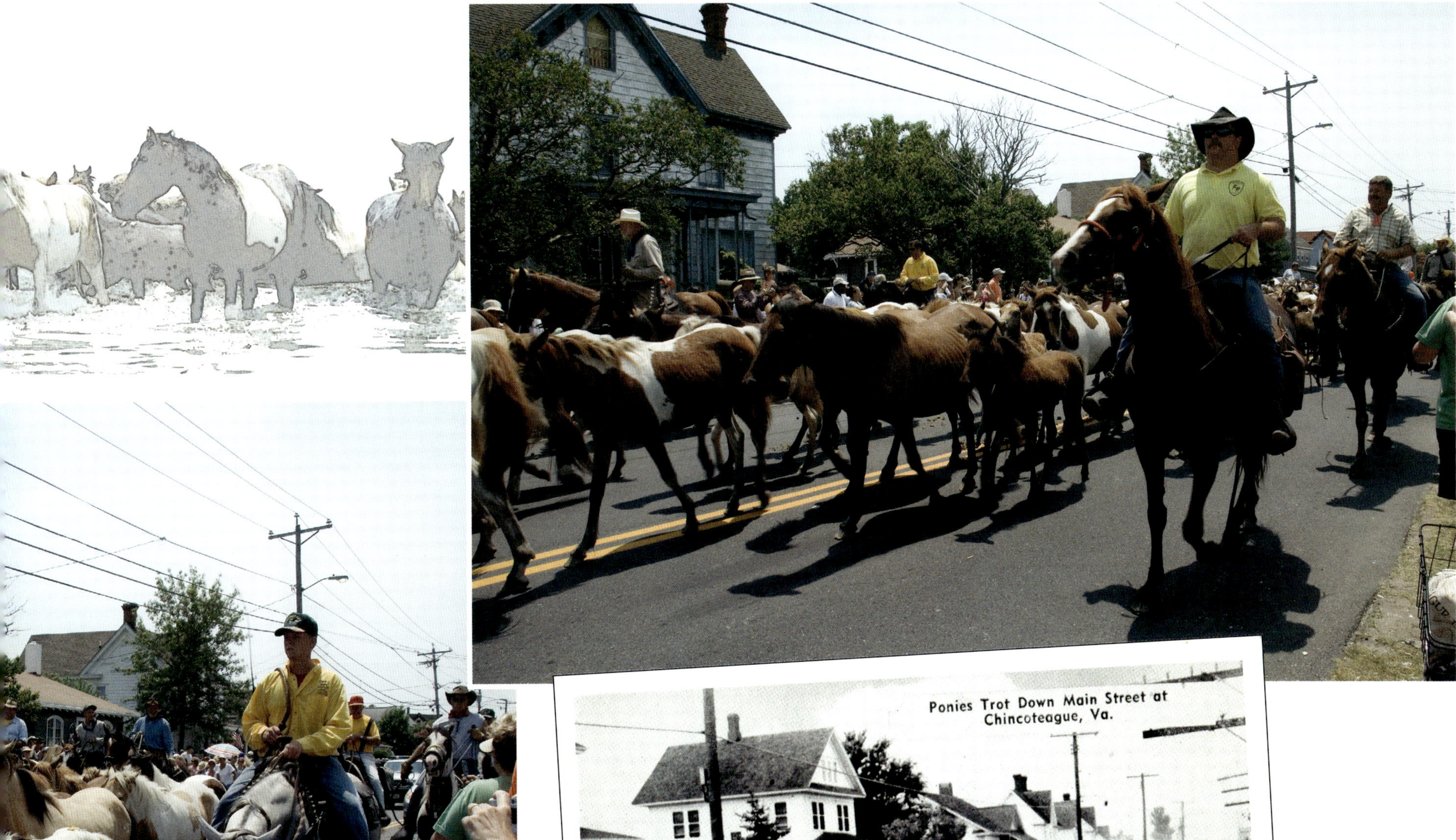

Ponies trot down
Main Street at
Chincoteague.
Circa 1940s.

113

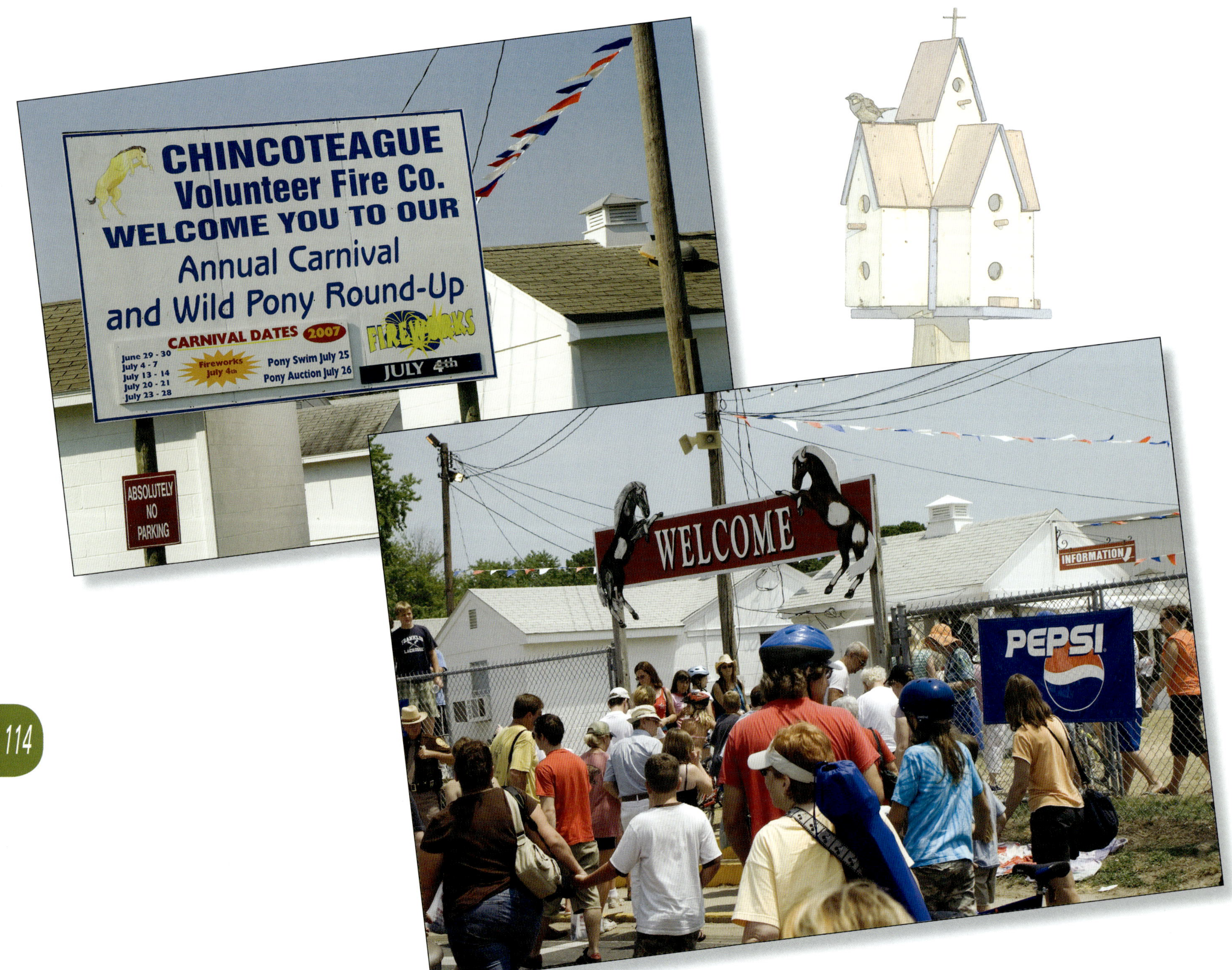

CHINCOTEAGUE
Volunteer Fire Co.
WELCOME YOU TO OUR
Annual Carnival
and Wild Pony Round-Up
CARNIVAL DATES 2007
FIREWORKS
June 29 - 30
July 4 - 7
July 13 - 14
July 20 - 21
July 23 - 28
Fireworks July 4th
Pony Swim July 25
Pony Auction July 26
JULY 4th
ABSOLUTELY NO PARKING
WELCOME
PEPSI
INFORMATION

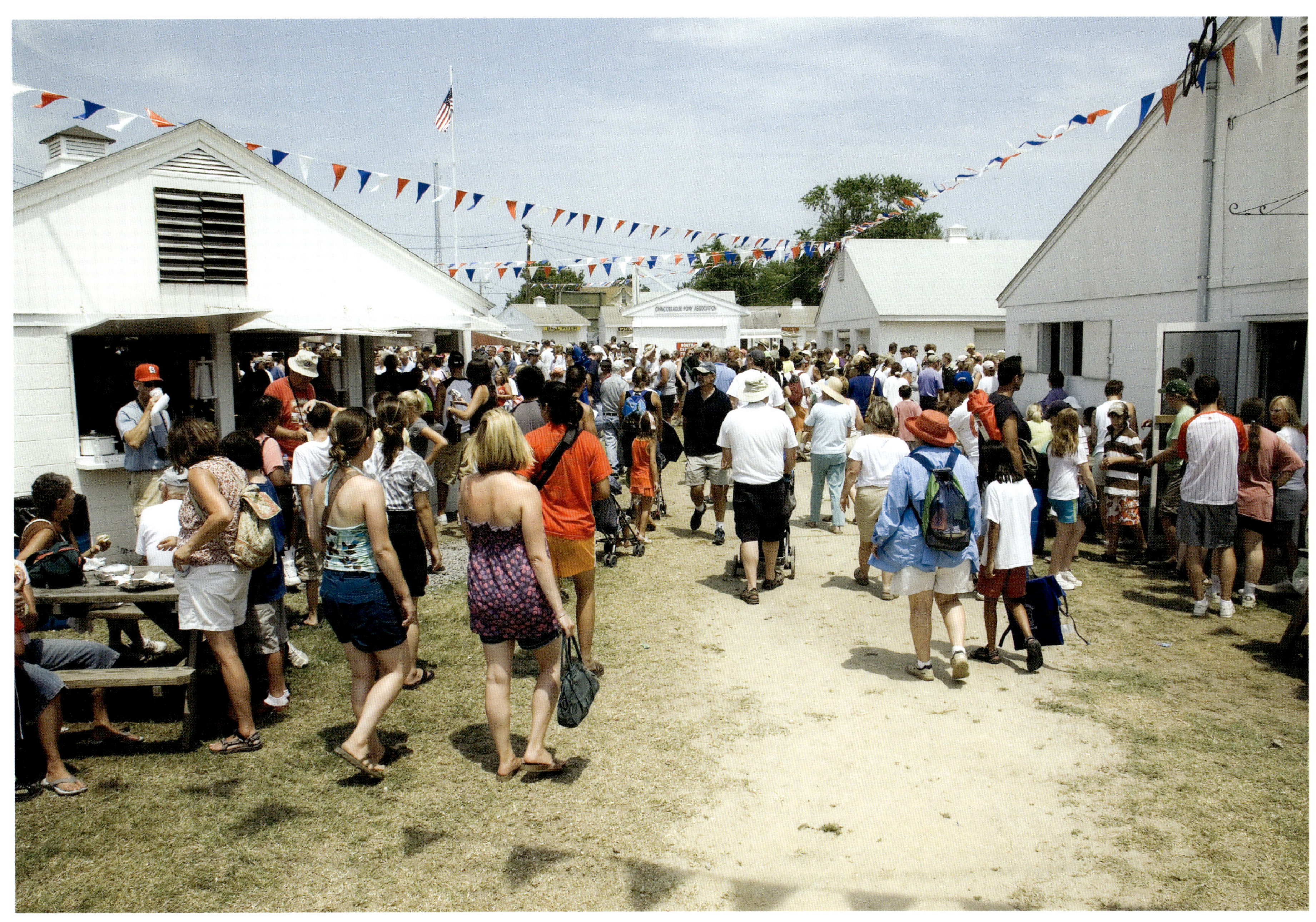
CHINCOTEAGUE PONY ASSOCIATION

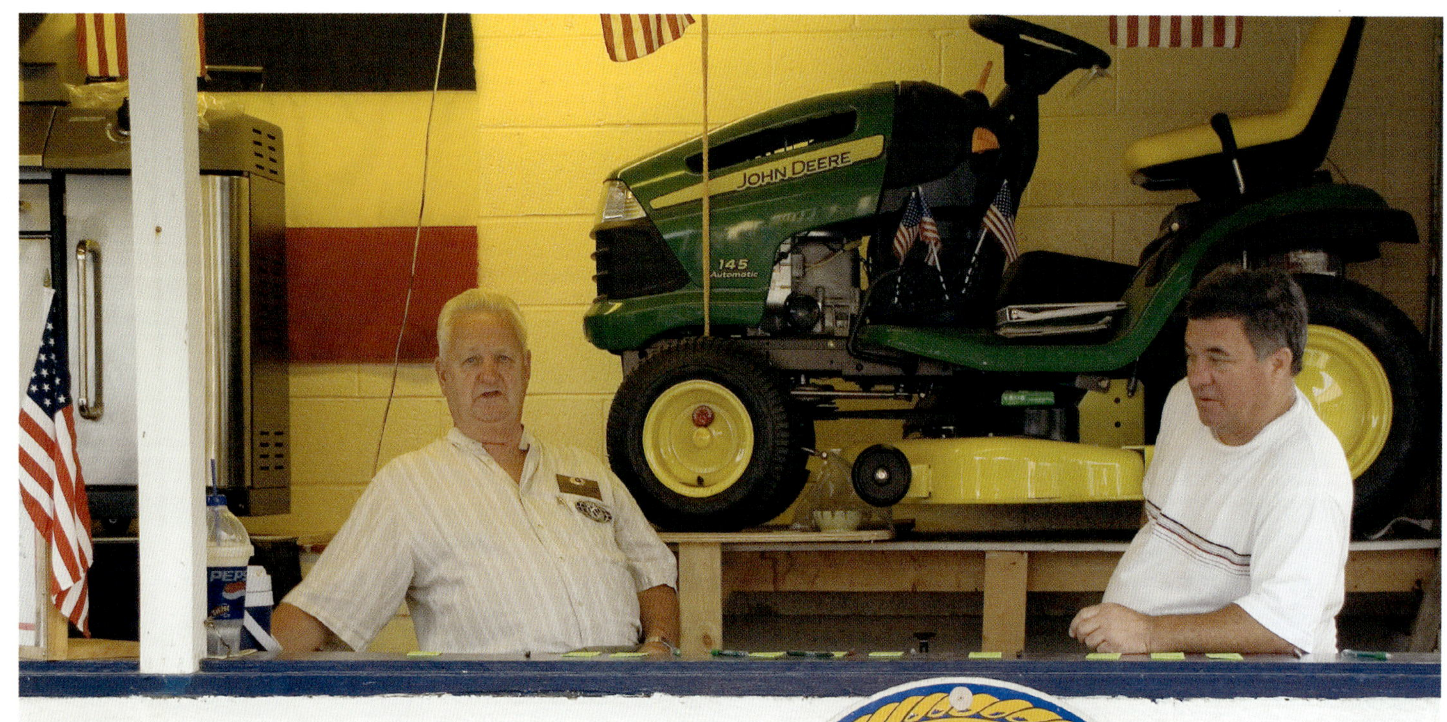
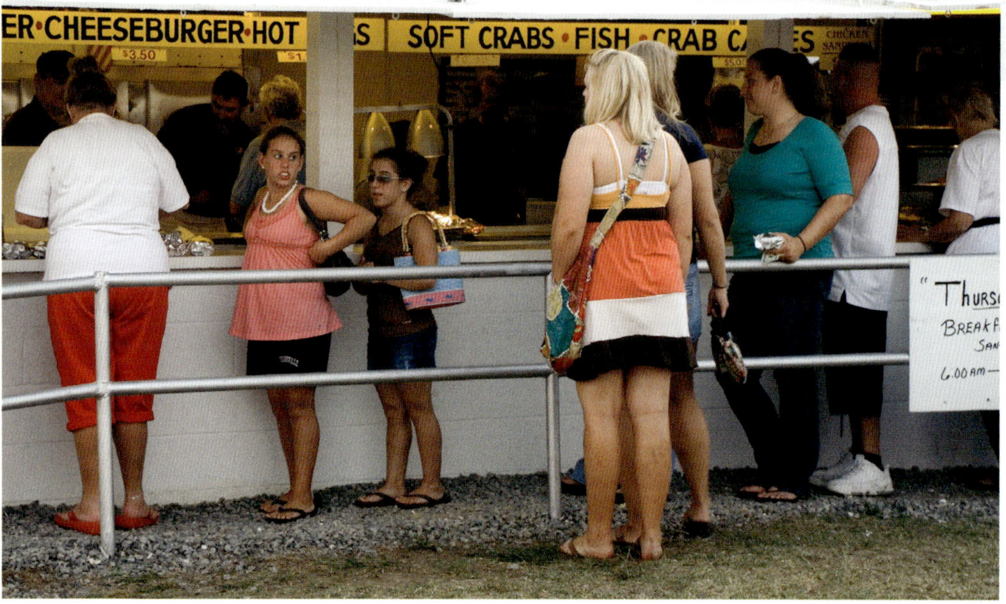
CHEESEBURGER • HOT
SOFT CRABS • FISH • CRAB C
$3.50
"Thurs
BREAK
6:00 AM
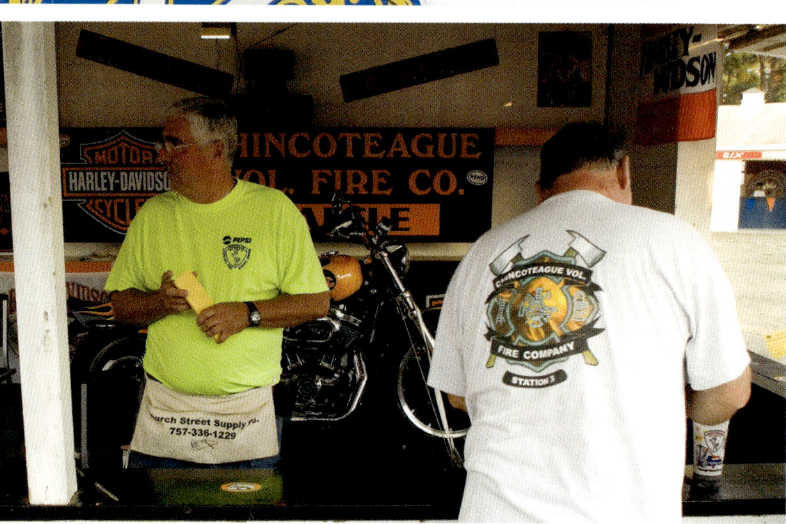
KIWANIS
HARLEY-DAVIDSON
MOTOR
CHINCOTEAGUE
FIRE CO.
CHINCOTEAGUE VOL.
FIRE COMPANY
757-336-1229

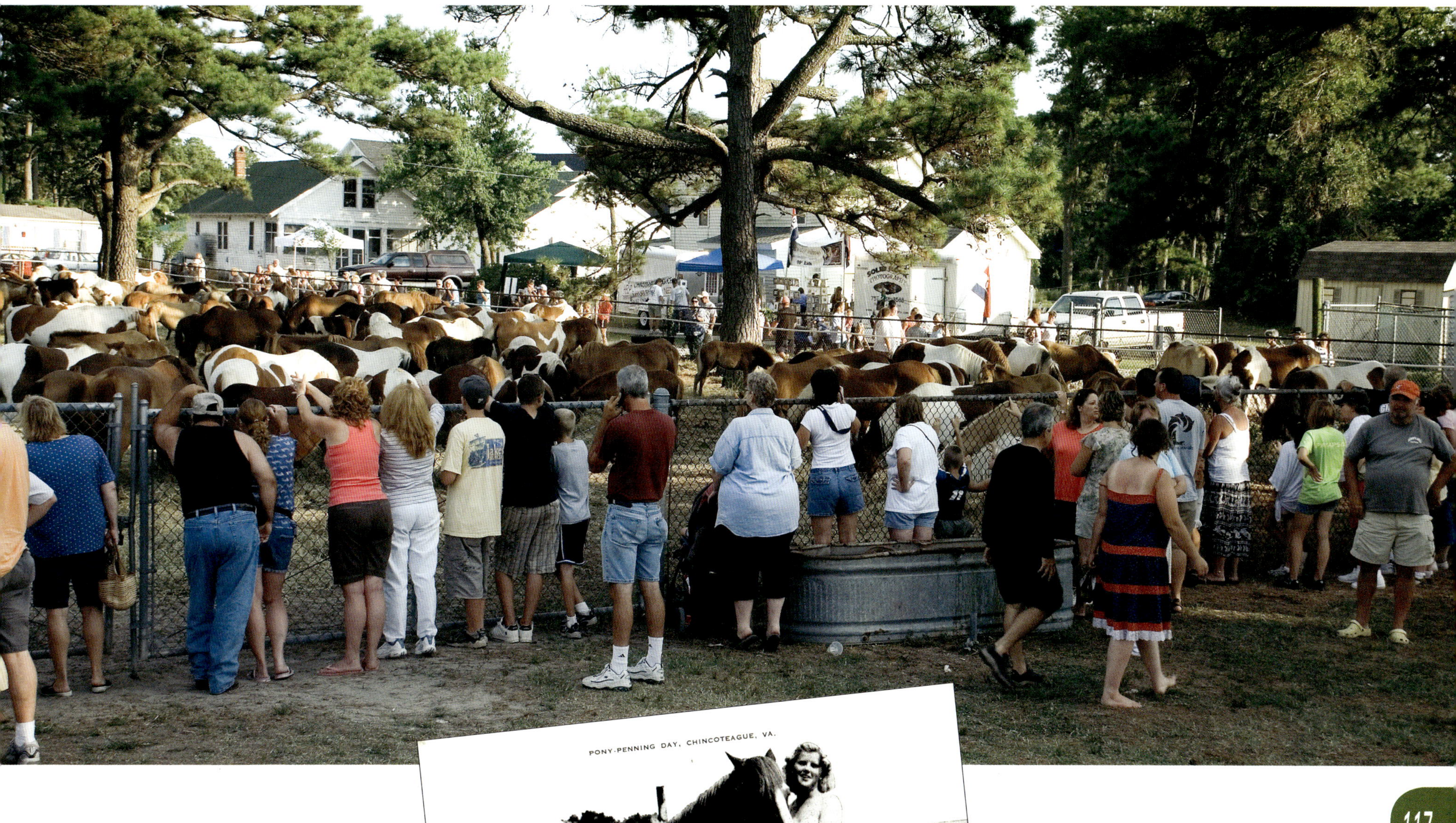

Pony Penning day.
Circa 1940s.

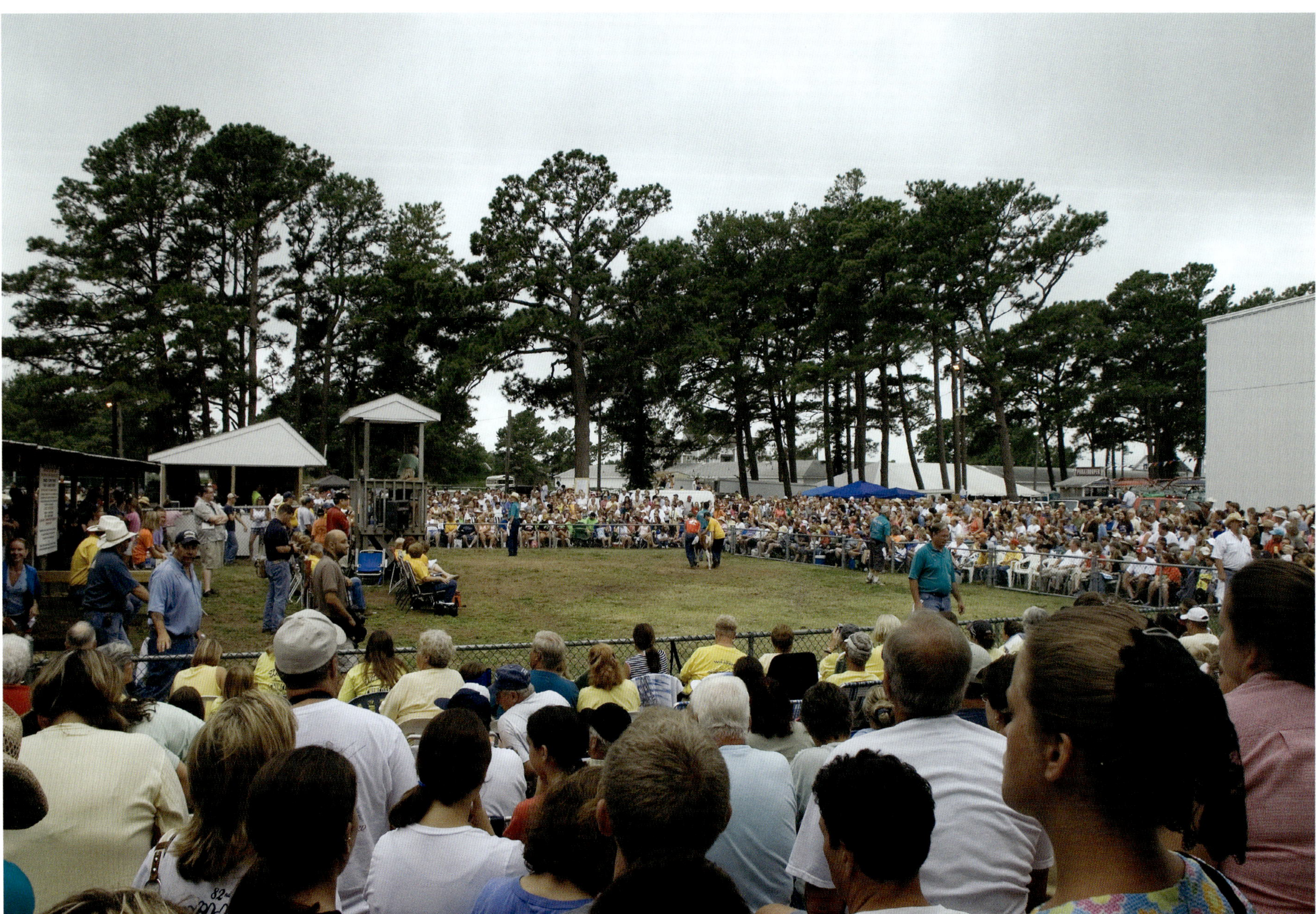

118

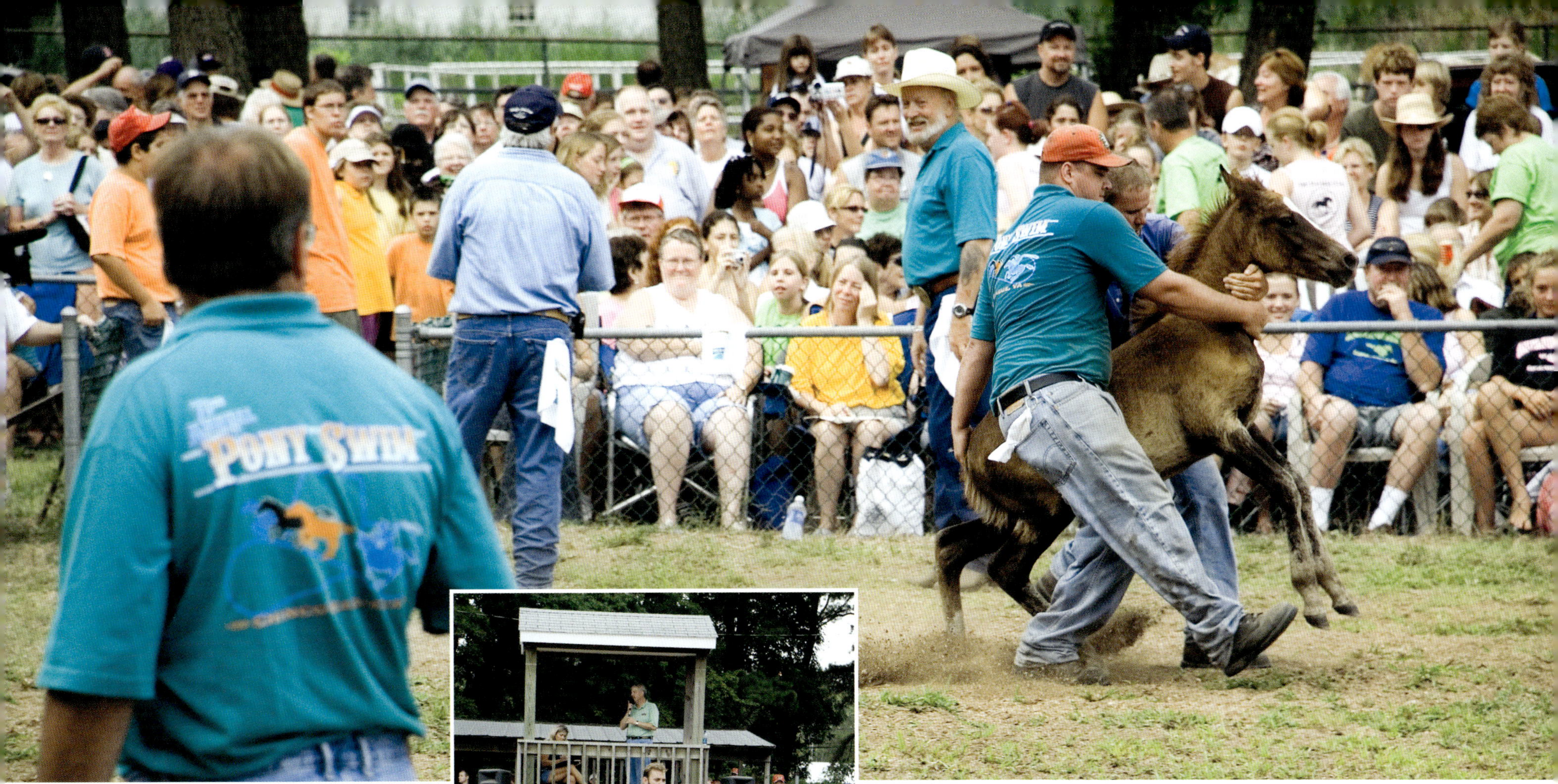

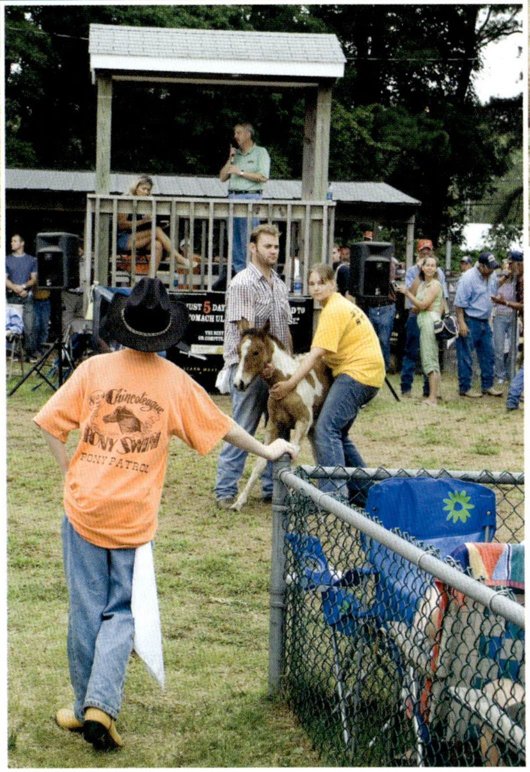

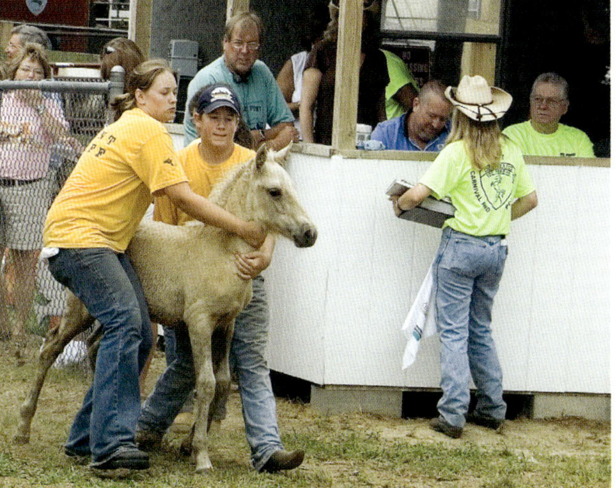

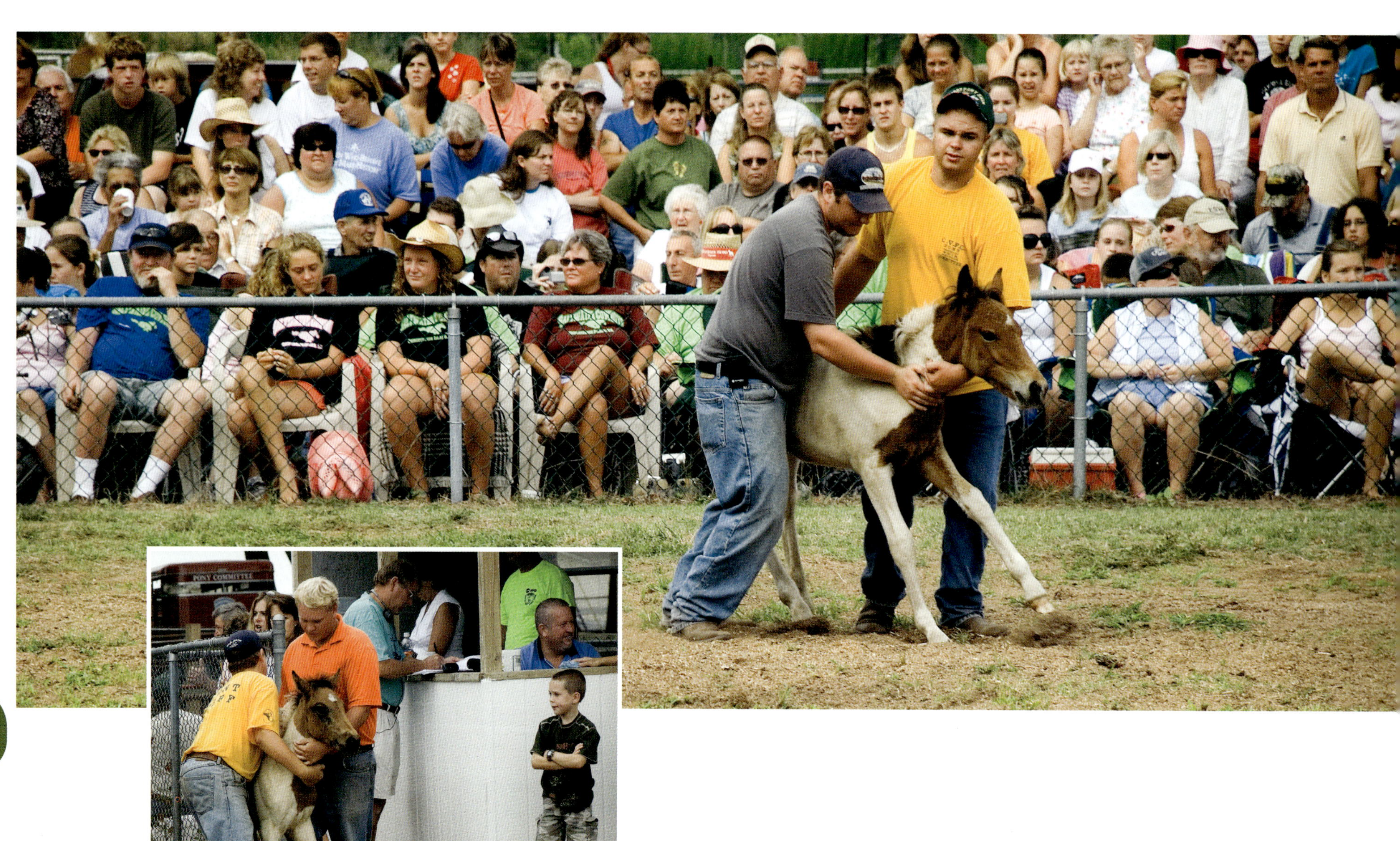

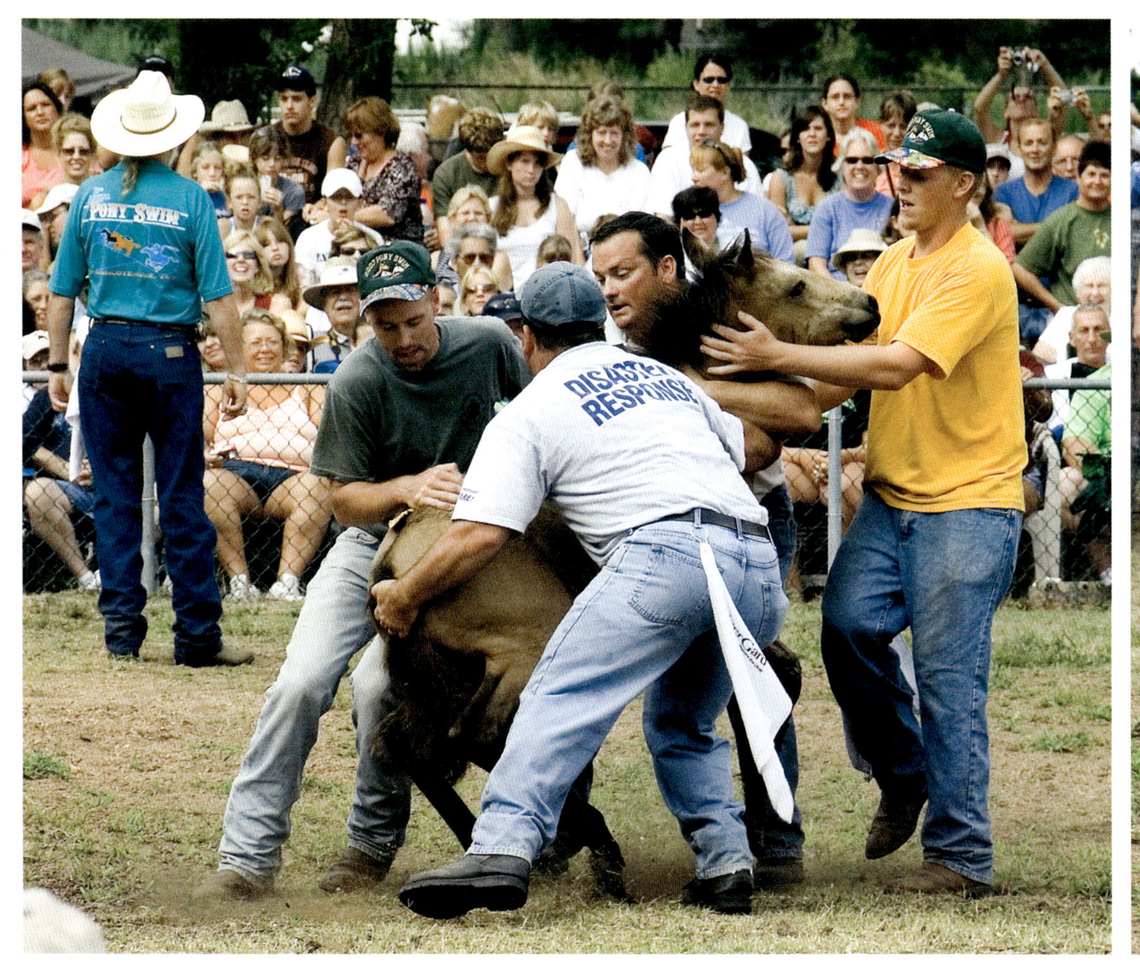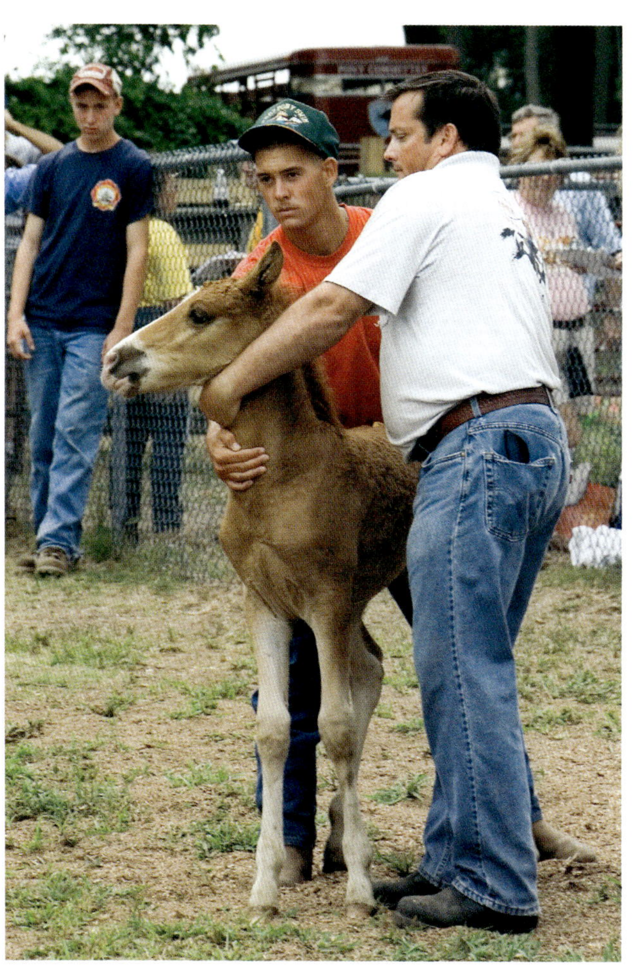

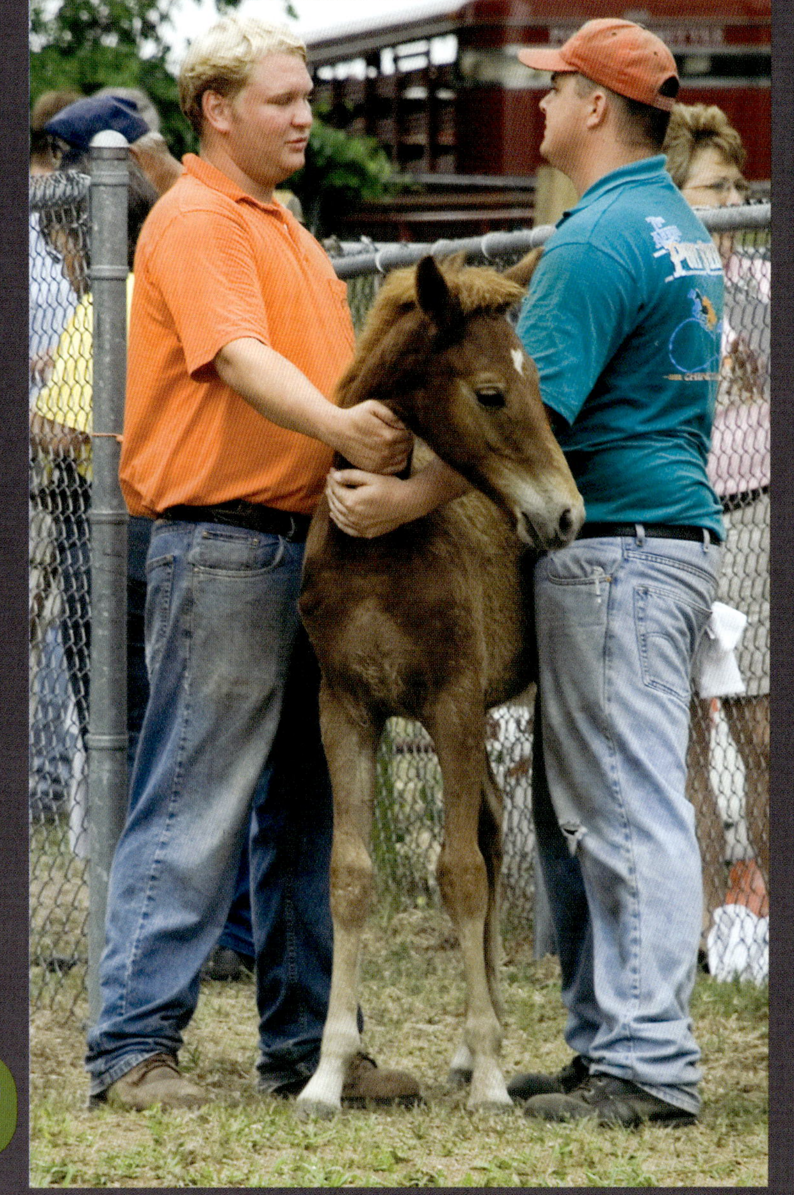

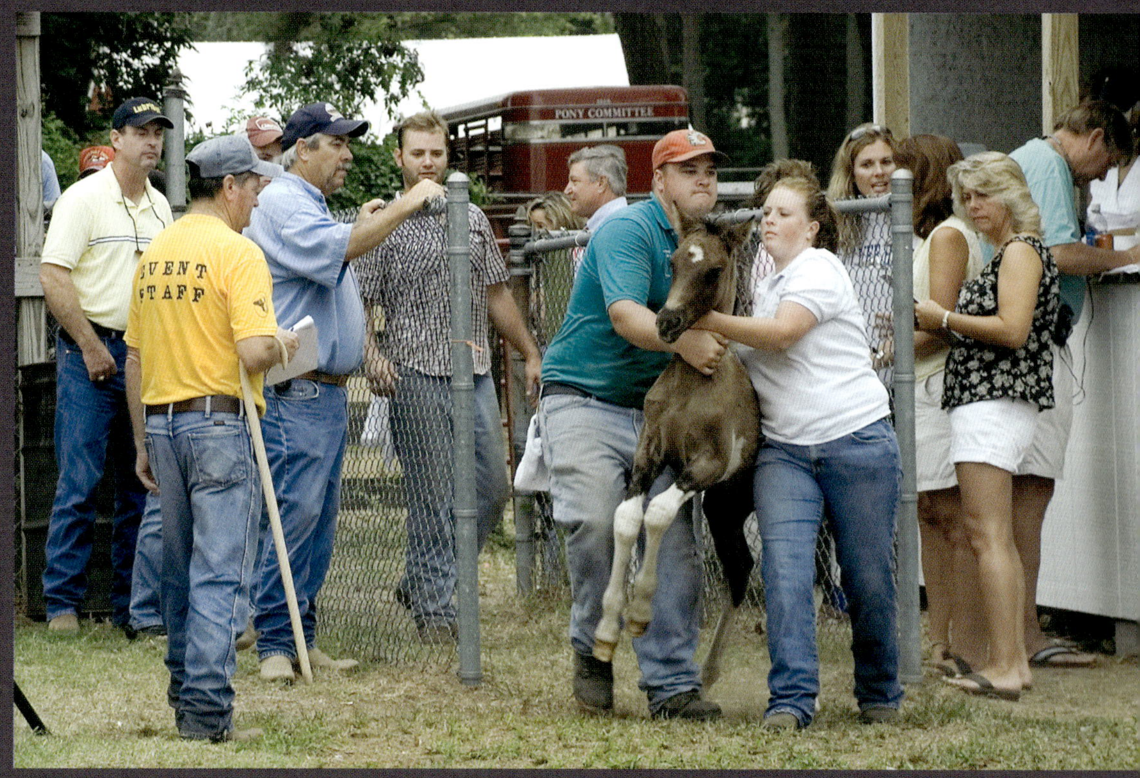

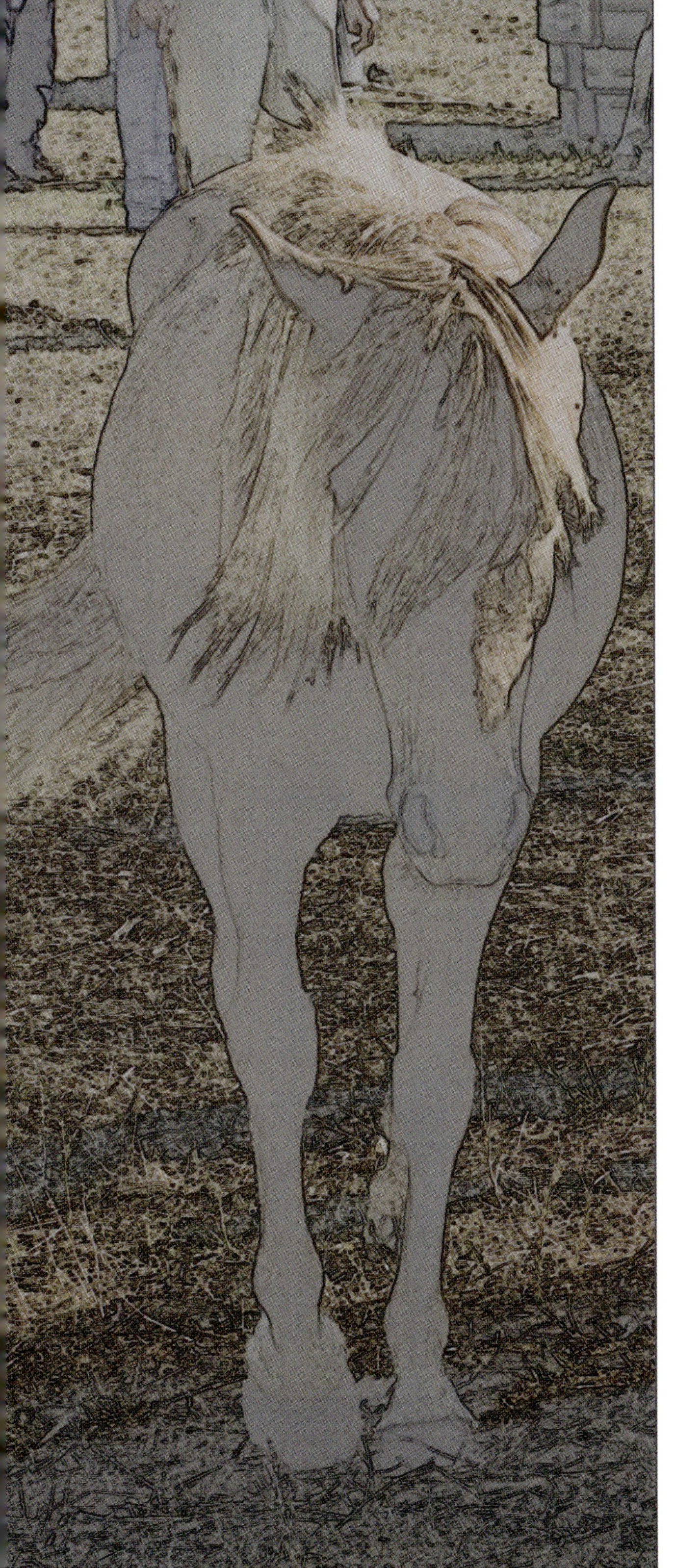

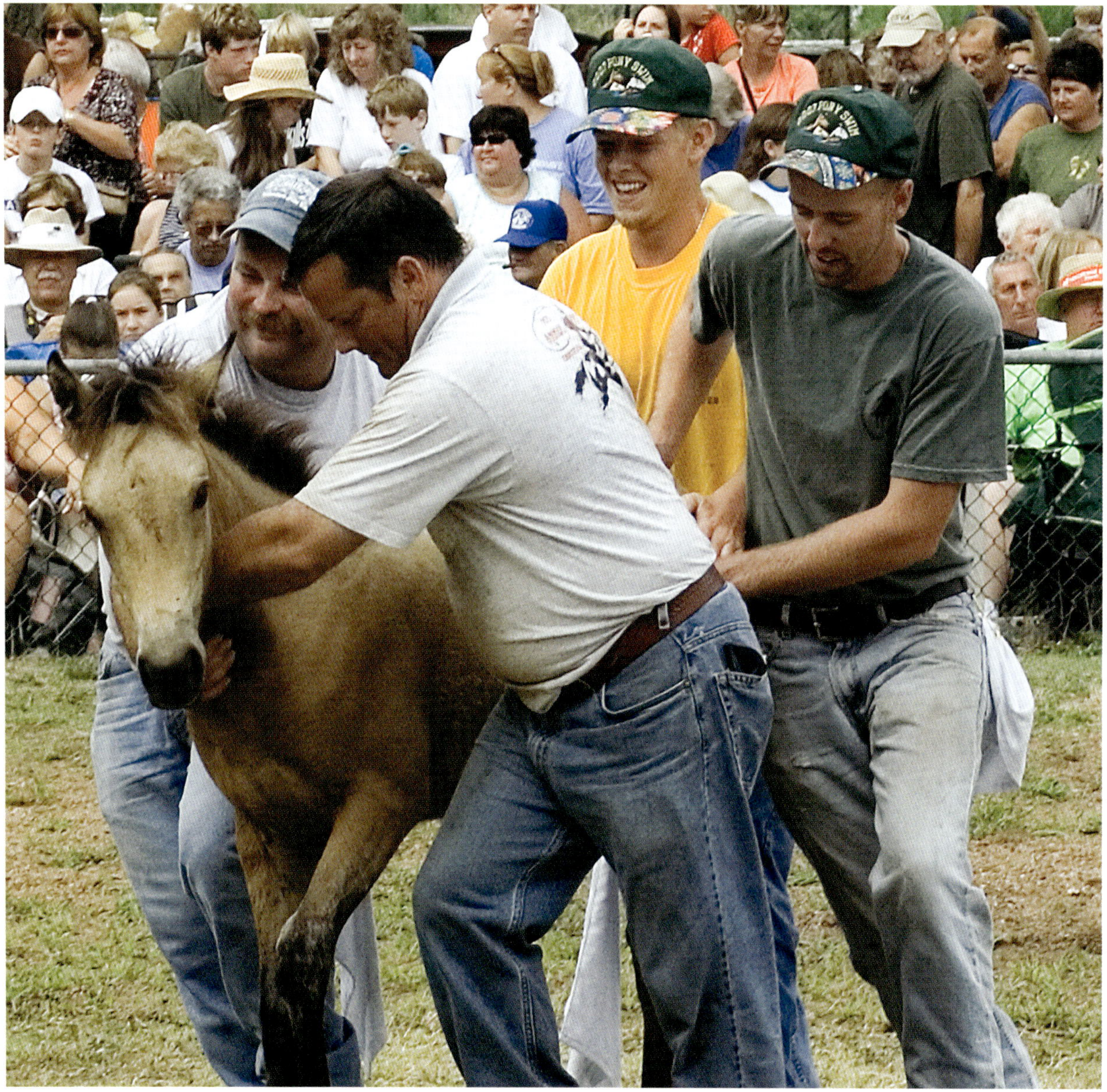

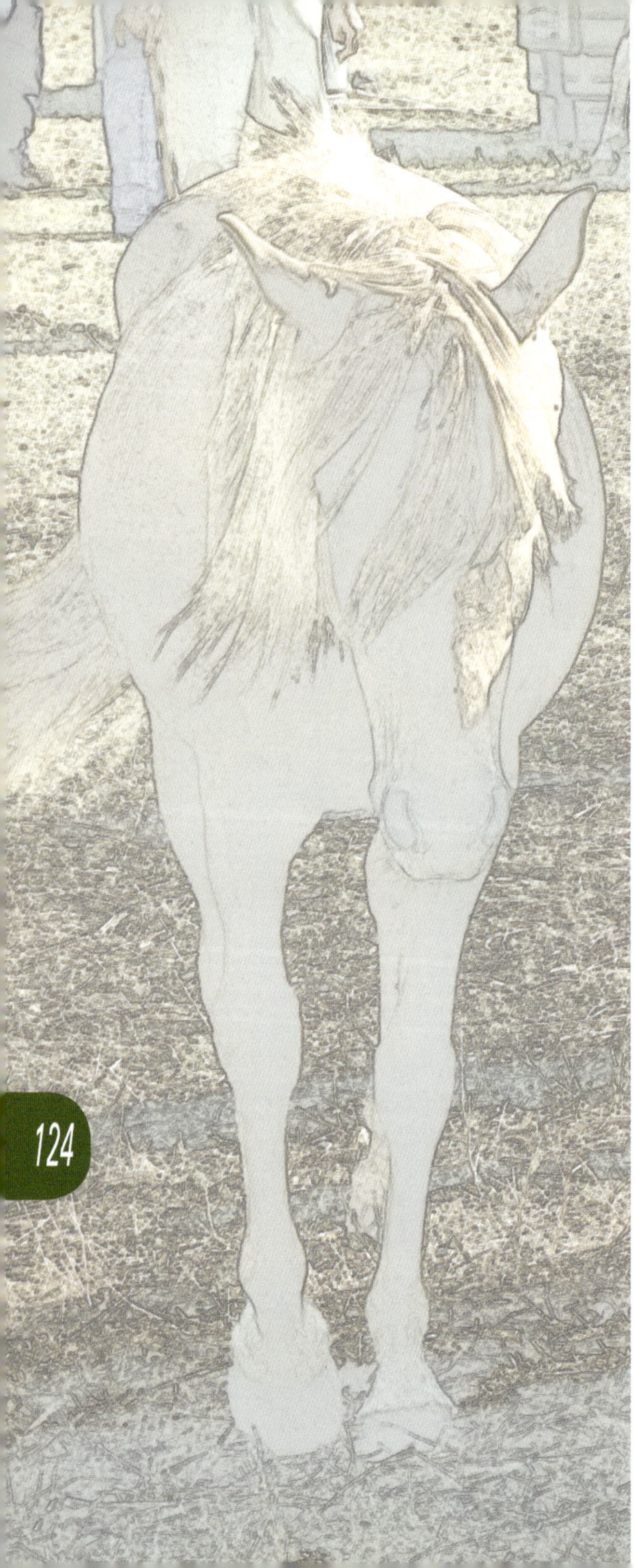

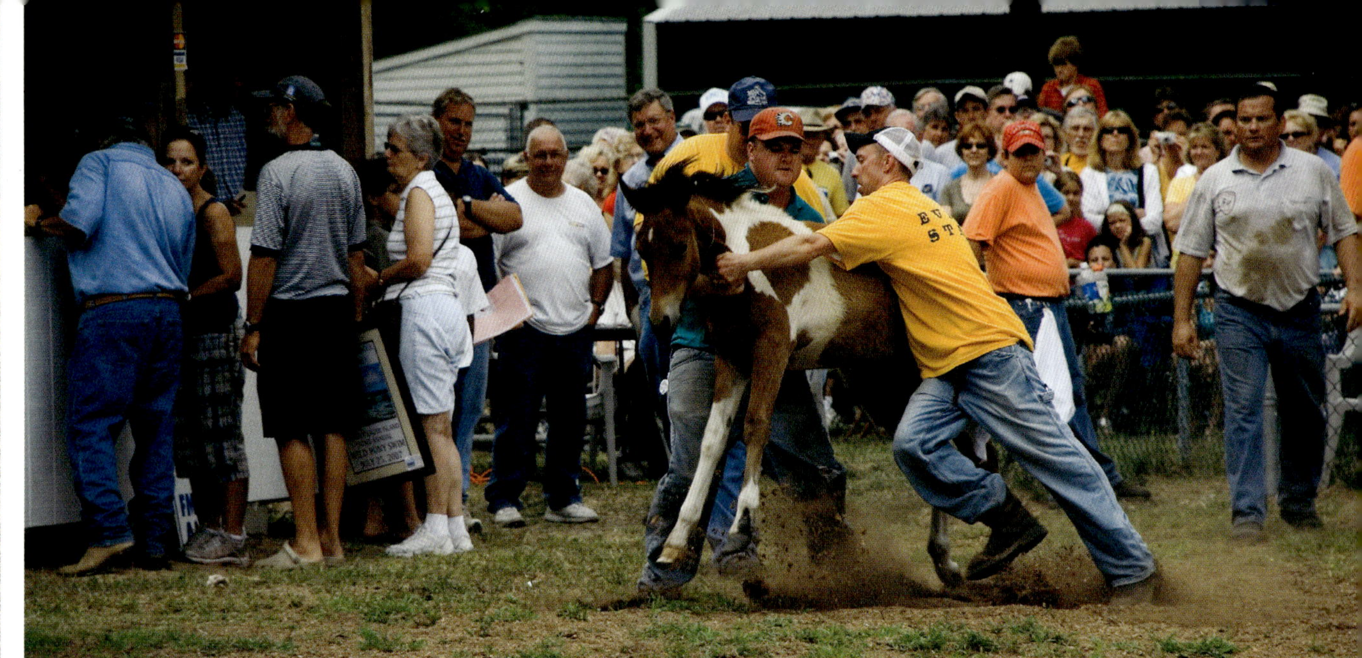
IN JUST 5 DAYS, STRESS CAN LEAD TO
STOMACH ULCERS IN YOUR HORSE.
THE NEXT TIME YOU TRAIN, TRAVEL
OR COMPETE, PROTECT YOUR HORSE WITH
UlcerGard
(omeprazole)

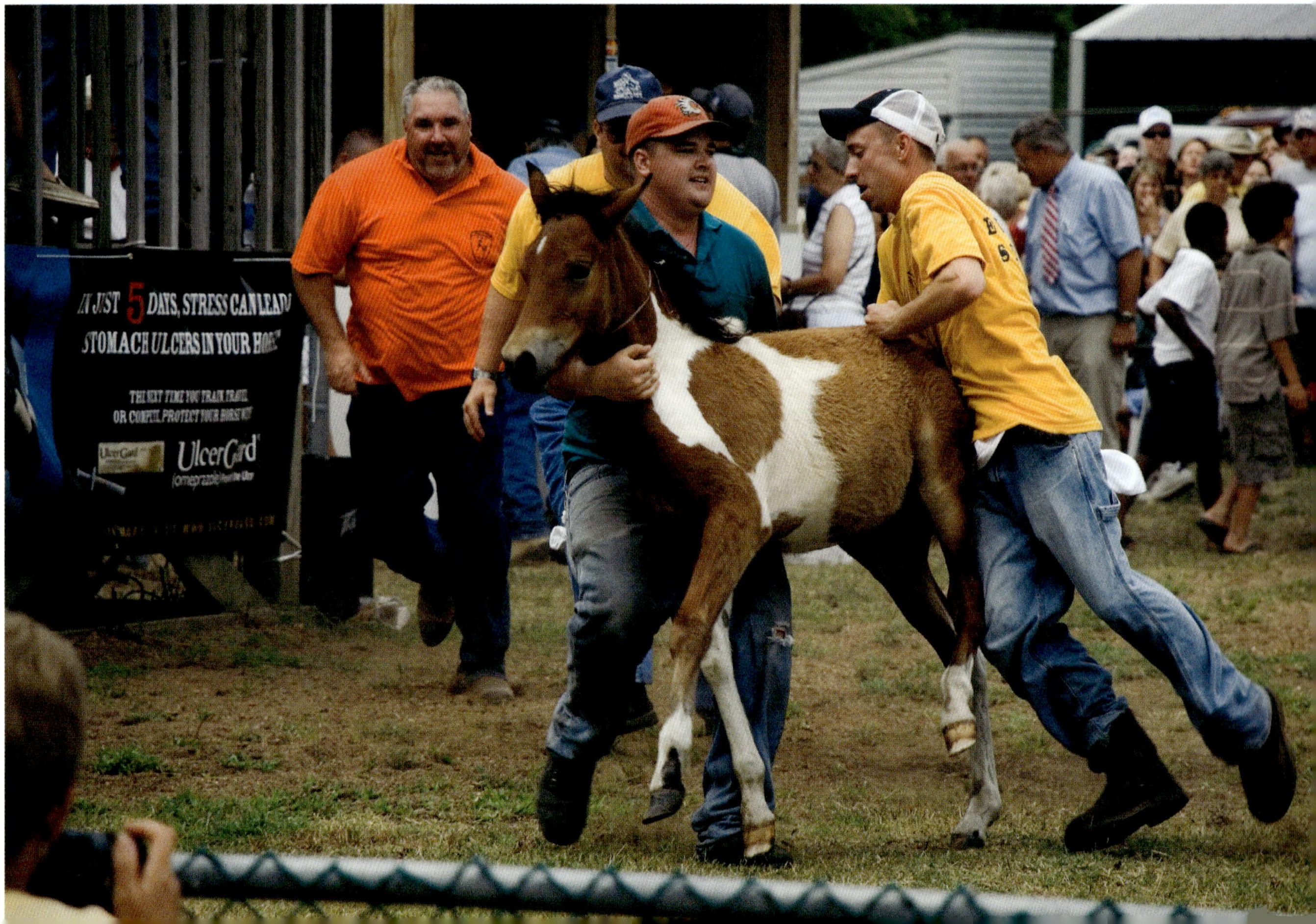

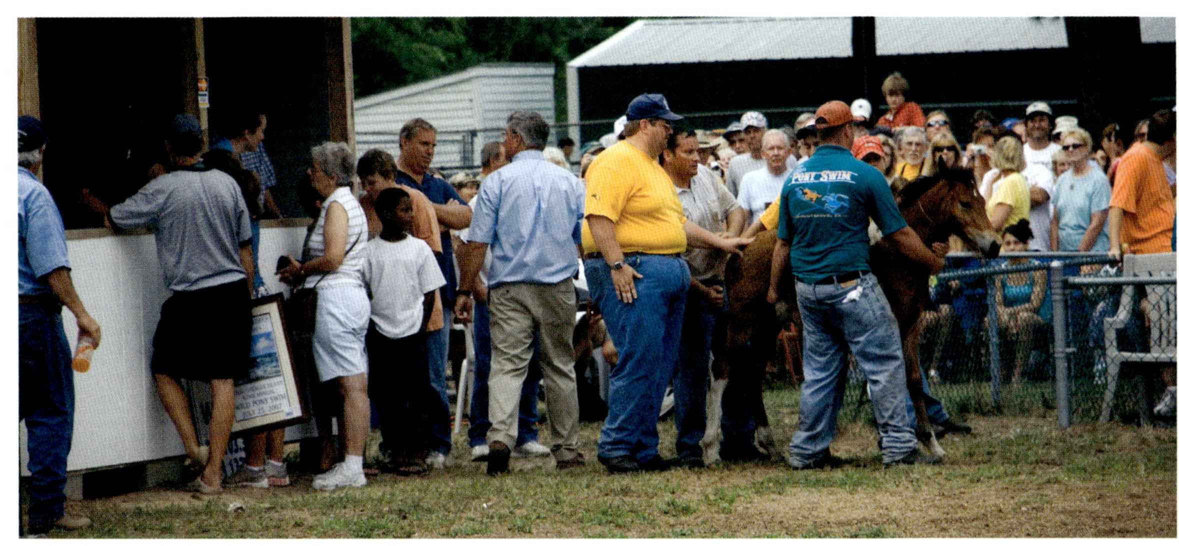

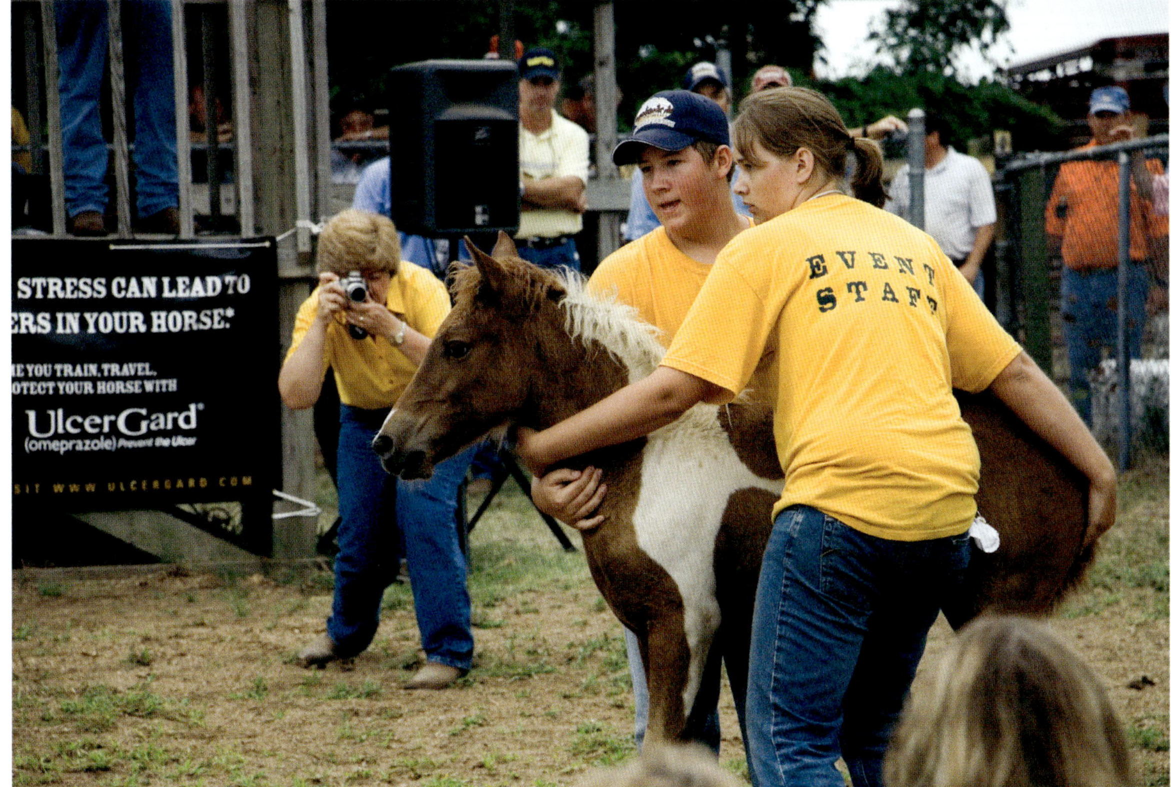
STRESS CAN LEAD TO
ERS IN YOUR HORSE.
ME YOU TRAIN, TRAVEL,
OTECT YOUR HORSE WITH
UlcerGard
(omeprazole) Prevent the Ulcer
SIT WWW.ULCERGARD.COM
EVENT
STAFF

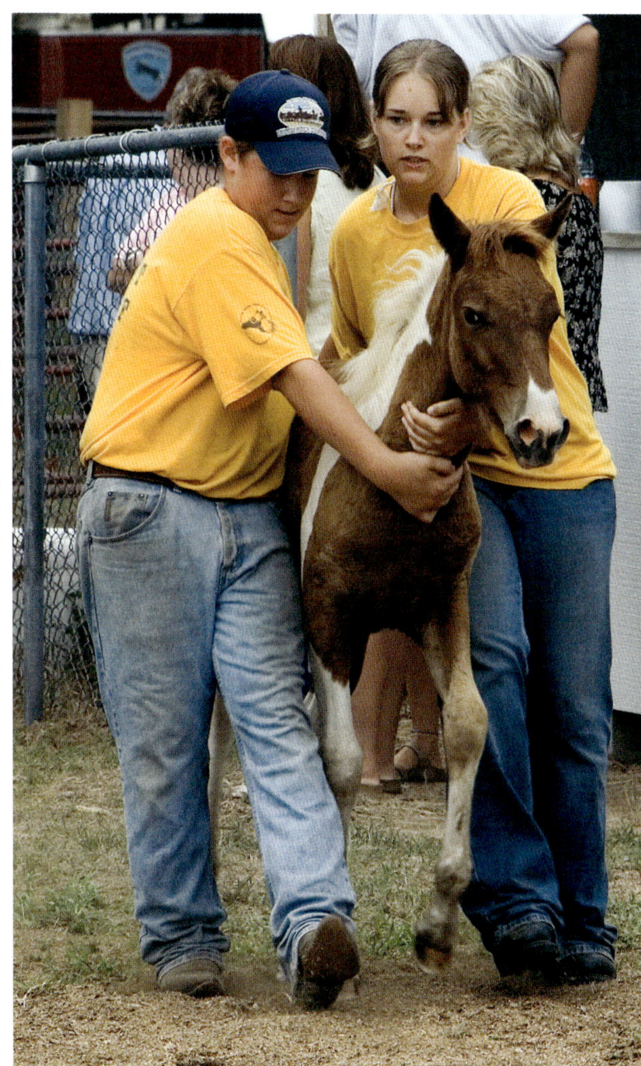

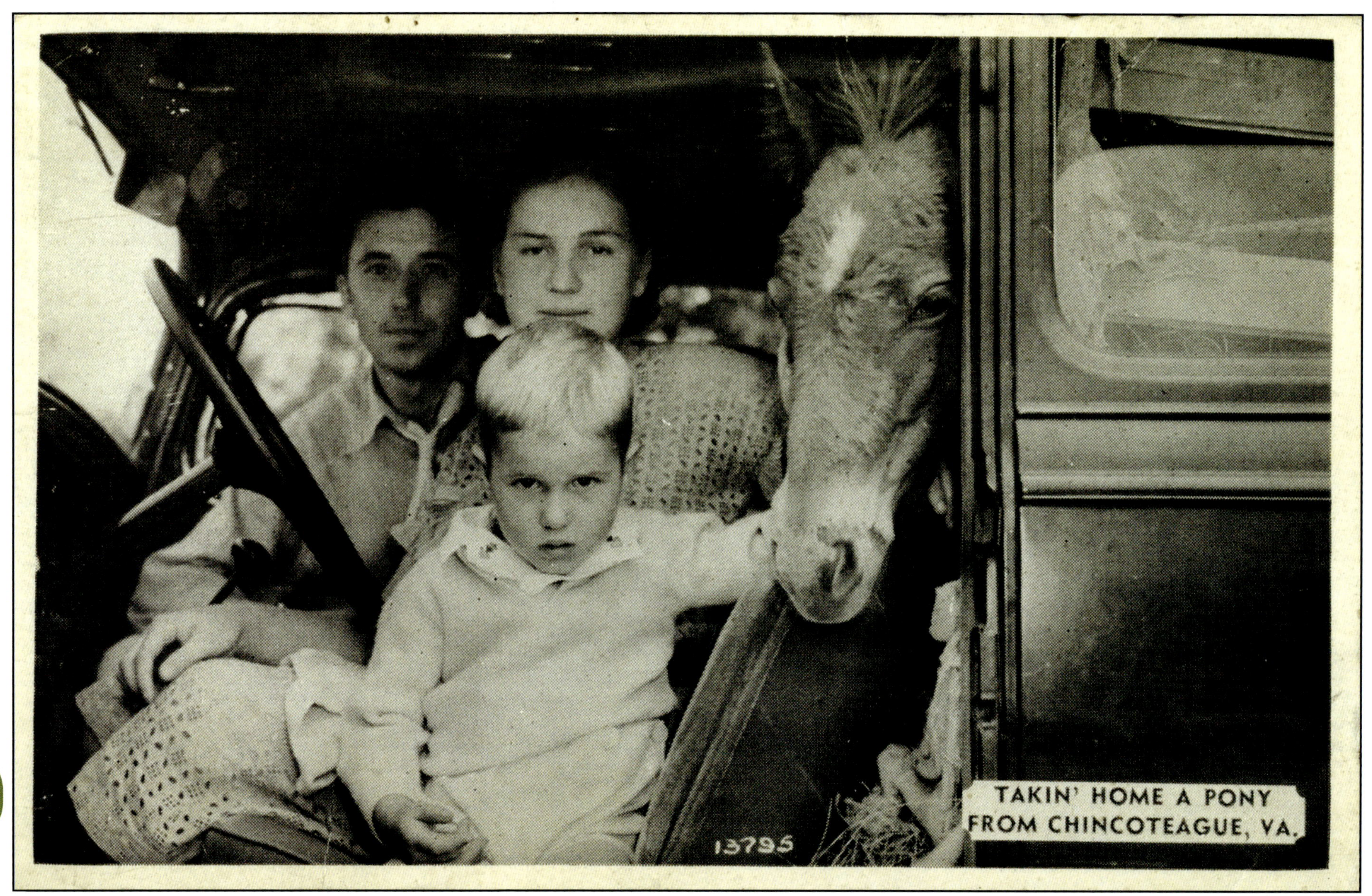

Taking home a pony from Chincoteague. Printed message on the backside reads: "On the annual pony penning day at Chincoteague visitors buy Chincoteague ponies in great numbers. Some for as low as $25.00. Here is the usual way the visitor takes his 'baby' home." Postmarked 1946.

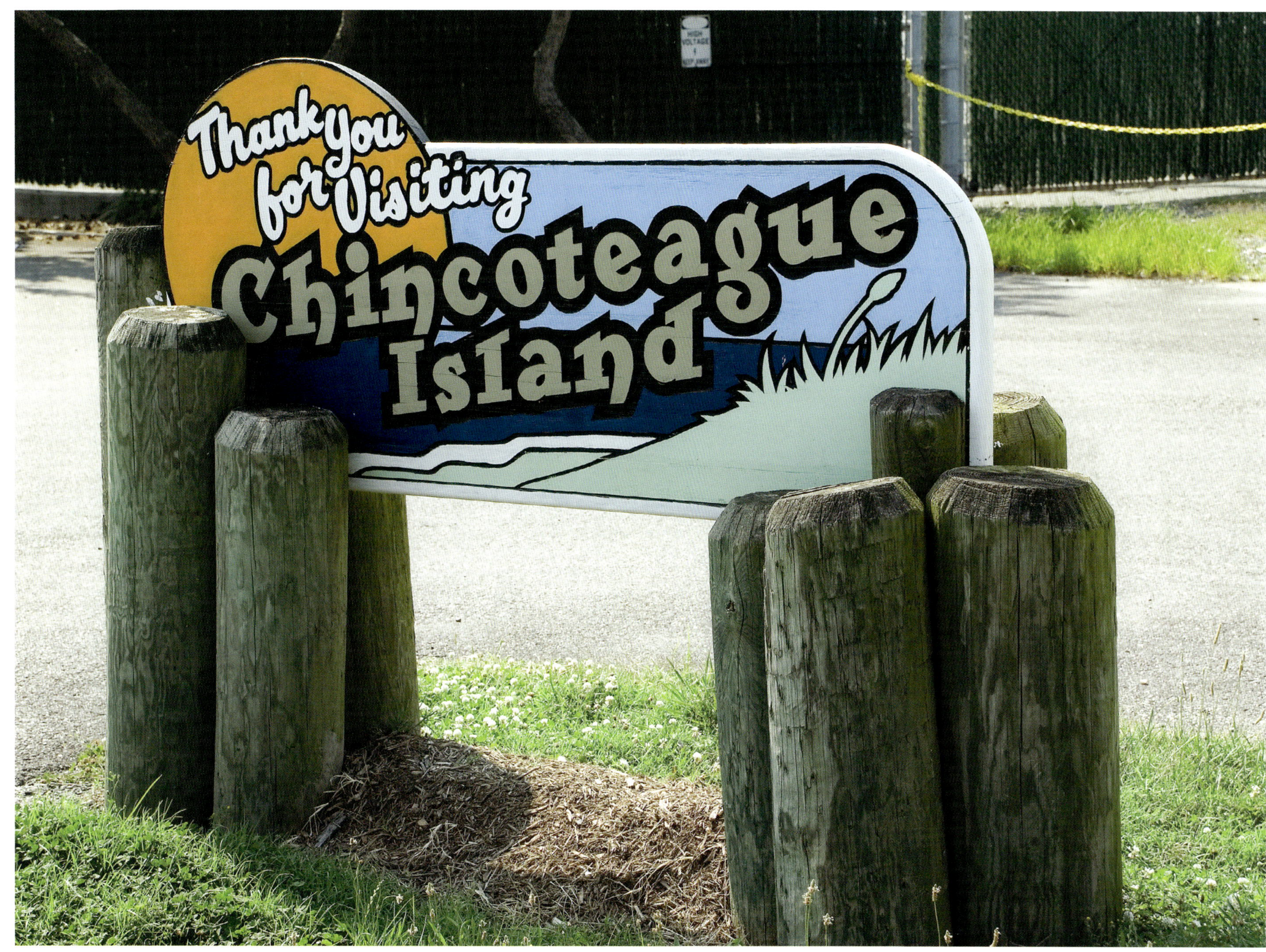

Thank you for Visiting
Chincoteague Island

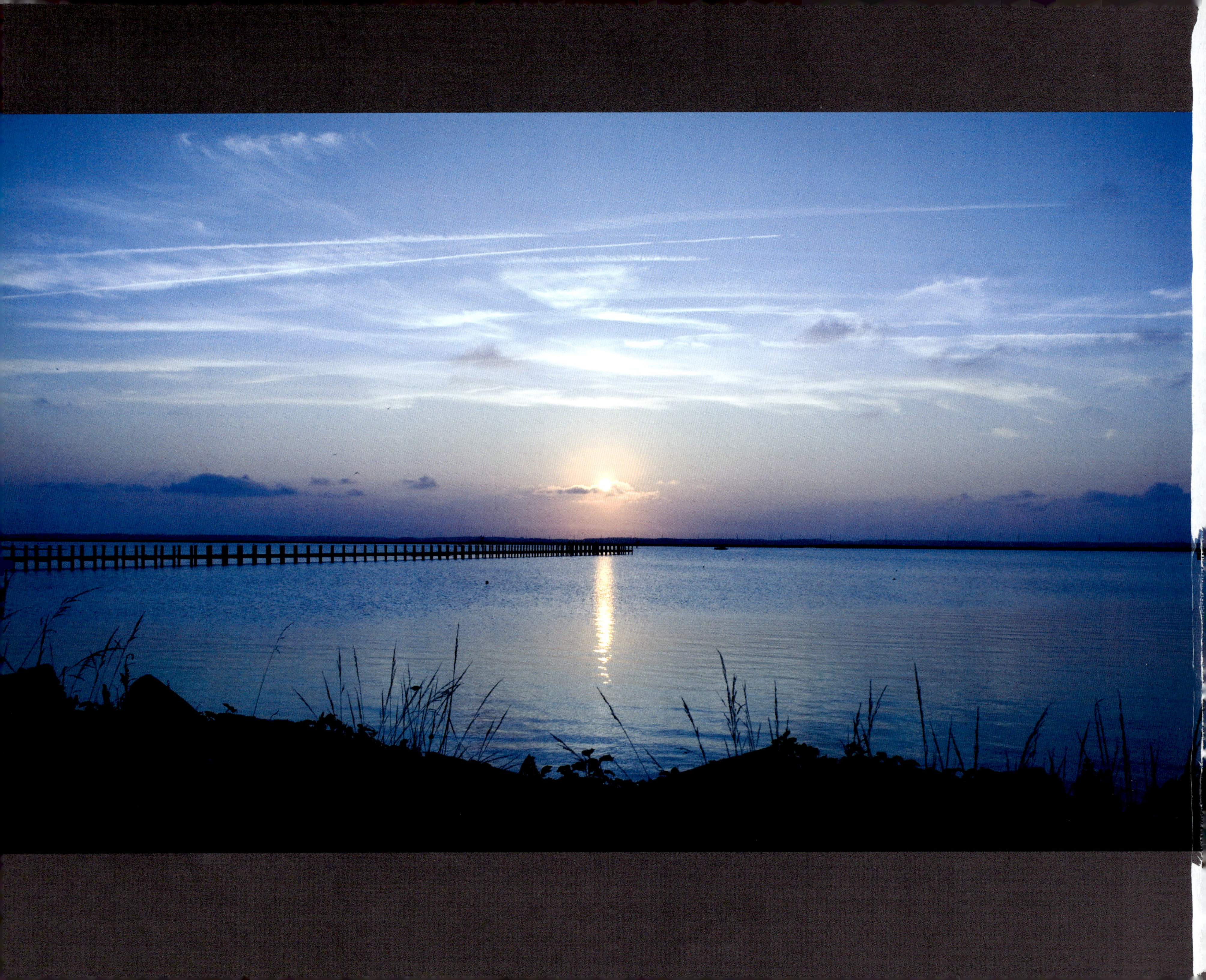

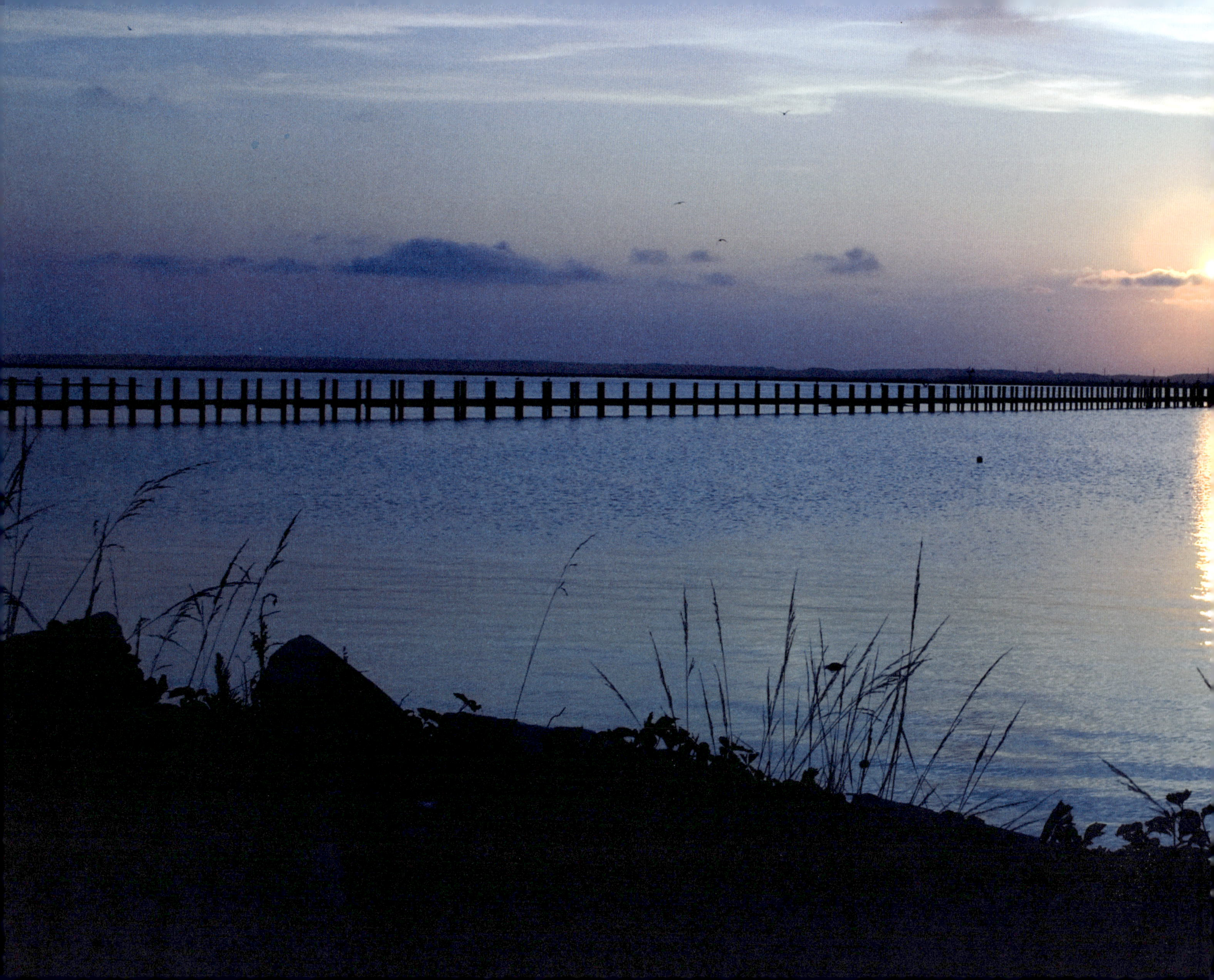